BEYOND TERMAN:

Contemporary Longitudinal Studies Of Giftedness and Talent

Creativity Research
Mark A. Runco, Series Editor

BEYOND TERMAN:

Contemporary Longitudinal Studies Of Giftedness and Talent

edited by

Rena F. Subotnik

and

Karen D. Arnold

ABLEX PUBLISHING CORPORATION
NORWOOD, NEW JERSEY

Second Printing 1995

Printed in the United States of America

Library of Congress Cataloging-in-Publication Data

Beyond Terman: contemporary longitudinal studies of giftedness and
    talent / edited by Rena F. Subotnik and Karen D. Arnold.
        p. cm.
    Includes bibliographical references and index.
    ISBN 1-56750-011-0
    1. Gifted persons—Longitudinal studies. 2. Terman, Lewis
Madison. 1877-1956. I. Subotnik, Rena Faye. II. Arnold, Karen D.
    BF412.B45 1993
    153.9'8—dc20   93-25250
                                                             CIP

Ablex Publishing Corporation
355 Chestnut St.
Norwood, NJ 07648

Contents

About the Authors

EDITORS

Rena F. Subotnik is Associate Professor in the department of Educational Foundations at Hunter College, City University of New York. Professor Subotnik, winner of the 1990 National Association for Gifted Children Early Scholar Award, has been principal or co-investigator of grants exploring talent in mathematics and science with the National Science Foundation, Spencer Foundation, and the U.S. Department of Education. She is on the editorial board of the *American Educational Research Journal*, is past Chair of the Research and Evaluation Division of the National Association for Gifted Children, and is first author, along with Lee Kassan, Ellen Summers, and Alan Wasser of *Genius Revisited: High IQ Children Grown Up* (Ablex, 1993).

Karen D. Arnold is Assistant Professor of Higher Education at Boston College. She received her PhD in Higher Education from the University of Illinois at Urbana-Champaign, where she held the John Corbally Fellowship. Arnold directs the Illinois Valedictorian Project, a 15-year longitudinal study of high school valedictorians. Her research areas include the higher education of women, the development of academic talent, and the social context of achievement. She is an advisory board member of the *Roeper Review* and Chair of the Committee on the Role and Status of Women in Educational Research and Development of the American Educational Research Association.

CHAPTER CONTRIBUTORS

Robert S. Albert is now Professor of Psychology Emeritus at Pitzer College, Claremont, California. After receiving his BA from Vanderbilt University, MA from The University of Texas, and PhD from Boston University he acquired clinical training at the Massachusetts Mental Health Center, Harvard University Medical

School. In 1965 he joined the faculty at Pitzer College where he remained until retirement. For the past 20 years he has written on and researched the areas of exceptional giftedness and the achievement of eminence, supported by grants from the Robert Sterling Clark and the John D. and Catherine MacArthur Foundations. Among his publications are *Genius and Eminence*, 2nd edition and *Theories of Creativity*, edited with Mark Runco.

Camilla Persson Benbow is Professor and Chair of Psychology at Iowa State University, where she co-directs the Study of Mathematically Precocious Youth (SMPY), the Office of Precollegiate Programs for Talented and Gifted (OPPTAG), and a post-doctoral training program in intellectual giftedness. She focuses her research efforts on conducting a 50-year longitudinal study of intellectually talented students, which began in 1972 and now involves over 5,000 individuals. She directs research-based summer programs, involving over 400 students per year and The Iowa Talent Search, which serves over 5,000 students annually. Dr. Benbow was the first recipient of NAGC's Early Scholar Award in 1985 and was inducted into Johns Hopkins University's Society of Scholars in May 1991.

Bonnie Cramond is an Assistant Professor in the Department of Educational Psychology at the University of Georgia where she is the Coordinator of the graduate program in Gifted/Creative Education. She is the Chair of the Research and Evaluation Division of the National Association for Gifted Children and a contributing editor of the *Roeper Review*. In addition to teaching and parenting gifted children, she has published papers and chapters on giftedness and creativity and presented at local, national, and international conferences. A former student of E. Paul Torrance, she was able to construct this chapter with his patient and wise assistance.

Lyle Davidson is chair of the Undergraduate Theory and Music Education Departments and member of composition and music education faculties at the New England Conservatory of Music. He is also a Research Associate at Harvard Project Zero at the Harvard Graduate School of Education, where he works with the Project Arts Propel group and Lincoln Center group. His research interests include portfolio assessment, musical cognition in child development, composition, and pedagogy.

Marcia Delcourt is an Assistant Professor at McGill University in Montreal, Canada where she teaches courses in the Department of

Educational Psychology and Counseling. She has been a Research Assistant Professor at the University of Virginia and a Principal Investigator for The National Research Center on the Gifted and Talented. Dr. Delcourt has been active in gifted education for over 13 years as a teacher, graduate-level program coordinator, curriculum and program consultant, and researcher. She is presently a board member for the Association for the Education of Gifted Underachieving Students, and has been program chair for the Divisions of Research and Evaluation and Counseling and Guidance of the National Association for Gifted Children. Her present research interests include creative behavior, social and emotional issues, program development and assessment, student learning outcomes, teachers as researchers, and computer technologies.

John F. Feldhusen is the Robert B. Kane Distinguished Professor of Education and Director of the Gifted Education Resource Institute at Purdue University. He is past president of the National Association for Gifted Children and Editor of the *Gifted Child Quarterly*. With Joyce VanTassel-Baska and Ken Seeley, he is author of *Excellence in Educating the Gifted*.

Elyse S. Fleming holds a PhD in educational psychology from the University of California, Berkeley. She is Professor Emeritus at Cleveland State University. She directed special summer programs for gifted elementary and high school students for many years. Her research and writing have centered on individual differences including issues of gender equity, and career development of the gifted with special emphasis on gifted women. She continues to write and consult in these areas.

Ernst A. Hany holds a post of Assistant Professor at the Institute of Educational Psychology at the University of Munich directed by Kurt A. Heller. He received his diploma degree in psychology in 1984 and his doctoral degree in 1987 (with a thesis on identification of gifted children). Together with Kurt Heller, he is involved in many large-scale research projects on giftedness and creativity. His scientific interests and publications cover cognitive processes of thinking and learning, expert system technology in identification of the gifted, evaluation of programs for the gifted, and leisure experiences as a background to creative thought.

Kurt A. Heller is Professor of Psychology and Director of the Institute of Educational Psychology and Psychological Diagnostics at the

University of Munich. His research and publications are in these fields, in the last years especially in cognitive competence (metacognition, etc.), technical creativity, gender-specific differences, and cross-cultural studies related to giftedness and talent. Together with Dr. Ernst A. Hany he organized the Third ECHA Conference in Munich, 1992.

Constance L. Hollinger holds a PhD in Educational Psychology from Case Western Reserve University. She is presently Professor of Psychology and Coordinator of the School Psychology Program at Cleveland State University. She has written extensively in the areas of the career development of gifted women, the assessment of ability, and the area of the gifted adolescents. She teaches and presents workshops on topics related to the psychology of women.

Eunsook Hong is Assistant Professor, Counseling and Educational Psychology, University of Nevada, Las Vegas. She received her MS and PhD in Educational Psychology from the University of Southern California in 1985 and 1990, respectively. Her work includes assessment, identification, and instructional application of mental models. She has been studying on the development and verification of psychometric inventory to be used in the identification of gifted and talented children. Currently she is expanding her research on mental models to the domain of creativity.

David Lubinski is Assistant Professor at Iowa State University, where he co-directs the Study of Mathematically Precocious Youth (SMPY). He received his BA and PhD degrees in psychology from the University of Minnesota and subsequently completed a two-year postdoctoral training program in quantitative methods in the Department of Psychology at the University of Illinois. Dr. Lubinski's research interests involve assessing individual differences in human behavior. He is especially interested in identifying different kinds of intellectual giftedness in young adults and in finding optimal ways to enhance their educational and vocational development. He has received two MENSA awards for research excellence.

Roberta M. Milgram is Associate Professor, School of Education, Tel-Aviv University, Israel. She has been studying creativity in children and adolescents in Israel and in the United States for more than 20 years and has published over 50 articles and two books on the topic. She has developed a theoretical model in which giftedness in its various forms and at its different levels is represented as being affected by home, school, and community environments, as well as by a wide variety of personality and other individual differences. She has developed two measures of creativity, the Tel-Aviv Creativity Test (TACT) that assesses original ideas in children and adolescents and the Tel-Aviv Activities Inventory, which measures genuine creative accomplishments in real world tasks.

Sidney M. Moon is an Assistant Professor, Department of Educational Studies, Purdue University. As the chair for research for the Indiana Association for the Gifted, she developed a statewide model for bridging research, theory, and practice in gifted education. She is Editor of *Quest*, the newsletter for the Research and Evaluation Division of the National Association for Gifted Children (NAGC), and *Research Briefs*, an NAGC Service Publication. She has published numerous articles on gifted education and research methods. She has experience with gifted youth in the roles of parent, teacher, coordinator, counselor, and researcher. She won the 1990 Hollingworth Award for the research reported in this volume.

Christoph Perleth, school psychologist, works as Research Assistant and Lecturer at the Institute of Educational Psychology and Psychological Diagnostics at the University of Munich where he has been engaged with Prof. Heller in the Munich Longitudinal Study of Giftedness. His fields of interests include metacognition and strategy training, cognitive abilities, educational–psychological diagnostics, research methods, and research on giftedness.

Rose A. Rudnitski taught at the elementary level for 18 years before coming to academe. She earned the doctorate in Curriculum and Teaching at Teachers College, Columbia University, where she studied with A. Harry Passow. She is now an Assistant Professor of Education and Coordinator of the Graduate Programs in Reading at State University of New York, New Paltz.

Larry Scripp is a member of the Music Education and Undergraduate Theory Departments at New England Conservatory and a researcher with Harvard Project Zero. At Project Zero he has focused on assessment of learning in the arts with the ARTS PROPEL project in the Pittsburgh Public Schools. He consults on arts assessment for various school districts and arts organizations in the United States. He has published numerous articles about assessment in the arts, children's musical development, computers and education, and the acquisition of music literacy skills. Mr. Scripp is also a composer and conductor.

Cynthia Steiner won a 1983 Westinghouse Science Talent Search award for her original research in population genetics. Her collaboration in this book, and in Runco's volume *Problem Finding, Problem Solving, and Creativity* (Ablex, in press) arose from her participation in Subotnik's longitudinal study of Westinghouse winners. Ms. Steiner currently works as a manager for an international accounting firm. She is interested in the value of mentoring in the development of science careers among young adults.

Foreword

Mention the phrase "longitudinal studies" to gifted educators, and immediately Lewis M. Terman's *Genetic Studies of Genius* comes to mind. This response has become so automatic and spontaneous that educators constantly need to be informed that Terman's, albeit one of the most important, is not the only longitudinal study that has been conducted in the field.

In his first report in 1925, Terman suggested that as more is learned about giftedness and how gifted children should be educated, more is learned about expanding the talent reservoir:

> When the sources of our intellectual talent have been determined, it is conceivable that means may be found which would increase our supply. When the physical, mental and character traits of gifted children are better understood it will be possible to set about their education with better hope of success. . . . In the gifted child; Nature has moved far back the usual limits of educability, but the realms thus thrown open to the educator are still *terra incognita*. It is time to move forward, explore, and consolidate. (pp. 16–17)

In recent years, Terman's study has been criticized and his findings questioned because of its geographically and socioeconomically limited sample and its research methodology. Whatever our concerns and reservations about the Terman studies, they do not detract from the seminal importance of his work and the impact it has had on research, theory, program, and practice in gifted education. A major significance of Terman's work is that it has spawned research and development that has led us "to move forward, explore, and consolidate." To assert that the field of gifted education has moved "beyond Terman" is to acknowledge the importance of Terman and his colleagues while recognizing the distance we have come from those beginnings.

Beyond Terman: Contemporary Longitudinal Studies of Giftedness and Talent is an important contribution to the literature in two fields—those of gifted education and educational research. It is

significant for the former in terms of the insights and understandings it provides about giftedness and its nurture. It is important for
the latter for its elucidations of the methodology associated with
longitudinal research. The editors point out that

> [the] volume presents recent collected works that demonstrate the fit
> between longitudinal methodology and the central issues of gifted
> education. Collectively, the studies investigate the early determinants
> of later academic and career achievement and creativity while employ-
> ing varied identification practices, perspectives, theoretical orienta-
> tions, and populations.

The studies described vary along many dimensions, including
research problem, sample size and character, length of study, data
collection procedures and sources, and longitudinal orientation
(i.e., emergent/developmental or retrospective). The studies deal
with a variety of talent areas, such as academic achievement, science, technical creativity, music, creative and productive thinking,
and career development. The samples include gifted and talented
children, youths, and adults, both males and females. Although
most of the studies deal with identified gifted/talented individuals,
one is a retrospective look at the achievements of graduate students
in a university-level leadership education program. Studies originat-
ing in Germany and Israel add an international flavor and, more
importantly, remind us that there is good research being conducted
beyond the borders of the U.S.

By having each of the contributors follow a similar format in their
presentations, the editors—both of whom report on their own longitudinal studies—made it easier for the reader to view the studies
cumulatively so that when the last chapter is reached, the "Lessons
from the Collected Studies" are clear and make good sense.

Having been involved in two major longitudinal studies myself,
one on the effects of ability grouping and the other on bright underachievers (neither of which are included in this volume because they
were published in 1966 and consequently do not qualify as "contemporary"), I resonate to the contributors' expressions of the joys and
pitfalls of longitudinal research. The grouping study was of two
years' duration, focusing on the effects of having gifted pupils present or absent, and incorporated more variables than any such
study before or since. The problems of attrition coupled with the
mass of data on more than 2,200 students were constant reminders
of the pleasures and pain of such research. The bright underachiever study was of three years' duration, and the findings
differed in each year of data collection: First the controls did better,

then the treatment group did better, and finally, neither group did very well! Had the study not been longitudinal, we would have reported very different findings and arrived at very different conclusions, as short-term studies may yield findings that are transitory and ephemeral. Certainly inherent problems of subject attrition, missing data, and changing outcomes exist, but there can be no question that, in the end, the findings are more meaningful, enduring, and significant than a good deal of the short-term research reported in the literature.

Rena Subotnik and Karen Arnold have broken ground by taking us *Beyond Terman*. One hopes that the field of gifted education will profit from the undertaking and reporting of other longitudinal studies inspired by this volume.

> *A. Harry Passow*
> *Jacob H. Schiff Professor*
> *Emeritus of Education*
> *Teachers College, Columbia University*

REFERENCES

Terman, L. M., et al. (1925). *Genetic studies of genius. Volume I: Mental and physical characteristics of a thousand gifted children.* Stanford, CA: Stanford University Press.

Acknowledgments

We were fated to meet because of our common interests in longitudinal research, talented adolescents, and the Pacific Northwest. *Beyond Terman* actually began at the 1989 meeting of the American Educational Research Association. A shared panel presentation sparked a brainstorming session of collaborative project ideas. While Rena was plotting tax-deductible trips to Oregon from New York, Karen moved to Boston, resulting in a much more realistic, in-person collaboration. Unlike most such partnerships, we wrote and edited together during long weekends in New York or Boston punctuated by walks, movies, and talks of future projects. Our major writing projects were born at annual retreats on the Atlantic Coast, where we communicated with our contributors via picture postcards. We recommend this collaborative style as intellectually stimulating and highly productive.

Collecting these studies and working closely with contributors through an arduous revision process reinforced our respect for this highly talented international group of scholars. We thank them for providing the research community with the first comprehensive view of contemporary longitudinal research on giftedness and talent.

Mark Runco, the Creativity Series Editor for Ablex, has encouraged this book since its inception. We are deeply appreciative of his insightful, timely, and rigorous editorial work on the volume. We were honored to have Harry Passow accept our invitation to write the introduction to this book. Dr. Passow's eminence in the field of gifted education gives him an unparalleled position to view the broad significance of the collected longitudinal studies. We are grateful for the financial support of a Boston College Research Expense Grant to fund the last stage of clerical costs. At Boston College, Ellen Nelson, Lynette Robinson-Weening, and Kay Feeley assisted in manuscript preparation.

We thank Oleg Davydenko and Jeff Arnold for their unfailing personal and professional support. We also cherished Oleg's good company on mutual hiking trips and Jeff's laughter, lunches, and patient understanding.

Setting out on a longitudinal exploration is an act of belief and patience, superbly modeled by our respective mentors, Mildred Kersh and Terry Denny. Among the many rewards of such research is collaboration with others who share a commitment to this exacting and rewarding methodology. We look forward to participating in an expanding community of researchers whose imaginations are captured by the unfolding lives of gifted individuals.

Rena F. Subotnik, New York, New York
Karen D. Arnold, Chestnut Hill, Massachusetts

1

Longitudinal Study of Giftedness and Talent

Rena F. Subotnik
Karen D. Arnold

We have seen that intellect and achievement are far from perfectly correlated. Why this is so, what circumstances affect the fruition of human talent, are questions of such transcendent importance that they should be investigated by every method that promises the slightest reduction of our present ignorance.
—Terman and Oden, 1947, p. 351

Lewis Terman heralded the field of gifted education in the United States by tracing the development of high-IQ children from their childhood in the 1920s to midlife and beyond (Burks, Jensen, & Terman, 1930; Oden, 1968; Terman, 1925; Terman & Oden, 1947, 1959). Terman and his research team posed the following questions about intelligence and achievement: Do precocious children become exceptional adults? Do high-IQ adults exhibit a disproportionate degree of mental health problems? Are brilliant children also physically superior? Does having a high IQ correlate with excellent school performance? Can gifted children be expected to display exceptional adult career achievements as eminent scientists, scholars, artists, and leaders? If high-ability children become extraordinary adults, what can be learned from the personal and educational antecedents that seem to nurture their development?

The contemporary field of gifted education, building on the work of Terman and others, presumes that gifted children become exceptional adults. Educators of the gifted further assume that highly intelligent children benefit from and may even require special educational opportunities that nurture their considerable potential. In the rush to identify and provide services to the exceptional child, however, gifted education has moved away from empirical investigation of the long-term effects of early promise and special educational opportunities.

This volume contains recent longitudinal studies of gifted individuals, highlighting the advantages of studying the same subjects over time. Longitudinal research offers the opportunity for critical examination of the way gifted children and adolescents are identified and illuminates the characteristics and experiences that affect sustained achievement.

Controversies over methods of identification point to the need for predictive validity studies to support labeling and services for exceptional people. Thus far there exists little empirical evidence that our interventions are accomplishing long-term educational goals. Indeed, educators of the gifted rarely set explicit goals of developing and sustaining achievement over the life span. Such goals may be too overwhelming for a classroom, school, or special program. They are certainly beyond the scope of most evaluation studies. At a time when educational policy issues are on the national agenda, resource and policy decisions must rely on research that demonstrates the efficacy of gifted education in providing adult national leadership. The National Research Center for Gifted Education has called for longitudinal studies as a top priority in the field (Reid, 1991). Only long-term studies can directly address whether or not gifted education is finding the right people and doing the right things.

This volume presents recent works that demonstrate the fit between longitudinal methodology. and the central issues of gifted education. Collectively, the studies investigate the early determinants of later academic and career achievement and creativity while employing varied identification practices, perspectives, theoretical orientations, and populations.

This introductory chapter provides the reader with a brief synopsis of early retrospective and longitudinal research in gifted education, a discussion of the strengths and weaknesses of longitudinal methodology, and a brief overview of the volume's other chapters. The studies in Part I investigate individuals identified as gifted on the basis of early demonstrated accomplishments—in academic achievement, science, music, and technical creativity. Part II presents reports on populations identified as gifted on the basis of intelligence and achievement test scores, leisure time activities, or tests of creativity. Included in Part III are long-term follow-ups of participants in gifted programs organized around conceptions of giftedness such as those proposed by Renzulli (1977, 1986) and Feldhusen and Kolloff (1979; Feldhusen, 1986), or multidimensional identification processes not directly tied to a single theory of giftedness. A final chapter summarizes the collected research and proposes areas for future investigation.

The diversity represented in this collection will allow researchers, policy makers, and practitioners to compare long-term effects of different identification procedures. Not only do researchers focus on different domains of talent, they follow individuals through varied points in the human life span: childhood, adolescence, and adulthood. Some studies include males and females, others one gender only. Investigations take place within schools and outside of academe. Samples comprise gifted individuals of different racial, ethnic, socioeconomic, and national backgrounds. The variety of domains and samples presented in this volume allows for the application of results to a wide array of populations.

A final dimension on which the studies vary reflects the type of data. Some investigators collected survey data, others conducted interviews, and still others observed subjects involved in specific activities. Most employed more than one form of data collection, triangulating their methods to increase the explanatory power of each. All of the researchers represented in this volume investigated factors that have an impact on the realization of promise among the gifted. Factors of interest included gender, family background, cognitive characteristics, and personality. In short, this comprehensive set of studies represents a wide range of research designs within the framework of longitudinal methodology of gifted individuals.

EARLY RESEARCH

Long-range studies comprised a significant proportion of important early investigations in gifted education. In order to put the present set of studies into a historical context, earlier important retrospective and longitudinal studies with gifted groups are briefly described below.

Retrospective Studies

Goertzel and Goertzel (1962) conducted a study of the emotional and intellectual family milieu in which eminent people of the 20th century were reared. Their subjects had made outstanding contributions in politics, social reform, music, and art. The investigators studied biographies of these individuals in order to explore the role played by parents in the development of their child's talent. Almost all the parents had their own strong drives toward intellectual or creative achievement and encouraged the development of their child's talent, sometimes at the expense of their own personal fulfillment.

Roe (1953) interviewed eminent artists about alcoholism in the world of the arts. In the process, she became interested in studying famous scientists in order to explore the relationship between personality and vocation. She identified 23 male scientists and conducted a retrospective study of their life histories including family, schooling, and outside interests. Roe traced the development of these men's careers in terms of postsecondary schooling and professional experience. She concluded that the ability to absorb oneself in one's work was a central factor in achieving recognition in science. Also essential was the skill of identifying a good scientific question.

The concept of "accumulation of advantage" (Merton, 1968) in the achievement of scientific eminence was examined by Zuckerman (1977) in a retrospective study of 74 Laureates who won the Nobel Prize between 1901-1972. Through extensive interviews, Zuckerman identified the process by which this select group of talented individuals was labeled "comers" and thereby gained privileged access to resources and mentors. A majority (59%) of the Laureates in the study attended one of 15 elite undergraduate institutions. For their doctoral degrees, 74% of her subjects attended either Harvard, Columbia, Berkeley, Johns Hopkins, or Princeton. According to Zuckerman, more professional advantage was provided by the novice scientists' choice of post-secondary school than their social origins. Over half of the Laureates had worked either as students, postdoctoral fellows, or junior collaborators under previous Nobel Prize winners. Through that apprenticeship they received an orientation to scientific standards and modes of thought, including the feel for elegant solutions or important problems.

From 1935 to 1940, Leta Hollingworth served as the educational advisor to a special enrichment program for high-IQ students at the Speyer School in New York City. Twenty-eight members from the population of 90 enrichment program participants were located in 1981, and 20 completed questionnaires designed to examine the impact of the program on their adult achievement and values (White & Renzulli, 1987). Eight subjects were selected for in-depth interviews, including three from among the children described in Hollingworth's (1942) *Children Over 180 IQ*. Criteria for selection of the interviewees included gender, geographic accessibility, and willingness to participate. The subjects reported that the school provided a highly enriched experience which led to lifelong love for learning, pleasure in independent work, and joy in interacting with similarly high-ability students.

Other long-term retrospective studies of high-IQ individuals were conducted by Subotnik, Karp, and Morgan (1989) and Subotnik, Kassan, Summers, and Wasser (1993). The subjects were graduates of Hunter College Elementary School from 1948 to 1960 with a mean IQ of 159. The purpose of the investigation was to compare the responses of the Hunter group at mid-life with those reported by the Terman (1959) cohort in the volume *The Gifted Group at Mid-Life: 35 Years' Follow-Up of the Superior Child.* Both sets of subjects had evolved into productive professionals with stable interpersonal relationships and good mental and physical health. However, gender differences were far less significant in the Hunter cohort in terms of reported life satisfaction and values associated with success.

Bloom (1985) and his associates conducted a retrospective interview study of high achievers in six talent areas. Ranging in age from late adolescence to their mid-30s, subjects were athletes (world-class tennis players and Olympic swimmers), artists (concert pianists and prize-winning sculptors), and intellectual achievers (research neuroscientists and prize-winning mathematicians). Investigators identified subjects according to criteria appropriate to each talent area, seeking individuals who could be classified at the top of their field by early adulthood. Interviews focused on the role of childhood experiences, family support, teachers and mentors, and the development of the subjects' personal identity as up and coming "stars."

Bloom and his colleagues reported a common pattern across talent areas, in which intrinsic interest gave way to intensive technical study and subsequent recapturing of initial enjoyment as the student reached mature mastery of the talent area. This common progression was made possible by an interpersonal network of support and challenge featuring, successively, parents, personally nurturing teachers, technique-oriented teachers, and master teacher/mentors. These relationships, as well as increasing public recognition, fostered an identity in the talent area that helped the gifted achiever to persist.

A small body of empirical research has investigated the relationship between grades and adult attainments such as employment level and income (Baird, 1985; Cohen, 1984). This literature found a positive relationship between academic success and adult career measures. Academic performance explains very little of the variation in adult career outcomes, however, and grades appear to influence career attainment only indirectly. Of particular difficulty, however, is the problem of separating the contribution of individual characteristics, such as motivation and ability, from the increased access to opportunities that results from high academic performance.

Longitudinal Studies

Retrospective studies of high achievers offer insight into the development of giftedness. However, such studies suffer from the distortions of hindsight. Furthermore, retrospective inquiry fails to illuminate the process by which eminent individuals develop differently from their peers who showed equally high potential at an earlier age. True longitudinal studies address those limitations by collecting data at multiple points in the process of subjects' development. Below are brief reviews of the few true longitudinal studies of gifted individuals available in the literature.

This chapter opened by recognizing the important questions addressed by Terman's research. A review of longitudinal studies of giftedness should begin with his findings. Terman and his colleagues followed the lives of a cohort of California school children who scored in the top 1% on the Stanford-Binet IQ test he had developed. Beginning in the 1920s, Terman followed subjects through clinical interviews and a variety of intelligence and personality tests (Terman, 1925). As adults, the Terman group generally reported outstanding health, social adjustment, freedom from delinquency and mental illness, educational attainment, and vocational achievement (Terman & Oden, 1947, 1959). The group was comprised overwhelmingly of middle- and upper middle-class Anglos whose superior life adaptation was probably attributable, in some part, to enriched home backgrounds.

Although Terman's subjects demonstrated variability in all measured outcomes, Terman and his colleague Oden maintained that intellectually superior children become gifted adults. The vast majority of male subjects were professionals, higher level businessmen, and occasionally semiprofessionals. The most frequently represented professions in the group were law, engineering, college teaching, science, and medicine. The group was well represented in *Who's Who*, in scholarly and scientific publications, and among prestigious award recipients. Oden (1968) wrote that "all the evidence indicates that with few exceptions the superior child becomes the superior adult" (p. 50).

Although the generalizability of the Terman studies is reduced by the single-cohort design, the reliance on IQ scores for identification, and the absence of vocational involvement by most female participants, the research demonstrates a relationship between early intellectual promise and life attainment. Terman's work reassured educators and parents that extremely high IQ levels were not inevitably accompanied by social maladjustment. Further, his later work particularly underlined the importance of personality and motivation factors in realizing high ability. In a review of Terman, Baird (1982) concluded: "Perhaps the most striking aspect of these results is the expectedly small role of intelligence scores, compared to the influence of social class, educational level attained, and personality traits reflecting personal stability, social impressiveness, and ambition" (p. 33).

The Grant Study of Adult Development traced the lives of 258 male Harvard undergraduates beginning in the early 1940s (Vaillant, 1977). Subjects were identified on the basis of their academic achievement and emotional stability. Vaillant, the most recent study director, reported on psychological defense mechanisms that appeared to relate strongly to the life satisfaction, health, and career attainments of the Harvard men. Of particular interest is his conclusion that the volume and severity of actual difficulties in the lives of gifted adult men is far less important in determining life outcomes than their repertoire of coping mechanisms. The Grant Study is a good example of a well-designed single-cohort investigation. Interviews, health and psychiatric records, survey data, and behavioral evaluations were all utilized in subjects' profiles. As a single-cohort study of males, the research is subject to historical effects that limit its generalizability to populations of different time periods, to women, and to nonwhite, nonelite gifted populations.

Getzels and Csikszentmihalyi (1976) published the results of a longitudinal study that identified problem finding as a key variable in the prediction of success in the art world. The two investigators, working with male fine arts students at a prestigious art institute in Chicago, observed subjects creating a problem from a given set of objects. The number of objects manipulated, the uniqueness of those objects, and the length of time that problem closure was deferred were all quantitatively reported. Getzels and Csikszentmihalyi classified the art students into problem finders and nonproblem finders. Seven years later, problem finders were evaluated as more successful artists than the comparison group by directors of major art galleries, art critics from influential national newspapers, and peers. Other variables that had earlier distinguished subjects from one another, such as values and personality traits, were not found to be predictors of long-term success. Between the 7- and 18-year follow-ups, however, problem finding was discovered to play a less prominent role in predicting recognition within the artistic community (Csikszentmihalyi, 1990).

A few large-scale national longitudinal studies have included gifted subsamples within their research populations. These data sets are ideal for comparing outcomes of gifted and nongifted individuals; however, they were not formulated as investigations of giftedness and leave unexplored many variables of interest. Below are selected examples of such studies.

Three studies of heterogeneous student populations include investigations of gifted and talented subgroups. The first, Project Talent, began in 1960 with the collection of varied data on the personal characteristics, achievement, and aptitude of approximately 100,000 secondary school students throughout the United States. Researchers periodically collected follow-up data on subsamples of these subjects. Among the Project Talent findings of interest to educators of the gifted was Astin and Myint's (1971) report that scholastic aptitude, especially in mathematics, and high educational aspirations were the best predictors of girls' career orientation in 5,000 female Project Talent subjects. A second study using the Project Talent data bank investigated differences in achievement in relation to early potential (Card, Steel, & Abeles, 1980). Card and his associates found gender differences favoring the achievement of males and attributed these findings largely to career and family conflicts for women. For high-potential males, achievement predictors included socioeconomic status and job-related experiences.

A third study analyzing a subgroup of talented subjects is a recent Educational Testing Service (ETS, 1991) project using data from two large-scale longitudinal surveys, the National Longitudinal Study of the High School Class of 1972 and the High School and Beyond study (high school class of 1980) to compare the educational pathways of high- and average-ability high school seniors. The report described the top quartile of 1980 high school seniors as somewhat more likely to begin undergraduate study than 1972 high-ability seniors. No progress was made in college graduation rates over this period, however. Only half of the high-ability seniors from each cohort had earned a bachelor's degree and only 12% were enrolled in graduate study seven years after completing high school, leading the ETS researchers to conclude "There are large losses of this talent at the higher levels of postsecondary education" (p. 30).

LONGITUDINAL RESEARCH AS METHODOLOGY

Longitudinal research follows the same persons over time. (Pre-post-test type studies generally focus on a limited number of observable behaviors, and use control groups to strengthen their validity. They are usually too limited in duration to be considered true longitudinal studies.) Two variations of cross-sectional design stand between single-measurement studies and true longitudinal research. The first calls for simultaneous cross-sectional measurement of two or more different age groups in order to impute developmental changes. A more common design in the gifted field is the retrospective study in which eminent achievers are investigated cross-sectionally and asked to reflect on their development. Cross-sectional and retrospective investigations cannot assess intraindividual change or the effects of early factors on later achievement.

In contrast, two major types of questions are ideally suited to longitudinal study: First, how do people change as they age? Second, what are the consequences of early experiences and characteristics on later functioning (Schaie, 1983)? The investigation of changes associated with aging draws from a developmental life-span perspective, usually tracing one or more life stages of infancy, early childhood, adolescence, and adulthood. The developmental approach is not only theoretically rich, but is essential in disentangling effects of maturation, personal and sociocultural experience, and aging. Longitudinal studies can demonstrate individual change over time and document the consequences of earlier experiences.

Researchers and educators interested in identifying and nurturing gifted individuals seek access to information about personal qualities and behaviors of school-aged children, adolescents, and young adults. They draw on such information, within a theoretical framework, to design programs for gifted individuals. The efficacy of identification procedures and educational services is best demonstrated by following individuals longitudinally and monitoring their experiences.

Longitudinal work captures variability in individuals over various occasions and life stages, whereas a cross-sectional view reveals only a moment in time. Take, for example, the case of one of the high school valedictorians in Arnold's study (Chapter 2). This valedictorian, "Ellen," turned down prestigious colleges to attend a small Christian fundamentalist institution in the South. A snapshot of her achievement at age 18 might have led to the conclusion that Ellen was unlikely to realize her enormously high academic potential as a graduate of a limited-curriculum, low-prestige undergraduate institution. A snapshot at age 20 would have yielded a far different prediction. Three years after high school, Ellen graduated early as a biology major with a perfect grade point average and planned to attend medical school. Ellen never became a doctor. A snapshot at age 23 showed her as the wife of a seminary student, taking courses in elementary education and contemplating a career as a teacher to alternate with full-time child raising. Ellen's traditional values, researchers might have concluded, would take precedence over using her ability in a high-level career. Ellen's story is still unfolding, however. Her most recent snapshot at age 28 shows Ellen as a minister's wife who is also a full-time doctoral student in science education.

There are several lessons about longitudinal inquiry that can be derived from Ellen's story. First, cross-sectional views of individuals can be limited and misleading. Ellen's snapshots were each incomplete; a full picture shows a rather consistent pattern in which she demonstrates both her traditional values and her intellectual and achievement strivings. Second, Ellen's participation in a longitudinal study provides rich contextual information for understanding her choices and perceptions of her own development. Third, the complexities of Ellen's life course have been captured only with multiple contacts over time.

Educators, developmental psychologists, and other longitudinal researchers follow the same general process of inquiry. After establishing the focus of a study, the researcher identifies and samples an appropriate population. A sample size large enough to address subject attrition and small enough to manage multiple contacts with subjects is needed. Like single-measurement studies, data may be qualitative or quantitative, collected using quasi-experiments, ethnography, survey, or other social science approaches. Some researchers, including those represented in this book, triangulate their methods and data sources, combining interviews, for example, with survey data, or standardized test scores with observations of program participants. Chapters by Moon and Feldhusen (Chapter 14) and Delcourt (Chapter 15) provide examples of triangulation methods used in evaluating the effects of special gifted programs. After identifying a sample, contact is made with potential study participants and, in some cases, schools, parents, or testing companies, to request their cooperation over the proposed study period. The number of contacts varies, although most longitudinal studies contain more than the two measurement points of a conventional pre- and posttest design. The data sources can be paper-and-pencil test administrations, interviews, observations, or examination of creative products such as scientific reports or artworks. Interim data analysis and interpretation normally occur following each data collection point. Researchers trace paths of individuals as well as patterns among groups and subgroups.

As the study progresses, the issue of subject attrition inevitably arises. Researchers attempt both to locate study members and to understand potential differences between active study participants and nonrespondents. Unique to longitudinal research, the focus or even the purposes of a study can change as the research progresses. Although limited to a certain extent by their initial designs, repeated-measures studies can expand to include new variables that reflect changes in the researcher's understanding and in the life stage or experiences of the study members themselves. Of particular value, participants can reflect back on their own experience from different vantage points and assist with the interpretation of their own data profiles.

The majority of longitudinal studies involve repeated personal contacts between researchers and their study members. Multiple contacts provide the opportunity to clarify and follow up on previous information. The close rapport and lengthy period of contacts with gifted and talented individuals is one of the joys associated with this methodological approach.

The pleasure of keeping in contact with talented people is balanced with the frustrations of keeping track of mobile individuals. A wealth of data can prove overwhelming in volume, complexity, and cost. Fleming and Hollinger (Chapter 12), for instance, found their data were too extensive for the local computing facility to process. They were forced to drive a car, sagging noticeably from the weight of innumerable IBM punch cards, to another state's flagship university for data analysis. Improvement in computing equipment and the obsolescence of punched data cards enabled the researchers to be reunited with their data several years later. Many researchers persist in spite of the pitfalls in order to investigate issues that can only be answered by studying the same individuals over time.

WEAKNESSES OF LONGITUDINAL METHODOLOGY

Those who have survived or are presently enduring the doctoral dissertation or the tenure processes will probably read with special understanding Wagner and Sternberg's (1986) discussions of tacit knowledge as a component of the Triarchic Theory of Human Intelligence. Their discussion focused on the decisions professionals must make based on a field's accumulated yet unwritten wisdom. When it comes to doctoral or pretenure academic research, it is considered unwise, for example, to select a research problem that cannot be addressed within a year or two because of the consequent delay this would have on the conferral of a degree or the acquisition of a publication. Longitudinal studies take time, particularly when data points are several years apart. A compensating element to keep in mind is that if all goes as planned, one does have a cohort of subjects from which to gather data over the course of years. This advantage is not something to be taken lightly given the difficulties associated with getting access and permission to study new groups of children or adults.

Overall, the commitment essential to conducting longitudinal research is immense, both in terms of time and money. Time is required for tracking down individuals who move and fail to send forwarding addresses, and for setting up interviews. Gifted individuals, such as the subjects of the studies described in this book, are often busy and active. Arranging time for a conversation can be extremely frustrating, especially within the constraints of a researcher's own schedule. Time is also needed to organize, code, or quantify the data needed to make comparisons across collection points. Finally, time is required for travel to meet with study subjects and to write funding proposals to continue the study.

Funds are needed to pay for transcriptions, mailing, copying, telephone bills, and travel expenses. Transcriptions of audio or videotapes alone can cost thousands of dollars. Some researchers might choose to purchase equipment to do their own transcription. One could also play the interview tapes repeatedly to extract anecdotal material verbatim and to classify the rest into categorical schemes or quantifiable variables. Some funding agencies, like the Spencer, Sloan, or the National Science Foundations, will support longitudinal research if they are interested in the study population. Although it is hard to predict what will be of interest to funding agencies in the future, work related to groups which are underrepresented in science, mathematics, and technology are current priorities, particularly if the proposed study's focus is on how to remove obstacles to active participation in these fields.

VALIDITY IN LONGITUDINAL RESEARCH

Schaie (1983) noted that, although longitudinal research offers significant advantages over cross-sectional designs, it suffers from methodological difficulties that can threaten the validity of the studies. (See Schaie for a more technical explanation of validity issues in longitudinal research.) We have already noted one potential threat to the internal validity of longitudinal studies: bias introduced by repeated exposure to researchers and to instruments. Campbell and Stanley (1963) referred to these as "testing effects," comprising practice effects and reactivity. Practice taking a certain test or completing a certain task might cause subjects to perform differently than if they had no prior exposure to the instrument or task. Similarly, participation in a study that encourages reflection or emphasizes given types of achievement might affect subjects' habits of reflection, insight, self-view, or even their subsequent decisions and behavior. The extent to which study members are affected by their participation in an ongoing research project cannot be measured and varies according to characteristics of individual study members and researchers and the nature of the contacts between them.

Difficult issues can arise in longitudinal research when, as is common, subjects ask researchers for advice or assistance. Occasionally, a researcher will feel it necessary to take an advocacy role for a study subject or gifted program. At other times, an investigator might act on information about a health or life-threatening situation or help a subject negotiate an obstacle to achievement. Such interventions, although rare, obviously contaminate study findings for affected individuals. Like many qualitative investigators, longitudinal researchers normally deal with concerns of researcher intervention and subject reactivity by acknowledging them to readers as potential sources of bias.

Subject attrition, or "experimental mortality," is a consistent threat to the internal validity of longitudinal studies. Subjects are lost through death or through geographic moves that leave them unreachable by researchers. Research on subject attrition suggests that experimental mortality of study participants is not random (Arzi, 1989). Subjects may withdraw when they perceive their lives are not going well: when they are unhappy, not achieving highly, or not leading the kind of life they think the research project values. Virtually every investigator represented in this book can describe specific instances of cases where subjects dropped out for one or more of these reasons.

Dealing with experimental mortality is difficult. Holmesian detective techniques are often required to find missing subjects (Call, Otto, & Spenner, 1982). (There are agencies that will trace research subjects for a fee.) Again researchers can, at a minimum, acknowledge attrition as a source of uncontrolled variability. Other approaches include matching the original study group with a more complete same-age control group, or extrapolating from subjects who rejoin studies the differences that might exist between study dropouts and persisters.

A third concern about validity in longitudinal research involves the generalizability of longitudinal study findings to other populations. The intensive study of highly unusual persons can make construction of control groups conceptually or logistically very difficult. Davidson and Scripp (Chapter 6), for example, use a control group in their investigation of musical reasoning development in gifted and nongifted preschoolers. It is unclear, however, how a control group could be formed for their second study, an investigation of musical thinking as it relates to performance of conservatory music majors (Chapter 7). Sample size and resources are already limited by the demands and costs of longitudinal inquiry; sometimes adding a control group is not practicable. The lack of comparison groups, however, confounds the effects of maturation with the effects of early characteristics and experiences. Further, as in all gifted research, the singularity or rarity of some highly gifted study samples prevents ready generalization, even to other gifted groups.

A related problem is the typically small sample size employed by many longitudinal studies of the gifted. Large sample designs, like those reported by Perleth and Heller (Chapter 4) and by Lubinski and Benbow (Chapter 10), require enormous resources from granting agencies. Some behaviors or abilities associated with giftedness or eminence are rarely exhibited and selective groups provide only small numbers of subjects for follow-up.

The validity of single-cohort longitudinal studies is threatened by historical effects. Single-cohort studies involve a research sample whose members are approximately the same chronological age. Since members of the same age group, or cohort, have experienced similar societal conditions (cohort effect) and identical historical events (time-of-measurement effect), their individual and group profiles might reflect their maturation in a common milieu rather than the impacts of the study variables. Another cohort with a different sociohistorical context might vary in its patterns of development. Fleming and Hollinger (Chapter 12), for instance, studied the careers of women who were high school students in the mid-1970s. Without question, the professional expectations and opportunities these women experience are different from those of their mothers or their daughters. Generalizing from the career development of the Project Choice subjects to women of other cohorts might be unwarranted. Single-cohort studies of programs for the gifted, like those of Delcourt (Chapter 15) and Moon and Feldhusen (Chapter 14), may suffer threats to validity from inconsistencies in the way programs are implemented as well as by a particular societal context.

Again, researchers use several means to deal with the threats to validity posed by single-cohort longitudinal studies. The best way, of course, is to replicate a longitudinal study with multiple cohorts. Subotnik, Karp, and Morgan (1989) created a multiple-cohort study by comparing their subjects with counterparts in Terman's study on matched IQ and survey instruments. In this volume, Lubinski and Benbow (Chapter 10), Perleth and Heller (Chapter 4), and Cramond (Chapter 9) used multiple-cohort longitudinal design. Other researchers compare longitudinal panels of same-age subjects from different sociocultural contexts. Single-cohort longitudinal studies can be justified in the case of populations that are previously unstudied and in intensive qualitative designs (Vaillant, 1977). Such studies generate information, questions, and hypotheses that serve as a foundation for future research using other cohorts, more limited variable sets, and larger samples. Care must be taken, however, to avoid generalizing single-cohort study findings to other populations with different surrounding circumstances.

STRENGTHS OF LONGITUDINAL METHODOLOGIES

We have presented a rationale for avoiding this time-consuming, expensive, and exhausting approach to conducting research. Now we want to convince our readers that the best way to answer vital educational questions is to extend, sometimes dramatically, the collection of data points used to measure the effects of an educational treatment or to determine the predictive validity of a standardized measure.

As responsible professionals, we want to be able to offer sound advice to children, teachers, and parents who pose questions that are of great concern to them. For example, how much of a role does doing well on an IQ or SAT test play in students' later accomplishment? How can we best assist students who achieve extremely high grade point averages to capitalize on the very academic talent and motivation that made them high school valedictorians? If winning a prestigious award for creative achievement in high school does not ensure outstanding accomplishment during early adulthood, what distinguishes the experiences of those who do fulfill their potential from those who do not? What role does gender play in the development of talent? These questions speak to the goals and expectations we have for young people in taking an active, constructive, and satisfying part in our society. The answers vary according to the developmental stage of the study subjects, as well as by societal expectations, historical events, and personal psychological predisposition. Longitudinal study, because of its sweeping chronological reach, can offer meaningful insights into the outcomes of earlier educational policies and help us plan interventions that more clearly fulfill societal and individual needs.

Maintaining control over constantly changing address lists of study participants can be frustrating, yet reuniting with individuals over more than one data collection point is extremely rewarding. Follow-up interactions result in strong bonds between researcher and subject, and the thrill of observing a growing and changing individual encountering the various challenges that are part of the developmental life span helps overcome some of the more frustrating aspects of the methodology. Interviews, whether in-person, on the phone, or in writing, offer a context for the quantitative data that usually serve as the structural base for a research project. For example, in the course of monitoring the educational decisions made by Westinghouse Science Talent Search winners, Subotnik and Steiner (Chapter 3) noted that the largest proportion of their subjects left the science pipeline during the first 2 years of college. They assumed, based on national reports on postsecondary science education, that this attrition was due to the large, impersonal, and demanding introductory classes traditionally designed to weed out those students not prepared to jump through intellectual and tradition-bound hoops to join the ranks of professional scientists. Indeed, the interviews supported this reasoning, but also showed how most undergraduate institutions systematically refused students opportunities for participation in research, the dimension of science that was most attractive to these students and for which they had achieved the most recognition. Furthermore, Science Talent Search winners were afraid to insist on being able to continue working at research because they now saw themselves as lowly freshman in a sea of equally talented individuals.

Follow-up interviews provide richer data by virtue of the heightened rapport between study participants and researchers, and increased comfort and openness of study members in talking or writing about themselves. Abundant anecdotal material aids investigators in triangulating data collection methods, thereby creating a three-dimensional view of study findings, enlivening written reports, and underlining the individuality of gifted persons.

Longitudinal researchers have seen teachers, gifted programs, and even school systems affected positively as a result of their ongoing research contacts. Terman enjoyed a warm relationship with many members of his study cohort. In fact, his interactions with them could be described in some cases as interference. He offered advice, made connections, and served as a reminder that they had been labeled as gifted. Similarly, Davidson's work on critical thinking in music in a Massachusetts school district resulted in expansion of the professional music staff in the schools (Davidson, 1992, personal communication). The impact of such relationships, which are inherent to the methodology, certainly compromises the rigor of the studies, but the rewards for both subjects and investigators are extraordinary.

OVERVIEW OF CHAPTERS AND THEIR ARRANGEMENT

The chapters in this volume have been organized into three categories based on the standard by which the study subjects were identified. The first cluster is organized around the criterion of demonstrated performance. Arnold (Chapter 2) identified Illinois high school valedictorians of the class of 1981. Her focus in this volume is on the career patterns and adult achievement aspirations of the males in the group. Subotnik and Steiner's study subjects (Chapter 3) were 1983 Westinghouse Science Talent Search winners who at age 17 competed successfully for America's most prestigious secondary school science prize. The investigators discuss the variables that differentiate those who have persisted in the field of science over time from those who have chosen a different path.

The region formerly called West Germany has an active scholarly community studying the development of talent in German youngsters. Two chapters in this section written by researchers from the University of Munich address the outcomes of experimental multidimensional identification procedures. Perleth and Heller (Chapter 4) report on a combined longitudinal and cross-sectional study of giftedness and achievement of German students from ages 6 to 18. Their large-sample, multiple-cohort study includes noncognitive, personality, and environmental determinants of educational achievement. Chapter 5 describes Hany's investigation into the development of technical creativity in German students.

Davidson and Scripp are musicians and scholars affiliated with the Harvard Project Zero, a developmental study associated with Gardner's (1983) theory of Multiple Intelligences, and the New England Conservatory of Music. They have contributed two chapters that explore musical giftedness. Chapter 6 looks at musical reasoning among preschool and early elementary school students. Chapter 7 introduces the evolution of advanced musical reasoning among performance majors at a distinguished conservatory. Finally, Milgram and Hong, in Chapter 8, report on an Israeli study that introduces the notion of leisure-time activity choice as a significant variable in predicting adult creativity and achievement.

Our second category of studies explores the predictive validity of various standardized tests that have been used extensively to identify giftedness. Cramond (Chapter 9) provides us with the historical context for the design of the Torrance Tests of Creative Thinking and a rationale for their continued use to recognize creative children who might otherwise be overlooked by IQ measures. Lubinski and Benbow (Chapter 10) have directed a comprehensive, multicohort study of individuals who reason extremely well in mathematics. The criterion of identification is a superior score on the SAT-M before the age of 13. In our only study of comparative identification procedures, Albert (Chapter 11) describes his work with high-IQ males and same-age males who were identified as math or science talented.

Our third section addresses the long-range effect of participation in gifted programs with unique identification procedures and programmatic designs. Highly able girls were the subjects of an experimental program in career development designed and conducted in 1977 by Fleming and Hollinger (Chapter 12). Their chapter describes the career patterns of women at the most recent data collection point. Rudnitski (Chapter 13) conducted a follow-up of Graduate Leadership Education Project (GLEP) fellows, all of whom had been labeled as potential leaders in the field of gifted education and were provided with a special experience by a consortium of universities. The Purdue Three-Stage Model was developed by Feldhusen and Kolloff as a pull-out enrichment program for gifted students. Moon and Feldhusen (Chapter 14) have conducted an investigation into the effects of the program on a group of its earliest graduates. A wide-spread enrichment program in the United States is the Renzulli Enrichment Triad which employs the Three Ring conception of giftedness as its identification method. Delcourt (Chapter 15) describes a 5-year follow-up of students in a program that implemented the Triad design in order to address the impact of the program on participating students.

The final chapter in this volume includes a synthesis of the reported research, identifies common themes, and suggests areas for future exploration. In that chapter we assess how far longitudinal research in gifted education has moved beyond Terman.

Chap-ter	Study	Sample	Data Collection Points	Primary Focus	Data Sources
2	The Illinois Vale-dictorian Project (Arnold)	Male high school valedictorians and salutatorians N=35	Began: 1981 Data Waves: annually 1981-1985 1990	Determinants of academic and career achievements in academically talented males	Interviews, college entrance examination scores, questionnaires
3	Adult Manifestations of Academic Talent in Science (Subotnik & Steiner)	1983 Male and female Westinghouse Science Talent Search Winners N=98	Began: 1983 Data Waves: 1984 1988 1990	Identification of variables associated with retention and attrition of science talent	Interviews, questionnaires
4	Munich Longitudinal Study of Giftedness (Perleth & Heller)	German elementary and secondary school students identified by teacher screening and test scores N=1414	Began: 1985 Data waves: 1986 1987 1988	Identification methods for gifted children and adolescents; Testing of multidimensional theoretical model of giftedness; genesis of achievement	Tests; questionnaires; interviews (of selected subjects)
5	Development of Technical Creativity (Hany)	German elementary and secondary school students N=195	Began: 1988 Data waves: 1988 1989 1990	Identification methods and testing of theoretical model of technical creativity	Tests, performance assessments, academic records

Figure 1.1. Overview of collected studies

6	Musical Giftedness in Pre-School Years (Davidson & Scripp)	First born preschool children ages 1-6 N=9	Began: 1978 Data waves: Twice monthly 1978-1982	Course of musical development in early childhood; development of musically gifted children	Observations; tapes and transcriptions of children's song singing
7	Giftedness and Musical Training in Conservatory Students (Scripp & Davidson)	Male and female music conservatory students N=120	Began: 1985 Data waves: Each cohort, twice yearly for two years Cohort I: 1986-1987 Cohort II:1988-1989	Relationship between music performance and cognitive structures of musical understanding	Observations; tapes and transcriptions of sight-singing and playing exercises; student reflective writing
8	Creative Thinking and Performance in Adolescents as Predictors of Adult Creative Attainments (Milgram & Hong)	Male and female 1973 Israeli high school seniors N=67	Began: 1973 Data waves: 1973 1990	Predictive validity of creativity test and leisure-time activities in predicting adult accomplishment	Tests of creative thinking; academic records; measures of activities and accomplishments
9	Torrance Tests of Creative Thinking: Design and Predictive Validity (Cramond)	1958-1964 Minnesota elementary and high school students (Additional small-cohort samples) N=500	Began: 1958 Data waves: 1958-1964 1969 1971 1979-1980	Development of creativity; measurement of creative potential; predictive validity of Torrance Tests of Creativity	Tests of creativity; indices of creative achievement
10	Mathematically Precocious Students (Lubinski & Benbow)	Five cohorts of 12-13 year-olds scoring highly on the SAT test in mathematics N=5000	Began: 1972 Data waves: Each cohort studied at ages 13, 18, 23	Determinants of achievement in science and mathematics among mathematically gifted students	SAT test scores, Psychological and ability tests, questionnaires, interviews (of selected subjects)

Figure 1.1. *Continued*

11	Gifted Boys and their Families (Albert)	High-IQ and mathematically gifted twelve year-old boys N=52	Began: 1977 Data waves: 1977 1982 1986	Effects of family, cognitive, personality, and creative factors on career choice and adult eminence	IQ and mathematics test scores; test battery; interviews
12	Project Choice: Gifted and Talented Women (Fleming & Hollinger)	1976 high school girls ages 15-16 in 2 public, 2 private, and 2 parochial high schools N=268	Began: 1976 Data waves: 1976 1978, 1979 1982 1990	Determinants of career achievements among gifted women; Outcomes of career program for girls	Tests; academic records; questionnaires
13	A Generation of Leaders in Gifted Education (Rudnitski)	1977-1981 Five cohorts of gifted education graduate student fellows at seven universities N=38	Began: 1977 Data waves: 1977-1981; 1990	Determinants of leadership in gifted education; Outcomes of Graduate Leader-ship Education Project	Interviews, academic and career achievement records, admissions materials
14	PACE Program: A Follow-Up Study Ten Years Later (Moon & Feldhusen)	Elementary school students who participated in PACE gifted program and parents of students N=23 students N=22 parents	Began: 1980-1985 Data waves: 1980-1985; 1990	Outcomes of theoretically-driven elementary gifted program	Family interviews questionnaires,
15	Characteristics of High Level Creative Productivity (Delcourt)	High school students (grades 9 to 12) from multiple schools/states who had been iden-tified according to the Renzulli Three-Ring Conception of Giftedness N=18	Began: 1987-1988 Data waves: 1987-1988; 1991	Determinants of creative and productive behavior; Outcomes of theoretically-driven gifted program	Document analysis, student interviews, questionnaires related to school, student, and parent characteristics

Figure 1.1. *Continued*

REFERENCES

Arzi, H. (1989). From short to long term: Studying science education longitudinally. *Studies in Science Education, 15*, 17–53.

Astin, H., & Myint, T. (1971). Career development of young women during the post-high school years. *Journal of Counseling Psychology Monograph, 18*(4), 369–393.

Baird, L. L. (1982). *The role of academic ability in high level accomplishment and general success* (College Board Report Vol. 82, No. 6). Princeton, NJ: Educational Testing Service.

Baird, L. L. (1985). Do grades and tests predict adult accomplishment? *Research in Higher Education, 23*, 3–85.

Bloom, B. S. (Ed.). (1985). *Developing talent in young people*. New York: Ballantine.

Burks, B. S., Jensen, D. W., & Terman, L. M. (1930). The promise of youth. *Genetic studies of genius* (Vol. III). Stanford, CA: Stanford University Press.

Call, V. R., Otto, L. B., & Spenner, K. I. (1982). *Tracking respondents: A multi-method approach*. Lexington, MA: Lexington Books.

Campbell, D. T., & Stanley, J. C. (1963). *Experimental and quasi-experimental designs for research*. Chicago, IL: Rand McNally.

Card, J. J., Steel, L., & Abeles, R. (1980). Sex differences in realization of individual potential for achievement. *Journal of Vocational Behavior, 17*, 1–21.

Cohen, P. (1984). College grades and adult achievement: A research synthesis. *Research in Higher Education, 20*, 281–293.

Csikszentmihalyi, M. (1990). The domain of creativity. In M. Runco & R. S. Albert (Eds.), *Theories of creativity* (pp. 190–212). Newbury Park, CA: Sage.

Educational Testing Service (ETS). (1991). *Performance at the top: From elementary through graduate school*. Princeton, NJ: Educational Testing Service Policy Information Center.

Feldhusen, J. F. (1986). A conception of giftedness. In R.J. Sternberg & J.E. Davidson (Eds.), *Conceptions of giftedness* (pp. 112–127). New York: Cambridge University Press.

Feldhusen, J. F., & Kolloff, M. B. (1979). A three-stage model for gifted education. *Gifted Child Today, 4*, 3–5, 53–57.

Gardner, H. (1983). *Frames of mind: The theory of multiple intelligences*. New York: Basic Books.

Getzels, J. W., & Csikszentmihalyi, M. (1976). *The creative vision: A longitudinal study of problem finding in art*. New York: Wiley.

Goertzel, V., & Goertzel, M. G. (1962). *Cradles of eminence*. Boston, MA: Little, Brown.

Hollingworth, L. S. (1942). *Children above 180 IQ*. New York: World Book .

Merton, R. K. (1968). The Matthew Effect in science. *Science, 159*, 56–63.

Oden, M. (1968). The fulfillment of promise: 40-year follow-up of the Terman gifted group. *Genetic Psychology Monographs, 77*, 3–93.

Reid, B. D. (1991, June). National research needs assessment process. *The National Research Center on the Gifted and Talented Newsletter, 1*(1), 8–9.

Renzulli, J. S. (1977). *The enrichment triad model: A guide for developing defensible programs for the gifted and talented*. Mansfield Center, CT: Creative Learning Press.

Renzulli, J. S. (1986). The three-ring conception of giftedness: A developmental model for creative productivity. In R. J. Sternberg & J. E. Davidson (Eds.), *Conceptions of giftedness* (pp. 53–92). New York: Cambridge University Press.

Roe, A. (1953). *The making of a scientist*. New York: Dodd, Mead.

Schaie, K. W. (1983). *Longitudinal studies of adult psychological development*. New York: Guilford Press.

Subotnik, R. F., Karp, D. E., & Morgan, E. R. (1989). High IQ children at mid-life: An investigation into the generalizability of Terman's "Genetic Studies of Genius." *Roeper Review, 11*(3), 139–144.

Subotnik, R. F., Kassan, L., Summers, E., & Wasser, A. (1993). *Genius revisited: High IQ children grown up*. Norwood, NJ: Ablex.

Terman, L. M. (1925). Mental and physical traits of a thousand gifted children. *Genetic studies of genius* (Vol. I). Stanford, CA: Stanford University Press.

Terman, L. M., & Oden, M. H. (1947). The gifted child grows up. *Genetic studies of genius* (Vol. IV). Stanford, CA: Stanford University Press.

Terman, L. M., & Oden, M. H. (1959). The gifted group at mid-life: 35 years' follow-up of the superior child. *Genetic studies of genius* (Vol. V). Stanford, CA: Stanford University Press.

Vaillant, G. E. (1977). *Adaptation to life*. Boston, MA: Little, Brown.

Wagner, R. K., & Sternberg, R. J. (1986). Tacit knowledge and intelligence in the everyday world. In R. J. Sternberg & R. K. Wagner (Eds.), *Practical intelligence: Nature and origins of competence in the everyday world* (pp. 51–83). New York: Cambridge University Press.

White, W. L., & Renzulli, J. S. (1987). A forty year follow-up of students who attended Leta Hollingworth's school for gifted children. *Roeper Review, 10*(2), 89–94.

Zuckerman, H. (1977). *Scientific elite: Nobel laureates in the United States*. New York: Free Press.

2

The Illinois Valedictorian Project: Early Adult Careers of Academically Talented Male High School Students*

Karen D. Arnold

OVERVIEW AND BACKGROUND OF STUDY

The earliest competition involving nearly all members of society takes place in the academic arena. The label "valedictorian" rewards the best grade earner in high school and constitutes a lifelong marker of success. The Illinois Valedictorian Project is in the thirteenth year of a projected 15-year study of high school valedictorians. The Project follows the academic and nonacademic lives of top high school achievers in order to understand academic success—its antecedents, prices, rewards, and relationship to career and personal life adaptation.

Aside from a yearly flurry of newspaper profiles and countless retrospective anecdotes, little is known about what really happens to high school valedictorians. No systematic study of valedictorians appears in the education or psychology literature. What are the consequences of graduating as the best student in a high school? Does stellar academic performance as a high school student translate into high achievement in postsecondary education? More importantly, what does scholastic achievement have to do with success outside academics? Such questions guide the longitudinal research which seeks to investigate the relationship between high school academic achievement and undergraduate and career attainment.

*The Illinois Valedictorian Project has been conducted since 1981 with Dr. Terry Denny, Professor Emeritus, University of Illinois at Urbana-Champaign. Partial funding for the study has been provided by the North Central Regional Education Laboratory, Boston College, and the University of Illinois Bureau of Educational Research.

The Project began with the identification of 82 valedictorians and salutatorians who graduated in 1981 from high schools throughout the state of Illinois. Researchers attended each of the graduation exercises of the participants, met with them, and conducted five or six extended interviews with each of the study members. Questionnaires, telephone conversations, letters, and other information supplemented the semistructured interviews.

Longitudinal Design

Following valedictorians through college and into early careers allows researchers to observe the change and continuity of individuals and group values, accomplishments, personality, and aspirations. Longitudinal study design also illuminates influences on achievement and issues of importance to students. Study members relate their perceptions and experiences as they occur, not in the tidied frame of retrospection. The participants' conception of their experiences over a crucial 15-year life period provides a developmental picture of academic achievers that is significantly richer and fuller than a cross-sectional view of a group of former high school valedictorians.

Single-cohort longitudinal studies such as the Illinois Valedictorian Project are vulnerable to time-of-measurement effects. In other words, the particular sociohistorical context surrounding Illinois high school students in the early 1980s may render this group incomparable to top achievers of a different time, region, culture, or age group. As the population of valedictorians is apparently unstudied, however, investigation must begin with intensive descriptive efforts. In addition, a single-cohort study can be useful in extracting information about a unique population (Schaie, 1983). Researchers conducting the longitudinal Grant Study of Harvard men, for example, extrapolated principles of optimal mental health and adaptive functioning from their highly atypical, intensively studied group (Vaillant, 1977). Similarly, the in-depth study of academically successful adolescents may provide patterns of successful adaptation that apply to more heterogeneous groups.

Related Research

The longitudinal Illinois Valedictorian Project draws from the literature of developmental psychology, particularly theory on meaning-making through intensive life-story narrative (Guba & Lincoln,

1989; Kegan, 1982; Lincoln & Guba, 1985). In addition, the research on high academic achievement is informed by other longitudinal studies of gifted individuals.

The developmental levels of late adolescence and early adulthood center on identity formation, which is related closely to the clarification of vocational purpose (Chickering, 1978; Erikson, 1968; Perry, 1970). An individual's approach to identity issues affects the relationship between educational achievement, career aspirations, and early vocational behavior through the way that individual makes meaning of his or her world (Kegan, 1982). Self-efficacy and cognitive development, for example, affect the formation of an adult work identity and mediate the direct relationship between academic and career attainment. Young people's perceptions of themselves and the world converge in the construction of a scenario or game plan for their future, a narrative picture of what they hope and expect from life (Whitbourne, 1987). Such narratives crystallize goals and offer a yardstick for measuring progress (McAdams, 1990). The longitudinal interview design of the Illinois Valedictorian Project elicits the development of these narratives over time.

Developmental theory provides a framework for the study of individual lives but longitudinal research on the gifted relates more directly to the valedictorian population. Despite several decades of studying the correlates of early achievement, present knowledge is not sufficient to understand fully, much less to predict, the achievement of outstanding individuals. Even Terman's widely quoted study of genius children included adults who worked as unskilled laborers (Oden, 1968). Longitudinal studies of the gifted offer a particularly rewarding insight into the development of outstanding human achievements.

Longitudinal research on the gifted focuses on intellectual ability and creativity as well as on outstanding performance in a single talent area. This volume includes, for instance, longitudinal studies of mathematically gifted adolescents (Lubinski & Benbow, Chapter 10) and scientifically talented high school students (Subotnik & Steiner, Chapter 3). The Study of Mathematically Precocious Youth (SMPY) is an example of a study whose gifted population was identified on the basis of tested ability, rather than school grades (Benbow & Stanley, 1983). Two major goals of the related educational efforts are early entrance into postsecondary education and facilitation of advanced, specialized work in mathematics and science. The mathematically talented students in the SMPY studies are frequently ineligible as high school valedictorians because of their early exit from high school. SMPY students and Westinghouse competition winners are encouraged to pursue talent areas rather than to excel in the complete range of high school subjects. In a retrospective study of top performers in athletic, artistic, and intellectual fields, Bloom (1985) reminded educators that exceptional talent development occurs with intense specialization. Such specialization normally takes place outside of, and sometimes in opposition to, the normal demands of group-oriented, multisubject schooling.

The longitudinal Grant Study, mentioned above, used identification procedures that resembled the valedictorian definition of talent as general academic excellence. The Grant Study of Adult Development followed the lives of 100 Harvard men for over 40 years, beginning in their college days in the early 1940s (Vaillant, 1977). The Grant Study identified subjects who seemed mentally and physically healthy—men who could be expected to make the best possible adaptation to life. The study followed the men's lives through questionnaire self-reports and interviews. The men were similar in intellectual achievement, physical and mental health, and stability of family background. Each man held the Harvard success label. Vaillant found that the differences that dramatically separated these men four decades after their identification as the best and the brightest were neither single traumatic events nor abundant problems. Instead, Vaillant concluded that adults change significantly over time and that eventual life success and adjustment results from superior abilities to adapt to the world.

The homogeneity of the Grant Study sample resulted in unanswered questions that can be profitably studied in a contemporary longitudinal study of more heterogeneously talented youth. The Grant Study defined giftedness as optimal adaptation. This definition of giftedness is not equivalent to academic performance; however, the Grant Study comes closer to a performance depiction of talent than most gifted studies that identify subjects on the basis of tested intelligence and ability.

An important example of a highly talented sample selected on the basis of measured intelligence was the longitudinal Terman study of 1,000 gifted California school children (Oden, 1968; Terman, 1959; Terman & Oden, 1947). Terman's group was selected in the 1920s from the top 1% in tested intelligence, contained males and females, and used clinical interviews and a variety of intelligence and personality tests. The findings from Terman's group and Grant's sample were similar on several counts. The principal differences occurred in academic achievement and career success, with Terman's group lagging behind the Grant group. The most apparent reason for these differences was the selection criterion of academic achievement present in the Grant study and absent in the Terman study. Terman's subjects varied widely on school performance, the identifying label of talent for the valedictorians. Findings from the Terman studies are only tangentially applicable to the valedictorian study because of the definition of giftedness as measured intelligence and the dissimilar historical context.

Few studies directly address the relationship of academic and adult attainment. It is unclear from the mixed results of these studies how closely high school and college grades relate to career success (Astin, 1977; Baird, 1982; Hoyt, 1966; Munday & Davis, 1974; Watley, 1971). Some indications are that scholastic performance does make a difference, for high academic achievers in general (Astin, 1977), and for women with high IQs (Sears & Barbee, 1977). Other studies found that success, especially life success but career achievement as well, related more closely to nonacademic factors such as extracurricular activities (Munday & Davis, 1974) or mature coping mechanisms (Vaillant, 1977).

A final category of related research is sociological and social psychological literature concerning determinants of adult vocational behavior. Basic status attainment models, for instance, hold that occupational attainment results from an individual's family socioeconomic level, educational level, and ability (Blau & Duncan, 1967), and from the influence on achievement of race, gender, and ethnicity. Social psychologists point to the importance of achievement motivation in determining academic and career behavior (Ames & Ames, 1984; Dweck & Elliot, 1983; Spence & Helmreich, 1983). Although achievement motivation has been shown to relate to real-world attainment, achievement behaviors are mediated by a constellation of other factors, including ability, personal values, and the actual and perceived occupational structure of opportunity (Astin, 1984). Sociological and achievement motivation research offer additional insight regarding adult behavior; however, such literature rarely highlights gifted populations.

Some definitions of gifted learners are stated in terms of abilities to make wise and personally rewarding adaptations to world demands (Sellin & Birch, 1981). How the valedictorians cope with these demands over time and, indeed, whether the research on talented and gifted applies appropriately to a group that achieves *within* the system are fascinating central questions to our study.

SAMPLE AND METHOD

The study members are 46 women and 35 men who were the best grade earners of their high school classes. The 51 valedictorians, 20 salutatorians, and 9 top honor students graduated in 1981 from public and private high schools in rural, town, city, and suburban Illinois. (The students will be referred to as "valedictorians" for the sake of conciseness.) The educational background and occupations of the students' parents vary considerably. The predominantly white group includes five African-American and three Latino/a students as well as one Asian-American student.

Sampling Procedure

The sample was drawn from a list of 270 Illinois high schools that publicly recognized valedictorians at commencement. The list of schools was obtained in response to letters of inquiry to all Illinois high school principals, half of whom responded. The scheduled times of the graduation exercises had a direct bearing on the sample, as a researcher attended the commencement ceremonies of each of the study participants.

Within the logistical constraints of attendance at graduation, high schools were chosen to include large and small schools; city, rural, and suburban; parochial and public; and schools with an African-American and Latino/a majority. Whenever a conflict arose in which more than one school was scheduled for a commencement ceremony at the same time, schools were chosen to provide the demographic characteristics which were otherwise underrepresented in the study. In this manner, 33 schools were selected, including six Catholic, one Lutheran, two nondenominational private, and 24 public high schools. Study members graduated at the top of classes of 25 students in farming communities and at the head of 650 students in suburban and city high schools. They achieved top high school honors in inner-city Chicago, in central and southern Illinois cities, and in university towns. One valedictory address was given in Spanish.

After attending the commencement exercises, letters requesting participation were sent to 90 students. Eighty-three replied, one of whom could not be convinced to join the study. Another died soon after the initial interview. In this fashion, the current 81 students were selected. In the first 10 years after high school graduation, all of the valedictorians remained active in the study.

The sample, in short, was designed to include students who were matched by a common criterion of publicly recognized academic success but who represented the widest range of possible settings for that success. Although the geographical distribution of the 33 schools roughly corresponds to the concentration of the state population in the Chicago area, the sample overrepresents Illinois students from high schools outside Chicago, from private high schools, and from predominantly African-American and Latino/a institutions.

The Participants

In addition to 51 valedictorians, participants include 20 salutatorians and 9 top honor students. Salutatorians were included on the urgings of members of a pilot study of high school valedictorians. A few top honor students were also included on the advice of informants who identified them as the actual top student at the school. Continued inclusion of these students has rested on analyses that show them to be similar to the rest of the group in ability, background characteristics, and college academic performance. Seventy-two of the valedictorians are white, five are African-American, three are Mexican-American, and one is Chinese-American. The parents of the valedictorians work in diverse occupations, from unskilled laborers to farmers, business owners, and professionals. Most of the valedictorians grew up in stable two-parent families. Only four students grew up in single-parent households because of divorce ($n = 2$) or death of a parent ($n = 2$). Parents were educated to the sixth grade in some instances, beyond the PhD in others. As they graduated high school, religion was at the center of some of the valedictorians' lives and outside of others. Among the believers are Catholics and Protestants, Baptists, Nazarenes, Mormons, and Jews. Some of the study group speak English as a second language; other native speakers of English speak a second language in the home.

Commencement Exercises

The sample was limited to high schools that recognized a valedictorian publicly with the traditional commencement address. Witnessing the moment of public anointment as valedictorian was, therefore, an important initiation to the Illinois Valedictorian Project. A Project researcher attended each of the 33 high school commencement ceremonies to get some sense of that significant day in the lives of the students as well as to introduce the study to them. Each valedictorian provided the Project with a copy of the valedictorian address. With a very few notable exceptions, these speeches were uninspired accounts of high school experiences, gratitude to adults, and vague calls to future leadership. In the first year of the study, researchers used the addresses and the field notes from commencement to initiate discussion about the background, meaning, and experience of being high school valedictorian.

Data Collection: Interviews and Quantitative Data Sources

The valedictorians participated in five or six semistructured interviews. In addition, questionnaire data were collected in 1981, 1984, 1985, and 1988.

In the academic year following their high school graduation, each valedictorian was interviewed about their high school and family experiences. Subsequent interviews dealt with adjustment to college, choice of major, and relationships. As the students left college, the focus of the interviews shifted to graduate school and early careers as well as dating, marriage, and parenthood. All the interviews feature questions aimed at identifying the participants' need to achieve and the source(s) of that need, influential experiences related to their academic achievement, and a sense of their general attitudes toward themselves, their families, their careers, and the future. Among the several questions that are repeated at each interview are queries about the students' ultimate goals, their struggles, and the meaning they give to having been valedictorian or salutatorian. Interviewers also read excerpts from past interviews to solicit current reactions of study members to earlier thoughts, feelings, and aspirations.

During the first year of the study, the Project collected survey information about student lifestyles and values that replicated items from a national sample of over 16,000 1981 high school seniors (Bachman, Johnston, & O'Malley, 1981). The same questions were posed to the study members in 1990. Researchers administered other normed survey instruments over the years that have facilitated the comparison of the high-achieving study group with national samples of heterogeneous and gifted age peers. In 1985, students completed instruments measuring gender role expectations and achievement motivation (Personal Attributes Questionnaire, Spence, Helmreich, & Stapp, 1974; Work and Family Orientation Questionnaire, Spence & Helmreich, 1983). Finally, study participants have completed Project-designed surveys regarding educational and employment experiences, and personal and occupational values.

FINDINGS FROM THE FIRST 5 YEARS

Participants in the Illinois Valedictorian Project identified themselves as top students long before high school. Half of the valedictorians considered themselves high academic achievers by the 5th grade, 75% by the 8th grade. Although Bloom (1985) found talent was developed by individualized instruction outside the school, academic achievers excelled in classroom group learning within school. In the first year of the study, it became apparent that the conception of the high school valedictorian as socially backward and exceptionally studious was a myth. Valedictorians were high school cheerleaders, football stars, and class officers. They played in school bands and wrote for school newspapers. Unlike Bloom's talented youth, who subordinated school to talent development, these academic achievers performed within the system of schooling and, for most, school was at the center of their lives. The valedictorians were not extraordinarily dedicated intellectuals, nor did they escape the materialism and vocationalism of their cohort (Levine, 1980). As they left high school, the valedictorians exhibited a low incidence of idealism and a high priority on materialism. For most, making a contribution to society and working to correct social and economic inequalities were not important goals. Instead, the majority of the valedictorians expressed their adult goals in terms of children, houses, and financial security.

As they left high school, both male and female valedictorians expressed basic insecurities about their abilities. A male valedictorian said: "I've never thought myself intelligent. I've always thought myself very stupid." A female honor-roll student at an elite institution told researchers: "I fear flunking out. I always fear that." Many students agreed with the study member who said: "I'm not the smartest student in my high school. I just know how to get good grades." Nearly all of the valedictorians were confident of their academic ability, yet most felt they were not actually the most intelligent student in their high schools.

Undergraduate Education

All of the valedictorians attended college in the Fall term following their May 1981 high school graduation. The group scattered across

the country to attend public and private institutions of widely varying selectivity and prestige. Most (70%) graduated in 4 years. One
male and three females did not attain undergraduate degrees and
have no plans to resume undergraduate study. Two other students—one male and one female—are unsure whether they will return to college. For each of these individuals, personal rather than
academic reasons led to dropping out. Their situations included
financial problems, pregnancy, early fatherhood, and dissatisfaction with career plans.

Sixty percent of the group completed their undergraduate work in
one of three fields: business (24%), engineering (19%), and science
(19%). Only six women and three men changed their majors during
college. The valedictorians excelled academically in college, earning
a mean grade point average of 3.6 on a 4-point scale. Three of four
study members received one or more academic honors during college. At least a dozen study members graduated Phi Beta Kappa,
three were cited as the outstanding student of their graduating
class, and six received all As in college.

Undergraduate Gender Differences

The first five years beyond high school showed significant gender
differences in intellectual self-esteem and career aspirations for the
former high school valedictorians. The first major gender difference
emerged in the area of intellectual self-esteem. Although men and
women participants received equally high college entrance examination scores and college grade point averages, women lowered their
estimate of their intelligence over their college years. The first drop
in self-estimated intelligence in relation to peers occurred between
the senior year of high school and sophomore year of college. The
women, but not the men, showed a sharp decline in their own
estimations of their intelligence. By the senior year of college, some
women had raised their self-ratings. Still, a significant difference
remained favoring males' intellectual self-estimate. Not one female
college senior said she was far above average in intelligence compared to her peers, while a quarter of the men said they were far
above average.

A second gender difference was women's concern about combining career and family. As college sophomores, six of the valedictorian
women abandoned their medical school aspirations, anticipating
the interference of professional demands on future marriage and
childraising. Women in all majors raised concerns about the merging of family and career, although none were married or engaged at

the time. Male study members did not raise these issues in relationship to their own educational and professional paths.

A third gender difference was the striking divergence in labor force participation plans of male and female valedictorians. As college seniors, two-thirds of the women valedictorians planned to reduce or interrupt their labor force participation to accommodate marriage and childraising. All of the men planned continuous, full-time labor force participation.

Finally, women's professional expectations as college seniors were more vague than those of the men in the study group. Women were also more likely than men to list multiple career possibilities when they reported their goals.

Gender Differences in Careers

The early research focus on gender differences masked the differences in career aspirations within genders. In the fifth year of the study, therefore, analyses concentrated on the career-related differences among the women. Two distinct vocational groups emerged among the female valedictorians. Discriminant analyses showed that women who aspired to high vocational levels were distinguished from less professionally ambitious women by work and family values, rather than by ability, family background, and college experiences. Valedictorian women's job values, mother's education, planned timing of marriage and childbearing, and job experience correlated with their 1986 professional level. These variables separated the two female vocational groups very accurately.

The variables that clearly separated women into two career groups, however, failed to explain men's vocational patterns. The current assessment looks more closely at the factors which appear to account for differences in the career attainment and aspirations of the male valedictorians.

POSTCOLLEGE STATUS: 1989

Marriage and Children

Nine men and thirteen women were married by January 1989, about one-third of the males and one-third of the females. One man was divorced, and one man and one woman were engaged to be married. Two men and four women were parents, including two of the study women who were not married. The three men who married before completing college were all parents and each was among the least vocationally and educationally achieving students in the study. For two of the three, the economic necessity of supporting a family clearly reduced educational and employment possibilities. The third chose a rural life centered on his family's fundamentalist Christianity. The first valedictorian woman to marry was the only study participant to plan not to participate in the labor force.

For valedictorians who married after college graduation, marriage has not been an equally dramatic factor in their professional lives. Of interest, however, is the fact that only one of the women pursuing a PhD or MD degree was married in 1989. One woman in a PhD program told us that she is not involved in a relationship because she is busy and needs to be geographically flexible. "Who has the time? I have had some opportunities, but right now school is my first priority. Also knowing I would be moving, I didn't want to get involved and then deal with a long distance relationship."

Graduate Study

The valedictorians now work and study around the country. Table 2.1 shows the activities of participants in 1989. One man completed college in 1989 under an engineering co-op program. In 1986, the year following their college graduation, women were more likely than men to be in graduate school. The percentage of men and women in graduate school in 1989 was relatively similar, with 20% of each group pursuing graduate degrees. However, the graduate fields still showed a gender difference. Men entered law school in greater numbers. Women only attended medical school. (One male study member was considering medical school.) Male PhD students were studying mathematics and science; women study members were also studying English, agriculture, political science, and Divinity. Seven women completed terminal Master's degrees or were enrolled in terminal Master's programs. In sharp contrast, only one man completed a Master's degree program.

Graduate school proved inspirational for some valedictorians and trying for others. Valedictorians entered programs at prestigious graduate institutions including the Wharton and Kellogg Business Schools, MIT, and the Harvard Law School. One male told us that the best part of the past two years was: "The discovery that I could be intellectually challenged and stimulated by legal work and realizing that I have the preparation and the ability to do very well professionally." A woman wrote that the best for her was: "Being recruited by

Table 2.1. Male and Female Valedictorians: Occupations in 1988

	Males	Females
Business:		
Accountancy, insurance,	11	7
retail management	(32%)	(15%)
Technical:		
Agronomist, architect,	10	5
computer science, engineer	(29%)	(11%)
Graduate study:		
Law, medicine,	7	10
Ph.D., M.A.	(20%)	(22%)
Helping professions:		
Nurse, physical therapy,	0	13
K-12 teacher		(28%)
Nonprofessional and	1	4
homeworker	(3%)	(9%)
Farmer	1	0
	(3%)	
Unknown	4	7
	(12%)	(15%)

professors for a PhD; finding out from my MS adviser and other professors that I do have what it takes to make it as a woman in this field. For a while I was doubting my abilities and this helped to boost my confidence. Pleasant surprise when they actually come out and say it." Other students found graduate school personally difficult. A male law student wrote that "competition at school makes me realize I'm no longer a big fish—just one of the masses." Another male law student was looking for a summer job when he wrote: "After 20 years of education, 7 of it 'higher,' they finally broke my spirit this spring. Problems because my record is not great on paper, but my references and my work are very good. Tough to break in. Also, my grades have suffered because of the need to work my way through school." Three students left graduate programs without degrees. One woman left a prestigious PhD program in chemistry and was teaching in a private high school. A male study member left a top MBA program after 3 weeks, saying "the program was just not for me." Another man left a PhD chemistry program at a top university after he "suffered a mental meltdown . . . Nothing serious really, just burned out on chemistry and took a leave of absence. A trying time."

Most graduate students wrote about their progress without commenting about extreme satisfaction or dissatisfaction. Many looked forward to completing their graduate programs and beginning to work in their professions.

Occupations

Male and female valedictorians were participating in male-dominated professions of science, math, business, engineering, and law. Although many females were pursuing male-dominated career fields, the group generally reflected the sex segregation of occupations found in the work place. Women only were employed in female-dominated jobs in precollege teaching, nursing, physical therapy, and secretarial work. No men were working in female-dominated professions. Sixty percent of the study men were working in business and technical fields. Two men majored in education; both were employed in business. Three study members were temporarily employed while they searched for something in their field of interest. Four men were working in insurance companies as accountants. One man managed a chain of four video stores; another was development director of a nonprofit institution. Three men and two women were certified public accountants with major accounting firms.

MALE VALEDICTORIANS

Combining employment and family has emerged as central to the career aspirations and attainment of gifted female academic achievers, as noted above. Men, however, have uniformly expected continuous full-time labor force participation. Most male valedictorians omitted family considerations in interview discussions of their professional plans and goals. The variables which accounted for women's early career paths failed to explain career differences among men. The early career patterns of the valedictorian men, therefore, merit separate attention and analysis. The analysis is based on a 1988 update of professional and personal activities.

Male valedictorians were not as distinctly separated into vocational groups as were females. A few men stood out as outstanding achievers in graduate education and employment. One law student was a clerk for a federal judge prior to joining a prestigious Chicago law firm. Another had completed a highly selective special MBA program and was one of the youngest account executives at a major advertising firm. A third man was teaching at a selective liberal arts college while he completed his PhD in mathematics. A few male valedictorians were working at distinctly lower occupational levels than most of the group. One college dropout was working as a nonprofessional for a delivery company. Another man was farming at a marginal profit level. Most of the male valedictorians, however, were working at responsible entry-level and mid-level jobs. They were computer scientists, engineers, accountants, and business managers.

Another trend which emerges from the findings on the male study participants is the early consistency of men's career choices. Most of the study group majored in technical areas. The first few interviews established the value placed by the men on choosing college majors that would prepare them for prestigious, high-paying, secure careers. Since high school graduation, the valedictorian group as a whole has been practical and career-oriented, rather than creative and intellectually oriented. As high school seniors, the valedictorians were largely uninterested in becoming active in their communities or working to change social and economic inequalities. In 1988, as several times before, each valedictorian discussed their ultimate goals. Some study members listed only professional aspirations. Many spoke of marriage and family goals as well as careers. Only one man, an African-American engineer, listed community service.

In this career-oriented, practical group, almost all of the men were working in the fields of their college majors and following the plans they articulated in their first year beyond high school. Some of the men were delighted with the reality of their early choices. The valedictorian who worked making training films for an insurance company had the job he wanted in the location he desired. This student described to an interviewer during the sophomore year of college his dream job as a media director of a company in a midsized midwestern city. In 1984, he described his professional expectations as "producing and directing educational videos." He wrote in 1986: "It's nice to slip into a job which fits perfectly the expectations I had." The student expected to move up in his current organization over the next several years. He married in the summer of 1988 and listed his ultimate goal as "a healthy, happy family and work that makes it a pleasure to get up in the morning." An architecture student expressed to us during college his ambivalence about the business aspect of architecture and design. In his junior year of college, he indicated an interest in urban planning. In 1988, this student was working as a project leader in a Chicago architectural firm. "I have a lot more responsibility in my work than most my age. Some of it was luck, but I'm starting to allow myself to respect my success." The student was still uncomfortable about the business side of architecture. "I'm still struggling with the conflict of art and business in architecture. Working now, I've come to detest some of the insensitivity and irresponsibility and simple boorishness of many of our clients. I'm becoming increasingly interested in urban planning and social issues. As you can see, I still can't commit to anything."

The architecture student represented a group of male study members who were considering job changes within the same basic area or cluster of occupations. Six of the men specifically stated their current goal as owning their own business. (Two of the study women listed owning their own business as a professional goal.) One began his entrepreneurship as an undergraduate student at his prestigious west coast university, establishing two successful businesses and working in the summers at a venture capital firm. This valedictorian was employed in 1988 as chief fundraiser for an organization in Chicago and planning to begin an MBA degree.

One-third of the valedictorian men either planned to advance in their current professional or academic field or to move from established businesses to owning their own business. A PhD student in medicinal chemistry wrote that he planned to "take a job in the pharmaceutical industry in Chicago, Indianapolis, Cincinnati, or the North Carolina area—have a couple of kids, house, you know, the WASP dream." In 1986, he named the company he wanted to join; speaking of his ultimate goal as "the means to support wife and kids and our parents (if they need it) and provide those 'sane' things which were given to me when I was growing up."

Another third of the men had entered tentative career paths which they were considering and evaluating for the future. One man in this group worked as an insurance analyst, planning to "evaluate my career direction. I would like to move out of the insurance field, probably into management consulting, if the opportunity arises. I'm working for something that I hope I would thoroughly enjoy. Also, I would like to think that serious relationship possibilities would arise." A PhD student, teaching mathematics at a college and folk dancing at a community center, saw the future as ". . . unclear. I have a wide variety of things I like, far more than I could do. One of my biggest highs is teaching people something so that they really learn it. In the long run I would like to be in a position where I could teach, say, math and folk dancing, but still be involved in challenging learning experiences and travel. I also expect to have a family at some point." An engineer wrote: "I hope to get married in a couple of years. I'm planning to take courses in education, possibly thinking about teaching at some point. I have to do some more soul searching before I decide if electronics is my star. I plan on joining a different department at [his current company], a venture which will lead to increased independence and self-confidence in teaching and training others." The men in this group had not yet committed themselves to specific occupational goals but did have professional direction. They were optimistic about the future, accumulating professional experience and weighing options before reaching final decisions about their career goals.

The final third of the male valedictorian group were either entirely unsure of their career direction or were very dissatisfied with their current activities. One Ivy League graduate cast his professional expectations in terms of his college major of philosophy: "If only the oracle would reveal the latent and benighted truth! (Or is a truth something already revealed? I think Plato might have problems with that one!)" Two public accountants with prestigious firms expressed the desire to leave accountancy and coach high school sports. Neither had any immediate plans to move toward their ultimate goal. One of the two wrote: "I don't like my job and work. Too many hours; consequently, my personal life is the pits . . . Part of my problem is I have no plan. I would say the immediate future involves finding a new job. I also plan to get involved in some type of coaching (on a volunteer basis) within the next year. I feel once I get a job I like, plans will flow much freer." For this student, the ultimate is: "To be happy. I realize this is vague, but given how unhappy I am, I long to be at peace with the world and myself. I'm sure that happiness will involve being part of a family I love and who love me." In 1984, as a college junior, this man discussed his ultimate goal as follows: "It's hard to say. If I follow my dream I'll be a high school history teacher and coach."

Two men wrote especially poignant statements of regret about their career choices. One student, who graduated from law school in 1988, told us that the worst thing about the past two years was: "Deciding on law school, because I finally realized, two years after graduating, that I should have been an engineer." A chemist wrote that his ultimate was: "Death of course. The penultimate would be to have enough guts (and talent) to write fiction for a living. Sadly, I lack one of the two, if not both."

The sense of being unable to reverse or modify early choices or to seek ideal goals was echoed by five men who expressed rather disturbing views of the future. One of these men returned after college to his rural hometown to work as a civil engineer with the state highway department. As a high school senior, this valedictorian chose not to enroll in the university where he had been accepted because he feared he couldn't measure up. He enrolled instead in a local community college, where he earned all As. He then transferred as a junior to the same university he had considered as a high school student, almost dropping out in the first few weeks of the university term because he felt he did not belong there. Much to his surprise, he earned all As in his first semester in engineering. Having achieved his educational goal with distinction, the engineering graduate took a job in his field. Two years later, he had a stomach ulcer, "caused by a stressful work situation compounded by a nagging, nontrusting new supervisor." Asked in 1988 to state his ultimate goal, the engineer wrote: "Cruising a faraway highway, good tunes up loud, in a restored muscle car, while catching admiring stares." An accountant in a prestigious firm also spoke of escape, writing that the ultimate for him was: "winning the lottery, quitting my job, driving down to the Keys, and not coming back." A law student wrote that the ultimate for him was to "recapture the youth I lost or never had."

MALE VOCATIONAL PATTERNS

The first four years of the Illinois Valedictorian Project concentrated on differences between the male and female academic achievers. The focus of the research subsequently moved to career-related differences among the study women. The analyses in this chapter focus on career differences among the gifted men.

Analyses relied on both qualitative and quantitative data. First, men were classified into two vocational groups according to a definition of vocational achievement which included aspiration level, professional and educational status in 1986, and professional and educational status in 1988. The men, unlike the women, uniformly planned continuous labor force participation and the combination of marriage and parenting with full-time employment. Labor force participation plans were therefore excluded from determination of the two male vocational groups. The classification into groups was initially carried out independently by three raters who had worked with the study group for a minimum of five years. Quantitative measures of the classification criteria were then used in a discriminant analysis to determine the appropriateness of the group assignments and to reveal the combination of variables which maximally differentiated the groups. This technique addresses directly the question of how exceptionally high-aspiring men differ from other men.

Three raters independently assigned the valedictorian men to groups using specified criteria: level of professional goal, level of professional or graduate school activity in 1986 and 1988, and expectations for graduate study. Raters also drew on interview and questionnaire data in assigning men to groups. The resulting groups classified 20 men as high vocational achievers/aspirers—the A group. The remaining 14 men fell into the B group of men who are planning lower levels of professional and educational attainment. (The analysis method follows Terman's comparisons of an A and a C group, representing the 100 most and the 100 least vocationally successful men in his sample; Oden, 1968).

The discriminant analysis which quantified the raters' classifications did an accurate job of predicting the a priori group membership. The discriminant analysis which quantified the raters' group assignments correctly classified 97% of the men in their a priori groups. One man who had been placed by the raters in the A, or high group, was classified by the discriminant function analysis in the B, or low group. He had attended a premier private technological university but left college after his sophomore year to concentrate on his burgeoning computer software consulting activities. At age 19, he was working with national firms around the country to develop business computer systems. This valedictorian found the theoretical emphasis of his college coursework frustrating and irrelevant to his computer consulting. The young entrepreneur saw the college degree as an irritating credential to show his capability for what he felt he could do without more formal education. Raters felt this study member was likely to achieve significant vocational success; the discriminant analysis evidently classified him in the low group based on his educational attainment and graduate school expectations.

The defining variables confirmed the group classifications of the three raters who had known the study members for 5 to 8 years. The first analysis, then, defined the groups more precisely. A second analysis addressed the more critical question: What pattern of variables is associated with membership in the A and B groups? Or, in the discriminant function language: What linear combination of variables separates the two vocational groups to the maximum extent? The variables for the analysis were chosen in response to theoretical and empirical considerations. The research literature suggests that the adult career attainment of men relates to the socioeconomic status (SES) of the family of origin, individual ability, and educational and job opportunities (Blau & Duncan, 1967). Achievement motivation also contributes to academic and nonacademic attainment (Spence & Helmreich, 1983).

The salience of intellectual self-esteem in the valedictorian study led us to include this measure in the analysis. A questionnaire item that measured optimism about reaching one's goals was included in response to the finding that many study males were dissatisfied with their current ability to move toward desired career ends. Finally, measures of work values were included in the analysis. Work values items showed strong bivariate correlations with current professional level and with career aspirations.

The variables and their associated labels which were included in the discriminant analysis were:

> *Background measure:* Socioeconomic status of family of origin (SES)
>
> *Ability measure*: American College Testing Service college entrance examination score (ACT)
>
> *Education and college work experience measures*: Selectivity of college or university according to institutional average ACT score (COL ACT); intellectual self-esteem according to self-estimate of intelligence in relation to peers in 1985 as college senior (SMART); professionally related work experience during the college years as an intern, paid employee, or college teaching or research assistant (JOB)
>
> *Achievement motivation measures*: Work and Mastery subscales of the Work and Family Orientation Questionnaire (Spence & Helmreich, 1983; WORK, MASTERY); perceived ability to reach one's goals (GOALS)
>
> *Job values measures*: Importance of prestige in choosing job (PRESTIGE); importance of using one's best talents in a job (TALENT)

The discriminant function, presented in Table 2.2, separated A men and B men with a significant discriminant function. The function, which accounted for 71% of the variability due to groups, placed the centroid of A men above the centroid of B men. The function showed high positive contributions from the ACT score, desire for career prestige, and professional job experience during college. Lesser positive contributions were made by college selectivity, intellectual self-esteem, motivation to master challenging material or tasks, and optimism about one's ability to meet personal

**Table 2.2.   Discriminant Analysis for A: High Vocational Level Men ($n = 20$)
and B: Medium and Low Vocational Level Men ($n = 14$)**

Eigen Value	Canonical Cor- relation Coefficient	Wilk's Lamda	Chi- Square	Degrees of freedom	p
2.6	.85	.28	34.27	10	.0002

Standardized Discriminant Function		Group Centroids	
SES	.06	Group A (2) = 1.29	
ACT	.61	Group B (1) = −1.85	
COLACT	.42	Predicted Group versus A Priori Group	
SMART	.38		
JOB	.73		Predicted Group
WORK	−.02		A B
MASTERY	.34		No. % No. %
GOALS	.33	A Priori A 1 (.05) 19 (.95)	
PRESTIGE	.62	Group B 13 (.93) 1 (.07)	
TALENT	.11		

Percent correctly classified: 94%

Note. Abbreviations are as follows: SES: Socioeconomic status of parents; ACT: College entrance examination score; COLACT: Average ACT at college attended; SMART: Self-estimate of intelligence in relation to peers; JOB: Professionally related work during college; WORK: Work motivation; MASTERY: Mastery motivation; GOALS: perceived ability to reach personal goals; PRESTIGE: Desire for high prestige career; TALENT: Desire for career that utilizes best talents.

goals. The A and B men were not separated by SES, motivation to work hard, or desire to use one's best talents in careers.

The variables separated the two male groups very accurately: The discriminant function correctly predicted the group membership of 94% of the study men. One man whom raters classified with the A group was classified by the analysis as a B group member. He worked as a systems representative for a Chicago computer company, reporting his ultimate goal as "owning and operating my own business and still having time to travel and enjoy work." Raters classified this former valedictorian in the high vocational group because of his steady advancement and high salary in his company and because he definitely planned to attend graduate school. He was not among the most promising A-group men, however, and his goals were not particularly focused or ambitious.

The second man whom the analysis misclassified was the Ivy League philosopher who whimsically awaited divine revelation to indicate his career path. Clearly among the few incontrovertible intellectuals among the males in the valedictorian study, raters classified him as a B-group member because his career plan was highly uncertain. This valedictorian has high career potential, however, based on his privileged family background, his high ability, and his degree from an elite private university. (Indeed, in 1990, researchers found him working from his parents' home as an off-the-floor commodities trader.)

The earlier analyses of the female valedictorians demonstrated that family expectations and related work participation plans accurately forecast gifted women's early career attainment and aspirations. Gifted men's patterns were unrelated to these family and participation factors. Instead, we now find, the valedictorian males were beginning their careers and forming their professional aspirations on the basis of those factors which have historically been associated with adult male career attainment. The 26-year-old male academic achievers were separated by ability, by early work experience, and by the desire for prestigious careers. As compared with lower achieving men, high career achievers attended more selective colleges, had higher intellectual self-esteem, were more highly motivated to master tasks, and felt more optimistic about reaching their goals.

DISCUSSION

Standard measures of career achievement seem to apply to the early adult lives of the male valedictorians. Ability, motivation, job experience, and college prestige accounted for differences in the male valedictorians' educational and professional activities seven years after high school graduation. Unlike the female valedictorians, the professional lives of the male young adults were not defined by expectations of marriage and parenting choices.

In particular, the male valedictorians were not affected at age 26 by the actual or anticipated need to balance career and family. This gender difference relates to the finding that the men formed a more homogeneous group than the women in their early career activities. The three independent raters who placed the males into vocational groups had greater difficulty determining the group assignments than was the case for the females. The differences between the two male vocational groups were not as striking or as clear as the differences among the female valedictorians. With few exceptions, the 26-year-old men were working full time in male-dominated professions closely related to their college majors. All the males anticipated continuous full-time labor force participation; all considered employment as a central focus of their lives.

The most interesting patterns in the early careers of the male valedictorians emerged in the qualitative interview and survey data. First, and perhaps most surprisingly, the top high school students were not achieving exceptional levels of early career attainment. Eighty percent had not gone on to graduate study. Only three male study members were pursuing PhD degrees. Only one of the three anticipated a career as an academic and none entered medical school.

Nearly all of the male valedictorians were beginning solid professional careers. All but two graduated from college and nearly all were working in positions which required their college degrees. Even the nonprofessionals were potentially high adult achievers. One of the nonprofessionals, in fact, was among the highest earners in the group, as a supervisor for a delivery company.

As a group, then, most of the male valedictorians began adult life with solid but not outstanding career prospects. Although the current activities of four or five men still placed them among the top levels of early professionals, the male valedictorians as a group did not appear to be the intellectual or professional leaders of the future. Should we have anticipated a different profile from the valedictorians in their mid-20s? What does this finding indicate about school achievement and the practice of recognizing valedictorians?

Two possible interpretations might account for these findings. First, the study was conducted in the state of Illinois in the early 1980s. Few of the students grew up in highly intellectual families, and all were products of an age group which valued a college education for job and income enhancement. The students entered the fashionable college majors of their college generation: business and engineering. The liberal arts were out of vogue, as were the college tasks of developing a philosophy of life and redressing social inequities. These trends, amply documented by Alexander Astin and others, were perhaps more pronounced in the midwest than on either coast (Astin, Green, & Korn, 1987; Bachman, Johnston, & O'Malley, 1981; Levine, 1980).

Second, these students were gifted as academic performers. The college entrance examination scores of the men varied far more than their high school or college grade point averages. The valedictorians were talented in school performance. Achieving a high grade point average requires organization, dutifulness, and comfort with structure and authority (Bloom, 1985). This performance definition of giftedness overlaps but is not identical to conceptions of giftedness as intellectual or creative ability. Always dutiful, perhaps these men were continuing to achieve within established social structures and within defined social pathways.

That these academic achievers were subscribing to the careerism of their generation and continuing to be solid contributors inside the system is an observation, not a criticism. However, important questions emerge from this interpretation. What does the valedictorian story mean in terms of school achievement and the practice of recognizing valedictorians? Are educators recognizing the right group of young people as the top achievers? Are they rewarding the right things in school performance? Should adult leadership be associated with school achievement? Is education's appropriate aim the training of solidly able individuals to make significant but not exceptional adult contributions?

Another set of questions emerges from the finding that many of the valedictorian men appeared extremely disillusioned for 26-year-olds who had arrived exactly where they aspired to be. What can high school and universities do to encourage academically talented men to explore their options fully? How can educators help young people to avoid the traps of narrow careerism?

The most fundamental question of the valedictorian study concerns the connection between school and life, and academic performance and adult attainment. The first decade of the Illinois Valedictorian Project demonstrated a strong connection between top academic achievement in high school and outstanding academic performance in college. The years after high school graduation also demonstrated that these former valedictorians were apparently not headed for stellar career achievements. Early adult achievements of this group of high school valedictorians reflected the influences of gender and social context rather than ability and academic performance.

LONGITUDINAL RESEARCH ON ACADEMICALLY TALENTED STUDENTS

Longitudinal methodology is uniquely suited to the exploration of change and continuity in development. The repeated measures design of the Illinois Valedictorian Project has proven valuable in tracing the early adult attainments of academically talented students. Cross-sectional study of the valedictorians would have obscured both the process and the substance of their career development. A snapshot of former valedictorians five years after high school, for example, would have found an unemployed philosophy major, an African-American college dropout, and a female doctoral student in agriculture. Within the next few years, however, the philosopher would become an aggressive commodities trader, the dropout would enter an engineering program at a historically Black college, and the agriculture student would leave graduate school and take a non-professional job. Qualitative longitudinal research illuminates both the antecedents and personal meaning of such apparent discontinuities. The research design also uncovers the personal turbulence that may accompany an apparently smooth career path.

Longitudinal research of the gifted offers the ability to see beyond short-term choices and adjustment to immediate circumstances. Researchers can also develop themes that originate from the valedictorians themselves. Admittedly, the Project's longitudinal design also poses some unique difficulties. First, the logistical demands and expense of repeated personal interviews of 81 mobile young adults is a constant challenge. The resolve of the researchers is regularly tested during the days on the telephone and the long drives home. Second, attrition is a constant concern in longitudinal research. Study participants move, change their names, or fail to respond to queries. The Valedictorian Project has lost subjects for periods of time. As researchers fear, attrition is not random. Valedictorians have stayed away from the study when they have dropped out of school, made a bad marriage, or suffered from alcoholism. All eventually returned to the study, usually as a result of immense effort on the part of the researchers. This high retention rate may be attributed to the bonds interviewers have created with the valedictorians and to the wealth of information about families, schools, and work places that we can use in locating participants.

The strong bond between researchers and valedictorians is both a strength and a possible methodological weakness of the study. From recurrent intensive discussions of their experience and feelings, participants come to know the researcher, the nature of the interview, and certain repeated questions. They become socialized to the mode of reflecting and articulating that the interviews elicit. It is impossible to estimate the magnitude of these practice effects in a repeated interview study or to understand what effect might result from periodic intensive review of one's life. Efforts to contain bias from interviewer and practice effects include the use of more than one interviewer and triangulation of interview information with quantitative data sources.

Longitudinal study offers the researcher an unparalleled opportunity to trace over time the personal meaning of achievement and the consequences of early academic success. The Illinois Valedictorian Project explored the meaning of achievement in the lives of academically talented students and addresses the fundamental educational issue of the relationship of school performance to life attainment. Such basic questions about academic talent are uniquely suited to longitudinal investigation.

AREAS FOR FURTHER INVESTIGATION

The valedictorian story is incomplete. The valedictorians are 81 individuals from one period of time and one state. Nine years beyond high school graduation, their plans and current activities did not reveal their actual life attainment. The valedictorians were talented at earning high grades but were not necessarily the most intellectually gifted high school students. Extremely talented students might have accelerated their schooling and been absent by their class commencement (Benbow & Stanley, 1983), or developed their talents outside of formal schooling (Bloom, 1985). The Illinois Valedictorian Project omits a control group of less highly performing students of equal intelligence, and the sample size precludes authoritative findings concerning the influence of socioeconomic, community, and school characteristics. These limitations suggest directions for further research. Needed are larger sample studies and multiple-cohort studies, investigations that compare students identified by ability and by performance measures, and research that singles out limited variables of interest. Whenever possible, such future research efforts should incorporate longitudinal methodology and the use of both qualitative and quantitative data.

In 1992, the Illinois Valedictorian Project received funding for two additional interview waves. Extending the study to a 15-year span will further illuminate the relationship between academic performance and occupational outcomes for gifted students.

REFERENCES

Ames, R., & Ames, C. (Eds.). (1984). *Research on motivation in education.* Orlando, FL: Academic Press.

Astin, A. W., Green, K. C., & Korn, W. S. (1987). *The American freshman: Twenty year trends.* Los Angeles, CA: The Higher Education Research Institute, Graduate School of Education, University of California, Los Angeles.

Astin, A. (1977). *Four critical years*. San Francisco, CA: Jossey-Bass.

Astin, H. (1984). The meaning of work in women's lives: A sociopsychological model of career choice and work behavior. *Counseling Psychologist, 12*(4), 117–153.

Bachman, J. G., Johnston, L. D., & O'Malley, P. M. (1981). *Monitoring the future: Questionnaire responses from the nation's high school seniors*. Ann Arbor, MI: Institute for Social Research.

Baird, L. L. (1982). The role of academic ability in high level accomplishment and general success. *College Board Report, 82*(6).

Benbow, C. P., & Stanley, J. C. (1983). *Academic precocity*. Baltimore, MD: The Johns Hopkins University Press.

Blau, P., & Duncan, O. D. (1967). *The American occupational structure*. New York: Wiley.

Bloom, B. S. (Ed.). (1985). *Developing talent in young people*. New York: Ballantine.

Chickering, A. W. (1978). *Education and identity*. San Francisco, CA: Jossey-Bass.

Dweck, C. S., & Elliott, E. S. (1983). Achievement motivation. In P. Mussen & E.M. Heatherington (Eds.), *Handbook of child psychology* (Vol. IV) (pp. 643–692) . New York: Wiley.

Erikson, E. H. (1968). *Identity: Youth and crisis*. New York: Norton.

Guba, E. G., & Lincoln, Y. S. (1989). *Fourth generation evaluation*. Newbury Park, CA: Sage.

Hoyt, D. P. (1966). The relationship between college grades and adult achievement: A review of the literature. *Educational Record, 47*, 70–75.

Kegan, R. (1982). *The evolving self*. Cambridge, MA: Harvard University Press.

Levine, A. (1980). *When dreams and heroes died*. San Francisco, CA: Jossey-Bass.

Lincoln, Y. S., & Guba, E. G. (1985). *Naturalistic inquiry*. Beverly Hills, CA: Sage.

McAdams, D. P. (1990). Unity and purpose in human lives: The emergence of identity as a life story. In A. I. Rabin, R. A. Zucker, R. A. Emmonds, & S. Frank (Eds.), *Studying persons and lives* (pp. 148–200). New York: Springer.

Munday, L. S., & Davis, J. C. (1974). Varieties of accomplishment after college: Perspectives on the meaning of academic talent. *ACT Research Report, 62*.

Oden, M. H. (1968). The fulfillment of promise: 40-year followup of the Terman gifted group. *Genetic Psychology Monographs, 77*, 3–93.

Perry, W. G. (1970). *Intellectual and ethical development*. New York: Holt, Rinehart & Winston.

Schaie, K. W. (1983). *Longitudinal studies of adult psychological development*. New York: Guilford Press.

Sears, P. S., & Barbee, A. H. (1977). Career and life satisfaction among

Terman's gifted women. In J. C. Stanley, W. C. George, & C. H. Solano (Eds.), *The gifted and the creative: A fifty-year perspective* (pp. 28–65). Baltimore, MD: Johns Hopkins University Press.

Sellin, D. F., & Birch, J. W. (1981). *Psychoeducational development of gifted and talented learners.* Rockville, MD: Aspen Systems Corporation.

Spence, J. T., & Helmreich, R. L. (1983). Achievement-related motives and behaviors. In J.T. Spence (Ed.), *Achievement and achievement motives* (pp. 7–74). San Francisco, CA: W.H. Freeman.

Spence, J. T., Helmreich, R. L., & Stapp, J. (1974). The Personal Attributes Questionnaire: A measure of sex-role stereotypes and masculinity-femininity. *JSAS Catalog of Selected Documents in Psychology,* 4(43).

Terman, L. M. (1959). The gifted group at mid-life. *Genetic studies of genius* (Vol. V). Stanford, CA: Stanford University Press.

Terman, L. M., & Oden, M. H. (1947). The gifted child grows up. *Genetic studies of genius* (Vol. IV). Stanford, CA: Stanford University Press.

Vaillant, G. E. (1977). *Adaptation to life.* Boston, MA: Little, Brown.

Watley, D. J. (1971). Career or marriage? A longitudinal study of able young women. In A. Theodore (Ed.), *The professional woman* (pp. 260–274). Cambridge, MA: Schenkman.

Whitbourne, S. K. (1987). Personality development in adulthood and old age: Relationships among identity style, health, and well-being. In K. W. Schaie (Ed.), *Annual review of gerontology and geriatrics* (Vol. 7, pp. 189–216). New York: Springer.

3

Adult Manifestations of Adolescent Talent in Science: A Longitudinal Study of 1983 Westinghouse Science Talent Search Winners*

Rena F. Subotnik
Cynthia L. Steiner

OVERVIEW AND BACKGROUND OF THE STUDY

The Westinghouse Science Talent Search was established in 1941 during a period when American corporations were becoming integrally involved with secondary science education (Duschl, 1990). The Talent Search was designed to recognize and reward adolescents who were creatively gifted in mathematics and science. Over the course of the last 50 years, it has become the single most prestigious secondary school academic award. Science Service, the agency employed by the Westinghouse Corporation to conduct the Talent Search, has reported intermittently on the number of significant prizes won by former finalists. The most recent list includes five Nobel Prize winners, two Field Medalists, two National Medal of Science recipients, eight MacArthur Fellowship winners, and two Albert Lasker Basic Medical Research awardees. However, the process by which these eminent scientists and mathematicians evolved from this pool of talented adolescents has not been documented. The objective of this longitudinal study is to monitor the academic growth and development of a cohort of Westinghouse Science Talent Search winners as they move from secondary school through the postsecondary experience into the development of their careers.

*This project was supported by grants from the Spencer Foundation and the Professional Staff Congress of the City University of New York. The authors would like to give special thanks to Karin Baerwald Johnson, Debra Kaplan, and Sylvia Schaindlin for their contributions to the study.

Each year 300 semifinalists are identified by Science Service on the basis of a technical paper describing an original and rigorously conducted science or mathematics project. From among that group, 40 are selected as finalists and invited to interview for ten scholarship awards. The semifinalist cohort was selected as the population for the present study because criteria for distinguishing finalists from semifinalists were not available to the public or the research community, and also to provide a large enough sample to withstand the attrition that might take place over the years. The study began in 1984 with the 1983 Westinghouse cohort. During the next eight years, members of this group participated in a series of surveys and interviews designed to identify the variables that lead to retention in the fields of science or mathematics. We also wanted to explore if and how the subjects had been encouraged to develop their creative talents within those two fields.

LONGITUDINAL DESIGN

The most direct way to investigate long-term outcomes is to study the same individuals over time. The drawbacks to longitudinal design, however, include threats to validity in the areas of maturation and attrition. Maturation refers to difficulty in identifying whether change is a result of natural development rather than a given experience or treatment (Campbell & Stanley, 1966). Typically, this potential problem is addressed by using a comparison group. In the case of the Westinghouse Science Talent Search cohort, finding a meaningful comparison group was problematic in that no other forum existed for adolescents to demonstrate, at a national level of competition, creativity in science. Looked at in another way, maturation could be redefined as the *focus* of longitudinal study, becoming, therefore, an important variable of interest rather than a handicap (Arzi, 1989).

Subject attrition, on the other hand, is a serious obstacle to the development of valid conclusions about a population. Attrition tends to be selective, with those discontinuing participation in a study being the ones most likely to have veered from what they interpret as the investigators' expectations for them (Arzi, 1989), in this case, a career in research or applied science or mathematics. We are therefore relatively confident that our report reflects the population of those who stayed in science more accurately than the subgroup that has left science for other majors and later careers.

The longitudinal design allowed us to explore the attitudes and experiences of 1983 Talent Search winners during a period of transition between their school and occupational lives. Is the Talent Search indeed a proving ground for future science researchers? Is the undergraduate and graduate academic environment as supportive as the one encountered in high school? What role did mentors play in the development of participants' creative gifts? Are there significant differences between the experiences of Talent Search men and women in their pursuit of success in careers and school? Longitudinal research describing the development of creatively gifted adolescents may help to answer these questions and provide insights into stemming the flow of talent out of the academic pipeline.

REVIEW OF RESEARCH

Reasons for Retention

Literature on the career development of scientists supports the role of mentors as catalysts in the process of movement from novice to expert. The influence of a mentor has been even more dramatically demonstrated in keeping women in the science pipeline (Berg & Ferber, 1983; Kenschaft, 1981; Lewis, 1991; Light, 1990; Widom & Burke, 1978). The master may serve as a role model, intellectual sparring partner, emotional supporter, or guide to important people in the field (Jacobi, 1991). The mentor advises the novice on how to recognize a good scientific question and an elegant solution (Kanigel, 1986), which areas get funded, and which methodologies should be used (Aikenhead, 1985).

The mentor typically begins to influence his or her mentee by setting high standards and acting as a role model of the professional scientist. Instruction in scientific "taste" transpires via example, discussion, and guidance. The novice learns to identify deep problems and elegant solutions and gains access to the nonacademic or tacit knowledge acquired by "insiders" in a professional field (Wagner & Sternberg, 1986). Finally, the mentor provides access to needed resources, both human and material, to conduct research and advance in one's career. At each stage, the mentor provides opportunities for the novice to successfully test him or herself against the best competition so as to develop the confidence needed to tackle big problems (Zuckerman, 1983).

The mentor-apprentice relationship tends to be less unidirectional at the postsecondary level. Mentorship programs for young adolescents often involve matching an active scientist with an academically talented or motivated high school student. At the graduate or professional level, however, mentors select students or apprentices who might be good investments of their time (Jacobi, 1991). Simply having a mentor may in fact not be a determining factor in predicting success at the graduate or professional level. Rather, whether a powerful mentor identifies a young scientist as having talent and invites that individual to work or study with him or her may be the better predictor (Jacobi, 1991; Zuckerman, 1983).

Reasons for Attrition

Poor quality instruction at the undergraduate level can serve as an obstacle to retention in science and mathematics. Women have responded more negatively than men to the lack of feedback for course assignments or lack of recognition for their individual accomplishments (Lewis, 1991). Course content, particularly in physics, has been described by both men and women as rules applied mechanically to a set of problems embedded in a distastefully competitive environment. In contrast, courses in the humanities and social sciences appear more intimate in size and more respectful of students' intellectual contributions (Tobias, 1990).

Even if undergraduates successfully negotiate these introductory courses and experience work in an active research laboratory, without the appropriate socialization, the lifestyle of the research scientist can appear to be overly isolated, requiring superhuman dedication and delayed gratification (Frieze & Hanusa, 1984). Recognition of less obvious social and intellectual rewards can be provided by an emotionally supportive mentor, graduate student, or more experienced peer.

After graduate school, scientists encounter a profession with slow promotion rates and low pay (Kahle, 1985). Women are not promoted as rapidly as men, even when matched by number of publications and the quality of the degree program from which they graduated (Cole, 1987). Overall, women scientists tend to publish less than their male colleagues (Cole, 1987). Further research is needed to explain the source of these gender differences. Zuckerman (1987) proposed that future investigations be conducted on whether the diminished success of women scientists is due to self-selection, discrimination, or accumulation of advantage by men. Cole and

Singer (1991) described a "kick" phenomenon in which lack of success in important career milestones such as acceptance of papers, getting grants, or admission into a chosen PhD program affect women by causing them to remove themselves from the "fast lane."

Sample and Method

The study members are 146 men and women who were among the 300 semifinalists and finalists of the 1983 Westinghouse Science Talent Search. As noted above, they became winners by submitting a technical paper on an innovative and rigorous mathematics or science project conducted on their own or under the auspices of a mentor. A panel of judges made up of highly respected scientists reviewed the papers and recommended the winners to Science Service.

Since the time they were recognized as Talent Search winners, the subjects have been contacted three times by the primary investigator. The original study cohort of 146 completed a mailed survey in 1984; 94 of these students completed a second mailed survey in 1988. Brief reports of the study outcomes of the first two collection points are described below. The current study describes the analysis of telephone and personal interviews conducted during 1990-1991 with 94 members of the original (1984) cohort and one additional 1983 Talent Search semifinalist who did not participate until 1988. Seven members of the original cohort joined the group after being "found" in 1991, but were absent from the 1988 collection point.

The interview consisted of questions related to the following issues:

1. Career choices;
2. Feelings toward science;
3. The degree to which undergraduate and graduate institutions recognized and nurtured their exceptional talent in science or mathematics;
4. Participation in research;
5. Involvement with mentors;
6. Reasons for remaining or leaving the fields of science or mathematics (from the social sciences, only experimental branches of the social sciences were included in the category of science).

BRIEF SUMMARIES OF RESULTS FROM PREVIOUS COLLECTION POINTS

1984 Questionnaire

One hundred and forty-six subjects (96 males, 50 females) completed a questionnaire exploring self-image as scientists, the qualities admired in scientific heroes, and personal motivations for conducting scientific research (Subotnik, 1988a, 1988b). Every member of the cohort group was attending college in 1984 and all but five (97%) planned careers in applied or research science or mathematics. These young men and women were recognized as creatively talented in science; however, most (61%) were not yet prepared to generate research questions entirely on their own. As secondary school students, they had selected an area to work on within the domain of questions being investigated by a mentor or advisor, usually a laboratory director, university professor, or high school teacher. Competing in the Talent Search served as a period of apprenticeship and initiation into the world of science although, as discussed later, this novice stage was experieced differentially by males and females.

Subjects' self-images as scientists were investigated as they began college, using a scheme devised by Mitroff (1974) for categorizing the intellectual and creative orientations of Apollo moon scientists. Members of the Talent Search cohort were presented with Mitroff's four categories: the "abstract theorizer" who likes to build theoretical models; the "humanistic scientist" who concerns him- or herself with the application of scientific discoveries; the "rigorous experimentalist" who indulges in carefully detailed experimental work and hard data gathering; and the "intuitive synthesizer" who speculates and extrapolates on existing data. While males were fairly evenly distributed over the four categories, 55% of the females described themselves as rigorous experimentalists, an outcome that reflected a limiting view of their place in the scientific enterprise. Ironically, Mitroff observed among his subjects a tacit hierarchy in which the rigorous experimentalist and humanistic scientist were ranked as less prestigious than the other two categories.

Sixty-one (42%) of the subjects responded positively to the question "Do you have a mathematical or scientific hero or heroine?" They were then asked to indicate the quality they found most admirable in their hero or heroine. The male respondents to this question ($n = 41$) distributed themselves evenly across a spectrum of descriptions including intelligence, overcoming adversity, creativity, ethical principles, and dedication to work. None of the females identified creativity as the quality most admired, and only two indicated that intelligence was primary. Of the 20 females who had a hero or heroine, 12 selected "dedication to work" as their hero's most admirable quality. Persistence and effort rather than intellectual or creative expression seemed to be the behaviors women associated with fulfillment in science or mathematics. Fifty-eight percent of the participants could not think of anyone they admired and wished to emulate. When asked to identify their primary motivation for conducting research, a majority of respondents (78%), both male and female, chose curiosity as their primary motivation over prestige, aesthetics, or bettering the human condition.

The following quotations derived from the questionnaires give a flavor of the self-reflection of these adolescents. When asked what advice they would give to other young people interested in pursuing a career in science or mathematics, they focused on the essential role of strong academic preparation, adult and peer support, and commitment to one's chosen field.

> Take something other than the typical series that goes from algebra to geometry to trig to calculus as soon as possible: i.e., number theory, graph theory, logic, group theory, etc. The "normal" math taught in the schools is simply techniques of calculation. Real creative math allows you to explore patterns and learn to ask good types of questions. (Female, mathematics major)

> Find a teacher who is interested in sponsoring you for science or math fairs, and get involved with any science or math clubs at your school. Also if you have the opportunity, work with a professional in your field, either as a job or summer program. Finally, and most importantly, never give up. My project was hardly recognized at the local science fair, but I surprised a lot of people when I was chosen as a Westinghouse finalist. (Female, biochemistry major)

> Be prepared to work alone. High school administrators do not wish to waste their time helping out innovative students. Other students will make fun of your ideas and research. Do not allow them to ridicule your project, show them you have other interests. Do not make friends with competitors, they will turn on you, and do not trust anyone but your parents. (Male, criminal justice major)

> Find a topic that interests you, learn all you can about it, and you will always still have unanswered questions. If you can't locate the answer in a book, but your intuition somehow tells you what it is, use all available resources to prove it. (Male, computer science major)

Take all the science or math courses offered, enter science projects in science fairs and symposia. Pursue the "connections" that you get by entering these contests and try to get involved in "real" research at a hospital or college. Talk to these people about career opportunities and necessary educational requirements. (Male, biochemistry major)

1988 Questionnaires

In 1988, 94 (57 males, 37 females) of the original cohort group completed a survey designed to serve as a follow-up to the questions posed on the instrument mailed in 1984. The objective was to monitor changes and consistencies in decisions to pursue or not pursue science as a field of study, area of research, or possible career (Subotnik, Duschl, & Selmon, 1993). At this data collection point, 22 of the participants (23%) had already chosen occupations or fields of study outside of science, including law, diplomacy, journalism, and creative writing. Of those 22, 15 were female.

The subjects were approximately 23 years old at this point. Twenty-two were employed full time and not attending school. Of this group, 10 were involved in physical or life science-related occupations, six in social science occupations, and six in other areas. Fifty-eight subjects were attending graduate school, 34 in applied science (medicine, engineering), 10 in social science (psychology), and 14 in life or physical science research programs (for example, PhD in the natural sciences). Fourteen were still completing their undergraduate studies in science. None were college dropouts (see Table 3.1).

Table 3.1.   Employment and Educational Status in 1988

Status	Males: Other Fields (n = 8)	Males: Science and Science Related Fields (n = 50)	Females: Science and Science Related Fields (n = 22)	Females: Other Fields (n = 15)
Employed Full Time	4	7	3	8
Graduate School: Applied Fields	1	26	8	4
Graduate School: Research Track	2	9	5	3
Undergraduate	—	8	6	—

Those subjects continuing to conduct science research described their motivation as derived from intellectual curiosity more than a need to help humanity, fulfill creative needs, meet academic requirements, or acquire prestige. In contrast, sociological studies of professional scientists report a motivational pattern based on competition for prestige, recognition, and grant money (Ghiselin, 1989; Knorr-Cetina, 1981; Ziman, 1980). It is possible that some of the subjects thought that "curiosity" was the most socially acceptable response. Whether the source of the response was social desirability or genuine feeling, the outcome revealed that the subjects had not yet been inculcated into the value system of the academic world of science.

There were no gender differences in the number of publications and awards achieved since high school within the group that stayed in science (n = 72). The mean number of awards among group members was 3.1 as compared to 1.7 in the nonscience group. Twenty-five of the subjects still in science had published at least one article (M = 2.1), while only three of those not in science had received public recognition via publication of their creative work.

Subjects who stayed in science were somewhat more likely than those who left to have had enthusiastic science professors who encouraged them to participate in competitions and projects leading to the development of a publication. All but one were able to identify an individual who served as a mentor. Those mentors were able to provide advice concerning research topics, access to equipment and facilities, and introductions to professionals in the field.

> For anyone who wants to pursue a career in science, I feel it is extremely important to work for at least a month or two with various different labs or professors before deciding on one area to pursue. Once that decision is made, it's good to try and find an advisor or mentor with whom to work at length on some in-depth project. It's important to try and work as closely as possible with this person, have regular meetings and make some definite long-term goals, like preparing papers, theses, presentations, etc. (Male, medical student)

There were no significant gender differences in the quality of relationship experiences with mentors. That is to say, whether the mentor or mentee was male or female, the relationship served the same purposes and provided the same access to some of the nonacademic, "tacit," or insider knowledge associated with success in any professional or academic field (Wagner & Sternberg, 1986).

> I think it's important to become an expert in a couple of subfields and, my personal bias, of course, make sure you are VERY strong in mathe-

matics. Seek out faculty members early on, particularly ones whose work and whose intelligence you admire, and learn how they think, how they approach problems and do research. (Female, mathematics/computer science graduate student)

Half of those who left the field of science to pursue creative expression in other fields had not found adequate role models in science for either emulation or support during their college experiences.

After beginning graduate school, I became very disillusioned with science and decided to switch from science to international relations and economics. The prospect of being paid by the Department of Defense for the rest of my life seemed quite unpleasant, and the humanism I had hoped to find in the scientific community was strangely lacking. Not only that, but many of the graduate students and professors were narrow to the point of being boring, and for me it seemed that this was not the type of environment I wanted to work in. (Female, international relations graduate student)

In sum, those individuals who had left science were much less likely to have been encouraged during their undergraduate years or provided with mentoring at least equal to that provided during high school, including exposure to nonacademic advising about "making it" in the world of scientific research (Subotnik, Duschl, & Selmon, 1993; Subotnik & Steiner, 1994).

CURRENT STATUS OF THE GROUP

In 1990, the cohort was contacted again and 98 interviews were conducted over the course of the next one and one-half years. Forty-nine of the remaining 60 male participants, now approximately 26 years old, could still be categorized as scientists or mathematicians because of their study or employment in scientific research or applied fields. Of the remaining 38 women, 25 were still in the science pipeline. The other 13, or over 34%, pursued other interests (see Table 3.2). The questions posed in the interview explored the role of mentors in their lives, reasons for retention or attrition in science, and the effects of labeling as a Westinghouse Science Talent Search winner.

Males Not in Science

Eleven male members of the study cohort were no longer involved with applied or research science at the time of their last interview

Table 3.2.   Employment and Educational Status in 1991

Status	Males: Other Fields (n = 11)	Males: Science and Science Related Fields (n = 49)	Females: Science and Science Related Fields (n = 25)	Females: Other Fields (n = 13)
Employed Full Time	6	18	4	8
Grad School: Applied Fields	2	8	8	4
Grad School: Research Track	3	21	10	1
Undergraduate	—	2	3	—

(1990-1991). Five subjects were in graduate school: One subject was in a doctoral program in social science, two were in humanities doctoral programs, and two more were in law school. Three other subjects identified themselves as businessmen. The remaining three included a novelist, a counselor for victims of bias crime, and a professional athlete.

Five of the 11 men reported having mentors in their lives after high school, although none in the science area. These five had experienced different relationships with their mentors. One mentor was primarily an intellectual sparring partner, another provided emotional support, a third served as a role model, and the fourth and fifth were actively involved in developing the subjects' professional lives. Five of the six subjects without mentors indicated that they did not miss that type of relationship. One, however, said he had been unsuccessful in his active search for an experienced professional to help guide him in his business career.

Why did these young men, all of whom had demonstrated extraordinary talent in science, leave the field? Nine made the decision during their undergraduate years, one even before entering college. In general, the decision was reported as being based on one of four rationales: low-quality science instruction, high interest in courses outside of science, discovery that the lifestyle of the scientist was unappealing, or realization that they had been blindly channeled into science by school or parents. Here are their own words:

When I got to college my intention was to major in biology or chemistry. When I was doing the Westinghouse project, I really enjoyed the whole process of doing scientific research, so that was where I was focused. When I got to college and went to some of the required science classes, like intro bio and chem, I realized I was going to be in for three years of memorizing scientific facts. At that point I said to myself, "I'm going to be miserable if this is what I do for the next three years."

Duke had a special freshman program in American Studies and really I liked history as much as biology. I did a semester of history and enjoyed it very much, and then I decided to check into biology courses, particularly pre-med. I took comparative anatomy and liked it very much, but the next year when I took chemistry, it really put me off and I didn't enjoy it. It might be because of the mathematical orientation. I've always been competent at math but not really very good at it. I always felt that I was driving on a very interesting country road where if someone pointed something out to me I could appreciate it, but could never see anything for myself. At the same time I was taking linguistics and it appealed to me tremendously.

My fifth semester was my last real chemistry semester and again I took 3 chem courses. But I knew this was the end, that I had lost what I came into MIT with, which was the desire to win the Nobel Prize in chemistry, become a prof at MIT, Cal Tech, Harvard, or Stanford and do this real pioneering fundamental chemical research. I don't know when it happened, but it was either before or after the fifth semester that I decided I would finish my chem degree because I was almost done with it anyway, and try to pursue other interests in the course of making a career. And chem wasn't a career for me . . . I started looking at what interests I had not pursued for years and years. The scientists that I saw that were successful did not have these interests. They were not interesting people. I was beginning to find scientists really dull and selfish in the sense of individual responsibility, saying things like "I would never let people inside my lab do recycling because it would take too much time away from work." Or my advisor in chemistry, who when I first voiced doubts about being a chemist, totally disaffiliated himself from me and I never saw him again.

By the time I got into college I was terribly burned out, both from academics and extracurricular activities, and also from being involved in science not because I liked it, but because there were all these other reasons which put you there [school and parental expectations]. So I tried to carry on in college. But Harvard is such a competitive place that if you're really not into it, focused, and enjoying it, you really won't last very long. You become very dissatisfied with yourself very quickly and you don't do well.

Seven of the 11 subjects expressed no regrets concerning their disaffiliation with science careers. Two of the subjects who are involved in the business world wish they had completed a science degree to give them more cache in their work with technology corporations. Two seemed to think they could have been talked into staying in science if they had had some of their doubts addressed. One said, "I never had the confidence to ask my profs if they ever had any doubts, and if they did, was that okay."

None of these young men were greeted as individuals with extraordinary talent when they entered their undergraduate institutions. Most went to prestigious private colleges where, it seemed, everyone was talented and, for this reason, seeking individual attention seemed inappropriate. Further, three members of this group felt that their high school coursework was not rigorous enough to prepare them for the level of difficulty they encountered in college.

When asked what it would take, if anything, to reinvolve these talented individuals in science, five said it was far too late to look back. An additional two subjects do not view themselves as having the kind of commitment to science that it would take to be successful. Two others hope to work actively with scientists as managers of entrepreneurial firms, but cannot imagine being directly involved in research. One subject who dropped out of medical school to become a writer has not discounted a return to medicine, and another who dropped out of a physical chemistry graduate program to go to law school said he could be tempted if offered a job with a good salary.

Females Not in Science

Thirteen female members of the study cohort were categorized as no longer involved directly with science. These women were generally more regretful about leaving science than were the males not in science. In fact, several, given the right conditions, would consider returning to the field. At the time of the interviews, five of these women were lawyers or attending law school, four were business consultants, two were preparing to be teachers, one was entering a clinical psychology program, and one was a writer and traveler.

One woman never even considered majoring in science. She participated in the Westinghouse competition just for the challenge. Four women had health-related reasons for dropping out of science majors: One had allergies, one had a learning disability, and the other two had chronic illnesses. Two other subjects had negative reactions to the lifestyle they witnessed in the labs. One reported that

> Science was fun, and I loved hearing about results and thinking of uses for those results, but the actual day-to-day lab work with very little "human" contact was boring to the point of distraction.

The six other females who took themselves out of the science pipeline as undergraduates blamed crowded, impersonal classes.

I was never particularly encouraged in any of my science courses in college. The professors, while good researchers and quite famous in their own right, were not particularly "personable" in many respects. I found them to be much more removed from their students than my professors in the social sciences.

I didn't feel like there was much room for creativity. I felt that the way we were being taught, everything was very objective in nature. I personally don't think science is an objective field. Once everything was reduced to numbers, symbols, and formulae, I just couldn't get as excited about learning those things. They didn't seem particularly relevant to everyday life, although obviously it certainly is relevant to everyday life.

Five of the women in this group could not identify a mentor that had played a role in their lives since high school. Seven had mentors, but all outside of science. Two of the mentors served as role models, two provided emotional support, and three, professional advice. Only one female subject who is no longer in science had a science mentor who was actively involved with her research in pathology. This mentorship ended when the student left medical school due to problems associated with learning disabilities.

When asked if they received any special treatment as undergraduates because they had been Westinghouse winners, five subjects said they had been placed in an elite group but did not feel that the special treatment was appropriate for their needs.

The Benjamin Franklin Scholar position I had at the University of Pennsylvania entitled us to a section of biology with only 20 people instead of the usual 200. We sat in on the regular lectures and the only difference was that we had double lab time with a special teacher and neat animals to put up. There didn't seem to be any guidance in what you should take or to track you into a particular field.

Two women described the lack of preparation they felt upon encountering the high-powered freshman class, including a woman who said "I kept thinking that the admissions committee was going to come and say they made a mistake!"
Six others felt ignored by their universities.

The guys I worked with at Columbia during high school [for the Westinghouse project] were like my friends. At Harvard I didn't really click with the people. The guy who ran the lab was really disinterested and didn't even know my name, and my job ended up being cutting out fish eyes.

I think it's very discouraging because I do have a deep interest and a deep love for science. No matter what I do, inevitably I come back to that. I want to have a career that relates to science in some way, and I'm sorry that there wasn't someone there, because I think you're so overwhelmed at college that you don't know what direction to head in or what you have to do to get to a certain destination. I wish there had been someone there who would have recognized that I was a little bit beyond what was going on in general courses and taken me under tow and gotten me more involved. I think you need that kind of figurehead when you're that age. There's so much going on and I was a thousand miles away from home. As a woman I don't think I was encouraged to participate in science and math.

Six of the women in this group of "nonscientists" expressed no regrets about abandoning a career in science. Another subject wished she hadn't been pressured by school and home to have been a science major.

I don't really regret the science training I've had—I think the thought processes it made me develop are still very useful to me. But I wish I had not felt so pressured into studying science—I might have majored in something I could have enjoyed more.

Three subjects discussed lifestyle issues. An example from the interviews:

I wonder what I could have done if I had gone into some field of science. Who knows what I could have achieved or invented, or how happy I would have been? But from what I have seen of the people that are still out in the lab, I don't think they're doing that hot. They're not that happy with it, not as happy as they once were.

Three of these young women blamed poor advice or decision making for their experience with science. One chose an undergraduate institution and another selected a graduate institution for its name, not for the quality of science instruction. The third felt she received little guidance in terms of coursework, and therefore felt as if she had neither engrossed herself in a major nor enjoyed a well-rounded liberal education. It appears as if at least seven of these women might have stayed in science had not circumstances or unwelcome educational experiences impeded their progress.

Males in Science

Forty-nine of the males in the study cohort have continued course-work in science or have pursued science or mathematics careers. Of the 31 men attending school at the most recent data collection point, 2 were completing bachelor's degrees, 5 were in master's programs, 16 in PhD programs, and 8 in medical school. Among those employed and not going to school, 16 were engineers, and one was an actuary. One subject had just completed his PhD and was in search of employment.

Thirty-five members of this subgroup were engaged in research at the time of the interviews, although three felt it was unlikely they would continue once they completed their schooling. Another 11 were unsure whether they would incorporate research into their future career. One of these young men related his dismay at what he perceived to be the lack of recognition received by scientific re-searchers.

> A lot of these companies, not just the one I work for, just don't recognize the contributions of researchers. When I hear, for instance, that there is a need for chemical engineering research, I laugh, be-cause if there really was a need for them, they would nurture the research engineers they have. Instead 50-year-old people are laid off because they don't want to pay for their health insurance.

Four participants who weren't sure about the role research would play in their lives once they had finished school, said it would depend on the flexibility and demands of their work schedules. Five others said they would consider the possibility if they were to en-counter a good idea they wanted to pursue. One member of this group discussed his impressions of how researchers spent their time.

> The closer you come to being a professor or someone who is in charge of a lab, the more you come to realize that there are a lot of politics going on. I see that a lot of professors, instead of using their time to deal with intellectual problems at hand, spend 80% of their time trying to win grants—writing proposals and worrying about getting money. I think that would be the main reason that would keep me from staying in science.

Twenty-one male members of the cohort who have remained in the science pipeline plan to incorporate research as an integral part of their professional work. Participants conducting research were asked whom they most wanted to impress with their work. Nine of the 35 expressed a lack of concern about impressing anyone but themselves, but the 26 others hoped to gain the respect and feedback of their professors, principal investigators, or the general research community, all of whom would play some role in influencing their future.

How were these gifted young men treated during their undergraduate years? Surprisingly, only 13 said they definitely felt prepared by their high school experience for the workload and level of competition they encountered in college. The participants were asked whether they received any special recognition for their scientific talent when they attended their undergraduate institution. Only two could recall being offered unique opportunities or programs. One participant expressed dismay about being ignored in college: "I was just sort of left alone and I think, actually, a lot of my enthusiasm died away because in high school I did have a lot of encouragement."

However, five of the remaining 47 men said they were just as glad not to have been treated differently;

> Not being treated as a person who had special talent in science probably contributed to my staying with it, because any kind of coddling would have probably annoyed me.

> I don't think I was "nurturable," because if a person had tried to nurture me too intensively, I would have objected. I was going to do what I wanted to do, and nothing they would have said would have changed me.

Seventeen of the men still in science have not, since high school, established a mentoring relationship with a professional scientist: "There were many times when I wished I could have approached someone with a question. I've really needed someone at different points to help me out."

The other 32 found mentors who offered them intellectual support, role modeling, and professional advice. Proportionally fewer males (13%) than females in science (30%) looked to a mentor for emotional support. More typically, the nature of the relationship was reflected in the following two quotations:

> They are interested in me and how well I do. They are almost universally enthusiastic, know what they know well, and are open about sharing it.

I have tried to find scientists who have been big names in their fields to work with because I feel that they are the ones with the best ideas and also the ones at the cutting edge of whatever they do.

When asked to reflect on any regrets they might have had about the status of their life thus far, half the participants in this group ($n = 25$) had none. The other half expressed various regrets, wishing they had worked or studied harder on the undergraduate level, had chosen more varied coursework, or had attended a different graduate or undergraduate institution.

Females in Science

At the time of the most recent set of interviews (1990–1991), 25 female members of the study cohort were pursuing coursework or careers in science. One member was about to begin graduate school. Three members were in the process of completing undergraduate programs, having taken time for commitments to political organizations or to their personal lives. Three women were science majors at the masters level, and six at the PhD level. Six were in medical school, one in optometry school, and one in veterinary school. Four were working in science/math-related jobs, specifically cytogenetics, engineering, and accounting.

With the exception of one cohort member, an accountant, all of the women in this group expressed varying degrees of interest in pursuing research at some point in the future, if they were not already doing so. Of these 24 women, however, 4 expressed concerns about the difficulty of getting grants. When asked what it would take for her to stay in research, one subject replied:

Originally I wanted to get a PhD and do research. Now I can't say that's still my goal just because I can't say I enjoy begging for grants all the time. I think it's a shame that grants are so competitive. There are so many bright scientists who are not being funded simply because they don't know the right people or they haven't been around long enough. Because of that maybe I'll go into industry.

Four women were disturbed by the low researcher salaries and two discussed what they perceived as the dilemma of wanting both families and careers in science.

I'd like to be back in it [research], but then the greed factor comes in. I am making a lot of money, and I like that check that comes every two weeks.

My mentor at Harvard runs the lab and she is very successful, but I don't think the wage is that high compared with a medical doctor. I think having financial support would be a big factor. For me that's the main factor actually.

I'm always battling with the conflict of having a family and doing research. There are three women in my department of 15 faculty. Only one is married and has a child, and she had it at 40. So they still don't have it all.

Thirteen of the 25 females in science are currently doing research. When asked whom they would most like to impress with their research work, eight named the research community, particularly their advisors, professors, or principal investigators of the grant projects with whom they were involved. Five felt that they needed only to impress themselves or family members.

When asked if they were treated differently as undergraduates because of their status as Westinghouse winners, 23 of the 25 participants said they had not received any special recognition. The two who did receive special recognition were placed in honors programs rather than in research-based projects. Many discussed their feelings of anonymity, lack of preparedness for both the work and the competition which they encountered among students, and the lack of support they received from professors and administrators.

Cornell threw you in a big pot with people who were just as smart as you were. Most of the pre-meds were out to do better than their classmates. It was paralyzing when my roommate and I were in all the same classes and she always did better than me, and after a while I just couldn't live with her.

I think I was intimidated because I came from a public high school and a lot of the others came from the prep or private schools. I think they were a little more prepared than I was.

There were a few people who were just so intelligent that I couldn't believe it. I think I was desperately intimidated by a few of them.

They had so many people who were stars in one aspect or another that everybody was put into a melting pot and left to sink or swim.

You were just a number. I didn't have contact with a teacher until my junior year. You didn't have to attend classes—no one would care. I felt like they wanted to get rid of you, they didn't want you to get As. They didn't want students to do well. Pre-med was "dog eat dog," very cutthroat.

Though 23 of the 25 women in science received no special recognition, 19 were able to find at least one person who served as a mentor. Mentors, as mentioned above, can serve four basic purposes: role model, emotional supporter, intellectual sparring partner, or active professional sponsor. Because most of these women had more than one mentor, they were able to obtain a wide array of positive effects from those relationships. Some of the subjects described their mentors:

> She was nice and kind of friendly, and she didn't look at students as pests in her lab. The whole lab was a very comfortable place, not high pressured and I felt at home there.

> Besides counseling me, being there when I needed her, and being a friend, I also worked for her in the genetics class and learned a great deal. She liked to challenge me.

> He is really supportive and paternal and has lots of interesting ideas. And he is very good at negotiating the politics. We were all very social with faculty members. It's very much a tight community.

Three had negative experiences with people who might have been potential mentors:

> The science department at the school where I went as an undergrad was very unsupportive of the students in that they felt that the students should learn by themselves. I don't believe that's what undergraduates need at that point.

> I had an interest in physics from high school, but one of the professors in the physics department, the one who was my advisor, was almost an adversary. The first day I met him he said, "Your name is Becky. That was my first wife's name."

When asked if they had any regrets they would be willing to share, two lamented not having taken time off from their studies for adventure and four regretted not having had more varied educational experiences, including the pursuit of other careers. Four rued not having studied harder, and three wished they had chosen other undergraduate programs.

DISCUSSION

The 11 men and 13 women who had left science by the most recent data collection point had, for the most part, found satisfying careers in other disciplines; the talents they displayed in science most likely were transferable to other disciplines. A few planned a possible reentry into science but their choices were necessarily limited to applied fields, such as medicine, because they had missed the sequence of connections, experiences, and time commitments needed to reach an optimal level in the research pipeline.

Except for health problems that prevented four women from persisting, reasons for leaving science were similar for both males and females. Their perception of the scientist's lifestyle as unappealing, along with their attraction to other fields, lack of mentors in science, inappropriate guidance by parents and school officials during adolescence, and low-quality or inaccessible science instruction, led to a change in life goals for this significant subgroup of the study cohort. Many made the realization late in their undergraduate years or during their graduate years, even after a considerable amount of time, effort, and money had been invested on their part and on the part of their parents or mentors.

At the time that these individuals entered the Westinghouse Science Talent Search, several factors helped maintain the extraordinary dedication required to produce a noteworthy piece of research and participate in the Talent Search. Parental and teacher guidance, idealistic views of a lifestyle and career in science, promise of prestige, and pure interest and curiosity were motivating forces for all but five to enter science careers. Sometime during their undergraduate and postgraduate years, extrinsic and intrinsic motivating factors were redefined. Particularly noteworthy is the fact that nearly half of this group found mentors who were outside of a science field.

The 49 men and 25 women still involved in science shared similar educational histories, and their assessment of what a career in science would be like was reinforced during their undergraduate years by courses, mentors, and laboratory experiences. Against sometimes overwhelming obstacles, they persisted in striving to fulfill their goals. For females, mentors were more likely to have been part of their educational history, and may in fact have been a more critical factor for their retention in science than for the men. Both males and females recognized the need to impress the research community of which they were part, and many learned to master the political games played in their respective laboratories. They assimilated the tacit knowledge and the value system necessary to survive in today's research climate.

Both the science and nonscience groups, regardless of gender, acknowledged the negative aspects of science careers. Those who have chosen to continue were, however, able to justify their reasons for staying by alluding to intellectual satisfaction and prestige associated with success in rigorous fields. The fact that careers in science research are low-paying has been universally discouraging. Time commitments are seen as greatly infringing on family life or, for women, possibly precluding childrearing altogether. Our subjects became familiar with these issues through experiences with mentors during high school or college.

Despite the above-mentioned drawbacks, all but one female in the science subgroup planned to continue in research. Conversely, less than half of the males in science reported wanting to persist in that direction. It is possible that men are more discouraged than women by the low income-earning potential of research science; however, the larger proportion of females considering a career in research is extremely hopeful for the science enterprise.

Special recognition was provided to only a few individuals in our study during their undergraduate years in the form of one or two accelerated classes, smaller sections, a longer lab time, or an honors program. These "extras" provided little individual attention or coursework guidance, and few opportunities to participate in research with a university professor or receive access to potential mentors. The results reported from this data collection point confirm the unfortunate picture described by other studies about the state of science education in the United States. The seriousness of the problems and potential opportunities for reform are highlighted dramatically when the results of those studies are replicated by the experiences of the nation's potential scientific elite.

FUTURE DIRECTIONS FOR RESEARCH

Upcoming efforts to identify sources of attrition and retention of science talent will take the following directions:

1. Continuing with the 1983 Westinghouse cohort, collecting data at approximately age 30 when most subjects will have completed school and embarked on a career path;
2. Including at least one other Westinghouse cohort to replicate and compare study outcomes with the 1983 group. One of the cohorts could be composed of newly identified winners and the other a group of winners in the middle of their undergraduate education, when science attrition has been most likely to occur.

JOYS AND PITFALLS OF LONGITUDINAL RESEARCH

Each study has its unique characteristics, yet the problems and satisfactions that we encountered in the process of this work are generalizable to most longitudinal investigations. A constant source of frustration, as mentioned at the outset of this chapter, is subject attrition. There are agencies available to help locate "lost individuals," but the expense can be quite large. The investment of time required to prevent subject attrition is enormous. Although the subjects of the present study have been contacted regularly over the years, 34 people moved from their most recent address without leaving forwarding instructions. To make matters worse, their parents' permanent addresses became obsolete as well. We now regret not asking for subjects' social security numbers, the most consistent source of location, and plan to do so during the next point of contact. A good source of information on lost subjects is the alumni association of the college a subject attended. Although the associations will not provide addresses, they will forward stamped mail to graduates.

Individuals who do not respond to repeated efforts at contact may believe that their lives will be judged to be disappointing in comparison to the rest of the cohort group. It is very important, therefore, that the investigators convey a genuine, nonjudgmental manner in their relationship with study subjects. Sometimes, however, subjects presume that researchers value particular outcomes. In our case, many subjects assumed that we viewed remaining in science as a positive outcome and, furthermore, that we would not be interested in them if they were undecided or if their talents were expressed in the worlds of journalism, law, business, or international diplomacy. Although the purpose of the study is to investigate the retention of individuals in science research, we are also interested in the development of other talents within this pool of exceptional individuals and in knowing whether their gift in science or mathematics has played a role in the expression of their talents.

These gifted individuals tended to be highly active and involved with work, hobbies, and relationships, which led to difficulties in scheduling interviews or completing questionnaires. We believe that interviews, although more difficult to arrange, establish more committed personal relationships on the part of subjects, leading to lower rates of attrition. Interviews do have two main drawbacks. One is the cost of transcription, travel, and telephone. The other is the complexity involved with quantifying or interpreting the data.

Overall, we believe that the costs in time and effort are worthwhile in order to elicit accurate and detailed information from study subjects.

By far the most rewarding aspect of longitudinal research is the relationship one engages in with the study cohort. In order to develop the original 1984 questionnaire, the first author conducted 40 in-person interviews with subjects in the New York City, Boston, and San Francisco Bay areas. Listening carefully to each 18-year-old, she noted many details, not only about their creative work, but also about appearance and manner. During the last collection point, she encountered sophisticated 25-year-olds with traces of former appearance and manner, and newfound levels of confidence and introspection. It was as a result of one long and interesting conversation that Cynthia Steiner, a member of the cohort, became the second author of this chapter.

REFERENCES

Aikenhead, G. S. (1985). Collective decision making in the social context of science. *Science Education, 69*(4), 453–475.

Arzi, H. (1989). From short-to-long term: Studying science education longitudinally. *Studies in Science Education, 15,* 15–53.

Berg, H. M., & Ferber, M. A. (1983). Men and women graduate students: Who succeeds and why. *Journal of Higher Education, 54,* 629–647.

Campbell, D. T., & Stanley, J. C. (1966). *Experimental and quasi-experimental designs for research.* Chicago, IL: Rand McNally.

Cole, J. (1987). Women in science. In D.N. Jackson & A.P. Rushton (Eds.), *Scientific excellence: Origins and assessment* (pp. 359–375). Newbury Park, CA: Sage.

Cole, J., & Singer, B. (1991). A theory of limited differences: Explaining the productivity puzzle in science. In H. Zuckerman, J. Cole, & J. Bruner (Eds.), *The outer circle: Women in the scientific community* (pp. 279–310). New York: W.W. Norton.

Duschl, R. (1990). *Restructuring science education: The importance of theories and their development.* New York: Teachers College Press.

Frieze, I. H., & Hanusa, B. H. (1984). Women scientists: Overcoming barriers. In M. W. Steinkamp & M. L. Maehr (Eds.), *Advances in motivation and achievement* (Vol. 2, pp. 136–163). Greenwich, CT: JAI Press.

Ghiselin, M. T. (1989). *Intellectual compromise: The bottom line.* New York: Paragon House.

Jacobi, M. (1991). Mentoring and undergraduate academic success: A literature review. *Review of Educational Research, 61,* 505–532.

Kahle, J. B. (1985). *Women in science: A report from the field.* Philadelphia, PA: Falmer Press.

Kanigel, R. (1986). *Apprentice to genius: The making of a scientific dynasty.* New York: MacMillan.

Kenschaft, P. C. (1981). Black women in mathematics in the United States. *American Mathematics Monthly, 88,* 592–604.

Knorr-Cetina, K. D. (1981). *The manufacture of knowledge: An essay on the constructivist and contextual nature of science.* Oxford, UK: Pergamon Press.

Lewis, D. J. (1991) Mathematics and women: The undergraduate school and pipeline. *Notices of the American Mathematical Society, 38*(7), 721–723.

Light, R. J. (1990) *The Harvard assessment seminars: Explorations with students and faculty about teaching, learning, and student life* (Part 1). Unpublished manuscript, Harvard University, Graduate School of Education and Kennedy School of Government, Cambridge, MA.

Mitroff, I. I. (1974). *The subjective side of science: A philosophical inquiry into the psychology of the Apollo moon scientists.* Amsterdam, The Netherlands: Elsevier.

Subotnik, R. F. (1988a). Adolescent attraction to scientific research questions: Guidance from without and choices from within. *Questioning Exchange: A Multidisciplinary Review, 2,* 61–66.

Subotnik, R. F. (1988b). The motivation to experiment: A study of gifted adolescents' attitudes toward scientific research. *Journal for the Education of the Gifted, 11,* 19–35.

Subotnik, R. F., & Steiner C. L. (1994). Problem identification in academic research: A longitudinal study from adolescence to young adulthood. In M. A. Runco (Ed.), *Problem finding, problem solving, and creativity.* Norwood, NJ: Ablex.

Subotnik, R. F., Duschl, R., & Selmon, E. (1993). Retention and attrition of science talent: A longitudinal study of Westinghouse Science Talent Search winners. *International Journal of Science Education, 15*(1), 61–72.

Tobias, S. (1990). *They're not dumb, they're different: Stalking the second tier.* Tucson, AZ: Research Corporation.

Wagner, R., & Sternberg, R. (1986). Tacit knowledge and intelligence in the everyday world. In R. Sternberg & R. Wagner (Eds.), *Practical intelligence: Nature and origins of competence in the everyday world* (pp. 51–83). New York: Cambridge University Press.

Widom, C. S., & Burke, B. W. (1978). Performance, attitudes, and professional socialization of women in academia. *Sex Roles, 4,* 549–562.

Ziman, J. M. (1980). *Teaching and learning about science and society.* Cambridge, UK: Cambridge University Press.

Zuckerman, H. (1983). The scientific elite: Nobel Laureates' mutual influences. In R. S. Albert (Ed.), *Genius and eminence* (pp. 241–252). Oxford, UK: Pergamon.

Zuckerman, H. (1987). Careers of men and women scientists: A review of current research. In L. S. Dix (Ed.), *Women: Their underrepresentation and career differentials in science and engineering* (pp. 27–56). Washington, DC: National Academy Press.

4

The Munich Longitudinal Study of Giftedness*

Christoph Perleth
Kurt A. Heller

From 1985 to 1989 an educational-psychological research project, the Munich Longitudinal Study of Giftedness (Heller, 1992; Heller & Hany, 1986), was carried out at the University of Munich. Data from gifted students were collected in three waves from 1986 to 1988 starting with a large multiregional sample of 26,000 students in six cohorts. In 1989, a replication study was begun in Moscow by a team of psychologists at the Academy of Pedagogical Sciences of the USSR under the leadership of Prof. Dr. A.M. Matyushkin (cf. Averina, Scheblanova, & Perleth, 1991; Heller, Perleth, & Sierwald, 1991; Perleth, Averina, & Scheblanova, 1991). A data collection point for the German sample is planned for 1993.[1]

---

*Financed by the German Federal Ministry of Education and Science, Bonn (B 3570.00 B). The authors would like to thank Stephen Powell for stylistic and grammatical assistance.

[1] Two follow-up studies on developmental aspects and conditions of metacognition investigate implications of the mother-child interaction on the metacognitive development in preschool children (main investigators Dipl-Psych. C. S. Browder & Dr. J. Kretschmer) and the metamemory of primary school children (main investigators: Dr. C. Perleth & Dr. E. Rader). This research is being carried out cooperatively between the University of Munich (project leader: Prof. Dr. K.A. Heller) and the University of Leipzig (project leader: Prof. Dr. G. Lehwald) and is financed by the Volkswagen foundation (Az: II/66 350).

A team of Korean educational scientists is planning to conduct a giftedness study with similar design to ours, using similar or even the same methods. As described in more detail in the design section, only relatively large studies starting with randomly selected samples are best suited to produce reliable results on complex intercorrelations between a variety of giftedness, achievement, personality, and environmental variables. On the other hand, the replication studies in Russia or Korea can give valuable hints for the generalization of findings in the field of giftedness over different cultures.

GIFTEDNESS MODEL UNDERLYING THE MUNICH LONGITUDINAL STUDY

Most modern conceptions of giftedness include multiple giftedness factors: intellectual, creative, motivational, social, and so on (e.g., Gardner, 1983). The Munich Study of Giftedness is similarly based on a multidimensional giftedness concept. More specifically, we define *giftedness* as an individual's cognitive, motivational, and social potential to attain excellence in one or more areas. Giftedness domains (cognitive competencies), personality characteristics, and environmental conditions served as predictors for performance behavior (see Figure 4.1).

Thus, in the Munich Longitudinal Study of Giftedness the following constructs were taken into consideration:

1. Giftedness exists in intellectual, creative, social, musical, and psychomotor domains. These giftedness domains were assumed to be independent.

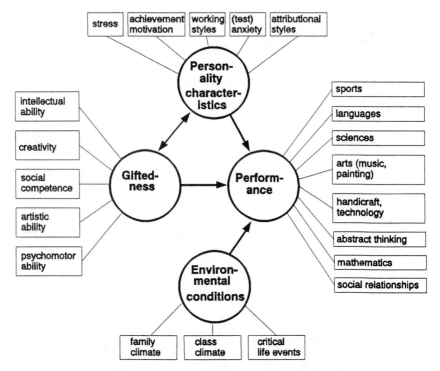

Figure 4.1. Giftedness model of the Munich Longitudinal Study of Giftedness

2. Academic and nonacademic achievements were observed in different areas corresponding to the giftedness domains.
3. Noncognitive personality traits under investigation were achievement motivation, working styles, (test) anxiety, stress, attributional styles, and so on. These variables were considered to mediate the giftedness-achievement relationship.
4. The main socialization factors were family and school climate as well as critical life events.

OBJECTIVES

Goals of the Identification Phase

The first phase of the study was dedicated to questions of identification and the validity of the giftedness model used. The goals of this identification phase (1986-1987) were the following:

1. Development and evaluation of a battery of tests and questionnaires for the identification of gifted students.
2. Testing aspects of the giftedness model underlying the study, particularly the independence of the domains of giftedness under investigation.
3. Analysis of the typological structure of the sample, especially identifying possible types of gifted students in different age groups.

Goals of the Longitudinal Phase

In the second phase of the project, the longitudinal phase, developmental, academic, and nonacademic achievement analyses based on the developmental models were computed. Essential goals of this second phase were:

1. The evaluation of the predictive validity of instruments employed during the first (Wave 1: 1986), second (Wave 2: 1987), and third (Wave 3: 1988) measurement periods for identifying gifted students in the 1st to 13th grades.
2. Longitudinal evaluation of the validity of the typological concept of giftedness and relationships between various types of giftedness and performance.
3. Evaluation of the effects of personality and environmental factors on the performance of gifted students over time.

4. Description and analysis of the developmental course of gifted children and adolescents in relation to changes in cognitive and noncognitive characteristics.
5. Analysis of the interaction between giftedness, achievement, personality, and environment.

In the limited frame of this chapter we can only give a general overview of some important results of these general research goals. We will feature findings concerning personality characteristics of gifted secondary school students. These results should contribute to answering the following specific questions:

1. Are there differences in personality characteristics between students of different levels of giftedness in intelligence and creativity?
2. Do underachieving gifted differ from other gifted students in terms of personality characteristics?
3. Are there relationships among intelligence and creativity, non-cognitive personality characteristics, and achievement?
4. What is the influence of intelligence, motivation, and other personality characteristics on the development of academic achievement?

In addition, we will present results of a small interview study conducted with a subsample of the secondary school students to obtain information on socioemotional problems and related counseling needs of gifted students.

DESIGN OF THE STUDY

Figure 4.2 shows the complete sample design as planned by Heller and Hany (1986). The numbers in brackets indicate the actual numbers of participants in the three waves. In the dotted boxes at the end of the shaded arrows we added a planned follow-up data collection point. The numbers indicate those students who voluntarily gave us their addresses and who were willing to answer additional questionnaires.

The "bandwidth-fidelity dilemma," formulated by Cronbach and Gleser (1965), stresses the fact that psychological tests cannot simultaneously measure a broad variety of characteristics with high precision (reliability). Bearing this in mind, a two-step identification process was employed in the first phase of the study as pro-

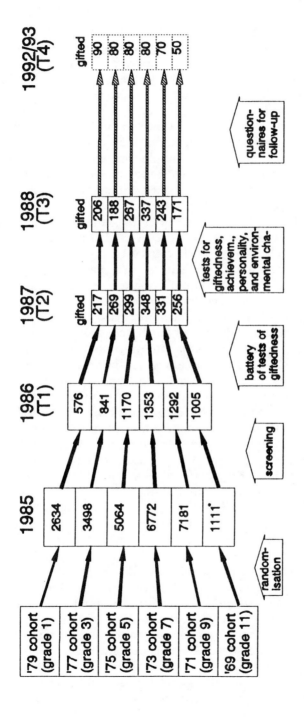

*Total evaluation without screening (since the 11th grade in Gymnasium consists of the most gifted students)

Figure 4.2.   Sample design of the Munich Longitudinal Study of Giftedness

posed by Heller and Hany (1986; Heller & Perleth, 1989). In the Fall of 1985, teachers were asked to nominate the most gifted students from their classes on a check list that covered the five dimensions of the study's giftedness model. Approximately 30% of the whole sample of about 26,000 students was preselected on the basis of these ratings. Although this screening procedure reduces the identification of underachieving gifted, it was practically and economically the only possible way to handle such a large sample. Second, the preselected 30% of the original sample were administered aptitude tests and questionnaires (Spring/Summer, 1986) in order to find the top 2-5% in each domain of giftedness. The top 10% of the preselected sample represented the top 2-5% of all students in the intellectual, creative, social, psychomotor, and musical domains. These top scorers among already preselected students were chosen for the longitudinal study. (Differences in Figure 4.2 percentage rates result from students refusing to take part in Wave 1 or the following waves.) The longitudinal sample selected by this two-step procedure were administered tests and questionnaires at two other measurement points in Spring/Summer 1987 and 1988.

The longitudinal design of the study reflected the nature of the research goals. There is no doubt that only longitudinal studies are appropriate for the study of developmental patterns. In spite of this, most research is done with cross-sectional designs. Schneider (1989) remarked that 99% of studies on memory development used cross-sectional design. As one focus of our study was the assessment of change using different developmental rationales, a longitudinal design was indispensable. Quite apart from the problems associated with retrospective studies, such attempts were not suitable for our purposes because the assessment of our giftedness factors required psychometric data.

The design, which combined cross-sectional and longitudinal sequences with six cohorts, facilitated control of age/grade and cohort effects. Time of measurement effects, however, could not be controlled (see Schaie & Baltes, 1975). The main focus was on the analyses of age/grade effects: at Wave 3 each cohort reached the grade the next older cohort had reached at Wave 1 (Figure 4.3a). This facilitated an extrapolation of the development of gifted students despite the relatively short duration of the study. Cohort effects were not analyzed because they were not likely to appear in our 3-year study which covered a decade between the youngest and oldest cohort.

Within each cohort, the design and the methods selected enabled analysis of the following developmental rationales (Buss, 1979;

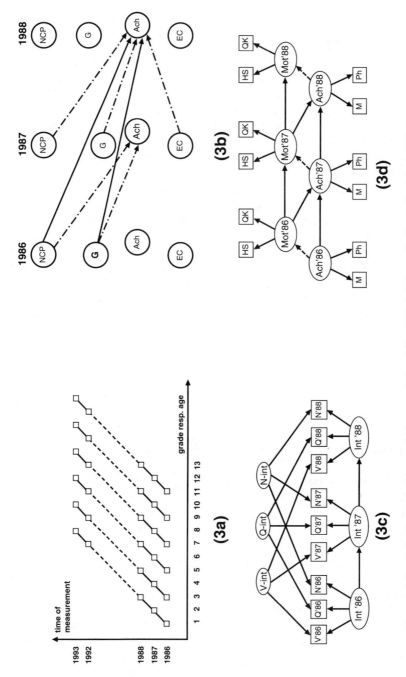

Figure 4.3. Developmental model/framework of the Munich Longitudinal Study of Giftedness

83

Schneider, 1989): (a) interindividual differences (at each time of measurement), (b) intraindividual changes (developmental functions), (c) interindividual differences in intraindividual changes, and (d) interindividual differences in interindividual changes (changes of relative position of individuals). Not all analyses were available for all variables in all cohorts, however. For example, with the scales used for measuring cognitive abilities (German CAT), we cannot analyze developmental functions in the sense of intraindividual changes.

Apart from these ANOVA-based approaches, the design allowed for the use of structural equation analysis for each cohort. Special attention was given to models that included latent variables. Figures 4.3b to 4.3d give examples of models adequate for: (a) analysis of predictive validity of tests (Figure 4.3b), (b) variability versus stability of traits (e.g., intelligence) including test-specific factors (cf. Jöreskog, 1979), and (c) nonrecursive models for analysis of interrelations between different constructs (i.e., reciprocal causal relationships between achievement and motivation). The structural approach also allows for future testing of the equivalence of the structural relations of two or more cohorts (Jöreskog & Sörbom, 1984).

SAMPLE AND METHOD

Sample Selection: Recruitment of Schools and Students

After receiving permission from the governments of the German federal states Baden-Württemburg, Bayern, and West Berlin, we asked a total of 1,020 schools to take part in our study. Schools of different types were selected randomly from the official catalogs of the respective states. Participation was voluntary for schools and teachers as specified by law. Only 210 (20.6%) of these schools agreed to participate in the study (participation rate for West Berlin primary schools was only 4.1%; participation rate without Berlin was 23.9%). One hundred and fifty-two schools were finally selected according to specific criteria, ensuring a representative sample (size of town, urban/rural town, schooltypes, region, and so on). After recruitment of the schools and classes, the parents of each of the students were asked to give permission for their children to participate in the study. Many parents refused to sign the relevant agreement. Reasons given were typical for such field studies in Germany: the parents' dislike of scientific testing of their own children and the fear that teachers might get the results of the tests of giftedness. Some properties of the sample of the first phase of the study are given in Table 4.1. As no standardized tests of general intelligence were used, we cannot give the exact mean IQ of our sample. Different comparisons of the respective means showed, however, that our sample of the identification wave was superior to representative samples by about one standard deviation in general intelligence and speed of information processing.

Some characteristics of the longitudinal sample (cohort, sex, school type) can be seen in Table 4.1. A total of 2,005 students were invited to take part in the longitudinal phase of the study. Unfortunately some students left the schools after Wave 1, and some schools or teachers did not want to participate in the longitudinal study. The figures indicate the numbers of completed results of intelligence testing for students who took part in at least two waves. Because of missing values, the number of cases is slightly smaller for each aspect of the reported results.

In the German school system, children attend primary schools for four years (grades 1 to 4). More academically able students then attend the 9-year grammar school ("Gymnasium"). This school type, the highest level, finishes with the "Abitur" after grade 13 and leads to university. The "Hauptschule" is aimed at the lowest academic level (grade 5 to grade 9 or 10 depending on the federal state). Hauptschule leads to blue-collar jobs, while a certificate from the intermediate schools or "Realschule," (from grade 5 or 7 to grade 10) is needed for most white-collar jobs.

Information Sources, Measured Variables, and Data Processing

Important sources of information, major research variables, and measurement instruments used—each related to the dimensions of the Munich Model of Giftedness (see Figure 4.1 above)—are summarized in Table 4.2. (Means, standard deviations, reliability coefficients, and so on of the different scales are not included because of the limited space.) In addition to the scales mentioned in the table, further tests were conducted to assess spatial thinking, verbal aspects of creativity, parents' ratings of activities and achievement outside school, parents' reports of socioemotional problems of their children, and their wishes for the counseling and support of their children, and so on.

In addition to the psychometric information, semistructured interviews were conducted with a small subsample of highly intelligent

Table 4.1. Description of the Sample of the Munich Study of Giftedness

Cohort 1	1986	1987	1988
Boys	259/102	100	89
Girls	296/113	102	102
Total	597/229	217	205

Cohort 3	1986	1987	1988
Boys	395/144	137	100
Girls	426/130	123	83
Total	856/280	268	187

Cohort 5	1986			1987			1988		
	School type			School type			School type		
	Haupts	Reals	Grammar	Haupts	Reals	Grammar	Haupts	Reals	Grammar
Boys	81/12	81/18	326/121	8	13	110	6	14	105
Girls	73/8	106/25	365/113	8	24	109	4	18	100
Total	227/23	190/43	780/249	19	37	232	11	32	217

Cohort 7

	1986			1987			1988		
	School type			School type			School type		
	HauptS	RealS	Grammar	HauptS	RealS	Grammar	HauptS	RealS	Grammar
Boys	87/5	203/49	352/106	3	39	100	4	44	97
Girls	71/3	193/48	400/143	3	46	133	1	43	127
Total	166/10	407/100	789/271	6	88	248	5	90	235

Cohort 9

	1986			1987			1988		
	School type			School type			School type		
	HauptS	RealS	Grammar	HauptS	RealS	Grammar	HauptS	RealS	Grammar
Boys	55/-	194/31	390/119	2	31	112		1	100
Girls	49/2	205/26	422/160	2	26	156			135
Total	109/2	413/60	817/287		59	268		1	239

Cohort 11

	1986	1987	1988
Boys	531/160	160	103
Girls	461/93	92	65
Total	1002/288	256	171

Note. Total in some cases bigger than Girls + Boys because of missing cases. For 1986, numbers of students in the sample of the identification phase (left side of slash) and the smaller number of participants in the longitudinal study (right side of slash) can be seen from the Table. HauptS = *Hauptschule* (lowest level, grade 5-9), RealS = *Realschule* (intermediate level; grade 5/7-10), Grammar school = *Gymnasium* (highest, most academic level, grade 5-13).

Table 4.2.   Information Sources and Measured Variables

	Information Sources	
Variables	**Students' Psychometric Scores**	**Teacher**
Intellectual Dimension	Tests: – KFT (German CAT) – ZVT (Numbers Connection Test)	Teachers' Checklist[3]: – T-Int
Creativity Dimension	Tests: – VWT (Unusual Uses) – TCT (Torrance Creativity Test – subtest Completion of Pictures) Questionnaires: – GIFT, GIFFI	Teachers' Checklist[3]: – T-Cre
Social Competence	Questionnaire: – Social Competence	Teachers' Checklist[3]: – T-SC
Psychomotor Dimension	Tests: – Computer Tests[1] – Construction Game Test – Paper-Pencil-Tests[2]	Teachers' Checklist[3]: – T-PM
Art (Music) Dimension		Teachers' Checklist[3]: – T-Mus
Noncognitive Personality Characteristics	Questionnaires: – QK (Thirst or Quest for Knowledge) – HS (Hope for Success) – FF (Fear of Failure) – Anxiety[2] – Self Concept[2] – Attribution[2] – Learning Styles[2] – Interests[2]	
Environmental Characteristics	Questionnaires: – Family Climate[2] – Class Climate[2] – Critical Life Events[2]	
Achievement	Questionnaire: – MAI (Munich Activity Inventory with subscales: Arts, Literature, Social, Science, Technology, Music, Sport	Teachers' checklist[3] School Marks

Legend: [1] = only at Wave 1; [2] = only at Wave 2 and 3; [3] = long and detailed checklist at Wave 1, short checklist at Wave 2 and 3.

students (10 girls and 10 boys) to obtain information about their early development and on the typical effects (over time) of personality and environment on performance. This interview study has a retrospective character. A second interview study was carried out with a sample of 18 students who seemed from their answers on an

Table 4.3.   Definition of Group Labels

Construct/variable	Label	Criterion (Sample)	Correspondence in population
General intelligence (KFT = German CAT), creativity (TCT, subtest completion of pictures)	Average	Percent rank < 70	
	Gifted	Percent rank — 70	Percent rank — 90-95
	Highly gifted	Percent rank — 85	Percent rank — 95-97
	Extremely gifted	Percent rank — 92.5	Percent rank — 97-98
Interests	Average	Percent rank < 70	
	Well interested	Percent rank — 70	
	Highly interested	Percent rank — 90	
Personality and environmental characteristics	Low	Percent rank — 50	
	High	Percent rank > 50	
Academic achievement	Underachiever	z-value (intelligence) – z-value (Mean of German, English, mathematics) > 1.5	

interest and activity inventory to be highly interested in specific fields. The theme of this retrospective study was the development of outstanding interests in particular topics and the identification of conditions that facilitate development.

In order to create dichotomous variables for specific analyses (e.g., comparison of achievement and personality profiles of different groups), we used the following cut-off points (see Table 4.3):

1. General intelligence, creativity, and nonacademic achievement: The criterion was the 70th percentile for high performance. The best 30% of our longitudinal sample in intelligence corresponded to the best 5-10% of the population. We formed more differentiated intelligence and creativity groups by establishing cutoffs at the 85th and 92.5th percentiles of the sample (so that we could also examine the best 15 or 7.5%). We will use the label "gifted" for the top 30%, "highly gifted" for the top 15%, and "extremely gifted" for the top 7.5% of our sample. The latter should correspond to the best 2-3% of the unselected population. By "average," we mean all students with a rank lower than 70% in our sample.
2. Interests: By "interested," we refer to the top 30% in each domain of interests, while we use "highly interested" for the top 10%.
3. Personality and environmental characteristics: Here we divided the subsamples at the median.

4. Underachievers were those students whose scores in z-transformed general intelligence exceeded their average school marks (German and English language, mathematics) by more than 1.5 standard deviations.

Practical Problems in the Execution of the Study

As in most cases, the first practical problem of our research was financial. The costs of the Munich Longitudinal Study of Giftedness could not be met at our institute and thus had to be financed by the Federal Ministry for Education and Science. However, this financial support was restricted to a maximum of 4 years. Given that the screening procedure (in 1985) needed to be completed first, this constraint cut the number of points of measurement down to three. From the scientific point of view, a longer study with the option of following the school careers of gifted students through the whole primary or secondary school process would have been desirable. This was a reason why cohort effects could not be analyzed. As the difference between the youngest and the oldest cohort was only 10 school years within a decade without major changes in society or in educational policy, however, we did not expect cohort effects at all.

At the time our study began, there was much debate about research and guidance of gifted students in German society. The conservative and liberal parties supported activities for gifted students, but the social democrats argued that this would support elitism and put the majority of children at a disadvantage. After we received permission to collect data in schools—which was only possible in German federal states governed by the conservative party—some schools and teachers did not want to participate. In many cases this was because of organizational problems. But some schools and teachers said frankly that the reason they would not participate was related to their viewpoint in the giftedness discussion. In many cases, unfortunately, it was not possible to get information on reasons why teachers or schools did not want to take part. A similar problem arose with parents refusing to give agreement, and unfortunately we do not know why. This general problem for any research conducted in schools in the former West Germany hinders precise judgment of the representativeness of field study samples.

A major logistical problem that arose in the course of the study was the enormous sample of schools spread all over south Germany and West Berlin. During the weeks before the data collection, the organizing staff completed the massive task of establishing a time schedule accommodating all the following constraints: the schools' requirements, region of the school, holidays, availability of the co-workers, availability of cars, size of the student groups, available number of booklets, and so forth. All in all, the data collection could not have been conducted without the effort and commitment of all coworkers. As our institute has no vehicles of its own, the car-owning coworkers had to change their personal plans in many cases. On top of this, part-time research assistants tend to have old and unreliable cars so that occasionally the time schedule was threatened because of breakdowns. Global political events almost endangered the time schedule as well. The West Berlin testing sessions took place during the last visit of U.S. President Ronald Reagan. Extremely strict police controls inspected cars and luggage at various checkpoints. When our coworkers' car was searched, the police found some metal boards which we needed for a sort-recall task. It was somewhat complicated to explain what these "suspicious metal objects" were needed for.

A more serious problem arose with the strict laws on data protection in the Federal Republic of Germany. The ministries of education did not allow our team to have the names and addresses of the participating children. We used identity codes for all the students. Lists matching codes to names were mostly in the hands of the class teachers at the schools. Unfortunately some teachers threw away these lists between two waves or took the list with them when they left the school. Sometimes, during the actual test sessions, wrong numbers were written on the answer sheets and booklets. After the phases of measurement, especially after Waves 2 and 3, we needed a specialized coworker to help clear up all these cases. Without the work of this "Sam Spade of the data archive" the sample sizes for the longitudinal analyses would have been much reduced.

Yet another problem was caused by the German school system. After grade 4, most children change schools and after grade 7 intermediate school ("Realschule") begins in Bavaria, so that it was quite hard to get parts of the sample for the testing sessions of the following waves. The Hauptschule and the Realschule finish at the end of the 9th and 10th grades, respectively, so that, with a few exceptions, these students were lost for Waves 2 and 3. At Wave 3, the students of some classes of the oldest cohort did not want to attend future testing sessions because they did not want to lose study time for their high school diploma examinations (Abitur).

Statistical-Methodological Problems Occurring in Investigations of the Gifted and in Studies with Special Selection Procedures

In the course of the study we had to deal with three major statistical-methodological problems. The first problem resulted from the differentiation power of the methods in the upper area of the distribution. As most giftedness tests are usually designed to differentiate best with normal, average gifted children, ceiling effects were likely to occur (see also Heller, 1989). Ceiling effects hinder discrimination, especially between highly and extremely gifted students. As an attempt to solve this problem we adapted the tests. With the intelligence test used, the multilevel KFT (Heller, Gaedike, & Weinläder, 1985), German version of the Thorndike and Hagen (1971) CAT for example, we combatted the ceiling effects of the test by giving items to the students which are normally attempted by students who are two years older. We also shortened the time allowed for certain speed tests and revised the items of some questionnaires in order to adapt them for our sample of above-average students.

The second major methodological problem concerned the distribution properties of the variables in the study, especially the variables which were used for the selection procedure. The investigation groups—average, highly, and extremely gifted—were defined in the longitudinal sample by using (multidimensional) cutoff points. The shapes of the distribution curves of the respective variables were affected and, as a consequence, normal distribution of errors was lost. As the assumption of normal distribution is essential for most parametric statistical methods, the results of the analyses may be misleading. We employed two approaches to solve this problem: First, we used nonparametric methods such as log-linear analysis (Perleth & Sierwald, 1988), and second, we conducted robustness studies to examine the extent to which the results were affected by the violation of the assumptions (Sierwald & Perleth, 1989).

A third problem arose from the fact that many variables, such as the winning of prizes, are of a genuinely qualitative character. In order to analyze such variables in complex interrelations, we employed nonparametric methods such as log-linear models (Perleth & Sierwald, 1988), which also allow for the use of recursive causal models (see Fox, 1984).

RESULTS FOR THE FIRST PHASE OF THE STUDY (IDENTIFICATION PHASE)

Several major results emerged from the first phase of the Munich Longitudinal Study of Giftedness (cf. Hany, 1987; Heller & Perleth,

1989; Heller, 1990). The instruments used to measure cognitive and noncognitive (especially motivational) dimensions of the gifted, together with relevant conditions of the social learning environment, were sufficiently reliable (see Heller, 1986). The five factors of the Munich Longitudinal Study of Giftedness (intelligence, creativity, psychomotor ability, practical intelligence/social competence, musical ability) were independent dimensions of giftedness (as indicated by the results of factor analyses). Thus the hypothesis of domain-specific forms of giftedness was confirmed.

Significant differences could be found between the highly gifted and average students in each domain of giftedness and among the various types of giftedness. For example, the intellectually (or academically) gifted had better school grades than the rest of the sample. The creative students were in some aspects more active and more successful in artistic and literary areas, the socially gifted in social areas, and so on. Multiple or many-sided gifted were found relatively infrequently in the selected sample ($N = 1,800$). If, however, one views those students (from ages 6 to 16 or 18 years), who were both highly intellectually and creatively talented, one sees that they were superior to all of the other students in important performance areas. From the methodological point of view, this finding is not too surprising, but nevertheless it underlines the point that the diagnosis of giftedness should not continue along single dimensions. Particularly capable students differed from the others in personality characteristics (in this case, motivational variables).

Research conducted to evaluate different strategies for the identification of gifted students using different statistical approaches (factor analysis, cluster analysis, regression analysis) and diverse sources of information (Hany, 1987) showed that both for practical purposes and with regards to our research, a multidimensional cutoff best optimized the different constraints (simplicity, practicability, effectiveness, efficiency). Cluster analyses seem to be more appropriate for the description than for the identification of gifted students (see Hany, 1987, for an extensive discussion of identification questions).

RESULTS OF THE SECOND PHASE OF THE STUDY (LONGITUDINAL PHASE)

The Predictive Validity of the Test Battery

Multiple regression analyses showed for primary school pupils that our giftedness tests, especially the intelligence test used, were able to predict academic achievement to an acceptable degree over periods of one and two years. Quite surprisingly, the tests (uncorrected multiple $r = .5 - .6$) were superior to teacher judgments (uncorrected multiple $r = .4$) especially in the major subjects (German language, mathematics, and natural sciences). Teacher judgments tended to be global, whereas our test battery tended to give differentiated results. For the primary school age range, the need for psychological diagnosis of giftedness was therefore well demonstrated. This finding is particularly important in Germany, as the decision about school career is based on teacher judgment and is made at the end of grade 4.

The creativity test used ("Completion of Figures" subtest of the Torrance Creativity Test) was—in contrast to the teachers' check lists—not a good predictor of arts and music in primary school, even though it might seem to have face validity. When analyzing nonacademic achievement in different areas, both tests and teacher judgments proved to be good predictors in discriminant function analyses.

The predictive validity of our tests seems to be a little weaker in secondary school (uncorrected multiple $r = .3 - .5$), decreasing somewhat from cohort to cohort. The teachers' ratings played a more important role here (uncorrected multiple $r = .4 - .6$). The increasing influence of the knowledge base for high achievement at this age could plausibly explain this finding. The intelligence scales used nevertheless turned out to be relatively good predictors (up to $r = .45$), especially for the most important school subjects.

In contrast to the results reported for primary school children, the creativity test, which was an "Unusual Uses" test for the respective cohorts, showed some predictive validity for arts (up to $r = .2$). Concerning nonacademic areas, teacher ratings play a much smaller role in predicting activities and achievement (tests: uncorrected multiple $r = .3 - .6$; teacher check lists: uncorrected multiple $r = .1 - .3$). Quite surprisingly, this even held true for activities in natural sciences and technology. In the latter, a larger part of the variance could be explained by including both tests and teachers' ratings in the analysis (uncorrected multiple $r = .4 - .6$). The inclusion of motivational variables in the regression analyses increased the portion of explained variance, especially in nonacademic domains. Quest for knowledge played an especially important role in the prediction of activities and achievement in natural sciences and technology.

Overall, the analyses confirmed our model of giftedness: Domain-specific giftedness tests were best able to predict domain-specific achievement, while personality characteristics (here: motivational variables) played a mediating role (cf. Gagné, 1985). Therefore, identification of gifted students should not simply rely on intelligence tests.

Results Concerning the Typological Concept of Giftedness

As mentioned above, one of the aims of the longitudinal phase of the study was to establish a typology of giftedness with an exploratory approach. Cluster analyses were conducted which included many factors extracted by factor analyses of test and questionnaire data from the first identification phase of the project. Equivocal results were obtained: No clear types of gifted students could be identified. It had been planned to construct the longitudinal sample according to a possible giftedness typology. As no clear typology could be found, we decided on multiple cutoff as the selection strategy for building the sample for the longitudinal phase.

In the course of the longitudinal phase of the project, some additional attempts were made to analyze types of giftedness and their stability over time. As it had not been possible to identify special types of giftedness by cluster analysis (k-way method, see Wisehard, 1984), the hypothesis arose that gifted students show such highly individual structures of giftedness that they differ from normal students in the very fact that they cannot be grouped at all. Accordingly, we applied Bergman's (1987) program to identify possible "singular types" of giftedness. This method tries to separate the possibly clusterable part of a sample from the nonclusterable residuum. Unfortunately, the residual of nonclusterable cases did not contain gifted students with special combinations of giftedness factors, but rather extreme cases of low-gifted pupils. Cluster analyses with the cases not in the residuum again showed no clear types of giftedness. In addition, the resulting types were not stable over the course of the three measurement points. This means that the students belonged to different clusters at different measurement points even though the giftedness traits in the analysis were relatively stable. All in all, from the cluster analysis point of view, the results show that, in our sample there were no typological differences between gifted and average students. The students were distributed continuously along the dimensions of giftedness, the samples of the different cohorts therefore being homogeneous and not divisible into clearly distinguishable groups. These findings strengthen the hypothesis that the different giftedness domains are relatively independent.

The Influence of Environmental Factors on the Performance of Gifted Students

Environmental factors, as measured by questionnaires of critical life events as well as family and school climate, did not show a great deal of influence or association on the performance of gifted and average students, especially in the older cohorts. These results are based on group statistics. We also conducted an interview study which showed the important role of environmental factors on the development of individual highly gifted students. The need for guidance and nurturing of the gifted was more obvious in the case study. Moreover, among students with extraordinary interests, the role of the family climate became apparent. A controlling, achievement-oriented family climate seems to favor the development of technical interests, while students with interests in arts and music came from families with ongoing, culturally oriented leisure-time activities, high independence, and an average level of parental control and achievement orientation. If one considers the whole sample, however, influences from socialization as well as critical life events seem to be of minor importance for the actual genesis of achievement. One interpretation is that these influences seem to become less significant, especially in the course of secondary school, in comparison with young people's perception of their degree of control over their own lives.

Reasons for these negative results include the fact that the instruments used covered only a segment of possible environmental features (family and school climate, critical life events). Further, the analyzed interrelations in the framework of the mostly linear models might have been too simple to capture the complexity of real life. Using the causal model and taking into account quite complicated interactions between intelligence, motivation, family climate, and achievement yielded some hints: Intelligence and motivation might, for example, have a direct impact on academic achievement, while family climate, itself influenced by school grades, has an indirect effect on academic achievement via motivation. These results should be treated as exploratory, however, because of the severe identification problems in estimating the structural model parameters.

Changes in Cognitive and Noncognitive Features

Differentiated analyses for the subsample of gifted primary school children showed that intelligence seems to be a relatively stable trait (e.g., $r = .75$ between the results of Wave 2 and 3 in the cohort of third graders). Recall that only the relative positions of the children in our sample were investigated. This does not give a developmental function of intelligence. Hence the stability of interindividual differences in our findings does not mean that there is no increase in intelligence in the primary school age. The structural model of Figure 4.3c applied on the KFT data of the cohort of third graders gave correlations between the latent variables "general intelligence" at the three points of measurement of $.71 \leq r \leq .87$.

The results indicated that the measured creativity variable was quite unstable. We cannot decide whether this was because of the low reliability of the test used (Completion of Pictures) or the instability of the measured trait. When similar findings from other studies (e.g., Sefer, 1989, who undertook a longitudinal study with primary school children) are taken into account, there is some considerable reason to doubt the theory and the quality of this type of test.

Concerning intelligence, the results for secondary school students were similar to those for children of primary school age. The interindividual differences in the German Cognitive Abilities Test turned out to be so stable (correlations $.65 \leq r \leq .77$ between results of Waves 1 and 3), that it was not possible to analyze simultaneous influence of more than one of the variables sex, constellation of siblings, or level of intelligence at the first point of measurement. Applying the structural model shown in Figure 4.3c to derive the "error-free" estimate of the stability of the latent variable general intelligence, we obtained for the cohort of ninth graders correlations of .76 (results of Waves 1 and 2) and .93 (results of Waves 2 and 3). Here the model explained 56-79% of the variance of the measured scales, showing a good fit to the data.

The "Unusual Uses" creativity test used for secondary school students turned out to have better properties than the "Completion of Pictures" creativity test used for primary school children. Although the examined interindividual differences were more stable, the use of such an instrument for important, irreversible selection decisions seems, in our opinion, to be neither possible nor warranted.

With secondary school students we were able to study developmental functions of the speed of information processing (Number Connection Test, i.e., German trail-making test). The findings indicated that performance on this task increased between grade 5 and grade 10/11 and remained stable for older students of grade 11 to 13. This finding is in accordance with the results of Oswald and Roth (1978), the authors of the test. Interindividual differences were extremely stable in this test of speed of information processing (correlations $.65 \leq r \leq .73$ between results of Wave 1 and 3).

A majority of the results reported up to this point indicate that most interindividual differences in giftedness domains are quite stable. We then investigated stability versus development of noncognitive personality characteristics. Consider one hypothesis as an example. For ninth graders, we analyzed the interrelation between motivation (here thirst for knowledge and hope for success) and academic achievement in science (mathematics and physics) with a structural model (see Figure 4.3d). The hypothesis was that motivation and achievement are to a certain degree stable constructs (arrows between the latent Mot and Ach variables). Motivation should influence academic achievement (one year later), while the impact of academic achievement on motivation should only be found in average but not in highly intelligent students. When interpreting the attained coefficients, however, we found that both motivation and achievement were stable characteristics in both groups, influencing one another only a little.

The Role of Interests

The first striking result, when analyzing the data of the interest questionnaire (secondary school) applied in Waves 2 and 3, was gender differences reflecting stereotyped patterns. Girls were more interested in music, arts and literature, and social activities, and boys showed more interest in natural science, technology, sports, and competition. These findings were reinforced when we examined the proportion of boys and girls in the top 30% of the interest range. Nevertheless, there are hints that girls who are particularly interested in technology do not lose their interest, while a decline in technical interest can be seen in boys or moderately interested girls.

Analyses of students highly interested in specific domains showed them to have a broader spectrum of interests than average. An exception to this positive finding of broad interest is given by the technically interested students, who describe themselves as significantly uninterested in the music, literature, and arts domains. This fits the common picture of the "techno freak" who is not interested in anything except computers. As mentioned above, we found only a few girls among the technically interested students, so our results for this group cannot be interpreted without consideration of the gender-specific findings.

The highly interested students (top 10%) showed specific profiles in cognitive and noncognitive personality characteristics including those aspects of their family climate mentioned above. The technically highly interested were success-oriented, curious, independent, and showed especially strong quantitative intelligence. Students highly interested in arts seemed to be positively motivated young people, brought up to think and act independently, with good school marks in German language and worse marks in English and mathematics. The musically highly interested earned quite good grades overall, their interests being the most stable. Finally, comparing the fields of interest with the areas of achievement, it became apparent that high interest is reflected in good academic and nonacademic achievement in corresponding fields. The interest questionnaire in the planned follow-up study will allow comparisons between the interests during school years and the choice of career/college and later life achievement.

Personality Characteristics of Gifted Secondary School Students

In our subsamples of seventh to eleventh graders, we were surprised to find no differences between the intellectually gifted and other pupils in curiosity and motivation. Although one could perhaps have expected that intelligence is not related to curiosity in the domains of science and technology, we were surprised that the means for hope of success and fear of failure also did not differ according to different levels of giftedness. Because the students in our sample had been preselected by teachers and selected by a test battery, the average members of the sample are not really representative of the general population. Our selection procedures and the study as a whole might have selected the more motivated pupils or those with a tendency to conformity.

The second interesting result concerned the groups considered creative: They also did not differ in personality characteristics from the other groups. Interpreting this, one should be aware that nearly all our variables on anxiety, coping with stress, self-concept, and learning styles are based on items that deal with situations in school or with homework and test preparation.

The most obvious and consistent result when investigating intelligence groups was the stronger academic self-concept of the gifted and highly gifted students. There were no differences in general or nonacademic self-concept. No differences were found on the variables of anxiety, but there seems to be a slight trend that the more gifted one is, the lower the anxiety scores are. This would seem to indicate that stressful situations, including tests, influence the quality of thinking of the gifted to a lesser extent than less gifted pupils. The gifted members of our sample also tended to attribute success and failure less to external causes when compared with average students.

We also found interesting differences between intellectually gifted and average students regarding learning styles. While the average and the moderately gifted did not differ, the highly and extremely gifted are much less likely to use simple learning techniques such as making a plan for homework or doing homework before playing. It seems as if older highly and extremely gifted students have no problems with homework and thus do not need simple techniques for successful homework management.

In addition, we found that the older intellectually gifted students prefer working alone and do not like to work cooperatively with pupils in their classes. This should not be interpreted as saying that the gifted do not want to work with other students; rather, they do not want to work with other members of the class who are usually not as gifted. It cannot be concluded from this that the gifted are socially isolated because the character of the items of the scale used is largely schoolwork related.

Comparing the intellectually gifted academic achievers and underachievers in our samples, we found many of the differences that are reported in the literature. Because of the small sample sizes, the results should not be emphasized, but nevertheless they may provide some important hints. Underachievers tend to be more anxious, their thinking is more disturbed by stressful situations, they tend to attribute academic success and failure externally, they have a weaker academic self-concept, and their motivational structure tends to be less favorable.

Two-way ANOVAs were computed to investigate the influence of specific noncognitive personality characteristics and intelligence on academic and nonacademic achievement. As described above, we regard personality characteristics as mediators between giftedness and achievement. In the field of academic achievement, intelligence has the greatest impact, but anxiety, stability of thinking, external attribution, and academic self-concept also play important roles. The same general pattern holds true for leisure time activities and nonacademic achievement in the domain of science. The influence of resistance to stress is particularly salient in highly intelligent students while average and moderately gifted students do not differ.

Similar ANOVAs showed no significant effects of personality characteristics on activities in the domain of literature and arts. In the field of social activities, willingness to cooperate with peers and a strong self-concept seem to be advantageous for high achievements, while intelligence seems to have a negative, but not very strong influence. This means that more intelligent students engage somewhat less in social activities.

The findings reported next should illustrate the role of cognitive and noncognitive personality characteristics in the development of academic achievement. In college-track students attending grades 5 to 7, no influences of personality characteristics on the development of achievement (ANOVAs with repeated measure design) could be found. However, in contrast to gifted students, the school marks of the averagely gifted decreased during this period of time. Between grades 7 and 9 (grammar school students only), intelligent students with strong academic self-concept and high stress resistance were able to improve their school marks while all other groups got worse results. In students attending grade 9 to grade 13 (grammar school students only) in the period of time under investigation, none of the effects was significant.

Overall, we can say that at the beginning of grammar school ("Gymnasium"), intellectually gifted students were better able to cope with the new tasks in German, English, and mathematics. In grades 7 to 9, personality characteristics gained more influence as mediators between giftedness and achievement. In these grades, German students learn a second foreign language; begin physics, history, and social sciences; and encounter more stress from outside school (e.g., puberty). After this period, changes in interindividual differences in academic achievement cannot, according to our results, be regarded as consequences of differences in personality characteristics.

RESULTS OF THE INTERVIEW STUDY

The research reported above draws from statistical analyses of test and questionnaire results using large samples. We were also interested in looking beyond these statistical findings to obtain information about intellectually gifted pupils whose questionnaires and test scores indicated high test anxiety, low stability of thinking in stressful situations, weak self-concept, high fear of failure, unfavorable causal attribution, or underachievement. We also included pupils in the interview study who explicitly sought psychological counseling.

In general, we found few gifted pupils in the top 5-10% of the intelligence range who suffered from these kind of problems, at least according to their questionnaire responses. Twenty students (10 girls and 10 boys) were finally included in an interview study carried out in 1988 (see Schmidt, 1989; see also Perleth & Sierwald, 1992, Ch. 9).

The interview study included among its goals the following:

1. Collecting information to achieve better insight about the validity of the questionnaires employed. This was realized by checking whether students with high scores on personality aspects of the questionnaires actually reported the respective characteristics.
2. Obtaining more information about the possible ways in which noncognitive personality and environmental characteristics mediate between giftedness and achievement. Here the focus was on constructs such as anxiety, self-concept, coping with stress, patterns of attribution, and task commitment.
3. Finding developmental conditions which cause low self-concept and underachievement.

Validity of the Questionnaires

When we compared the statements the pupils made in the interview study with their scores in the 1987 questionnaires, we were surprised that in some cases there was little correspondence. However, when we then compared the statements with the scores of the 1988 wave, which was carried out two months before the interview study, we realized that the statements were consistent with these latter results. Moreover, the pupils told us in the interviews that many of the problems they had reported in the questionnaires in 1987 had disappeared in the meantime. In general, the validity of our questionnaires was well demonstrated.

Pupils with high test anxiety or low self-concept were more evasive than the others in the interviews. Sometimes pupils denied having such characteristics, had inhibitions in speaking, or gave evasive answers. Only after the pupils had gained more confidence in the interviewer were they able to speak more freely about their problems. Thus, interview studies can also have validity problems, because it seems to be easier for some pupils to be open in questionnaires than in an interview.

Moderating Effects of Personality Characteristics

The interviews revealed a great variety of interactions among intelligence, noncognitive personality characteristics, environmental variables, and achievement. A comprehensive summary of the results of the interview study is hardly possible. Nevertheless, we will cautiously try to outline some constellations which seemed to us to be typical.

We found gifted students who are underachievers, who regarded this as a problem, and who are helpless. Because of impulsiveness, for example, they could not control careless mistakes. Other students viewed their own underachievement positively: Underachievement was preferred to "learning senseless things." These students seemed to be sure of their ability to get good grades, saying "If I wanted to, I could get better grades." It is interesting that some of these students were willing to try to improve their grades for the "Abitur" (high school diploma) and were convinced of reaching that goal. It is important to know that German grammar schools have a course system in which every single mark during the last two years (grades 12 and 13) goes toward the final diploma mark. Since some subjects at university require a minimum diploma grade, this is quite meaningful. These students began to put more effort toward improving academic achievement at the beginning of grade 12. If underachievement, as in these cases, is not accompanied by helplessness, we have to question whether this sort of underachievement is really a cause for counseling. A follow-up study will determine whether or not these students were indeed able to increase their academic achievement.

A similar situation to underachievement was found concerning anxiety variables. Some pupils experienced physical symptoms of test anxiety or worried about school grades only before the test. In these cases, anxiety seemed to have no negative influence on their performance. With other students, anxiety appeared during the test itself, sometimes only in certain subjects. A typical statement was: "If I see that I can't manage the last problem which is the most difficult, I can't concentrate any longer, even on the easiest problem." These were the pupils who received low scores on scales such as stability of thinking and who regarded their test anxiety as a problem. Some seemed to have developed coping strategies: They consciously talked to themselves during the test in order to calm themselves or, as in the above-mentioned case, they told themselves to ignore the problems not yet worked on.

Other students considered their problems "normal." For example, they judged their "butterflies" as not being unduly important. They were convinced that their performance was not affected because anxiety wears off as soon as they start working on a problem. These pupils seemed to place little importance on possible failure because they were certain of doing better the next time. Furthermore, these students seemed to be less anxious in the social domain. They did not judge it as very problematic to confess a failure to their friends or their parents. Where anxiety existed about reporting bad marks to parents, friends, or teachers, it seemed to be especially detrimental to concentration during examinations.

According to Pekrun (1983), who used similar quantitative methods, academic and general self-concepts correlate well. However, we found a gap between academic and general self-concepts in strongly achievement-oriented pupils in the interview study. There were students who had a strong academic self-concept because of good grades, but who had a weak general self-concept. These seemed to be pupils who had few social contacts. This was not surprising because we know from developmental studies that peers are important for the formation of self-concept. Learning theory explains this in terms of the absence of reinforcement from others. Aside from this, pupils with few social contacts have fewer opportunities to compare their achievement with each other, so they develop unrealistically high standards for themselves. With one girl, these high standards could be seen in her role models, who were "nonexistent fantasy persons." This distance from reality could also be another hindering factor in making close friends.

Gifted students seem to set high standards for themselves outside school because they are used to achieving brilliantly in school. That could mean that students with extremely high grades are quite vulnerable concerning criticism outside school. They have not yet learned to cope with failure. They are not, as Schwarzer (1987) expressed, immune (see also Seligman, 1979). Other students, who have extensive social contact but nevertheless have a weak self-concept and consider themselves average, seem to be much less concerned. They do not have the drive to change themselves.

We cannot answer the question of why some gifted students had a weak general self-concept and were also failure oriented. One girl who was failure oriented in the domain of school and career said, "I tend to be a bit pessimistic," and believed she had inherited this from her mother. However, to give a general explanation of all personality characteristics is beyond the scope of this chapter. With regards to our practical psychological and educational aims, we see it as our task to be able to help these students attain a realistic view of their own potential and abilities. Whether a student remains "a bit pessimistic" or not is, in the end, up to him or her.

Developmental Conditions

One way that weak self-concept could arise in highly intelligent pupils is the following: Some pupils in our study had, because of their more unusual interests, little social contact with peers in earlier years. Because of this they did not receive reinforcement from their surroundings, which seems to have resulted in weak self-concept in further development. However, weak general self-concept was not problematic for all affected students, especially if they had ways of compensating.

In some cases pupils suppress their potential in order to avoid being seen as pushy by their peers. Negative consequences for their development followed, especially if a student had no chance to pursue his or her interests outside school. Some attended adult education centers, for instance, but that is not possible everywhere, especially in rural areas. More individually centered lessons could prevent understimulation with its negative impacts on gifted students.

Students who attract attention with their outstanding abilities, for example by mastery of mental arithmetic, are not usually regarded as pushy by their peers. Other good pupils who do not show such outstanding skills develop social problems if they are particularly hard workers in classes with a low achievement-oriented class climate. Pupils who are able to compensate for this lack of social acknowledgment on the basis of their high performance are not bothered so much by this. Some students found that their friends were only interested in them because of their knowledge. They might indeed have contact in class, but, according to their statements, the academically weaker pupils only cultivated them in order to profit for their own school tasks. This, again, seems to be unfavorable to general self-concept.

DISCUSSION AND CONCLUSIONS

Selected results of our research suggest practical and pedagogical applications for parents, teachers, and counseling psychologists. Possible consequences for the identification and support of gifted children and adolescents also follow from the Munich Longitudinal Study of Giftedness.

Giftedness Identification as a Necessary Prerequisite for Individual Development Support

The results of the investigations, especially of the identification phase of the study, pose new challenges. The most important consequences are summarized below.

First, giftedness *is* clearly a highly complex phenomenon. Multidimensional constructs (cf. Hany & Heller, 1991; Sternberg, 1990) are required, together with hierarchical giftedness models, in which general intelligence at the highest level could perhaps mediate between the generalist and the structuralist positions. Heller (1989) defined giftedness as a hierarchy of correlated but clearly distinguishable intellectual ability constructs and area-specific creativity potentials. This model would seem to be compatible with Guilford's (1967) threshold hypothesis, according to which exceptional creativity and giftedness, at least as far as academic performance is concerned, are to be expected predominantly in the upper intelligence range. Moreover we share the opinion of those who expect both theoretical and practical results with a research approach combining psychometric (trait-oriented) and cognitive paradigms. The results presented in this chapter represent the first of these paradigms. There are, however, further complementary, individual studies which have not yet been completed and which belong to the second paradigm. In general it must be said that the psychometric diagnosis approach is more directly relevant to giftedness identification practice at present.

A further consequence would be to stress the importance of defining the concept of giftedness differently for different purposes. This also applies to giftedness diagnoses, which alongside cognitive and motivational personality characteristics, should assess relevant socialization factors. Information on the individual case, reinforced by diagnostic techniques, forms an indispensable starting point for preventative measures, developmental intervention, and psychological counseling.

In a similar way, satisfactory results in giftedness identification, for instance during "talent searches," are only possible when all available information sources have been accessed. These include both formal and informal measuring instruments (for instance, teacher check lists or questionnaires on giftedness features). We do not agree with the wholesale condemnation of psychometric diagnostics. Testing must be refined, however, by the inclusion of process analyses, such as within the framework of learning test (pretest/treatment/posttest design) or experimental diagnostics. This refinement is particularly important when conditional analyses are necessary, for instance, for intervention and preventative purposes in supporting gifted children and youth.

Reliable prognoses on the personality development of gifted children and young people and on their school achievement and leisure-time activities require not only an appropriate prediction model and relevant decision strategies for classification, placement, and selection, but also empirically backed giftedness indicators and usable criterion variables for individual performance, not to mention suitable conditions in the social learning situation.

Among the high-risk groups—those young people whose giftedness is easily overlooked or recognized too late—are, above all, gifted girls and also the underachievers, whose number is, according to experts, not to be underestimated (cf. Mönks & Heller, 1992). The latter group comprises those school children whose performance at school clearly lags behind what could be expected from their intellectual ability. Their psychological and social situation presumably does not allow their giftedness potential to be converted into adequate performance. Experts estimate that up to 50% of gifted children remain unrecognized through underachievement and are therefore not faced with challenges fitting their individual abilities (e.g., Mönks, van Boxtel, Roelofs, & Sanders, 1986).

Further investigations stress very heavily the importance of early recognition and support of especially able children, above all with regard to the establishment of a suitable learning environment and favorable socialization conditions. Here the development of giftedness must be understood from the start as an interactive process. Gifted children exert influence on their environment actively and spontaneously, often from a very early age, in order to satisfy their considerable urge to learn. Curiosity, as a preliminary form of striving for knowledge, and creativity in play are important giftedness indicators of later excellence (Lehwald & Friedrich, 1987; Mönks & Lehwald, 1991).

Giftedness support is valuable for all school children and does not put support for the disabled under threat, as some critics have claimed. Instead it has a complementary effect, often opening up new and useful aspects for mainstream teaching or for special needs classes. The legal right to educational opportunity appropriate to giftedness, in the form of appropriate socialization conditions, corresponds well to the measures suggested by developmental and educational psychology.

Recommendations to Schools and Teachers

The need for giftedness-specific socialization conditions has already been addressed on a number of occasions. This thesis is not only theoretically well based, but it has also been empirically confirmed. Its translation into practical educational measures must take into account the following points.

Giftedness is initially a relatively nonspecific set of individual pre-dispositions which interact with the social learning environment—that is, with concrete educational and socializing influences—right through the developmental process. Giftedness represents an inter-action product at every instant of the individual's development.

Variations in giftedness between individuals are observable in the first years of life, expressed, for example in play by the desire to learn, outstanding memory performance, learning and work styles, problem sensitivity, originality of problem solving, and so on (Leh-wald & Friedrich, 1987).

Once the differences in forms of giftedness have been acknowl-edged, along with the now generally accepted fact that most school learning processes are not additive but cumulative, the respon-sibility of educational policy becomes clear: to provide appropriate educational and socialization conditions for the different forms of giftedness in each individual. In practice, this involves providing differentiated giftedness-specific learning environments and curric-ula. No matter how varied the organizational and institutional frameworks may be, they must all follow the principles mentioned above: developmental support of children and young people appro-priate to different forms of giftedness.

We see diagnosis and support as a functional unity. Diagnostic investigations of the gifted primarily serve the interests of the indi-vidual and support his or her development. It should be clear from the above that we doubt the value of one-dimensional definitions of giftedness and call for multidimensional definitions (e.g., profile analyses). Giftedness diagnosis relying on a single IQ threshold should be abandoned in favor of analyses which take in the most important cognitive and noncognitive personality and process fea-tures in the most differentiated way possible. The analyses should also include the influence of such variables as the social learning environment on the development and achievement of the gifted. Individual diagnoses should be based on information from all avail-able sources: life, questionnaire, and test data in Cattell's (1965) terminology. Here the measurement scale level must, of course, be borne in mind. Status diagnostic procedures should be comple-mented (not replaced) by process diagnostic approaches as far as possible.

A special problem in diagnosis of giftedness arises with the use of standardized tests. Due to variance limitations on psychometric measures in the upper ranges of the scale, so-called "ceiling effects" arise in which there is an insufficient discrimination of the given feature. These can be combated with performance tests, including intelligence and ability tests in the narrower sense, by administering items from tests for an older age range (up to 3 years' difference); the "acceleration principle." However, many tests on the market are not fully standardized; moreover only "level" or "multilevel" tests such as the Cognitive Abilities Test (CAT), which performed well in our giftedness investigations, are really suitable (see also Hagen, 1989).

In addition, teacher and parent check lists with appropriate categories and rating scales (e.g., operationalization of observable behavior features) have proved useful in our investigations, providing certain criteria are fulfilled. When choosing the raters, careful attention must be paid to their individual area of experience. Seen in this light, it is not just assessments by teachers and parents which complement one another well but also self and other ratings (e.g., in talent searches for particular support programs). Since "soft" data such as these are usually less reliable, checks on reliability are indispensable. On the other hand, ecological validity, which must also be empirically checked, is often better than with fully standardized measuring procedures (tests). For these reasons, along with decision theory considerations of the bandwidth-fidelity dilemma and the well-known error risks associated with selection decisions, the importance of a broad combination of methods in giftedness diagnosis is essential.

The bandwidth-fidelity dilemma, applied by Cronbach and Gleser (1965) to diagnostic personnel decisions, is also relevant to giftedness identification. It highlights the tension between the desired wide range of data gathering—as many giftedness features as possible—and the related criterion, accuracy (reliability) of the diagnostic information sources or test results. Both criteria cannot be simultaneously optimized. For this reason, we recommend a sequential decision strategy in giftedness diagnostics. First, a wide-range giftedness survey (rough sorting) is employed as means of screening with the help of rough check lists, observation techniques, ratings, nomination procedures, and so on. In this way, no form of giftedness should remain unidentified. Inclusion of a number of not highly gifted testees in the first selection group leads to deliberate α-errors. In a second and perhaps third stage, increasingly accurate but more area-specific diagnostic instruments (e.g., tests) are applied. The risk of making β-errors is also reduced, minimalizing incorrect labeling.

Another question concerns the timing of identification. Developmental psychologists tend to argue for early giftedness diagnoses, in spite of methodological objections concerning the unreliability of intelligence tests in the preschool and in the first school years. According to empirical studies, these objections are less relevant with gifted children. On the other hand, the fears of educators (only partly confirmed empirically; Robinson, 1986) about the danger of negative labeling effects cannot be dismissed completely. In this connection, arguments for an optimization of individual socialization opportunities have been strongly advanced (Lehwald & Friedrich, 1987; Mönks & Lehwald, 1991). The need for an early giftedness diagnosis must be carefully assessed in each case, even where this would present practical difficulties.

FURTHER INVESTIGATIONS

As the opportunity arose to collect additional data on the school and university careers of some members of the sample within the following year, we were able to analyze the further development of gifted students. Some of the participants of the oldest cohorts are now at university, in some cases having already taken their Part I examination ("Vordiplom"), while students of other cohorts have had to make important decisions about their school careers. Thus, the planned follow-up study will concentrate on the investigation of the school, university, and vocational careers of some students from our sample. A total of about 450 students from all cohorts agreed to answer further questionnaires. These questionnaires will cover (if funding can be obtained): (a) personality characteristics, primary working styles, (achievement) motivation, curiosity, and thirst for knowledge; (b) interests with respect to motivation, emotion, action and other aspects; special attention will be given to field of university study and vocational interests in the oldest cohorts; (c) indicators of academic achievement such as school grades, decisions in school career, results of diplomas, and so on, as well as indicators of achievement outside school and university; (d) motives and reasons for the chosen university studies or professions (only oldest cohorts); (e) indicators of success in "real life." In addition, we plan to conduct follow-up interviews with subjects of the initial interview study. Using these data we seek to determine (a) the stability of personality characteristics and interests across critical life transitions, (b) the predictive validity of our giftedness tests and questionnaires of personality characteristics and interests for academic and nonacademic achievement (and, in the long run, success in real life), and (c) interrelations between giftedness, personality characteristics, interests, and decisions about school and vocational career in longitudinal designs.

As a second enlargement of the body of longitudinal research in the field of giftedness, a cooperative study is being carried out between our Institute and the Institute of General and Pedagogical Psychology of the Academy of Pedagogical Sciences in Moscow. The Moscow-Munich Study of Giftedness is the first Russian empirical investigation to cover multiple factors of giftedness. It should be possible to reveal for the first time in Russia the interrelations and intercorrelations between different factors of giftedness development at various ages and also to follow the special features of this development with regard to different motivational and social contexts.

The joint study is also planned as a replication of parts of the Munich Longitudinal Study of Giftedness, the main variables under investigation being intelligence and creativity, (achievement) motivation, thirst for knowledge, working styles, other noncognitive personality characteristics, aspects of the social environment, and achievement indicators in different areas. The first wave of data collection was completed in Spring 1991. By enlarging the body of evidence, the Russian data should enable us to assess our confidence in the present findings and to deepen our understanding of the general meaning of the results of the Munich Longitudinal Study of Giftedness.

REFERENCES

Averina, I. S, Scheblanova, H. I., & Perleth, C. (1991). Adaptatsia Miuncheskich testov posnvatelnich sposobnostej dlja odarennich utshashichsja [Adaption of the Munich cognitive abilities test for gifted students]. *Voprosii Psichologii, Nor. 5*, 151–156.

Bergman, L. R. (1987). *You can't classify all of the people all of the time* (Rep. No. 662). Stockholm: University of Stockholm, Department of Psychology.

Buss, A. R. (1979). Toward a unified framework for psychometric concepts in the multivariate developmental situation: Intraindividual change and inter- and intraindividual differences. In J. R. Nesselroade & P. B. Baltes (Eds.), *Longitudinal research in the study of behavior and development* (pp. 41–59). New York: Academic.

Cattel, R. B. (1965). *The scientific analysis of personality*. Chicago, IL: Penguin.

Cronbach, L. J., & Gleser, G. (1965). *Psychological tests and personnel decisions* (2nd ed.). Urbana: University of Illinois Press.

Fox, J. (1984). *Linear statistical models and related methods. With applications to social research*. New York: Wiley & Sons.

Gagné, F. (1985). Giftedness and talent: Reexamining a reexamination of the definitions. *Gifted Child Quarterly, 29,* 103–112.

Gardner, H. (1983). *Frames of mind. The theory of multiple intelligences.* New York: Basic Books.

Guilford, J. P. (1967). *The nature of human intelligence.* New York: McGraw-Hill.

Hagen, E. (1989). *Die Identifizierung Hochbegabter* [Identification of the gifted]. Heidelberg, Germany: Asanger.

Hany, E. (1987). *Modelle und Strategien zur Identifikation hochbegabter Schüler* [Models and strategies for identification of gifted students]. Munich, Germany: University of Munich.

Hany, E. A., & Heller, K. A. (1991). Gegenwärtiger Stand der Hochbegabungsforschung. Replik zum Beitrag Identifizierung von Hochbegabung [Current state of giftedness research. Reply to the contribution "Identification of giftedness"]. *Zeitschrift f. Entwicklungspsychologie u. Pädagogische Psychologie, 23,* 250–262.

Heller, K. A. (1986). *Zweiter Zwischenbericht zum Forschungsprojekt "Formen der Hochbegabung bei Kindern und Jugendlichen"* [Second report of the research project: "Forms of giftedness in children and young people]. Munich, Germany: University of Munich.

Heller, K. A. (1989). Perspectives on the diagnosis of giftedness. *The German Journal of Psychology, 13,* 140–159.

Heller, K. A. (1990). Goals, methods and first results from the Munich Longitudinal Study of Giftedness in West Germany. In C. W. Taylor (Ed.), *Expanding awareness of creative potentials worldwide* (pp. 538–543). New York: Trillium Press.

Heller, K. A. (1992). *Hochbegabung im Kindes- und Jugendalter* [Giftedness in children and young people]. Göttingen: Hogrefe.

Heller, K. A., Gaedike, A. K., & Weinläder, H. (1985). *Kognitiver Fähigkeitstest (KFT 4 − 13 +)* [Cognitive Abilities Test] (2nd ed.). Weinheim: Beltz.

Heller, K. A., & Hany, E. A. (1986). Identification, development, and achievement analysis of talented and gifted children in West Germany. In K. A. Heller & J. F. Feldhusen (Eds.), *Identifying and nurturing the gifted* (pp. 67–82). Toronto, Canada: Huber.

Heller, K. A., & Perleth, C. (1989). Forms of giftedness in children and adolescents: Current results of a longitudinal study. In M. A. Luszcz & T. Nettelbeck (Eds.), *Psychological development: Perspectives across the life-span* (pp. 241–249). North-Holland: Elsevier Science Publishers.

Heller, K. A., Perleth, C., & Sierwald, W. (1991). Longitjudnoje issledovanije odarennosti [Longitudinal study of giftedness]. *Voprosii Psichologii, Nor 2,* 120–127.

Jöreskog, K. G. (1979). Statistical estimation of structural models in longitudinal-developmental investigations. In J. R. Nesselroade & P. B. Baltes (Eds.), *Longitudinal research in the study of behavior and development* (pp. 303–351). New York: Academic.

Jöreskog, K. G., & Sörbom, D. (1984). *LISREL VI - Analysis of Linear Structural Relationships by the Method of Maximum Likelihood User's Guide* (3rd ed.). Mooresville, IN: Scientific Software.

Lehwald, G., & Friedrich, G. (1987). Entwicklungspsychologische Probleme der Früherkennung von Begabungen [Developmental psychological problems in the early identification of giftedness]. *Psychologie für die Praxis* (special issue, 5-12). Berlin: VEB Deutscher Verlag der Wissenschaften.

Mönks, F. J., van Boxtel, H. W., Roelofs, J. J. W., & Sanders, M. P. M. (1986). The identification of gifted children in secondary education and a description of their situation in Holland. In K. A. Heller & J. F. Feldhusen (Eds.), *Identifying and nurturing the gifted* (pp. 39–65). Toronto: Huber.

Mönks, F. E., & Heller, K. A. (1992). Identification and programming. In M.C. Wang et al. (Eds.), *International encyclopedia of education* (2nd ed.). Oxford: Pergamon Press.

Mönks, F. J., & Lehwald, G. (Eds.). (1991). *Neugier, Erkundung und Begabung bei Kleinkindern* [Curiosity and giftedness in young children]. Munich: Reinhardt.

Oswald, W. D., & Roth, E. (1978). *Der Zahlenverbindungstest (ZVT)* [Numbers connection test]. Göttingen: Hogrefe.

Pekrun, R. (1983). *Schulische Persönlichkeitsentwicklung* [Personality development at school]. Frankfurt/M.: Lang.

Perleth, C., Averina, I., & Scheblanova, H. (1991). *Measuring intelligence in gifted German and Russian students: Results of a cross-cultural project.* Munich, Germany: University of Munich, Institute of Educational Psychology and Psychological Diagnostics.

Perleth, C., & Sierwald, W. (1988, June). *Logit and loglinear models for the analysis of developmental data as applied to students' development of giftedness, motivation, and achievement.* Poster presented at the third European Conference on Developmental Psychology, Budapest, Hungary.

Perleth, C., & Sierwald, W. (1992). Entwicklungs- and Leistungsanalysen zur Hochbegabung [Developmental and achievement analyses of the gifted]. In K. A. Heller (Ed.), *Hochbegabung im Kindes- und Jugendalter* [Giftedness in children and young people] (pp. 165–350). Göttingen: Hogrefe.

Robinson, A. (1986). The identification and labeling of gifted children. What does research tell us? In K. A. Heller & J. F. Feldhusen (Eds.), *Identifying and nurturing the gifted* (pp. 103–109). Toronto: Huber.

Schaie, K. W., & Baltes, P. B. (1975). On sequential strategies in developmental research: Description or explanation. *Human Development, 18*, 384–390.

Schmidt, H. (1989). *Schulische Persönlichkeits- and Leistungsentwicklung intellektuell hochbegabter Gymnasiasten—eine exploratorische Studie unter Berücksichtigung möglicher Beratungsanlässe* [Personality and achievement development of intellectually gifted grammar school students, with special reference to counseling indications—An exploratory study]. Munich: University of Munich, Institute of Educational Psychology and Psychological Diagnostics.

Schneider, W. (1989). Problems of longitudinal studies with children: Practical, conceptual and methodological issues. In M. Brambring, F. Lösel, & H. Skowronek (Eds.), *Children at risk: Assessment, longitudinal research, and intervention* (pp. 313–335). New York: De Gruijter.

Schwarzer, R. (1987). *Stress, Angst and Hilflosigkeit* [Anxiety, stress, and helplessness]. Stuttgart, Germany: Kohlhammer.

Sefer, J. (1989). *Measuring divergent abilities.* Presentation at the XII International School Psychology Colloquium in Ljubljana, Yugoslavia.

Seligman, M. E. P. (1979). *Erlernte Hilflosigkeit* [Learned helplessness]. Munich: Urban & Schwarzenberg.

Sierwald, W., & Perleth, Ch. (1989, September). *Ein Vergleich unterschiedlicher Methoden zur Testung rekursiver Modelle für die Entwicklung hochbegabter Jugendlicher* [A comparison of different methods for testing recursive models of the development of gifted young people]. Poster presented at the 8th Tagung Entwicklungspsychologie Münich, FRG.

Sternberg, R. J. (1990). What constitutes a "good" definition of giftedness? *Journal for the Education of the Gifted, 14,* 96–100.

Thorndike, R. L., & Hagen, E. (1971). *Cognitive Abilities Test.* Boston: Houghton-Mifflin.

Wisehard, D. (1984). *Clustan Benutzerhandbuch (3. Ausgabe)* (CLUSTAN user's guide, 3rd version). Stuttgart: Fischer.

5

The Development of Basic Cognitive Components of Technical Creativity: A Longitudinal Comparison of Children and Youth with High and Average Intelligence

Ernst A. Hany

This chapter reports on a 3-year study of the cognitive development of German children with high and average intelligence in order to investigate creative problem solving in technological domains. Levels of intelligence, gender, and age were considered in analyzing interindividual differences in developmental patterns. Following a brief outline of the relevance of technology for human life and the status of research in creative problem solving, study goals and methods are described. The chapter then presents empirical data testing a theoretical model of the correlation between several ability components of creative problem solving. This model is followed through several subgroups and age levels. Time-related changes in the patterns of correlations are explained by effects of schooling, particularly in terms of students' changing knowledge bases and strategic skills as subjects become more experienced with technology.

This chapter was partially prepared on the basis of a grant provided by the Volkswagen Foundation (Germany) to Kurt A. Heller. The assistance of Stephen Powell with the preparation of the English version was of invaluable help. The editors' comments and the suggestions made by the series editor contributed substantially to the clarity of the presentation. David H. Feldman, Franz J. Mönks, Julian Stanley, and several other distinguished researchers provided valuable comments on preliminary results reported to a symposium concerning the entire underlying research project which was organized by Kurt A. Heller and cochaired by Zi-xiu Zha from the Chinese Academy of Sciences, in The Hague, Netherlands, in August 1991.

TECHNOLOGY AS A RELEVANT TOPIC
FOR EDUCATIONAL PSYCHOLOGY

Technology can be defined as the management and control of nature by artificial means (Walther-Klaus, 1987). The development of technological devices as a better way of reaching given goals can be seen as the definitive human achievement. For this reason, archeologists consider the appearance of tools as an indicator of the appearance of human life (Sachsse, 1987). The human world today consists largely of technological products. Even cultural reality, defined and transmitted as a system of knowledge, is a form of a technological construction designed to make life in society easier and to give direction to individual existence (Meehan & Wood, 1975; Oerter, 1988; Schelsky, 1965). From this perspective, humanity's task today is not only to develop technological products but also to find effective ways of relating to the technological environment. The task of education is to foster the necessary skills. Education for technological creativity, therefore, encompasses not only knowledge and ability in the natural sciences and technology (Gardner et al., 1990), and a feel for appropriate technological solutions to human problems, but also insight into the supporting role of technology in humanity's interaction with nature. Technical creativity thus includes an understanding of technology as a subordinate tool for the benefit of superordinate human goals; technology is a necessary but not sufficient condition for human existence (Walther-Klaus, 1987). Education for technology ought to counter the oft perceived danger that technology can become an end in itself and that human adaptation to the demands of technology can lead to spiritual poverty. Some German educators fear the loss of responsibility, feeling, social relationships, and a holistic awareness of self as consequences of the technological transformation of everyday life (see Forneck, 1986; Nicklis, 1985; Von Hentig, 1984).

TECHNICAL CREATIVITY AS A MATTER
OF RESEARCH

When one bears in mind that technology and technical education are particularly important today, it is extraordinary to think that technology exists as a school subject only in vocational schools. There has been no comprehensive psychological research on socialization in relation to technology. The concept of "technological creativity" is not usually found in journals of educational psychology.

There is certainly a connection between this deficit and the lack of adequate creativity research outside the psychometric paradigm. The wide variety of theories on special aspects of creativity (see Glover, Ronning, & Reynolds, 1989; Runco & Albert, 1990; Sternberg, 1988), sharp criticism of older approaches (e.g., Weisberg, 1986), doubts about the effectiveness of creativity training (Hany, 1992; Mansfield, Busse, & Krepelka, 1978), and the paradigm shift in educational psychology research from problem solving to expertise (Glaser & Bassok, 1989; Resnick, 1989) have all contributed to the fact that creativity currently seems to be of only minor research interest for educational psychology. Concepts such as learning transfer, problem solving, and knowledge application are currently used to denote topics which were, until recently, dealt with under the heading of creativity. The concept of creativity seems to be particularly avoided in studies on problem-solving processes in technological areas (e.g., Kieras & Bovair, 1984; Morris & Rouse, 1985; Neber, 1987; Rasmussen, 1986), even in investigations on the productive performance of designers (Arndt, 1990; Dylla, 1990). Some researchers even seem to assume that creative processes are not possible in technical areas because technological problem solving is widely restricted by the laws of physics and the attributes of the materials used.

Effective education for technical creativity requires the identification of personal factors which are required for creative technical performance and the understanding of the development of these factors during childhood and youth. However, research in these areas has had mixed results. Several personal factors have been postulated as necessary for technical creativity: creative abilities which are largely independent of intelligence (such as ideational fluency and flexibility), a certain cognitive style or special abilities (such as imagination, analogous thinking), information-processing strategies and metacognitive skills, and performance-related personality traits (such as endurance and topic-specific interests). Recently, the way in which information is organized in memory and subsequently used in problem solving has been postulated as the basis of individual creativity (see reviews by Barron & Harrington, 1981; Brown, 1989; Hennessey & Amabile, 1988; Perkins, 1990; Taylor, 1988).

The existence of specific creative abilities has been questioned in recent years, in spite of good prognostic results achieved with tests designed to measure them (Torrance, 1988). Their interaction with general intelligence has not been completely clarified (Haensly & Reynolds, 1989; Tannenbaum, 1983; Wallach, 1985), and the required theoretical basis in cognitive psychology is still lacking. Group comparisons (Runco, 1986; Runco & Okuda, 1988) and correlation studies (Michael & Wright, 1989) will probably be important for the progress of creativity research in the near future.

Ambitious theories have been presented on the development of creative abilities, domain-specific expertise, and outstanding achievement (e.g., Csikszentmihalyi & Robinson, 1986; Feldman, 1986). In most cases where empirical methods have been applied, the studies concentrate on individuals already publicly recognized as outstanding, investigated either retrospectively or projectively. Sternberg and Davidson (1985) reported a substantial deficit in empirical investigations on the development of highly gifted children:

> Empirical studies of the development of the gifted and talented have been illuminating with respect to childhood correlates of adult giftedness, but they have revealed little about development. Even studies that have included multiple age groups—whether longitudinal or cross-sectional—have been focused upon states of performance rather than its development. It is difficult to find studies that could be seriously viewed as strongly testing a theory of cognitive development in the gifted. (Sternberg & Davidson, 1985, p. 64)

There is a real need for longitudinal studies of the development of creative abilities and characteristics which are related to creative problem solving in the technological domain. These studies have to be based first on a model of the relationships between relevant personal and environmental factors on the one hand and the development of creativity on the other hand. Second, they have to specify a model of the relevant mechanisms for the development of creative thinking. In light of this goal, the reported study concentrated on psychometrically defined personal characteristics which were considered to be the cumulative products of learning and developmental processes. These processes are difficult to assess; the products in terms of abilities, however, can be measured more easily because of their intermediate stability. Furthermore, these abilities may be of more relevance and of higher validity for achievement in later life than are short-term cognitive processes.

THEORETICAL BACKGROUND

Our own study begins from the assumption that creative performance is possible in technical areas and that it requires the following intraindividual features: cognitive abilities, creative thought strategies, technical knowledge, and interest in technical issues. These factors develop during childhood and youth and interact with one another. If children are faced with technical objects in their environment and try to analyze their function in order to use them effectively, they need to be able to think in technological terms and to maintain their interests. This process of learning, in turn, promotes the acquisition of technical knowledge and domain-specific problem solving strategies. In addition to intraindividual factors, the following features are also important for the development of technical ability: (a) the technological features of the personal environment, (b) the opportunity to try out and experiment with technological items, and (c) introduction and instruction from parents, teachers, and media.

The study presented here concentrates on individual differences in the development of technical competence; environmental factors are covered by another study which is still in progress (Heller & Hany, 1991). Cognitive abilities are of particular interest because they are connected to differences in learning speed (Kyllonen & Woltz, 1989) and can lead to the growth of different interests (Klix, 1983). In addition, it may be supposed that highly intelligent pupils tend to develop general problem-solving strategies or find it easier to transfer domain-specific strategies to new knowledge areas (Lohman & Kyllonen, 1983). The study described here investigates whether highly and averagely intelligent children show different patterns of relationships between abilities, strategies, and performance.

Any investigation of ability and interest in physics and technology must also take into account gender differences revealed in numerous studies with respect to spatial and quantitative skills (Feingold, 1988; Halpern, 1986; Hyde & Linn, 1986; Linn & Petersen, 1985; Maccoby & Jacklin, 1974) and with respect to technical interests (Burns & Homel, 1989; Faulstich-Wieland, 1987; Heller, 1992b). It could be supposed that the differences often observed between girls and boys in the area of technical interests (Lubinski & Humphreys, 1990) and spatial and quantitative ability would be less pronounced among the highly intelligent, since differences in experience could perhaps be compensated by means of inductive knowledge generation, or the substitution of nonverbal with verbal problem-solving strategies (Goldstein, Haldane, & Mitchell, 1990; Halpern, 1986). A number of relevant studies, however, report that gender differences exist as well among the gifted (Eccles, 1985; Terman & Oden, 1947), some studies indicating that gender differences are even stronger in extremely gifted subjects due to gender-specific variances of the ability distributions (Benbow & Stanley, 1984).

The levels of those skills, interests, and knowledge areas that are important for performance in physics and technology can be expected to be highly age dependent, resulting in age-dependent interaction patterns between the components of technical creativity. The importance of general thinking skills ought to decrease with age, accompanied by an increase in the relevance of domain-specific factors (knowledge, motivation, strategies). As far as developmental psychology is concerned, it must be borne in mind that the teaching of knowledge relevant for the solution of technical problems as part of the school curriculum could tend to equalize prior differences in interests and knowledge, for instance between girls and boys. Phenomena of this kind, which affect the developing individual during a particular age range, can best be captured with a combined longitudinal/cross-sectional design, in which cohorts with and without physics training are studied. This study focuses on physics training because specific technical instruction is provided only in a few schools. Physics lessons are the only formal means by which society teaches technology to young people. Certainly, technology can be regarded as applied physics. Therefore, compared to all other school subjects, physics instruction is most relevant for understanding technology.

In the present study, young people's technical creativity is compared according to gender, age, and intelligence level. The study is being carried out as a cross-cultural investigation of German and Chinese subjects (Hany & Heller, 1990), allowing the inclusion of cultural context as an additional factor in the comparisons. The cultural aspect is not presented here, as the results are still being discussed with our Chinese research colleagues. This presentation will therefore deal only with the German sample.

CENTRAL QUESTIONS OF THE STUDY

The main aim of the study was to test a model of how creative performance in technical areas comes about. The general model, which is restricted to intraindividual factors (see Figure 5.1), can be described by means of the following hypotheses.

1. Creative technical performance depends on technical problem-solving ability and flexibility of knowledge application.
2. Problem-solving ability in physics and technology arises when comprehensive experience in technical areas is processed using inductive and deductive thinking strategies.

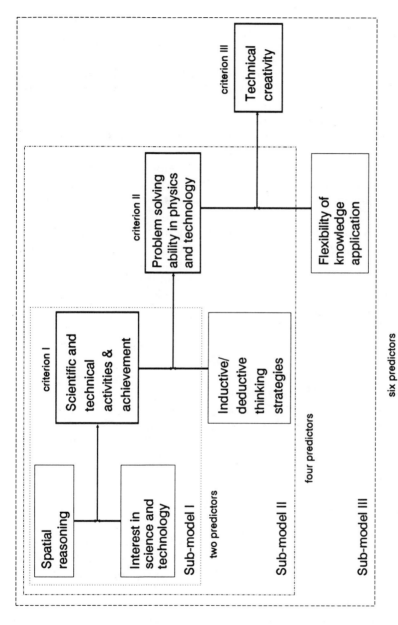

Figure 5.1. Hypothetical model of the causal factors of technical creativity to be tested empirically in the present investigation; the entire model is divided into three submodels to facilitate statistical evaluations

121

3.   Individuals become most involved with technical topics if they possess the relevant abilities and interests.

These hypotheses were suggested by results in expert-novice research (Chi, Feltovich, & Glaser, 1981; Chi, Glaser, & Farr, 1989; Larkin, 1985), in research on the development and application of technical knowledge (Gitomer, 1988; Neber, 1992), and in educational psychology (e.g., Bransford, Franks, Vye, & Sherwood, 1989). An additional topic of investigation was the extent to which interest in technical and scientific questions, involvement with technical problems, and problem-solving ability in physics and technology are less pronounced among girls than boys.

We expected that age, gender, and intelligence would affect the causal relationships in the model. Identifying different patterns of relationships between the factors would assist in the development of differential educational programs. There has been wide discussion in recent years of whether coeducation in science disadvantages girls (Heller, 1992a), and whether pupils should be taught in homogeneous ability groups. The identification of a variety of technical creativity development profiles could inform the development of differential teaching programs that take gender and, perhaps, intelligence into account.

METHODS

In the years 1988, 1989, and 1990, 195 children ages 11 through 13 were tested using paper-and-pencil group tests. The sample included equal proportions of highly and averagely intelligent children of both sexes and of two age cohorts. Subjects were taken from 11 higher level German schools and were tested yearly in their classrooms.

Experimental Design

A combined longitudinal and cross-sectional design was adopted for the investigation. Two age groups were measured over three years at intervals of one year. Since the gap between the age groups was on average two years, the younger testees were, at the time of the last measurement, as old as the older testees at the first measurement point. The two age groups were the fifth and seventh grades of the Bavarian school system, 11 and 13 years old, respectively. The longitudinal design enabled the influence of physics lessons, which begin in the eighth grade, to be measured. At the same time, it was possible to observe developmental factors (such as changes in interests) connected with the onset of puberty.

In addition to the two age groups, gender and intelligence variables were used to make two further binary distinctions. Averagely intelligent and highly intelligent testees formed experimental subgroups (see Sample section). The aim was to vary each of the three factors—intelligence, gender, and age cohort—independently, resulting in a factorial design with eight cells containing equal numbers of testees.

Instrumentation

Psychological constructs were assessed on the basis of paper-and-pencil group tests. For the measurement of creative technical performance, the testees received two written tasks, only one of which will be described and analyzed here. (The second task could only be completed by a part of the sample.)

The testees were given approximately 20 minutes to design a cart for the convenient transport of articles required for a day at the beach (towels, bathing suits, refreshments, games, etc.). The cart had to fit into the trunk of a car. The testees were advised to make labeled sketches. The subjects saw this as an attractive task which they felt they could solve. The sketches and commentaries were scored according to two groups of criteria. First, productivity was assessed (e.g., the number of finished sketches, the number of words written, etc.). The resulting indices were subjected to a factor analysis from which three readily interpretable factors were obtained: (a) quantity of production, (b) technical elaboration, and (c) feasibility. The second group of indices evaluated technical problem-solving quality. Rating scales were used to assess if the cart could be stowed in the car, the transport volume of the cart, its steering facility, and so on. The eight criteria were reduced by factor analysis to three cart design quality features: (a) ease of handling, (b) suitability as a means of transport, and (c) locomotion. The two sets of scores were then summed to give an overall production score and an overall quality score, which were processed in the statistical analyses.

For the measurement of problem-solving ability in physics and technology, 15 problems from the *Mannheim Test of Problem Solving in Physics and Technology* (MTP; Conrad, Baumann, & Mohr, 1980) were selected. The multiple-choice items (five possible answers, one correct) are similar to well-known tests for mechanical reasoning (e.g., *Bennett Tests of Mechanical Comprehension*). However, the *MTP* is carefully designed to measure problem-solving ability rather than knowledge.

Flexibility of knowledge application was measured with a "Uses test" in the style of Guilford (1967). Two tasks were set which involved thinking of as many uses as possible for everyday objects. The number of different categories into which the answers could fall was used to derive a measure of flexibility in use of knowledge, with the help of an evaluation technique developed by Facaoaru (1985). Producing many uses in this task was interpreted as the result of applying strategies for constructing rich semantic networks in memory. These strategies have been proposed as the basis of domain-specific creativity (Findlay & Lumsden, 1988; Krems, 1990). Knowledge representation in a dense semantic network facilitates flexible access to knowledge, thus promoting productivity (cf. Pettigrew, 1982).

The extent of prior involvement with scientific and technical objects and topics was assessed using a biographical inventory, from which the two scales "technical and craft activities" (seven items) and "mathematical and scientific activities" (15 items) were taken. The items covered extent of activity, performance, and frequency of involvement on a four-level scale. The scales were originally developed on the basis of American questionnaires (IBRIC, 1978; Payne & Halpin, 1974; Schaefer, 1970) and then tested and revised in several studies.

Inductive and deductive thinking strategies were measured using two nonverbal tasks, each of which presented 30 geometrical figures. The task was to choose as many groups of four figures as possible which were related to one another in the form of a geometrical analogy (A:B::C:D). Each figure could be used in more than one group. The solution of this problem involved the inductive extraction of the features of the individual figures, and then deductive reasoning from solution principles. The significance of the use of suitable strategies for working on the problem has been shown in a separate analysis of this "analogy test" (Hany, 1991). The final score was obtained by adding the total number of correct solutions in each of the two tasks.

Spatial reasoning was measured using a subtest of the WILDE intelligence test (Jäger & Althoff, 1983). This "unfolding" test consisted of 23 items, in which a flattened-out view (a "net") of a three-dimensional object is shown, together with sketches of five objects, only one of which could be made by folding the flattened-out shape. A time limit was set, as with all the other tests, in order to standardize test application as much as possible for the cross-cultural study. This may have resulted in the dominance of the speed component versus the power component of the test.

Scientific and technical interest was measured using the "Thirst for Knowledge" questionnaire, a shortened version of the 41-item test developed by Lehwald (1985). Each item consisted of a single self-assessment, to be evaluated on a four-level Likert scale. The instrument was subjected to thorough prior testing by our research group (in previous studies) and shortened with the help of factor and reliability analyses.

For the measurement of intelligence and also for the selection of the testees, the short form of the "Kognitive Fähigkeitstest 4-13" (KFT; Heller, Gaedike, & Weinläder, 1985) was used, a licensed German adaptation of Thorndike and Hagen's *Cognitive Abilities Test* (1974). The short form of the *KFT* consists of two scales for each of three dimensions—verbal, quantitative, and nonverbal—all of which test reasoning ability. Each scale consists of 20-25 items. The test is comprehensively standardized; there are norms for each type of material for each age and each German school type.

Three parallel forms were developed for each of the scales of problem-solving ability in physics and technology, inductive and deductive thinking strategies, and spatial reasoning. They were distributed randomly to the whole sample; each group took different test forms at each subsequent measurement point.

Sample

The sample consisted of 195 pupils at 11 Bavarian academic high schools ("Gymnasien"). It was expected that this school type would provide many highly intelligent pupils and also a sufficient number of averagely intelligent pupils.

Intelligence level was determined according to the age specific percentile rank scores of the German Cognitive Abilities Test *KFT* (Heller et al., 1985). Those pupils were defined as highly intelligent who achieved a percentile rank (PR) of 95 or over in at least two of the three areas of testing (verbal, mathematical, and nonverbal reasoning) and who achieved a percentile rank of at least 84 in the other dimension. Average intelligence was attributed to those who achieved scores within one standard deviation above or below the mean in all three areas of testing. The pupils assessed as highly intelligent achieved IQ scores mainly between 135 and 140. The averagely intelligent pupils scored, as expected, a global mean of about 100 IQ and a standard deviation of about 10.

Because of limited funding, it was not possible to reach the desired sample size. Of the 715 pupils tested at the beginning of the study, only 195 were suitable for the longitudinal investigation, that is, fit either averagely intelligent or highly intelligent categories. During the course of the subsequent survey a large part of the sample was lost. From the 195 subjects included in the first data collection, only 136 continued to the third assessment. Subject attrition is further discussed in the last section of this chapter.

Procedure

The survey was carried out on normal school days. At the first measurement point, the *KFT* was given during the first two 45-minute school periods, followed by a break. During the following two school periods, the tests described in the Instrumentation section were carried out. At the second and third data collection, the intelligence test was omitted. A time limit was set for most of the tasks. An explanation was provided at the beginning of each test, including examples.

It was explained to the testees that participation was voluntary. They were not explicitly told who belonged to which intelligence group, nor that one of the aims of the survey was the comparison of these groups. They were, however, given written feedback on their results at the end of the tests, which gave their approximate position in the relevant age group. Shortly before the second measurement point, all the pupils and interested teachers received an information packet with sample problems and materials from the first data collection and from our institute, in order to inform them about the aims of the survey and to motivate them to continue to participate.

RESULTS

The results of the statistical evaluations are presented below. All evaluations focus on the variables and their relationships as depicted in Figure 5.1. The mean values of the variables are compared on the basis of the subgroups organized by gender, level of intelligence, and age cohort (this last evaluation representing a cross-sectional analysis). In addition, variable means are compared over time. Special consideration is given to the relationships between the variables. In order to get a clear picture of the relationships, the complex model of Figure 5.1 is considered as consisting of three submodels, the first using scientific and technical activities as criterion, and spatial reasoning and interest in science and technology as the two predictors. The second submodel includes these three variables and inductive/deductive thinking strategies as predictors for problem-solving ability in physics and technology. The third submodel, takes all the previously named variables together with flexibility of knowledge application as predictors for technical creativity. Only those 136 testees who had taken part at all three measurement points were included in the evaluation. The significance level was set at alpha = .05.

Test of the Causal Submodels Including the Whole Sample

The explanatory model of technical problem-solving performance was tested with three regression analyses (Table 5.1). The extent of scientific and technical interest proved to be an exceptionally good predictor of scientific/technical activities (submodel I; β = .71; $p < .001$), whereas spatial reasoning showed no predictive power (β = .07; ns). The postulated relationship between scientific/technical activities and inductive/deductive thinking on the one hand and problem-solving ability in physics and technology on the other (submodel II) was not confirmed; however, spatial thinking proved to be a good predictor (β = .45; $p < .001$). The two technical creativity variables (submodel III) were generally poorly explained by the predictors used; none of the regression coefficients were significant. Most importantly, it was necessary to reject the hypothesis that technical creativity (as measured with the above pencil-and-paper problem) depends on problem-solving ability in physics and technology and on flexibility of knowledge application: The regression coefficients for these predictors were close to zero or negative.

From the point of view of expertise research, this is not an unexpected result. The argument would be that for the task given (the construction of a beach cart), domain-specific experience would be of particular importance, while general abilities or unspecific knowledge would hardly function as predictors (Chi, Glaser, & Rees, 1982; Rabinowitz & Glaser, 1985). On the other hand, it could be argued that general abilities do indeed suffice, but the fact that only a single task was used masked the correlations through inaccuracies of measurement. Before such interpretations can be accepted, it is necessary to examine causal models on a subgroup level. This procedure could rule out the thesis that the causal model cannot be confirmed for the whole sample because striking differences between the subsamples (e.g., of higher and average intelligence),

Table 5.1. Statistical Evaluation of the Hypothesized Model Explaining Technical Creativity: Results of the Multiple Regression Analyses for the Total Sample (Standardized Regression Weights are Depicted)

	Submodel I	Submodel II	Submodel III	
	scientific/ technical activities/ achievement	problem solving competence in ph & t	technical creativity: productivity	technical creativity: quality of solutions
Sample size	134	134	119	119
spatial thinking	.07.	.45*	.14	−.01
interest in science & technics	.71*	.12	.05	0.00
scientific/technical activities		.07	.23	.04
strategies of thinking		.14	.18	.16
competence in solving problems in ph & t			−.19	.08
flexibility of knowledge			.01	.06
Explained variance				
R^2	.52*	.34*	.13*	.05

Note: ph & t = physics & technology
   $p < .05$

might lead to an unexplainable picture at the level of the whole sample.

Comparison of Subgroup Means of All Variables of the Causal Model

If patterned subgroup differences underlie the nonsignificant total sample results, then the subgroups defined by age, gender, and intelligence would differ not only in the relationships between the variables but also in their mean values. In order to test this, three-factor variance analyses were calculated, revealing not only the main effects but also higher order interactions (Table 5.2). The individual variables all had in common nonsignificant three-way interactions between intelligence, age, and gender. Only in the case of problem-solving ability in physics and technology was there a significant interaction between intelligence level and gender ($F = 7.6; p < .01$). As for the main effects, the gender groups differed significantly in six of the eight variables considered, the intelligence groups in five, and the age groups in three. Figure 5.2 shows the mean values of the variables for the eight subgroups; the variables were previously

Table 5.2. Results of the Multifactor Analyses of Variance (F values): Influences of the Factors Age Cohort, Sex, and Level of Intelligence (a) on the Variables Predicting Competence for Problem Solving, and (b) on the Additional Variables

(a)	spatial thinking	interest in science & technology	scientific/ technical activities/ achievement	strategies of thinking
sample size	134	135	136	136
main effects				
intelligence (I)	26.9*	4.0*	2.2	28.7*
sex (S)	4.8*	11.7*	17.8*	.9
age cohort (A)	1.7	5.1*	.5	17.6*
interactions				
I × S	.8	0.0	0.0	.5
I × A	0.0	.7	0.0	1.8
S × A	.7	.9	0.0	.2
I × S × A	.3	3.7	.1	1.0

(b)	problem solving competence in ph & t	flexibility of knowledge	technical creativity: productivity	technical creativity: quality of solutions
sample size	136	135	135	135
main effects				
intelligence (I)	30.9*	0.0	0.0	4.6*
sex (S)	55.6*	4.1*	7.2*	0.0
age cohort (A)	14.9*	.6	1.8	0.0
interactions				
I × S	7.6*	.3	.1	.3
I × A	3.5	.7	1.6	0.0
S × A	0.0	.1	.9	0.0
I × S × A	1.7	2.4	.3	.3

Note: ph & t = physics & technology
   $*p < .05$

standardized over the entire sample, so that the feature profiles of the eight subgroups can be clearly seen. For example, the gifted boys of the older group were outstanding in problem-solving ability, strategic thinking, and spatial reasoning. The gifted older girls on the other hand were characterized by very good strategic thinking and by productivity on technical problems, but also by a level of interest in scientific and technical questions that was strikingly low for gifted pupils in general. The younger gifted girls showed a clear deficit in technical problem-solving ability, which was almost as pronounced as with the averagely intelligent girls of the same age.

The younger gifted boys scored highly in spatial reasoning, were very interested in scientific questions, (as were their less gifted classmates), and showed good problem-solving ability. These results offer some support for the present hypothesis that the relationships between the variables differ according to subgroup.

Submodel I. For this reason, the regression analyses shown in Table 5.1 were calculated separately for boys and girls, and were also split into highly and averagely intelligent testees. The explanation of the extent of science and technology activities is about as successful in all four subgroups as in the whole sample (Table 5.1): Interest in science and technology proves to be a powerful predictor, whereas spatial reasoning only plays a role in the averagely intelligent boys ($\beta = .30; p < .05$).

Submodel II. Explanation of problem-solving ability in physics and technology by the given predictors was successful in all sub-groups with the exception of the averagely intelligent girls. In the same three groups, spatial reasoning was a good predictor. The predictors particularly assumed to be relevant (i.e., scientific and technical activities and thinking strategies) seemed to have a certain relevance only for the highly intelligent girls.

Submodel III. Of the two indicators of technical creativity, only the productivity score, and this only for the boys, can be explained on the basis of the predictors. Less gifted boys were especially productive if they had substantial experience with technical questions and equipment ($\beta = .68; p < .01$), and if they showed less flexibility of knowledge application ($\beta = -.42; p < .05$). Among the more gifted boys, concrete experience was less important for the explanation of productivity; they seemed to rely more on general thought strategies ($\beta = .27; p < .10$) and flexibility of knowledge application ($\beta = .30; p < .10$).

The performance of the girls on the technical creativity task cannot be adequately explained by means of the predictors used. There are some weak indications that averagely gifted girls managed the problem especially well if they could rely on good general thinking ability (e.g., on spatial reasoning: $\beta = .38; p < .10$). Highly intelligent girls, on the other hand, seemed to be especially productive if they had sufficient experience with technical devices and mathematical problems ($\beta = .57; p < .05$). Their solutions were of high quality if they showed high problem-solving ability in physics and technology ($\beta = .45; p < .10$).

Integrating the Results of the Comparisons of Means and the Tests of the Causal Models

The subgroups defined with the variables gender and intelligence clearly differed in the extent of their experience with scientific and technical problems and objects, as can be seen in Figure 5.2. Interestingly, the more topic-specific experience the subgroups showed, the less successful was the explanation of the problem-solving quali-

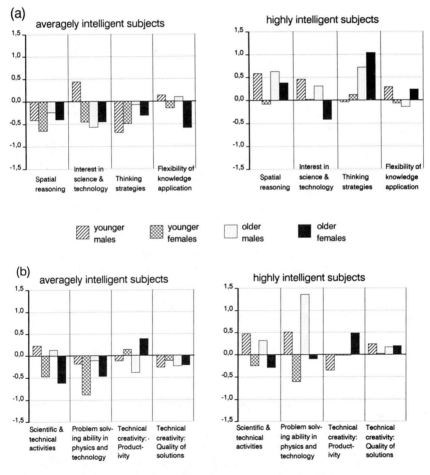

Figure 5.2. Mean values for the subgroups of the factorial combinations of age cohort, gender, and intelligence level (a) of the predictor variables, and (b) of the criterion and moderating variables of the model (means are computed on the basis of the third data collection)

ty. The squared multiple correlation coefficients for the problem-solving quality were lowest for the groups with the most extensive technical experience. The significance of this observation can be enhanced by reference to the research on expertise. Averagely gifted girls—the group with the least practical experience—had success in problem solving if they could rely on general thinking strategies. The highly intelligent girls, who had more practical experience, achieved their results by deploying physics problem-solving ability. The groups with even more experience—the boys—no longer needed to resort to general abilities. They could use domain-specific knowledge or special skills, which were not captured by the predictors adopted here. Insights from recent work in the psychology of problem solving corroborate the difficulty of explaining topic-specific performance by means of general predictors.

Conclusions of the Cross-Sectional Tests of the Causal Model

The results presented in the above section make it clear that the postulated causal model cannot be accepted in its most general form. Instead it seems possible to identify the following two mutually independent developmental tracks. The first involves activities and experiences with technical objects which, on the one hand, are dependent on technical interest, and on the other hand, contribute to productivity in dealing with technical problems. The other aspect concerns problem-solving ability for technical questions, which is dependent on more general (e.g., spatial) abilities, and which, in certain circumstances, can increase the quality of problem solving in general. The first developmental track would then lead to expert knowledge in the sense of rules of thumb and general routines, whereas the second would lead to strategic approaches and logical thinking on technical problems.

In the following section, the development of the investigated components of technical problem solving during youth will be presented.

Developmental Changes of Means Considered for the Entire Sample

Figures 5.3 and 5.4 show the changes in the mean values of the six creativity components, measured at three points in time. Clear linear changes over time can be seen when calculations are based on the entire sample. The components, standardized with respect to the means and standard deviations of the variables of the last measuring point, showed a variety of gradients; only the changes in the

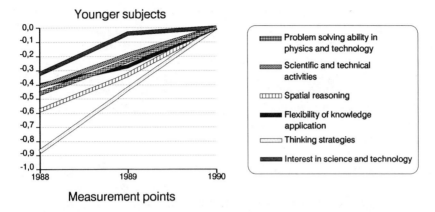

Figure 5.3. Changes in the predictor components of technical creativity for the younger age cohort (fifth grade). All scores are standardized in relation to the mean and standard deviation of the variables at the third measurement.

mean for flexibility of knowledge application (measured from the productivity score on the Unusual Uses Test) were not significant for the whole sample when tested with a multivariate variance analysis (for all other tests, Wilks' Lambda $< .90$; $p < .001$). It seems, therefore, that thinking skills and level of activities still undergo substantial changes in the years considered.

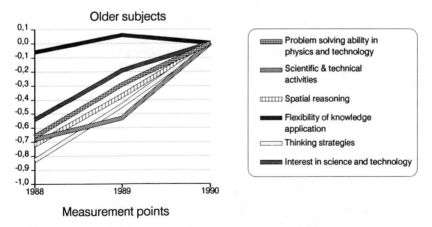

Figure 5.4. Changes in the predictor components of technical creativity for the older age cohort (seventh grade). All scores are standardized in relation to the mean and standard deviation of the variables at the third measurement point.

In Figures 5.3 and 5.4 the changes are shown separately for the *two cohorts*. The scores at the third measuring point were subtracted from those for the first and second, and these differences were then divided by the standard deviation of the measurements at the third measuring point, thus giving standardized variables, as is usual in meta-analyses of gains. Whereas the ability features (spatial thinking, thought strategies, problem-solving ability) climbed evenly in both cohorts, the other variables showed differing change profiles. Particularly striking is the growth in the level of scientific and technical activity in the older cohort between the eighth and ninth grades. The corresponding level of interest increased noticeably a year earlier (between grades 7 and 8) whereas, in contrast to the younger cohort, there was no growth on the knowledge flexibility scores.

Developmental Changes in the Causal Models: Submodel I for the Entire Sample

Considering the relationships between scientific and technical activity and its predictors, broken down by cohort and measurement point, we find that in both cohorts the relationship between scientific/technical activity and interest increased with age. This could indicate that the older testees were better able to pursue their interests than the younger testees and that they were more able to shape their free time in accordance with their own interests.

Spatial thinking only played a role in the explanation of activity in the older cohort, and here only in the eighth grade ($\beta = .26$; $p < .05$), that is, at the point at which physics lessons began. It is possible that physics study tended to have a more stimulating effect on the free-time activity of those with a suitable learning profile, for example, those with better spatial thinking skills.

Submodel II for the Entire Sample

The extent of scientific and technical activity had only a slight influence on the development of problem-solving ability in science and technology. Only at the first measuring point and only for the older cohort was the β weight significant ($\beta = .32$; $p < .05$). Ignoring this measuring point, since the explanation of the criterion was weakest here, spatial thinking proved to be consistently the best predictor of problem-solving ability (β's between .36 and .48; all with $p < .01$). In contrast to the postulated causal model (see Figure 5.1), inductive/deductive thinking strategies did not play a significant role in the development of technical problem solving ability in any of the age groups considered.

In summary, for the age group investigated (11 to 15 years) there did not seem to be any outstanding changes in the relationships between the variables considered. The mean values increased in the expected way, indicating the influence of maturation, teaching, and learning. The pattern of interconnections between the components of technical creativity seemed, however, to be invariant with respect to age group. Before this interpretation is finally accepted, however, gender and intelligence should be considered once more. These factors could act as differential filters on the effects of both the introduction of physics lessons in the eighth grade and also on age-related changes in interest.

Developmental Changes of the Means, Considering Subgroups by Intelligence, Age, and Gender

Table 5.3 contains the results of the multifactorial multivariate variance analysis conducted for the six components of technical creativity. In the upper half of the table, the mean values at the three points in time were tested for differences on the three factors. The results were very similar to those in Table 5.2, in which only the scores from the third measuring point were included. In the lower half of the table, the influence of the factors on the change of the scores over time was examined. In the line labeled changes, the changes in the mean values (already shown in Figures 5.3 and 5.4), were tested. Of particular importance for our investigation were the relationships between changes in the scores and the factors of gender and intelligence. In the case of problem-solving ability in physics and technology, there was a significant three-way interaction ($F = 5.4$; $p < .01$). As can be seen in Figure 5.5, this is mainly due to differences between the changes for the averagely intelligent and highly intelligent subgroups. Especially with the older pupils, the highly intelligent boys showed a more marked increase at the second and third measurement points than did their averagely intelligent colleagues. It is possible that they are better able to exploit school physics lessons to increase their ability. In contrast, the highly intelligent girls were not able to strengthen the clear advantage in ability over their averagely intelligent colleagues that they had at the first measuring point. In fact, they even dropped back slightly at the second measuring point and improved only slightly after that. The less intelligent older girls, who actually scored lower

Table 5.3. Influences of the Factors Age Cohort, Sex, and Level of Intelligence on Average Means and Changes of Means of the Components of Technical Creativity: Results of the Multifactor Multivariate Analyses of Variance Including Three Repeated Measures of Each Dependent Variable (F values are depicted)

	spatial thinking	interest in science/ technics	activities in s & t	strategies of thinking	competence in solving problems in ph & t	flexibility knowledge
Sample size	131	134	135	134	133	134
constant	1231.2*	7160.9*	996.0*	570.0*	895.1*	1529.7*
main effects						
intelligence (I)	32.5*	3.6	2.0	52.8*	31.0*	2.5
sex (S)	5.6*	8.4*	14.5*	1.5	60.9*	4.1*
age cohort (A)	2.2	12.5*	4.2*	21.9*	12.2*	.8
interactions						
I × S	1.6	3.4	.1	.5	4.7*	1.0
I × A	0.0	.7	.4	.5	2.5	.7
S × A	.1	1.2	.2	.1	0.0	.3
I × S × A	.5	5.3*	0.0	1.6	.1	.9
changes	32.8*	19.9*	40.3*	75.8*	27.2*	3.2*
main effects for changes						
intelligence (I)	1.4	.8	.4	5.2*	2.5	2.6
sex (S)	.3	1.1	3.8*	0.0	3.3*	.9
age cohort (A)	0.0	.5	2.8	4.4*	1.8	1.9
interactions with changes						
I × S	.1	1.9	1.0	.8	4.2*	.3
I × A	.8	.8	1.3	5.1*	.6	2.9
S × A	.3	.3	.7	.6	.2	.5
I × S × A	0.0	.2	0.0	.6	5.4*	1.3

Note: ph & t = physics & technology
s & t = science and technology
*p < .05

at the first measurement point than those two years younger, showed a substantial improvement over the following years. This exemplifies the "drama of the gifted girl": At 13, in the seventh grade, she has substantial potential in physics and technology problem solving, differing only slightly from the boys of both intelligence groups, yet in the two years following—in which puberty and physics lessons can be expected to begin more or less simultaneously— she showed little further development, in contrast to the considerable improvement shown by the highly intelligent boys.

With regard to the development of inductive/deductive thinking strategies, the interaction between cohort and intelligence ($F = 5.1$; $p < .01$) proved to be significant; lower order effects were not calculated. As is shown in Figure 5.6, the older highly gifted testees diverged sharply in their (higher) developmental rate from the other comparison groups. With scientific and technical activities we found gender-specific developmental curves ($F = 3.8$; $p < .05$). The boys improved between the second and third measuring points,

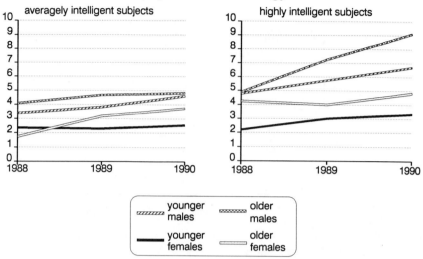

Figure 5.5. Changes in the mean values of problem-solving ability in physics and technology for (a) averagely intelligent, and (b) highly intelligent students broken down according to age cohort and gender.

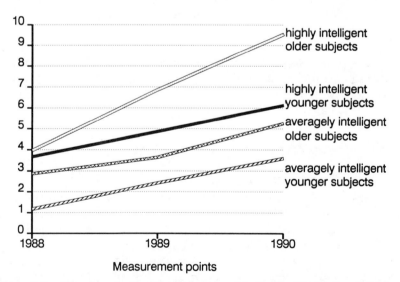

Figure 5.6. Changes in the mean values of inductive/deductive thinking strategies, broken down according to age cohort and intelligence level.

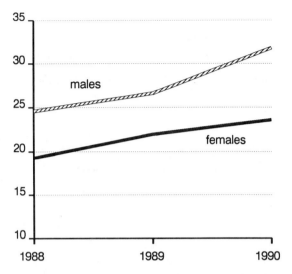

Figure 5.7. Changes in the mean values of scientific & technical activities for the male/female subgroups.

whereas the girls dropped back (Figure 5.7). Perhaps school was a reason for these patterns: In the seventh grade of Gymnasium, a second foreign language is introduced, and in the ninth grade, in some school types, a third is introduced. Since girls tend to follow linguistic interests much more than scientific interests, these results might reflect differing enthusiasm for different school subjects (sciences versus languages). With the variables spatial reasoning, scientific and technical interest, and flexibility of knowledge application, no connections were found between the factors considered and the changes in the measured values over time.

Developmental Changes of the Causal Models

Submodel I in the Subgroups. In addition to changes in the variables, changes in the pattern of relationships between the variables over time may also be considered. Due to the small size of the sample, it did not seem advisable to define four subgroups using the factors gender and intelligence. Instead the comparisons were limited to one factor in each case. For boys and girls at the different age levels, the regression of scientific and technical activity and performance on the variables spatial thinking and scientific and technical interest did not show significant differences.

When, however, highly intelligent and averagely intelligent testees were compared, different patterns of change in the relationships resulted for the older cohort. Whereas for the highly intelligent testees, domain-specific interest was almost always the only essential predictor for performance-oriented activity, the predictor weightings were almost reversed with the averagely intelligent pupils. At older ages, scientific and technical activity depended more strongly on spatial thinking than on relevant interests.

Submodel II in the Subgroups. The model for the prediction of scientific and technical problem-solving ability is substantially affected by the factors gender and intelligence. The criterion was only successfully explained in the case of male testees; spatial reasoning was the most powerful predictor at all age levels. The influences on scientific and technical problem-solving ability for girls remained unclear.

When the sample was split according to intelligence, it became clear that for the younger, highly intelligent, testees of both genders—as was previously noted for the boys in general—there was a strong interdependence between problem-solving ability and spatial reasoning. Among the older, highly intelligent testees, motivational factors seemed to increase ability (e.g., interest, 8th grade: $\beta = .61$; $p < .05$). Among the averagely intelligent testees, the explanation of problem-solving ability was less successful with the predictors considered; concrete experience seemed to play a role (e.g., scientific and technical activity, 8th grade: $\beta = .66$; $p < .05$). Spatial thinking, on the other hand, did not once reach a significant β coefficient.

Comparisons of the Subgroup Means of the Residuals of the Criterion Variables

It was then tempting to assume that the age, gender, and intelligence differences in scientific and technical activities (i.e., primarily non-school work and achievement in science and technology) and problem-solving ability, were due to the relationships between the variables included in the regression model. However, the assumption that the three grouping factors did not exert any independent influence on the criteria considered except via motivation, activity, and various abilities and skills, was not supported by the facts. On the contrary, although the inclusion of the predictors as covariates in the multivariate analyses (as in Table 5.3) gave a number of significant regression effects, the original factorial effects generally remained even after these regressions were taken into account.

Developmental Changes of the Subgroup Means of the Residuals of the Criteria

Figure 5.8 shows the change over time of the residuals for the variable "scientific and technical problem-solving ability" after the extraction, using a regression analysis, of the linear influence of the predictors (interest, spatial reasoning, flexibility of knowledge application, thought strategies) and the three factors age cohort, gender, and intelligence. The graphs display interaction effects only; differences in mean values have been equalized. (Figure 5.8 is, in effect, a further development of Figure 5.5, except that the individual graphs are split here by age and not by intelligence.) The following results appear:

1. In the younger cohort, boys in the two intelligence categories no longer differed, whereas the highly gifted girls scored lower (negative scores) and the averagely gifted girls scored higher than would be expected after main effects and predictors had been taken into account.
2. In the older cohort, strong, uneven changes appeared between the first and second measuring points (though not between

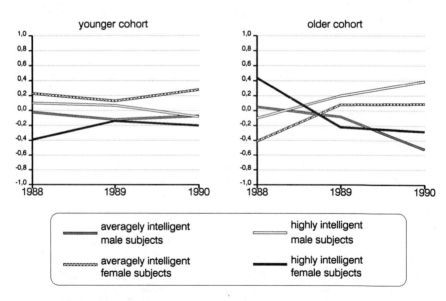

Figure 5.8. Changes in the residuals of problem-solving ability in physics and technology for the subgroups after deleting the main effects of age cohort, gender, and intelligence, and the regressions on the predictors (in order to analyze interaction effects).

the second and third) which were not predictable using the considered factors and predictors. It can be assumed that the introduction of physics lessons in the eighth grade was substantially responsible for these changes.

3. The effects specific to cohort and measurement point appearing between the seventh and eighth grades differed according to gender and intelligence. They lead to increased problem-solving ability among the highly intelligent boys and the averagely intelligent girls, but to lower ability than expected among the highly intelligent girls and averagely intelligent boys. The interaction between measuring point, age, gender, and intelligence level, calculated on the residuals of the problem-solving ability variables as shown in Figure 5.8, proved to be significant (multivariate analysis: Wilks' lambda = .93; $p < .02$; averaged test of significance: $F = 4.67$; $p = .01$).

DISCUSSION

Disconfirming the Causal Model

On the basis of the results from the statistical calculations, the postulated "causal" model for the explanation of creative technical performance could not be accepted. Technical creativity, as measured in this study with a paper-and-pencil test, cannot be adequately explained through an additive combination of general scientific and technical knowledge, more general thought strategies, or even technical interest and experience. It is possible that very different problem-solving strategies are used for different tasks, compensating for deficient skills by individually higher abilities. If this is true, such changes of strategy use could not be identified within the framework of a linear model.

Poor reliability of items or subjects' lack of familiarity with the "theoretical" solution of technical problems on paper could conceal any connections existing between the factors investigated and practical problem-solving ability. For this reason the discussion of appropriate measurement of creative performance must be reopened (Hocevar, 1981; Taylor & Barron, 1963; Wallach, 1985).

Post-Hoc Explanations of Disconfirming Results

However, the analysis of the relationships between predictors and criteria for each of the various subgroups gave a number of indications that these relationships are moderated by the extent of prior experience and technical expertise. The importance of individual components of technical creativity would, according to this supposition, vary substantially with increasing expertise acquisition and also in relation to the cognitive abilities of the sample. It might therefore be necessary to develop models of the relationships between the components of technical problem solving for the various levels of skill acquisition. This would mean changing the existing longitudinal experimental design with fixed intervals between the measuring points, so that measurements could be carried out at exactly the point at which the pupils had made a qualitative step to the next stage of expertise. Investigations of this kind are complicated by the fact that children and young people undergo changes in the level of knowledge acquisition parallel to making progress in general cognitive skills; and both kinds of change interact with one another (see the review in Sincoff & Sternberg, 1989).

A further argument for the inadequate empirical confirmation of the component model could be that brief exposure to a complex task, which the testees at the third measurement experienced, might depend on a large number of relatively time-invariant personality features and on situation-dependent (and variously active) motives, work strategies, knowledge contents, and problem-solving techniques. The low interrelations between problem-solving performance and the predictors investigated could then be interpreted as due to the failure to include a number of important variables. Of greater interest to developmental psychology for the analysis of technical creativity, however, are analyses of relationships and of progress of more stable personality features such as those defined as components of technical creativity.

Given the research on expertise, it was surprising to find that problem-solving ability in physics and technology was not dependent on the extent of the testees' relevant free-time activities or interests—either for the sample as a whole, within the subgroups, or in the individual age groups. It can be argued that problem-solving competence was measured using a paper-and-pencil test instead of a practical task, testing formal abilities rather than practical knowledge. However, the relationships to the scores on the tests for inductive and deductive thought strategies did not prove to be very strong either. Only the relationship with spatial reasoning proved to be significant in nearly all analyses and explained a considerable proportion of the variance of problem-solving ability in physics and technology. The measuring procedures for both constructs involved a large speed component, which could mean that the strong connections were effects of the test method used.

On the other hand, there are plausible reasons for the observed relationships by looking at the contents and forms of presentation of the items of the instruments. To take gender specific differences with quantitative ability tests as an example, it can be argued that to a large extent these are caused by differences in spatial reasoning (Halpern, 1986). With scientific and technical tasks, especially when they are presented graphically, as was the case here, and not in text or numerical form, spatial thinking could play a significant role. This may explain the high correlations as observed between spatial reasoning and problem solving in physics/technology. Concrete scientific and technical activities, in contrast, appeared to be only weakly dependent on spatial thinking. Since the scales used for measuring activities (and achievement) put more emphasis on time taken for technical activities than on the skill level reached, their dependence on scientific and technical interest rather than on spatial thinking (as was observed in most subgroup analyses) is easy to understand.

Conceptualizing a New Model

On the basis of the statistical results, enriched with a little creative interpretation, the following model of creative technical performance can be presented based on the predictors which were considered here (see Figure 5.9). According to the model, "divergent" and

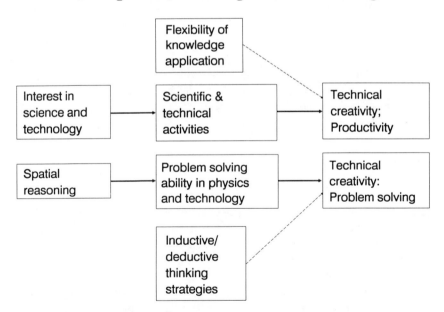

Figure 5.9 Hypothetical model of causal factors of technical creativity as suggested by the statistical results. A separate empirical investigation would be required to test this mode.

"convergent" aspects of technical problem-solving ability should be considered separately via separate treatment of quality and quantity of solutions. Quantity would depend more on motivational factors, practical experience, and flexibility of knowledge application acquired through a rich variety of activities. Quality of solutions, in contrast, would be more dependent on problem-solving ability, spatial thinking, and thinking strategies. Here it must be remembered that the variable of problem-solving ability is based, above all, on domain-specific knowledge. This model seems to be valid at least for the younger testees. For the older pupils, the two forms of problem solving seemed to interact more strongly. This could be because higher standards are set for activities in physics and technology at this age, and so these activities are more influenced by the ability level of the testees.

The Influence of Intelligence

Highly intelligent young people differed the most from averagely intelligent same-age peers on the predictors and components of the quality of technical problem solving (Table 5.2). They scored highly in spatial thinking, spatial reasoning, and in problem-solving ability in physics and technology and, therefore, also differed in the technical quality of their solutions from the comparison group. Highly intelligent children do not need extensive practical experience in order to cope with technical problems. They should be able to combine formalized instruction (as in school), with paradigmatic learning experiences, and then, in turn, to flexibly combine the resulting physics and technology knowledge with more general problem-solving strategies.

Gender Issues

The influence of gender on the scores and on the pattern of the relationships between the variables is at least as important as that of intelligence. There were clear differences in solution of the technical problems between averagely and highly intelligent girls. Whereas the less intelligent girls relied on general skills of thinking and combination, the more gifted girls used their practical experience with technical problems and their problem-solving competence. Thus the girls were able to score better than the boys in solution quantity, independent of their level of intelligence. Their failure to score better than the boys on solution quality seemed to be related to their clear deficit in spatial thinking and problem-solving ability in physics and technology.

The Role of School

Turning now in particular to the promotion of problem-solving ability in physics and technology, it seems that school lessons play a rather sad role here. The longitudinal/cross-sectional design used revealed a remarkable change between the seventh and eighth grades which cannot be explained purely as a result of familiarity with the test problems or of changes in activities, interests, and so on. The analysis of the measurement value residues from problem-solving ability in physics and technology (Figure 5.8) showed strong interaction effects between factors of intelligence and gender; highly intelligent girls in particular and to a lesser extent less intelligent boys show a clear drop in problem-solving ability during the 8th grade.

These results are particularly surprising, since at the beginning of the study it was assumed that girls with higher intelligence could perhaps compensate for gender-specific deficits in technical ability and interest—in other words, that gender differences would be less clear among highly intelligent young people. The results of this study show the opposite to be the case (see also Figure 5.5). The transition from the seventh to the eighth grade, accompanied by the beginning of physics lessons, seems to act among the highly intelligent boys as a strong stimulus for the growth of problem-solving ability in physics and technology, but among the highly intelligent girls, it seems to have an inhibitory effect. (Contrary to the hypotheses offered by Harvey & Goldstein, 1985, clear gender-specific differences were apparent even before the onset of physics lessons.) The exact reasons for this differential effect of physics lessons were not revealed. A study which was carried out on the same sample, with the encouragement of the present author (Kommissari, 1991) showed that girls performed lower than boys above all on abstractly formulated physics problems, but less so on problems which were taken from everyday life (see also Kaiser, Jonides, & Alexander, 1986). Following the results from the research into intuitive physics, it would seem that boys are able to integrate the knowledge taught in physics lessons with their subjective physics images and ideas, since the latter are already present in abstract form. Girls, on the other hand, are more likely to have stored their physics knowledge in concrete/verbal form, giving rise to problems with the abstract form of presentation in physics lessons. Less gifted girls may deal with the information presented in physics lessons in a way quite independent of their everyday thinking. Thus, due to lack of transfer, no conflicts arise (diSessa, 1982). More gifted girls, in contrast, are perhaps adversely affected by processing problems which arise out of the conflict between concrete everyday knowledge and abstract school lessons. This would explain why less intelligent girls profit from physics lessons more than highly intelligent girls. These suppositions are of course highly speculative; to test them would require a new investigation using special methods.

Developmental and Instructional Issues

On the whole, the investigated components of technical creativity develop in late childhood and early adolescence without any marked changes. Gender-, intelligence-, and age-related differences remain largely stable over the years. Only school physics lessons seem to have any significant influence on ability in physics and technology. Even though the present investigation highlighted unfavorable effects for highly gifted girls, it should not be forgotten that these effects are statistically so striking only because of the contrast to the positive effects achieved with the highly intelligent boys. So physics lessons do have positive effects; at present, however, it is mostly the boys who benefit. The international debate on the design of school science is very lively at present—even if differing motives are involved (see Gardner et al., 1990, where gender differences are not discussed). For this reason one may hope to see improvements within a relatively short time.

The *longitudinal design* of this study provided us with the insight that focusing on developmental sequences averaged for an entire sample may not be sufficiently sensitive to intraindividual differences in the pace of learning and knowledge acquisition. Instead of looking to entire cohorts and their changes, it would be more promising to focus on learning processes of individuals and their development over time and then to summarize those processes over a larger sample even if the same learning processes do not take place at the same time. It would be naive to expect, for example, that all 5th graders experience the same growth in technological skills in the same period of their adolescent lives.

This study reinforced the fact that interindividual differences play an important role in the explanation of problem-solving ability among young people and their development, and that these differences should be taken into account in lesson planning. Although expert-novice research reports that differences in knowledge are better predictors of performance than ability differences, this thesis remains to be proven in relation to knowledge acquisition in school-age children. The results presented here seem to give more support to the thesis that school programs must be differentiated according to different forms and levels of giftedness and interests.

At the beginning of this study, it was argued that the investigation into the development of technical ability was an essential prerequisite for the promotion of technical understanding and creativity. Physics lessons were regarded as the most significant effort of society to enhance young people's understanding of technology. However, we were able to observe that (a) physics lessons do not contribute to the acquisition of problem-solving ability in physics and technology in all subgroups, and that (b) this ability is not of great importance for the solution of (somewhat artificial) technical problems. If young people are to be prepared in school for the demands of a technological world, then according to these results, traditional physics programs must be extended to include special treatment of technology. This demand is difficult to reconcile with traditional educational theory in Germany (Dohmen, 1989). Nevertheless, physics education that is independent of the context of technology runs the risk of preaching only an archaic, naturalistic view of an innocent world. The control of technology and its humanization require abilities which can be acquired inside of school. Young people, especially girls, are extremely interested in the social consequences of technology (Subotnik, 1988), and would, without a doubt, respond well to technology education related to their own lives. Targeted educational programs and also the dovetailing of science and social science education should help to achieve the aim that

> the individual as a person asks him- or herself the right questions and retains the right to decide the aims and goals, which technical means are there to serve. To retain spiritual independence from the pressures and temptations produced by secondary systems which are, after all, human creations, is perhaps the greatest challenge for education today. (Dohmen, 1989, p. 49, trans. by Hany)

JOYS AND PITFALLS OF LONGITUDINAL RESEARCH

This study was conceived as a classical longitudinal study including representative samples of special populations. Therefore, the personal contacts between subjects and researchers were not emphasized or nurtured by special means. With each repetition of the test procedure, the team of researchers gained valuable insights into factors that might be relevant to the course of development but were not included in the research design. Some of these elements included the achievement orientation of the school, the personal interest of the school staff in their students, educational opportunities available outside schools, and differences in the onset of puberty-related phenomena.

This study was confronted with one of the main problems of longitudinal research, the loss of subjects. Because of limited funds, the intended sample size could not be realized, even at the beginning of the study. After the first point of measurement, 10% of the subjects were lost. An additional 15% were lost after the second data collection. Further, 10% of the cases could not be used for the longitudinal analyses because of missing values, as attrition was not equivalent for all experimental subgroups. Many of the averagely intelligent students suffered performance problems and had to repeat a school year, or had to change schools at the end of grade 6 (or in some cases after grade 7). Unfortunately, the schools involved did not report these changes to us in time, thus we were not able to include these pupils in subsequent data collection.

Our study was paralleled by data collection in the People's Republic of China. This research was undoubtedly severely affected by historical events. Shortly before the second data collection point, the university students' desire for reforms ended with the events on Tiananmen Square in Beijing. On the surface, these events only delayed data collection in China (most subjects were students in Beijing) yet it is very hard to say what effects these events had on the minds of our Chinese subjects.

It can be concluded that longitudinal research is burdened with special risks and with difficult methodological and organizational problems. Technical creativity research is at the stage of construct definition and experimentation with measurement instruments. At this point, it might be useful to carry out a series of cross-sectional analyses to improve instrumentation, design, and, above all, generate theory. A follow-up longitudinal study might then be more fruitful.

REFERENCES

Arndt, M. (1990). Zum Zusammenhang von intern repräsentiertem Wissen und Problemlöseerfolg beim Konstruieren [On the correlation between internally represented knowledge and success in solving design problems]. *Wissenschaftliche Zeitschrift der Humboldt-Universität zu Berlin - Reihe Mathematik / Naturwissenschaften* [Scientific Journal of the Humboldt University in Berlin – Mathematics / Natural Sciences Series], *39*, 51–58.

Barron, F., & Harrington, D. M. (1981). Creativity, intelligence, and personality. *Annual Review of Psychology, 32*, 439–476.

Benbow, C. P., & Stanley, J. C. (1984). Gender and the science major: A study of mathematically precocious youth. In M.W. Steinkamp & M.L. Maehr (Eds.), *Women in science* (pp. 165–196). Greenwich, CT: JAI Press.

Bransford, J. D., Franks, J. J., Vye, N. J., & Sherwood, R. D. (1989). New approaches to instruction: Because wisdom can't be told. In S. Vosniadou & A. Ortony (Eds.), *Similarity and analogical reasoning* (pp. 470–497). Cambridge: Cambridge University Press.

Brown, R. T. (1989). Creativity: What are we to measure? In J. A. Glover, R. R. Ronning, & C. R. Reynolds (Eds.), *Handbook of creativity* (pp. 3–32). New York: Plenum.

Burns, A., & Homel, R. (1989). Gender division of tasks by parents and their children. *Psychology of Women Quarterly, 13*, 113–125.

Chi, M. T. H., Feltovich, P. J., & Glaser, R. (1981). Categorization and representation of physics problems by experts and novices. *Cognitive Science, 5*, 521–152.

Chi, M. T. H., Glaser, R., & Farr, M. J. (Eds.). (1989). *The nature of expertise*. Hillsdale, NJ: Erlbaum.

Chi, M. T. H., Glaser, R., & Rees, E. (1982). Expertise in problem solving. In R. J. Sternberg (Ed.), *Advances in the psychology of intelligence* (Vol. 1, pp. 7–76). Hillsdale, NJ: Erlbaum.

Conrad, W., Baumann, E., & Mohr, V. (1980). *Mannheimer Test zur Erfassung des physikalisch-technischen Problemlosens (MTP)* [Mannheim Test of Problem Solving in Physics and Technology (MTP)]. Göttingen, Germany: Hogrefe Verlag für Psychologie.

Csikszentmihalyi, M., & Robinson, R. E. (1986). Culture, time, and the development of talent. In R. J. Sternberg & J. E. Davidson (Eds.), *Conceptions of giftedness* (pp. 264–284). New York: Cambridge University Press.

diSessa, A. (1982). Unlearning Aristotelian physics: A study of knowledge-based learning. *Cognitive Science, 6*, 37–75.

Dohmen, G. (1989). Bildung und Technik [Education and technics]. In L. Boehm & C. Schönbeck (Eds.), *Technik und Bildung* [Technology and education] (pp. 37–55). Düsseldorf, Germany: VDI.

Dylla, N. (1990). *Denk- und Handlungsabläufe beim Konstruieren* [Patterns of thought and action in design]. Unpublished dissertation, Technical University of Munich, Department of Design in Mechanical Engineering.

Eccles, J. S. (1985). Why doesn't Jane run? Sex differences in educational and occupational patterns. In F.D. Horowitz & M. O'Brien (Eds.), *The gifted and talented. Developmental perspectives* (pp. 251–295). Washington, DC: American Psychological Association.

Facaoaru, C. (1985). *Kreativität in Wissenschaft und Technik. Operationalisierung von Problemlösefähigkeiten und kognitiven Stilen* [Creativity in science and technology. Operationalization of problem solving abilities and cognitive styles]. Bern: Hans Huber.

Faulstich-Wieland, H. (1987). "Mädchenbildung und neue Technologien"— Ein Forschungs—und Entwicklungsprojekt in Hessen ["Education of girls and new technologies" - A research and developmental project in Hessen]. *Frauenforschung* [Women's Research], *5*, 75–95.

Feingold, A. (1988). Cognitive gender differences are disappearing. *American Psychologist, 43*, 95–103.

Feldman, D. H. (1986). *Nature's gambit: Child prodigies and the development of human potential.* New York: Basic Books.

Findlay, C. S., & Lumsden, C. J. (1988). The creative mind. *Journal of Social and Biological Structures, 11*, 3–56.

Forneck, H. J. (1986). Krise des Bildungssystems? Die Herausforderung unserer Schulen im 'Computerzeitalter' [Crisis in the educational system? The challenge to our schools in the 'computer age']. *Pädagogische Rundschau* [Pedagogical Review], *40*, 719–743.

Gardner, M., Greeno, J. G., Reif, F., Schoenfeld, A.H ., DiSessa, A., & Stage, E. (1990). *Toward a scientific practice of science education.* Hillsdale, NJ: Lawrence Erlbaum.

Gitomer, D. H. (1988). Individual differences in technical troubleshooting. *Human Performance, 1*, 111–131.

Glaser, R., & Bassok, M. (1989). Learning theory and the study of instruction. *Annual Review of Psychology, 40*, 631–666.

Glover, J. A., Ronning, R. R., & Reynolds, C. R. (Eds.). (1989). *Handbook of creativity.* New York: Plenum.

Goldstein, D., Haldane, D., & Mitchell, C. (1990). Sex differences in visual-spatial ability: The role of performance factors. *Memory & Cognition, 18*, 546–550.

Guilford, J. P. (1967). *The nature of human intelligence.* New York: McGraw-Hill.

Haensly, P. A., & Reynolds, C. R. (1989). Creativity and intelligence. In J. A. Glover, R. R. Ronning, & C. R. Reynolds (Eds.), *Handbook of creativity* (pp. 111–134). New York: Plenum Press.

Halpern, D. F. (1986). *Sex differences in cognitive abilities.* Hillsdale, NJ: Lawrence Erlbaum.

Hany, E. A. (1991). Strategien der Komplexitäsbewältigung bei induktiven Problemen in Abhängigkeit von Intelligenz und Alter [Strategies of coping with complexity in inductive problems in relation to intelligence and age]. *Zeitschrift für Differentielle und Diagnostische Psychologie* [Journal of Individual Differences and Diagnostic Psychology], *12*, 77–92.

Hany, E. A. (1992). Kreativitätstraining [Training of creativity]. In K. J. Klauer (Ed.), *Kognitives Training* [Cognitive training] (pp. 189–216). Göttingen: Hogrefe.

Hany, E. A., & Heller, K. A. (1990). Entwicklung kreativer Fertigkeiten bei deutschen und chinesischen Kindern: Ergebnisse einer explorativen

Längsschnittstudie [Development of creativity skills in German and Chinese children: Results of an exploratory longitudinal study]. In D. Frey (Ed.), *Bericht über den 37. Kongress der Deutschen Gesellschaft für Psychologie in Kiel 1990. Band 1: Kurzfassungen* [Report on the 37th conference of the German Society of Psychology in Kiel 1990. Vol. 1: Abstracts] (p. 542f.). Göttingen: Hogrefe Verlag für Psychologie.

Harvey, J., & Goldstein, S. (1985). Sex differences in science and mathematics for more able pupils. *Gifted Education International, 3*, 133–136.

Heller, K. A. (1992a). Koedukation und Bildungschancen der Mädchen [Coeducation and career opportunities for girls]. *Bildung und Erziehung* [Educatedness and Education], *45*, 5–30.

Heller, K. A. (Ed.). (1992b). *Hochbegabung im Kindes- und Jugendalter* [High ability in childhood and adolescence]. Göttingen: Hogrefe Verlag für Psychologie.

Heller, K. A., Gaedike, A. K., & Weinläder, H. (1985). *Kognitiver Fähigkeitstest KFT 4 − 13 +. (2nd ed.)* [Cognitive Abilities Test 4 − 13 +]. Weinheim, Germany: Beltz.

Heller, K. A., & Hany, E. A. (1991). Freizeitgebundene Technikerfahrung von Kindern und Jugendlichen als Vorbedingung für technische Kreativität [Technical experiences of children and adolescents during leisure time as preconditions for technical creativity]. In VDI Technological Centre (Physics Technology) (Ed.), *Technikfolgenabschätzung. Projektpräsentationen zum Förderschwerpunkt "Wechselwirkungen zwischen Arbeit, Technik und Freizeit"* [Assessment of consequences of technology. Presentation of research projects in the domain "Interaction between work, technology, and leisure time"] (pp. 23–27). Düsseldorf: Author.

Hennessey, B. A., & Amabile, T. M. (1988). The conditions of creativity. In R.J. Sternberg (Ed.), *The nature of creativity. Contemporary psychological perspectives* (pp. 11–38). Cambridge: Cambridge University Press.

Hocevar, D. (1981). Measurement of creativity: Review and critique. *Journal of Personality Assessment, 45*, 450–464.

Hyde, J. S., & Linn, M. C. (1986). *The psychology of gender. Advances through meta-analysis.* Baltimore, MD: Johns Hopkins University Press.

IBRIC (1978). *Biographical Inventory Form U.* Salt Lake City: Author.

Jäger, A. O., & Althoff, K. (1983). *Der WILDE-Intelligenztest* [The WILDE intelligence test]. Göttingen: Hogrefe Verlag für Psychologie.

Kaiser, M. K., Jonides, J., & Alexander, J. (1986). Intuitive reasoning about abstract and familiar physics problems. *Memory & Cognition, 14*, 308–312.

Kieras, D. E., & Bovair, S. (1984). The role of a mental model in learning to operate a device. *Cognitive Science, 8*, 255–273.

Klix, F. (1983). Begabungsforschung − ein neuer Weg in der kognitiven Intelligenzdiagnostik? [Research on giftedness − a new approach in the cognitive diagnosis of intelligence?] *Zeitschrift für Psychologie* [Journal of Psychology], *191*, 360–387.

Kommissari, B. (1991). *Interventionsstudie zu subjektiven physikalischen Konzeptionen bei Jugendlichen aus differentialpsychologischer Sicht* [An intervention study of adolescents' subjective conceptions in physics from the perspective of interindividual differences]. Unpublished diploma thesis, University of Munich, Germany.

Krems, J. (1990). *Zur Psychologie der Expertenschaft. Kompetenzmoderierte Urteilsbildung in semantisch vielschichtigen Domänen* [On the psychology of expertise. Competence based judgments in semantically multifaceted domains]. Unpublished postdoctoral qualification thesis, University of Regensburg.

Kyllonen, P. C., & Woltz, D. J. (1989). Role of cognitive factors in the acquisition of cognitive skill. In R. Kanfer, P. L. Ackerman, & R. Cudeck (Eds.), *Abilities, motivation, & methodology: The Minnesota Symposium on Learning and Individual Differences* (pp. 239–268). Hillsdale, NJ: Lawrence Erlbaum.

Larkin, J. H. (1985). Understanding, problem representations, and skill in physics. In S. F. Chipman, J. W. Segal, & R. Glaser (Eds.), *Thinking and learning skills, Vol. 2: Research and open questions* (pp. 141–159). Hillsdale, NJ: Lawrence Erlbaum.

Lehwald, G. (1985). Zur Diagnostik des Erkenntnisstrebens bei Schülern [Towards the diagnosis of thirst for knowledge in pupils]. *Beiträge zur Psychologie, Bd. 20* [Contributions to psychology, Vol. 20]. Berlin: Volk und Wissen.

Linn, M. C., & Petersen, A. C. (1985). Emergence and characterization of sex differences in spatial ability: A meta-analysis. *Child Development, 56*, 1479–1498.

Lohman, D. F., & Kyllonen, P. G. (1983). Individual differences in solution strategy on spatial tasks. In R.F. Dillon & R.R. Schmeck (Eds.), *Individual differences in cognition* (Vol. 1, pp. 105–135). New York: Academic Press.

Lubinski, D., & Humphreys, L. G. (1990). A broadly based analysis of mathematical giftedness. *Intelligence, 14*, 327–355.

Maccoby, E. E., & Jacklin, C. N. (1974). *The psychology of sex differences*. Stanford, CA: Stanford University Press.

Mansfield, R. D., Busse, T. V., & Krepelka, E. J. (1978). The effectiveness of creativity training. *Review of Educational Research, 48*, 517–536.

Meehan, H., & Wood, H. (1975). *The reality of ethnomethodology*. New York: John Wiley & Sons.

Michael, W. B., & Wright, C. R. (1989). Psychometric issues in the assessment of creativity. In J. A. Glover, R. R. Ronning, & C. R. Reynolds (Eds.), *Handbook of creativity* (pp. 33–52). New York: Plenum Pless.

Morris, N. M., & Rouse, W. B. (1985). Review and evaluation of empirical research in troubleshooting. *Human Factors, 27*, 503–530.

Neber, H. (1987). Beschreiben und Verstehen technischer Sachverhalte durch Berufsschüler [Description and comprehension of technical facts by vocational school students]. *Psychologie in Erziehung und Unterricht* [Psychology in Education and Instruction], *31*, 115–121.

Neber, H. (1992). Wissensnutzung: Förderung durch ein Training des situativen Wissenszugangs [Knowledge Usage: Promotion by situated knowledge access training]. *Zeitschrift für Pädagogische Psychologie* [Journal of Educational Psychology].

Nicklis, W. S. (1985). "Antiquiert" oder "informiert"? ["Outmoded" or "informed"?] *Vierteljahrsschrift für die wissenschaftliche Pädagogik* [Scientific Pedagogical Quarterly], *61*, 390–408.

Oerter, R. (1988). Wissen und Kultur [Knowledge and culture]. In H. Mandl & H. Spada (Eds.), *Wissenspsychologie* [Psychology of knowledge] (pp. 333–356). München: Psychologie Verlags Union.

Payne, D., & Halpin, W. (1974). Use of a factored biographical inventory to identify differentially gifted adolescents. *Psychological Reports, 35*, 1195–1204.

Perkins, D. N. (1990). The nature and nurture of creativity. In B. F. Jones & L. Idol (Eds.), *Dimensions of thinking and cognitive instruction* (pp. 415–443). Hillsdale, NJ: Lawrence Erlbaum Associates.

Pettigrew, T. (1982). Cognitive style and social behavior: A review of category width. In L. Wheeler (Ed.), *Review of personality and social psychology* (Vol. 3, pp. 199–224). Beverly Hills, CA: Sage.

Rabinowitz, M., & Glaser, R. (1985). Cognitive structure and process in highly competent performance. In F. D. Horowitz & M. O'Brien (Eds.), *The gifted and talented: Developmental perspectives* (pp. 75–98). Washington, DC: American Psychological Association.

Rasmussen, J. (1986). *Information processing and human-machine interaction*. Amsterdam: North-Holland.

Renzulli, J. S. (1978). What makes giftedness? Reexamining a definition. *Phi Delta Kappan, 60*, 180–184, 261.

Resnick, L. B. (Ed.). (1989). *Knowing and learning: Essays in honor of Robert Glaser*. Hillsdale, NJ: Lawrence Erlbaum.

Runco, M.A. (1986). The discriminant validity of gifted children's divergent thinking test scores. *Gifted Child Quarterly, 30*, 78–82.

Runco, M. A., & Albert, R. S. (Eds.). (1990). *Theories of creativity*. Newbury Park, CA: Sage.

Runco, M. A., & Okuda, S. M. (1988). Problem discovery, divergent thinking, and the creative process. *Journal of Youth and Adolescence, 17*, 211–220.

Sachsse, H. (1987). Zur Anthropologie der Technik [On the anthropology of technology]. In A. Menne (Ed.), *Philosophische Probleme von Arbeit und Technik* [Philosophical problems of work and technology] (pp. 122–135). Darmstadt: Wissenschaftliche Buchgesellschaft.

Schaefer, C. E. (1970). *Biographical inventory: Creativity*. San Diego, CA: Educational and Industrial Testing Services.

Schelsky, H. (1965). Der Mensch in der wissenschaftlichen Zivilisation [Human beings in scientific civilization]. In H. Schelsky (Ed.), *Auf der Suche nach der Wirklichkeit. Gesammelte Aufsätze* [In search of reality. Collected papers] (pp. 439–480). Düsseldorf: Diederichs.

Sincoff, J. B., & Sternberg, R. J. (1989). The development of cognitive skills:

An examination of recent theories. In A. M. Colley & J. R. Beech (Eds.), *Acquisition and performance of cognitive skills* (pp. 19–60). Chichester, John Wiley & Sons.

Sternberg, R. J. (Ed.). (1988). *The nature of creativity: Contemporary psychological perspectives.* Cambridge: Cambridge University Press.

Sternberg, R. J., & Davidson, J. E. (1985). Cognitive development in the gifted and talented. In F. D. Horowitz & M. O'Brien (Eds.), *The gifted and talented: Developmental perspectives* (pp. 37–74). Washington, DC: American Psychological Association.

Subotnik, R. F. (1988). The motivation to experiment: A study of gifted adolescents' attitudes toward scientific research. *Journal for the Education of the Gifted, 11,* 19–35.

Tannenbaum, A. J. (1983). *Gifted children: Psychological and educational perspectives.* New York: Macmillan.

Taylor, C. W. (1988). Various approaches to and definitions of creativity. In R. J. Sternberg (Ed.), *The nature of creativity: Contemporary psychological perspectives* (pp. 99–121). Cambridge: Cambridge University Press.

Taylor, C. W., & Barron, F. (Eds.). (1963). *Scientific creativity: Its recognition and development.* New York: J. Wiley.

Terman, L. M., & Oden, M. H. (1947). *Genetic studies of genius: Vol. 4. The gifted child grows up: Twenty-five years' follow-up of a superior group.* Stanford, CA: Stanford University Press.

Thorndike, R. L., & Hagen, E. (1974). *Cognitive Abilities Test. Technical Manual, Multi-level edition (Form 1 - Levels A-H/Grades 3-12).* Boston: Houghton-Mifflin.

Torrance, E. P. (1988). The nature of creativity as manifest in its testing. In R. J. Sternberg (Ed.), *The nature of creativity: Contemporary psychological perspectives* (pp. 43–75). Cambridge: Cambridge University Press.

Von Hentig, H. (1984). *Das allmähliche Verschwinden der Wirklichkeit* [The gradual disappearance of reality]. Munich: Hanser.

Wallach, M. A. (1985). Creativity testing and giftedness. In F. D. Horowitz & M. O'Brien (Eds.), *The gifted and talented: Developmental perspectives* (pp. 99–124). Washington, DC: American Psychological Association.

Walther-Klaus, E. (1987). Begriffsbestimmungen der Technik [Definitions of technology]. In A. Menne (Ed.), *Philosophische Probleme von Arbeit und Technik* [Philosophical problems of work and technology] (pp. 203–213). Darmstadt, Germany: Wissenschaftliche Buchgesellschaft.

Weisberg, R. W. (1986). *Creativity: Genius and other myths.* New York: W. H. Freeman.

6

Conditions of Giftedness: Musical Development in the Preschool and Early Elementary Years*

Lyle Davidson
Larry Scripp

OVERVIEW AND BACKGROUND OF STUDY

The two examples in Figure 6.1 represent what two first-born 3-year-olds sing when asked to perform "Somewhere Over The Rainbow." The two versions share the words, the initial ascending contour, but little else. A first impression suggests that one child does not know the song while the other does. Although the first impression raises questions about what it means to "know" a song, greater knowledge alone fails to account for all the differences. The abundance of nuances in the second performance, and other related issues lead to a more penetrating understanding of the performances. The first example (Figure 6.1a) represents a performance by an eager singer—always willing to sing for his "playmate" researcher and his parents (who are not musicians). The other child (Figure 6.1b) is equally eager to sing, but her parents are musicians. A simplistic explanation would attribute the difference to genetics or early family environment. However, these two versions of "Somewhere Over The Rainbow" raise complex questions for the musician and researcher interested in the psychological nature of giftedness. This chapter explores differences between extraordinary and more ordinary musical performance in young children.

Psychometric studies of giftedness have dealt with the question of giftedness in isolation of normal development, and have largely ignored the necessary conditions of support when considering the

*The longitudinal research reported in this chapter has been supported through grants from the Carnegie and Spencer Foundations and the National Institute of Education.

Figure 6.1. Two versions of "Somewhere Over the Rainbow" (at age 3)

nature of giftedness. Our discussion of creativity and talent in this chapter differs from those discussions in two ways: First, if we are going to shed light on the mystery and wonder of talent, we need to consider it in relation to everyday expression of normal capacity; second, talent needs to be considered in the context of the conditions which support it. Thus, we will consider giftedness using a model of cognitive development based more on social interaction than individual trait. The musical development of average preschool children will be contrasted with the singing of a gifted child. Various support conditions will be considered as contributing to differences between the average and gifted children.

The metaphor of concentric circles (see Figure 6.2) represents the relationship of conditions necessary for the identification of musical talent: The individual gift is revealed because it contrasts with immediate conditions and expectations, it requires various forms of support in order to survive and mature, and the larger community provides the defining properties which make the effort and investment worthwhile. These conditions, in short, must be considered when addressing the question of giftedness.

TALENT: IN THE MIND OR IN THE CULTURE?

Much of the research work carried out with gifted and talented subjects has been conducted in a psychometric tradition. The focus of research is on how information is taken in, processed, and integrated. Speed of access, encoding, and retrieval are assumed to indicate unusual ability (Davidson, 1985). The assumption that

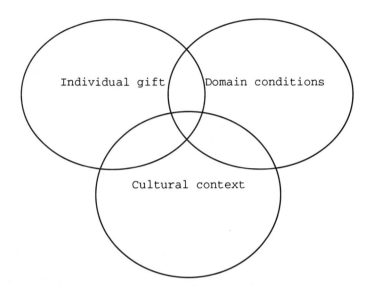

Figure 6.2. Concentric circles of conditions of giftedness

these characteristics predict a superior ability to learn, solve novel problems, show high levels of adaptability, and form sensitive judgments is fundamental to this approach. It assumes that giftedness is collateral with, if not dependent on, high general intelligence (Terman, 1925). It posits further that these traits can be observed in young children.

The notion that giftedness is distinct from general intelligence is important for two reasons. It suggests that giftedness, or at least its manifestations, can be seen very early in life—before IQ-type skills are developed. Second, if giftedness appears very early, the evolution of giftedness can be tracked through longitudinal studies of individuals in whom those traits first appear.

This perspective on giftedness reduces the scope of its study to those domains which are easily measured by tests of intelligence—typically pencil-and-paper tests which are verbal and mathematical in nature. These tests have little to do with other important issues, such as one's affinity for specific materials, feelings about one's identity, or attachment to a mentor—issues which may play major roles in one's choice of work and talent domain. Finally, by defining giftedness as a trait that involves above-average ability, unusual commitment to a chosen task, and a high level of creativity (Renzulli, 1986), the conditions of support, as well as the context within which one's gift is used, can be ignored or relegated to a minor position.

Predominantly psychological conceptions of giftedness (Stern-berg & Davidson, 1986) share the perspective that giftedness, tal-ent, and genius are seated within the individual whose products attract attention. Another point of view has begun to take shape wherein the gifted individual is placed at the center of a broadly conceived support system that includes peers, family, community (Walter & Gardner, 1986), and the culture (Csikszentmihalyi & Rob-inson, 1986). These researchers are advocating a shift of focus from the isolated individual within whom the gift emerges to the social individual within whom the gift is developed (Bamberger, 1986, 1991; Feldman, 1980; Gruber, 1986).

The perspective taken in this chapter is based on assumptions shared by developmental psychologists. Two major questions follow from that perspective: How can we best describe the changes we see in capacities essential to expression and production in a domain, and how much change has to occur in order to "count"? Change can be measured quantitatively, or as changes in the hierarchical struc-tures which coordinate central behaviors and thoughts (qualita-tively).

Developmentalists are interested in functioning processes rather than underlying traits of various kinds and sizes. Developmentalists also believe in the importance of charting or describing sequential levels of mastery rather than measuring amounts of general ability. Also, they are coming to see giftedness as connected to domains, rather than as a single, cross-domain trait (Feldman & Goldsmith, 1986). More recently, researchers working from Vygotsky's theory of development (Vygotsky, 1978) have emphasized the role of support-ing conditions (Newman, Griffin, & Cole, 1989; Rogoff, 1990).

This perspective of giftedness requires studying the constructive interaction of individual and social forms of knowledge. From this point of view, strength of expression depends less on the innate ability of the individual than on the interaction of the individual possessing various potentials and a world replete with possibilities.

Accordingly, a fuller explanation of giftedness will depend on several factors, including propensities such as talents and other individual differences; characteristics of the setting within which a person pursues mastery of a domain; those who provide critical influences such as peers, parents, and teachers; and the current state of the field being chosen as the arena of engagement.

The usefulness of this point of view about giftedness is evident when we take another perspective of intelligence itself, that of Multi-ple Intelligence theory (Gardner, 1983). Gardner argues that cultures maintain resources, provide opportunities for work and expression in, and reward achievement in seven intelligences: language, logico-mathematical, spatial, kinesthetic, musical, intra-personal, and interpersonal arenas of life. Gardner argues that the "pure" form of these intelligences does not appear except perhaps in unfortunate circumstances (as in idiot savants or cases of organic brain damage), but instead are components in individual profiles of abilities and propensities. For example, any lawyer must be able to think logically, but while a lawyer without an interest in interpersonal relationships or a flair for performance may have a career as a tax attorney, a trial lawyer must possess a higher degree of social intelligence in order to play his or her audience—the jury. Gardner's perspective immediately makes the limitations of the single dimension view of giftedness clear, while at the same time providing a way to describe the conditions of giftedness in more real-life terms.

The concentric circle view of giftedness includes a description of giftedness as it is seen in the individual, the conditions of support enabling its development, and the community or culture, both extended and local, which supports its specific expression. These three components enable us to describe the symptoms of an individual's gift, monitor its development throughout the formative years and beyond, and witness its reception in the world of mature achievement.

INDIVIDUAL DEVELOPMENT IN MUSIC

Let us turn to the innermost circle—the development of the individual. Most recently, significant work has addressed three perspectives of music: studies of the perception of elements of music (Deutsch, 1982), studies of graphic representation of music (Bamberger, 1991; Davidson & Scripp, 1988), and a very few studies of musical performance (Sloboda, 1985, 1986). Summaries of work in the field have been carried out by Dowling and Harwood (1986), Hargreaves (1986), and Shuter-Dyson (1968).

Giftedness and its relation to the development of normal musical ability is rarely considered. There appear to be at least two reasons for this: the assumptions limiting the scope of psychological research itself, and the culture's willingness to sustain an unarticulated model of extraordinary achievement and performance. These combined tendencies make it difficult to achieve an integrated view of musical development, especially one which includes the gifted and talented.

Several problems arise from assumptions which form the basis of psychological research. For example, the psychologist's assumption that the study of mind takes place in isolation of a given discipline, field of work, or domain makes it easier to conduct research in contexts from which it is difficult to generalize. This yields results which are difficult to observe in everyday life. Second, the reliance on the assumptions of inferential statistics in framing and reporting psychological studies, for example: (a) the need to identify a priori the salient dimensions necessary for testing null hypothesis models, (b) that one can correctly infer paths of change from the static observation of differences, and (c) that identified populations can provide "an unchanging universe of scores," make it difficult to observe the development of ability or skill (Wohlwill, 1973). These assumptions about questions, methods, and populations channel away from the unusual, the unique, and the gifted.

From another point of view, the culture's belief in inspiration, gift, and extraordinary ability oversimplifies the situation of giftedness. For example, the concept of "gift" stands in place of acknowledging the nearly impossible-to-imagine dedication to one's work, mastery of specific modes of thought, and ability to negotiate complex and sensitive issues having to do with one's self and others, which probably play a critical role in the life of every master. For example, if a business person or other professional produces a plan which requires an investment of 60 to 90 hours a week over a period of several weeks, no one is surprised. It is assumed that such extraordinary effort is necessary to carry off extraordinary work. On the other hand, an audience rarely questions the number of hours, weeks, and years that precedes a 60-minute concert. The nonmusician appears more ready to credit the musician with talent, rather than with the same extraordinary capacity for sustained effort that may be required to support the products of the marketplace.

Finally, because there are so few tools available for thinking about giftedness in a unified way, it is difficult for the psychologist, musician, and layperson alike to see beyond the "folk" psychology of talent. There is no single or sophisticated organizing framework which enables the interested reader, whether artist or not, to integrate the various findings and issues raised. This chapter represents an attempt do just that, to frame the achievements of clearly precocious and gifted children in a context of average achievement reflected in the song singing of less gifted children.

LONGITUDINAL STUDIES OF CHILDREN'S SONG SINGING

The framework and constructs guiding any investigative effort are extremely important. The framework guiding the work reported in this chapter is based on the assumption that one must study knowledge within the context of its everyday use or occurrence. This point of view takes full advantage of the concept of ecological validity.

The assumptions supporting developmental work (and longitudinal designs) are not symmetrical with those of cross-sectional studies typical of experimental work. Following the same subjects over an extended period of time allows the observer to see change and continuity within individuals as well as across individuals. This approach to research portrays the individual propensities for the domain as well as whatever giftedness may appear over the critical early years of life.

Descriptive studies are particularly useful as ways of beginning to study development in a specific domain (Wohlwill, 1973), but there are certain cautions to note. Studies, like this one, which focus on small numbers of subjects over an extended period of time, may reflect only the particular characteristics of the particular group being studied. However, studying a single group not only provides information about a single (and perhaps unique) population, it provides a descriptive base from which further and more refined investigation may take place.

Another important consideration is the difference between the methods of data collection represented by the cross-sectional view of an ability or capacity and the clinical approach to questioning and research. By design, cross-sectional studies typically "wash out" important individual differences in favor of differences between the mean scores of cohort groups. A longitudinal study, in contrast, generates much of its power from the attention given to individual differences. By design, longitudinal research seeks overlaps, parallels, and contrasts among individuals studied.

While these considerations represent some of the issues to consider when thinking about longitudinal designs, they entirely miss the quality of life these designs provide—the excitement of beginning a long study without knowing exactly where you will end up. Often during a longitudinal study one yearns for the clarity of a simple cross-sectional design with stable conditions and crisply framed independent and dependent variables. Instead, the researcher has to sustain tremendous amounts of ambiguity over long periods of time, and ignore the ever-tempting siren that taunts with forecasts of never being able to make sense out of the unformed mess of information being collected, some of which is hoped to support a comprehensive story. A story, carefully constructed one week, is often abandoned for what appears to be a more powerful explanation the next week. The research process makes severe demands on one's mental flexibility and ability to maintain multiple perspectives. Casting and recasting interpretations becomes a constant source of frustration, anxiety, and pleasure. However difficult it may be, the fun and excitement of discovery and the deep pleasure that comes from being engaged in the quest for rigor are equal to the commitment and passions found in any other rigorous pursuit, including those of the musical life.

Collecting Songs and Forming a Database

The following composite picture is based on the findings of a longitudinal study of nine first-born children plus a second cohort of 69 children who formed the cross-sectional study. The children were selected from a pool of respondents to ads taken out in a local paper. Agreements to participate were made on the basis of interviews and a mutual sense of a "goodness of fit." The intrusion on a family participating in the longitudinal study was significant; the researchers saw the children every other week for 5 years and became, in effect, "part of the family." The first visits were made shortly after the children's first birthdays. The findings from the longitudinal sample became the theory which was tested in the analysis of the cross-sectional study of 69 children drawn from the same age range and socioeconomic class. In all cases, the songs on which this study is based were collected in natural settings—in children's homes.

What counts as a song in this study? Although the data are rich with performances collected under informal conditions, the corpus of songs analyzed includes only standard and invented songs which consisted of two or more phrases. The children in the cross-sectional sample were seen three times. They were asked to sing their favorite songs and a song was taught to them by a researcher during the first visit. They were asked to sing the new song during each visit. The entire corpus of songs were transcribed by experienced musicians and checked by outside experts. The transcription and the analysis of the songs were separate processes. All analysis was conducted from both the notation and a tape of the child's performance. The songs from the cross-sectional cohort were tape recorded and later scored on the same measures as the songs from the longitudinal study.

Sorting out stable behaviors from random occurrences is critical in developmental research. We adopted a conservative rule of acquisition. In order for a musical shape to be counted as a stable part of a child's repertoire of pitch and rhythm relationships, it had to appear twice in different songs and in different sessions. Separate analyses were carried out on each group of songs, invented and standard. Davidson (1985) contains a more detailed description of the scoring process.

DEVELOPMENT OF PITCH AND RHYTHMIC RELATIONSHIPS

Pitch

Three components are basic to the control and understanding of pitch relationships on which song singing depends: (a) the capacity to grasp the figurative shape or contour of a phrase, (b) the ability to match individual pitches, and (c) sufficient memory or organizing structure to maintain key stability across the phrases of a song. Past research reveals contradictions about the manner in which these various aspects of pitch relations develop. Some research suggests that knowledge of pitch relations develops through a series of phases: Children first grasp the contour, then specific pitches, more precise centered pitches, and finally, stability of key (Moorehead & Pond, 1941; Shuter-Dyson, 1968; Teplov, 1966). Other research suggests that tonal knowledge may develop out of the ability to match specific pitches (Wing, 1963), while Sargeant and Roche (1973) report that children's ability to match pitches even declines as their ability to match contours improves. By and large, researchers report that the ability to sing in key appears late— children of five years of age are unable to sing scales at more than chance levels (Bridges, 1965). On the other hand, Michel (1973) reports that by the end of the preschool years, children are able to perform music in major and minor scales.

Beneath these descriptions lie two difficult, but highly significant problems in analyzing children's tonal knowledge: the size and the scope of the unit of analysis. First, the focus of many analyses has been too narrow. Either the development of interval matching or the growth of the ability to seize the figural shape of a melody have been examined, but not both at once. The exclusivity of the focus threatens the validity of findings because melody is reduced to fit the analysis. For example, if one studies tonal development by analyzing melody as intervals (i.e., by breaking up musical performances into their smallest units), one loses the ongoing motion of the melodic impulse. On the other hand, if one analyzes only the contours (the up-and-down motion of unfolding melodies), one misses the development of individual intervals. This Escher-like focus on either intervals or contours needs to be framed in a more comprehensive way; the phenomenon of melody need not be reduced to either one or another. If the analysis is going to remain faithful to music as we know it in everyday contexts, it must include both contour and intervals, thereby capturing essential features of melody.

The second difficulty arises because studies of children's song singing are often based on an inappropriate unit of analysis (Wertsch, 1985). It is evident that the tonal knowledge of musicians reflects the control of individual contours, pitches, intervals, and keys. However—and this is critically important—these musical organizers are the by-products of considerable and protracted activity constructing pitch relations. Children's early song singing simply does not depend on linking fixed pitches or key structures. Because of this, there is little reason to analyze their productions in those terms. Indeed, to analyze the songs of a 3-year-old in these terms is akin to applying the rules of point perspective to early drawings or the rules of transformational grammar to one-word utterances.

In effect, the key to understanding the development of musical ability lies in formulating a unit which captures the melodic aspect of children's songs but which does not presume that children organize their songs in terms of notes, contours, or keys from the outset. Thus, an early and major focus of our work was to develop a way of describing children's growing understanding of pitches, intervals, and contours which did not assume that the child used fixed pitches, measured intervals in diatonic terms, or organized performances based on knowledge of keys.

In the following sections, we will show how normal children's knowledge of musical elements appear in first draft form and develop into various levels of mastery. This will provide a context against which it will be possible to appreciate better the achievements of the gifted child.

Contour Schemes: The Developing Sound of Singing

Even when only a few days old, humans are extremely sensitive to pitch relations. Infants can be conditioned to respond to a melodic change, change of pitch, and contour (Chang & Trehub, 1977a,

1977b). Provided that the notes of a song (or the sung example) fall within the tonal frames in their repertoire, young children can match pitches (Fox, 1990; Updegraff, Heileger, & Learned, 1938). The ability to sing standard songs or invent novel songs which show a grasp of the tonal materials of music requires much more than these raw abilities.

Psychologically, the challenge facing the toddler is how to measure in performance what is first an unarticulated and undefined tonal space. Systematic observation suggests that *contour schemes*, rather than gradual refinements in the overall contour or interval matching, normally account for the route of emerging tonal knowledge (Davidson, 1985). The term "contour" conveys the importance of the figurative shape of melody—its up-and-down motion—while "scheme" conveys the presence of different levels of mental organization (Bartlett, 1958). A model suggesting four specific levels of pitch development in young children's singing between the ages of 1 and 6 years emerged out of the Project Zero research. These levels characterize children's knowledge of tonal relationships as expressed through their song singing. The arrows connecting the contour schemes indicate the sequence of the children's acquisition of levels of tonal knowledge.

Children's mapping of the tonal space proceeds along three lines: the establishment of the limits of the highest and lowest notes of phrases—the register or tonal frame, the appropriate melodic motion or direction, and the stability and relationship of individual pitches to one another—and the scalar organization of song.

Register or Tonal Frame

Phrases of songs have contours of up-and-down motions. The distance between the top pitch and the bottom pitch can be used as a measure of the range of a phrase. For example, in the song "Happy Birthday," the range of each of the first three phrases is larger than the one before it: The range of the first phrase is a fourth; the second a fifth; and the third phrase spans an octave (or eight notes lie between the top and the bottom notes). The last phrase, like the first, has a register of only a fourth.

In their earliest songs, children do not sing the phrases with those ranges. At first, children compress the range of the phrases and songs they sing to the span of a third. Heather's "Happy Birthday" illustrates this compression. (See Figures 6.4 and 6.5.)

Children generate this first leap-based scheme of a third through a process of increasing differentiation of the top and bottom of the

Levels of Contour Schemes

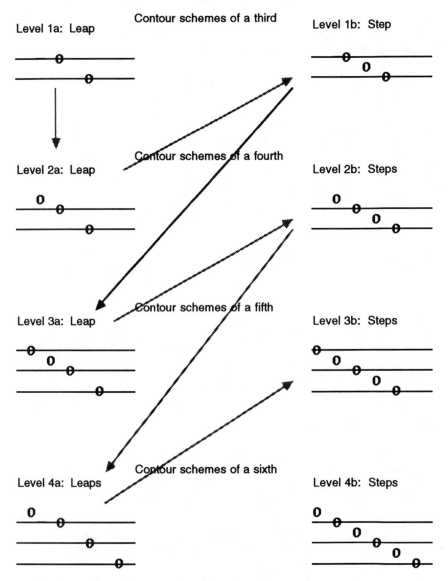

Figure 6.3.   Contour scheme chart '

diffuse glissandos common to their very earliest songs. What emerges over time might be called the first "rule" for generating a song: Sing a discrete pitch, then switch to a lower pitch without stopping the sound and without blurring the sound of either pitch.

Figure 6.4.   Canonical "Happy Birthday"

Figure 6.5.   Heather (1:6) "Happy Birthday"

Figure 6.6.   Max (3:0) "Somewhere Over the Rainbow"

Thus, they sharpen the limits of the range. This sharpening yields the top and the bottom boundaries of the contour scheme.

Children's repertory of tonal structures increases next by the addition of the contour scheme of a fourth. They create this new scheme by adding an outside step to one of the boundary notes of the earlier scheme of a third. Thus, they form either a descending step-leap motion or a leap-step motion. The result in either case is a framing interval of a fourth. The song in Figure 6.6 illustrates this type of melodic motion.

In this example Max flattens or reduces the octave span of the first phrase of the song's melody to accommodate his most stable mental structure for pitch, the contour scheme of an unfilled fourth. He sings subsequent phrases with equal or greater compression, performing each using schemes of a third and a fourth.

Children organize the tonal relationships of their songs using the available mental representations: contour scheme knowledge. When a model song contains leaps larger than a fifth, children who have acquired only that level compress the larger intervals to fit. Similarly, a given contour scheme is often generalized; smaller melodic intervals are often expanded to the span of a fifth. Although a child on occasion may appear to use scale-based knowledge when singing, these choices are not stable or generalized. For instance, a child may give an appropriate ending note (e.g., a tonic) when supplying the end to a familiar song or phrase figure begun by someone else, yet her own invented songs still lack such organization.

In summary, looking at the register or tonal frames children use when singing songs, we see that between the ages of one and five, children build an increasingly broad repertoire of melodic units (contour schemes). These schemes develop in a remarkably ordered manner independent of whether children sing standard or invented songs.

Direction and Contour

The use of contour schemes establishes criteria for normal development—in contrast to gifted development. Another such criterion is development of the direction and contour of the contour scheme, and here the information is straightforward. The ability to match the direction of the notes (or the up and down of the contour) within phrases of melodies is something children have to acquire. It does not develop easily. The melodic motion of the phrases of early invented and conventional songs is from high to low. Regardless of the actual contour of the model song (e.g., "The Alphabet Song" which goes up at first), children will start singing higher and move lower. If they continue singing more of the song, children generate phrases by using the same rule: high to low.

The "Alphabet Song," with its descending third units, shows the degree to which children substitute descending motion for ascending motion. The later ability to perform ascending motions, either modeled or invented, suggests that a certain degree of operational knowledge is available.

There is one more important issue. Even though normal children may be taught to repeat larger intervals or melodies which contain larger intervals by rote, without continued support they lose these intervals rapidly in subsequent performances. During the preschool years, a stable octave and a filled scale which can be sung in both directions, down and up, still remain outside the average child's vocabulary.

Figure 6.7. Heather (1:6) "Alphabet Song"

Stability of Pitches

Another criterion for assessing giftedness is the extent to which the pitches a child sings are stable. In normal children's first songs pitches are merged, often rendered as diffuse swoops up and down— the pitches are uncoordinated and extremely local. As the boundaries of more contour schemes are established, the distinctiveness of notes becomes increasingly clear. For example, when children first sing more than one phrase of "Happy Birthday," they do not return to the starting note for the second phrase. The result is a sing-song, up-and-down contour that sounds unfocused, off-key, or "microtonal" to adult ears.

Their initial grasp of music is one-dimensional—they focus on range at first. As they become increasingly able to define the high-low boundary points, children begin to sing using increasingly focused, though not yet hierarchically organized, pitches. This process may be analogous to the process of early sound articulation in language learning. In language, infants begin to differentiate among the phonemes by producing those at the extremes of the scale, such as the open and closed sounds that occur in "mama," "papa," or "baba." As in linguistic development, musical growth and development lies in the direction of filling in the sounds that lie between highly perceptible extremes, the boundary interval which frames the tonal motion of the phrase.

Because children do not treat individual pitches as fixed identities, their songs may contain as many pitches as notes or syllables. For example, the first phrase of the "Alphabet Song" (the same tune as "Twinkle, Twinkle, Little Star" and "Baa, Baa, Black Sheep") contains seven different notes, but only three different pitches (Do, Sol, and La).

With development, however, the story changes. Gradually over the course of the preschool years, children's ability to conserve pitches (return to the same pitches appropriately when singing songs) becomes more consistent. A specific set of pitches tends to be present throughout an entire song, and from this point on, songs are much less chromatic than during previous levels of ability.

In the earliest contour schemes, relatively few pitches are shared from one phrase to another. By contrast, children operating with the contour scheme of a fifth in their vocabulary exhibit greater stability of pitch, and more sharing of pitches across and within phrases. Consequently, a child at this level of development may sing a song like "Twinkle, Twinkle Little Star" appropriately with as few as five different pitches. Also, during this intermediate level, a child can sing a pitch in a given register, continue singing in a different register, and then return to the original pitch in the first register (as when singing "Old McDonald Had A Farm").

None of the average children in the longitudinal study organized their song structures using scale structures before their sixth year. However, a few outstanding instances show how children first achieve octaves by combining smaller contour schemes already in their vocabulary. When constructing the octave span, Maya (age 5:4) uses two contour schemes, an unfilled fifth and a filled fourth. The top note of the unfilled fifth is used as the bottom pitch of the fourth.

Once they have the capacity to conserve pitch, the only notes in children's standard or invented songs are those of the musical scale. Their songs tend to begin and end on the tonic of the scale, and they use a register bound by the frame of an octave. Notes on either side of leaps are stable. Children rarely sing contours, pitches, and intervals with a diffuse sound or connected by glissandos. When children complete songs started by others, they infer the appropriate tonic.

Figure 6.8. Maya (5:4) Invented song

SUMMARY: TONAL UNDERSTANDING

These longitudinal data suggest that prior to organizing their songs around the culture's scalar structures, children move through two broad periods of tonal understanding. During the periods when children sing using a tonal frame of a third or a fourth, they rarely duplicate pitches in the course of a song. Instead, they appear to have little ability to return to pitches previously sung. By comparison, when their tonal frame expands to a fifth or sixth, this multiplication of pitches (beyond those of the model song) within a single performance disappears. Individual pitches become stabilized and children frequently return to a specific tonal position several times throughout a song. However, it is not until still later that children understand that each note has a unique position and plays a specific role in the scale.

As each interval or tonal frame becomes crystallized, it is used in a widening set of melodic contexts. At first, it appears in its sparest form, the unfilled interval. Subsequently, the child fills in the pitches between the note at the upper boundary and the lower boundary. Particularly during the earliest efforts to carve up the intervening tonal space, these intermediate notes have no fixed positions. Instead the tonal space is mapped out anew each time the interval is negotiated in performance. As the individual frames mature, the intermediate space is mapped with increasing articulation and stability. While knowledge of an interval is in the process of being constructed, the child uses that interval only in the construction of descending or falling contours. Finally, in the last stage of its articulation, a particular interval can be used in forming an ascending melodic contour. At this moment the interval is finally reversible and thus a part of tonal space that can be negotiated in whatever direction a melody requires. Given this understanding of normal development, it should be clear how the gifted child would be distinguished—either by speeding through the developmental sequence of steps or by following a unique path.

Measuring Time: Regulating the Rhythmic Flow

Accomplished singers integrate many aspects of rhythm into single performances. Singers produce or match a range of different speeds (tempi); maintain a regularly occurring unit of measure, the pulse; sing notes of different durations which create the surface pattern of the song; and coordinate the pulse and surface rhythms as they coincide or contrast with one another.

For children, vocal performance is still more demanding when the natural pattern of the words and syllables contrast with the surface pattern of the song. Even in relatively simple songs, there are patterns of rhythmic surface which cross-cut the syllabic patterns of the text. For example, in the song "Happy Birthday," the first word is sung within the duration of a single pulse, the second word across the duration of two pulses—one pulse for each syllable, "birth" and "day." The remaining syllables of the phrase all coincide with the pulse. But the final syllable of the first, second, and final phrases is sung differently. The duration of the final syllable is approximately three times as long as that of the single pulse (see Figure 6.4 above).

A cogent understanding of these interlocking temporal patterns enables a singer to reproduce the rhythmic pattern of familiar songs. A singer must generate these temporal relationships moment to moment. The listener with even a tacit perception of these interlocking temporal patterns can infer much of the rhythmic blueprint of the music. Based on this perception, a listener can anticipate the repetitions on which the possibility for making internal reference rests, and appreciating the deviations can create surprise and renewed interest.

Researchers have sketched a clear-cut outline of the rhythmic structures children use in their songs: single pulse durations, subdivisions of the pulse duration, and ability to hold durations through or across a pulse. During the first year, children typically sing words or syllables using a single note value or duration. Rests which occur between or within phrases, performed without reference to the underlying pulse, sound free and outside the rhythmic structure of the sung portion of the song (Moog, 1968). By the third year, children begin to group successive notes into patterns of twos (Moog, 1968). At this age, rhythms and durations are closely linked to words. Children of three can neither speak a rhythm and then clap it, nor keep a steady pulse to recorded music (Rainbow, 1977). Even children as old as four experience difficulty clapping a steady pulse to ongoing music (Moog, 1968).

Between the ages of 4 and 6, children's rhythmic abilities undergo dramatic changes. At this age, children respond to rhythm patterns without words and pitches as though they were music, whereas between 3 and 4, children treat these same stimuli as though they were words. This suggests an increasing ability to separate words from the more musical aspects of songs, specifically temporal patterns. There is some indication that standard songs may provide practice models or templates for rhythmic structures which are later tried out in invented songs. The rhythms of the invented songs of 4-

to 6-year-olds resemble those of standard songs learned earlier at the ages of three and four (Moog, 1968).

Thus, there is a broad consensus about some general outlines and issues in the development of rhythmic understanding. It appears that children initially use the rhythms of speech in their songs and depend on note values of the same duration. With development, rhythmic patterns consisting primarily of duple subdivisions are differentiated from the pulse of the words, as children are able to focus on the musical, rather than the narrative aspects of songs. Finally, it appears that the rhythmic vocabulary grows from the standard songs which children are taught. In summary, there are three critical levels of rhythm: the pulse, the subdivisions of the pulse or activity within the pulse or subdivisions, and the activity which takes place across the pulse. We will consider each of these in turn.

Pulse and Tempo

Children between the ages of 1:0 and 2:8 are alive to some fundamental qualities of sound patterns. However, for such young children, rhythm is not a separable dimension of musical performance. It is fused with other qualities for example, loudness. Moreover, children have little that approaches metric organization—the length and number of groupings are determined much more by breathing, speaking, and the rhythm of motor activity than by any interest in a maintaining a steady pulse or engaging the interaction of that pulse with a surface or figural pattern. These qualities show up clearly in Kori's phrase at 1:6. This bit of melody contains an accelerando and a crescendo which makes it more of a dynamic "gesture" than a conventional musical phrase. Even though the song continues for two more phrases—each like the first—no regular pulse occurs.

At this level, children organize their singing on the basis of a regular pulse. While children create a pulse that is regular within phrases, they do not hold this pulse constant across phrases. Consequently, the rests between phrases are not determined by rhythmic pulse. Instead, they are controlled by extramusical factors (e.g., how long it takes to breathe, or to think up the next phrase). This ability

Figure 6.9. Kori (1:6) Song

to generate a regular pulse is analogous to the emergence of the two discrete boundary pitches from the undifferentiated cooing in the first level of contour schemes. While children may match the tempo of particular songs, they still reduce any song's specific surface pattern (typically involving subdivisions of the pulse) to a series of even pulses. Consequently, at this level, children's renditions of standard songs, as well as their own compositions, lack the interplay between an underlying pulse and surface figural patterns.

During their early years, children can imitate changes in pace or tempo, speeding up or slowing down their singing in response to someone else's modeling. However, they only rarely imitate a specific tempo or pulse. Instead they appear to catch on to a broad quality of quickness or slowness. In a similar vein, children don't repeat the exact number of pulses or figural groupings. Nor do they treat the tempo of their performances as a separate dimension of performance. When children occasionally imitate changes in dynamics, these imitations usually affect the tempo of their performance so that softer phrases tend to be slower while louder phrases are apt to be faster.

Later, children match the pace of songs accurately, particularly when they mimic another's tempo while they chant or sing recitatives. Similarly, when children echo parallel motor activity with vocal patterns for example, chanting as they draw dots or stripes), they exhibit this same ability to change pace easily. In singing standard songs, children are able to preserve the characteristic pattern of subdivisions or the surface rhythms within phrases. However, in invented songs, children frequently mix subdivisions of two and three units suggesting that the notion of using a specific subdivision to guide a phrase is still unstable.

Rhythmic Patterns Within a Pulse

A major milestone of rhythmic development occurs when children begin to perform songs using both an underlying pulse and a differentiated rhythmic figure occurring within the duration of a pulse. As in the previous level, children hold the pulse within phrases constant. However, they modify the steady pulse by subdividing it into two or three parts. With the appearance of this ability, young children acquire the rhythmic knowledge necessary for most of the vocal music they will be taught. However, during this period, one finds songs that show normal children mixing up duple and triple subdivisions of the pulse.

Rhythmic Patterns Across Pulse

This level represents another major change in children's mastery of temporal relationships. At this level, children's song performances show that they can maintain a pulse even without sounding it. Thus, a rhythmic pattern can be draped over an ongoing pulse, creating smoother and more dynamic groupings. This is a strong indication that songs are not merely carefully pitched and regulated speech.

Now the normal child begins to deliver the words in line with musical concerns. The duration of the pauses between text phrases is dictated by the pulse of the music. Put differently, children have now acquired the ability to sing phrases regulated by the same pulse. For example, when Jonathan composes a song about a marble machine (one of his toys), he shows more than phrase-specific awareness of rhythmic organization in the second phrase, "He was goin' down the thing." His ability to suspend marking every pulse in this phrase creates a rhythmic effect which contrasts with that of the initial phrase where each pulse is realized in the surface.

SUMMARY: RHYTHMIC UNDERSTANDING

In both standard and invented songs, children between one and three years organize their performances using single-level, phrase-specific rhythmic structures. By about age three, they begin to use a regulating pulse within individual phrases, first matching and then differentiating surface figures from the underlying beat. Finally, during their fifth year, the children in this study were able to ignore the pull of the pulse and sustain a duration across pulses. From our perspective, this signals the onset of songwide rhythmic structures. It is at this level that children can achieve the overall rhythmic organizations that will evoke listeners' expectations of culturally familiar songs. It is also at this moment that young singers are in a position to manipulate the rhythmic elements of their songs in such a way that internal reference becomes a possibility.

Just as the ability to sing the contour of a melody is a developmental achievement, so is the ability to realize its rhythmic shape. These data show that children construct an understanding of rhythmic structures in ways which parallel their construction of pitch structures: by establishing boundary areas and then articulating the space between the limits of the boundary. For rhythm, children first reduce the rich figural surface of a song to a single periodic unit—the pulse. After they establish this regulating unit they eventually divide the space between the units into durations of even and uneven lengths, thereby creating the varied surface patterns of songs. These abilities carry with them certain other musical skills such as the ability to control the endings of phrases and songs for expressive purposes.

Although 5-year-olds have most of the elements of rhythm in hand, there is clearly some distance between what they achieve and mastery of the full complexities of rhythmic organization. Specifically, there is still little evidence that they can group pulses into patterns which reflect the accented-unaccented shapes. They work at the level of sequences of pulses not yet organized by meter. Pflederer (1964) reports that this ability will not emerge for some time.

The analysis of the rhythmic development shows that 5-year-olds begin to distinguish between the materials of speech and the materials of music. At first, each syllable is sung to a single pitch, forming a one-to-one correspondence between the text and the melodic-rhythmic shape. By the end of the preschool years, however, children begin to sing melodies in which a many-to-one relationship obtains. The performance of many notes on a single syllable marks a major achievement in the musical development of the child. It signals the beginning independence of music from lyrics.

Finally, based on these findings, there is no significant relationship between the levels of contour scheme and the levels of rhythmic control. The two scales are independent. Although they share a common source, standard songs of the culture, pitch, and rhythm develop in their own time.

PERFORMANCE BY A GIFTED CHILD

So far, this report has traced the musical development of the average child. What about the gifted child? How does a child of unusual musical talent develop? To consider this question, we were fortunate to have access to the rich documentation of an unusual child from the first songs she sang at around the age of 2 to her early school years. The richness of her range of activities, the focus on vocal performance (and not the more typical instrumental performance), and the quantity of available material made considering her musical development irresistible.

Ashima, the singer of the second version of "Somewhere Over the Rainbow" cited in the beginning of this chapter, is an only child. Her parents are both practicing musicians. Growing up in a musical household, she regularly witnessed the many private lessons her parents taught in their home. As soon as she could talk, Ashima learned to sing using Solfege syllables. By the age of 2, she was singing children's songs and traditional songs with adult-like competence in rendering the pitches and rhythms. Music making was the primary activity for both parents and everyone was expected to take part in performances. She studied the cello for a time after her fourth birthday, and she has studied piano for several years. At 9 years of age, she begun studying composition, and at ten she was invited to play the lead role in "Annie," now performing music she has been singing since she was 3 years old.

In sharp contrast to the picture of normal development sketched above, the song performances of this musically gifted child differ on nearly every dimension—faithfulness to the contour of the model song, awareness of direction, stability of pitch, and an extraordinary capacity to realize, invent, and use nuance and drama to support an interpretation. The songs below illustrate (as well as can be accomplished on paper) these characteristics.

"Nelly Was a Moo Moo"

One of the songs she invented is for an opera she is making up with her animal dolls: "Nelly Was a Moo Moo" is sung by the cow. The remarkable quality of this song is the contrast between her grasp of text and her ability to coordinate the musical elements of the song.

Figure 6.10. Ashima (2:4) "Nelly was a Moo Moo"

The rhythm may have its origin in the text, "Nelly Was a Moo, Moo." But even if that is the case, she need not have elongated the note values on "moo," nor did she need to repeat "moo," thereby extending the phrase. Is it possible that she is in some tacit way aware of balance? Whether or not she is aware of musical structure she is certainly able to control the pitches of the song. In performance, she is clearly able to perform notes in a way that projects a stable key— quite unlike average children of her age and older. Furthermore, she appears to understand the importance of emphasizing certain notes rather than others. Here we need to be very cautious because it is easy to infer that she already understands and uses knowledge of the harmonic structure of music (the first phrase ends on the dominant; the second on the tonic). Caution in this regard is rewarded. Further investigation reveals that she is unable to use that "knowledge" in other settings. If she could harmonize a melody, sing appropriate notes to form a counterpoint, and so on, one might be more willing to credit her knowledge of harmonic structure.

"Hockett Games"

Over a period of years, Ashima and her father played a musical game which reveals a great deal about her ability to perceive and construct musical relationships. Her father would usually begin, often to refocus her attention on a given musical task. He would sing the beginning of a phrase and then leave the ending or the final few notes for

Ashima sings the notes on the treble staff. Her father sings the notes on the bass staff. Typically, there are small pauses between the notes that are passed.

Figure 6.11. Ashima (2:6) and her father "Hocketing"

Ashima to finish. Occasionally, Ashima would turn the tables on him and leave him with the task of completing the melodic phrase. Two things about her performance of this game are remarkable: her ability to quickly recognize the melody being modeled and her capability to match the key of the piece while filling in the necessary notes to complete the section. She delighted in this game, often smiling slyly while singing "false" notes which failed to complete the phrase or segment. For example, sometimes in response to a portion of a major scale her father would begin, Ashima would finish it, but purposely sing scale degree two or three instead of closing on the expected first scale degree. This indicates that her knowledge of tonal structures even at 3 years old is far beyond the contour scheme knowledge typical of normal children of that age, and even older.

"Tomorrow"

Ashima's rendition of the song "Tomorrow," from the musical "Annie" is always remarkable. For one thing, she is able to sing the octave with ease. Intervals occurring later in the song are even more difficult to negotiate, yet she does so with unerring accuracy and, therefore, stability. Indeed, in performance she is more like an adult than a child. She can transpose the song up or down. There are versions during the "Hocket Game" in which her father begins the song on notes in the standard key of the song. Ashima immediately adjusts and effortlessly continues the phrases.

To- mor- row,

Figure 6.12. Ashima (2:6) "Tomorrow"

"Iguana"

Several things make this performance special. First, the absolute confidence with which she performs the song is unusual. It is possible to consider her delivery of the song on a scale not tailored to capture children's typical style—a scale used for evaluating adult performers. Her performance has "class"—dramatic flair, a sense of delivery. Her singing and accompanying movements are not only coordinated, they reinforce one another. This young singer is really performing. The first phrases are sung legato, smooth, and con-

IGUANA

Words and Music by
DAVID S. POLANSKY

Figure 6.13.   Ashima (2:8) "Iguana"

nected. The dynamic level is generally soft. She gently turns to the left and right as she sings. Her delivery and use of nuance of the song reflects its structure. She coordinates her posture and dynamics to good effect—bending down and getting soft for the scary part and standing straight up and delivering the final refrain full voice.

She transposes up and down easily. Unlike normal children who tend to sing in their own register, she is able to adjust her voice to the needs of the specific accompaniment, and she is able to pick out her starting note from the introductory chord or phrase.

WHAT MAKES IT POSSIBLE FOR A CHILD TO DO THIS?

Normal children's mastery of tonal space proceeds along three lines: establishing the limits of the highest and lowest notes of phrases, which was discussed as the register or tonal frame; establishing the appropriate melodic motion or direction of the notes within a phrase; and the stability and relationship of individual pitches to one another required to project the scalar organization of the pitches of a song. But Ashima's development shows no signs of traversing such a path. Register and tonal frame, direction and contour, and the stability of the pitches she sings by the age of 3 all reflect adult standards of performance. After that, her focus in musical performance is on learning repertoire and exploring tonal and rhythmic nuance.

So far we have considered the innermost of the three concentric circles in some detail—the development of Ashima's individual talent. While it would be convenient to attribute Ashima's musical ability to innate gifts inherited from her parents and close this chapter, that story needs to be followed by the question: Is it the whole case? We think not. Because talent withers without necessary and sufficient scaffolding, we need to consider the second of the circles, the support conditions which contribute to the growth of the individual's gift.

CONDITIONS OF SUPPORT

This level consists of the local factors which surround, guide, and stimulate the flowering of whatever special capacities a child possesses. At first, these factors are limited to what the family and home provide. As the social world of the individual expands, they include a wider range of conditions and people.

The home conditions supporting musical development differ widely. They were remarkably different for the children in the longitudinal study described earlier and this gifted little girl. The children of the longitudinal study grew up in average homes, households in which musical expression was not common among the adults, where the children's primary musical activity was limited to listening to recordings and singing children's songs. Unlike the cross-sectional cohort, their musical activity was supported beyond the average by a researcher's visit twice a month.

In contrast, Ashima grew up in a home where musical expression—performance, listening, and discussion—was a normal part of everyday life for everyone in the household, children *and* adults. The conditions of her preschool years supported musical practice in its richest forms. This aspect of gift, the conditions of support, is rarely discussed in the literature. It is worth elaborating some of them here: environments and tools, and community and peers.

Environment and Tools

Supportive environments and tools abound during the preschool years: Parents are concerned that their children have ample opportunities for exploration and provide toys, tools, and playtime; support groups are formed to ensure children develop inter- and intra-personal skills and confidence. The array of occasions for development plays a significant role in the growth of a latent gift. Within the home and before the onset of schooling, many supports are possible: recordings of songs, tape and video playback/recording equipment to document important performances, singing games with parents (like the "hockett games" Ashima played with her parents), as well as a variety of musical instruments.

Making music in a variety of settings is also important. It encourages generalizing musical materials and repertory. Building personal relationships and performing with a variety of people are important when developing skills. In these settings musical standards are negotiated and defined.

In a context of rich musical engagement, the scope of activity extends beyond the more obvious manifestation of giftedness—the performance. In Ashima's case, performances took place in a context where her ability was buttressed by imitation and modeling, games involving skills of discrimination, and lots of discussion about what she was doing musically. Her perceptual and reflective skills were engaged in contexts where critical judgment and discriminations were part of everyday practice and experience (Davidson & Scripp, 1992).

Community and Peers

It is becoming clearer that genius depends on the conventions of the culture, its distribution systems, evaluative criticism from many sources including critics, and support of various kinds from all quarters, including patronage systems and so on (Becker, 1982; Csikszentmihalyi, 1987). Analysis of the workings of the art world supports Gardner's claim that giftedness shows itself in combinations of intelligences rather than within a single intelligence (Gardner, 1983). Finally, what appears to be intelligent behavior, giftedness, or propensity for a domain may only appear under conditions which may, but often may not, be supported by the academic structure of schools (Newman, Griffin, & Cole, 1989).

The influence of more and less capable others, even within a peer group, cannot be underestimated. The support of one's fellow students or workers is important because discussions, criticisms, and suggestions create conditions which make it possible to establish and refine goals, develop working habits, and form one's own identity and relation to a chosen field of activity.

The children in this report were all first-borns so they were not influenced by older siblings. What was their view of their performances during this time? The children in the cross-sectional study frequently interacted with other neighborhood children; sometimes the song the researchers taught the week before sounded through the streets as they went to see one of the young subjects. During her preschool years Ashima appeared to have no knowledge that her performance ability was any different from that of other children. Indeed it was not until two or three years after she started elementary school that she began to evaluate and compare her experience with that of other children—her classmates. One day, without being asked, she reported on what she observed in school. The day's activities had included singing familiar and new songs. She commented to her father, "These kids don't sing very well."

REFERENCES

Bamberger, J. (1986). Cognitive issues in the development of musically gifted children. In R. Sternberg & J. Davidson (Eds.), *Conceptions of giftedness* (pp. 388–413). New York: Cambridge University Press.

Bamberger, J. (1991). *The mind behind the musical ear: How children develop musical intelligence.* Cambridge, MA: Harvard University Press.

Bartlett, F. C. (1958). *Thinking: An experimental and social study.* New York: Basic Books.

Becker, H. S. (1982). *Art worlds.* Berkeley, CA: University of California Press.

Bridges, V. A. (1965). *An exploratory study of the harmonic discrimination ability of children in kindergarten through grade three in two se-*

lected schools. Unpublished doctoral dissertation, Ohio State University.

Chang, H., & Trehub, S. E. (1977a). Auditory processing of relational information by young infants. *Journal of Experimental Child Psychology, 24,* 324–331.

Chang, H., & Trehub, S. E. (1977b). Infant's perception of temporal grouping in auditory patterns. *Child Development, 48,* 1666–1670.

Csikszentmihalyi, M. (1987). Society, culture and person: A systems view of creativity. In R. Sternberg (Ed.), *The nature of creativity* (pp. 325–329). New York: Cambridge University Press.

Csikszentmihalyi, M., & Robinson, R. E. (1986). Culture, time, and the development of talent. In R. Sternberg & J. Davidson (Eds.), *Conceptions of giftedness* (pp. 264–284). New York: Cambridge University Press.

Davidson, L. (1985). Tonal structures of children's early songs. *Music Perception, 2*(3), 361–373.

Davidson, L., & Scripp, L. (1992). Surveying the coordinates of cognitive skills in music. In R. Colwell (Ed.), *The handbook of music research and learning* (pp. 1293–1328). New York: Macmillan Press.

Davidson, L., & Scripp, L. (1988). Young children's musical representations: Windows on music cognition. In J. Sloboda (Ed.), *Generative processes in music* (pp. 195–230). Oxford: Oxford University Press.

Deutsch, D. (Ed.). (1982). *The psychology of music.* New York: Academic Press.

Dowling, W. J., & Harwood, D. L. (1986). *Music cognition.* New York: Academic Press.

Feldman, D. H. (1980). *Beyond universals in cognitive development.* Norwood, NJ: Ablex.

Feldman, D. H., & Goldsmith, L. T. (1986). *Nature's gambit: Child prodigies and the development of human potential.* New York: Basic Books.

Fox, D. B. (1990). An analysis of the pitch characteristics of infant vocalizations. *Psychomusicology, 9,* 21–30.

Gardner, H. (1983). *Frames of mind: The theory of multiple intelligences.* New York: Basic Books.

Gruber, H. E. (1986). The self-construction of the extraordinary. In R. Sternberg & J. Davidson (Eds.), *Conceptions of giftedness* (pp. 247–263). New York: Cambridge University Press.

Hargreaves, D. (1986). *The developmental psychology of music.* New York: Cambridge University Press.

Michel, P. (1973). The optimum development of musical abilities in the first years of life. *Psychology of Music, 1*(1), 14–20.

Moog, H. (1968). *The musical experience of the pre-school child.* London: Schott.

Moorehead, G. E., & Pond, D. (1941). *Music of young children.* Pillsbury Foundation Study.

Newman, D., Griffin, P., & Cole, M. (1989). *The construction zone: Working for cognitive change in school.* New York: Cambridge University Press.

Pflederer, M. (1964). The responses of children to musical tasks embodying Piaget's principle of conservation. *Journal for Research in Music Education, 12*, 251–268.

Rainbow, E. L. (1977). A longitudinal investigation of the rhythmic abilities of pre-school aged children. *Council for Research in Music Education Bulletin, 50*, 55–61.

Renzulli, J. S. (1986). The Three-Ring conception of giftedness: A developmental model for creative productivity. In R. Sternberg & J. Davidson (Eds.), *Conceptions of giftedness* (pp. 53–92). New York: Cambridge University Press.

Rogoff, B. (1990). *Apprenticeship in thinking*. Cambridge, MA: Harvard University Press.

Sargeant, D. C., & Roche, S. (1973). Perceptual shifts in the auditory information processing of young children. *Psychology of Music, 1*(1), 39–48.

Shuter-Dyson, R. (1968). *The psychology of musical ability*. London: Methuen.

Sloboda, J. (1985). *The musical mind: The cognitive psychology of music*. Oxford: Oxford University Press.

Sloboda, J. (Ed.). (1986). *Generative processes in music*. Oxford: Oxford University Press.

Sternberg, R. J., & Davidson, J. E. (1986). *Conceptions of giftedness*. New York: Cambridge University Press.

Teplov, B. M. (1966). *Psychologie des aptitudes musicales*. Paris: Presses Universitaires de France.

Terman, L. M. (1925). Mental and physical traits of a thousand gifted children. *Genetic studies of genius* (Vol. I). Stanford, CA: Stanford University Press.

Updegraff, R., Heileger, L., & Learned, J. (1938). The effect of training upon the singing ability and musical interest of three-, four-, and five-year-old children. *University of Iowa Studies in Child Welfare, 14*, 83–121.

Vygotsky, L. S. (1978). *Mind in society: The development of higher psychological processes*. Cambridge, MA: Harvard University Press.

Walter, J., & Gardner, H. (1986). The crystallizing experience: Discovering an intellectual gift. In R. Sternberg & J. Davidson (Eds.), *Conceptions of giftedness* (pp. 306–331). New York: Cambridge University Press.

Wertsch, J. V. (1985). *Vygotsky and the social formation of mind*. Cambridge, MA: Harvard University Press.

Wing, H. D. (1963). Is musical aptitude innate? *Psychology of Music, 1*(1).

Wohlwill, J. F. (1973). *The study of behavioral development*. New York: Academic Press.

7

Giftedness and Professional Training: The Impact of Music Reading Skills on Musical Development of Conservatory Students

Larry Scripp
Lyle Davidson

In the last chapter we considered the differences between the development of normal children and the musically gifted. This chapter considers what happens to the musically gifted as they continue their development, honing their skills to enter the highly competitive life of the professional musician. To help set the parameters of the training, we will first consider the autobiographical account of a great pianist, Arthur Rubinstein. We will then consider what implications his account has for the professional training of musical talent. Data collected from a longitudinal study of gifted musicians' music reading skills provide fresh evidence that neither early detection of giftedness nor intensive early training in an artistic domain such as music assures smooth passage through later, equally essential, levels of development.

DEFINING THE PARAMETERS OF MUSICAL
THOUGHT AND TRAINING

Rubinstein's parents, aware that he possessed a keen interest in playing the piano, went to master violinist Joseph Joachim to determine the extent of their child's musical gifts (Rubinstein, 1973). Although still very young, Rubinstein had already developed considerable expertise in piano performance skills. Nonetheless, Joachim wanted to know more about the scope of the precocious child's musical development. He asked Rubinstein to name and repeat specific notes after they were played, play back notes and melodies which were hummed, harmonize melodies, and transpose passages from one key to another. Concerned about the scope of the young pianist's knowledge, Joachim recommended that the child be taken to concerts of good vocal singing, and that his sightreading be improved.

Joachim was concerned with far more than the prodigy's facility on the piano. His view of musical ability extended well beyond the demands of the instrument and immediate needs of the instrumentalist. He was concerned with several different areas of musical thought, its transfer across different contexts (performance, perception, and composition), and the integration of skills into a network of relationships which reflect a coherent understanding of the domain.

Following Joachim's advice, Rubinstein did learn to sightread, compose, and improvise music. He did listen to a wide variety of music during his early training. We cannot tell what impact this training had on Rubinstein, but we can ask how Rubinstein's experience compares to the experience of the average music student of today. For example, by looking carefully at the development of music reading skills in conservatory training, we can begin to infer the changes and transformations Joachim sought to bring about when he recommended that Rubinstein learn to sightread. In other words, how do musical capacities develop when those who possess a talent for performing music begin to master the additional skills Joachim recommends?

WHAT MUSICAL TRAINING CONTRIBUTES
TO MUSICAL INTELLIGENCE OF THE GIFTED

Gifted children can be distinguished by their ability to approach music from multiple perspectives. According to Bamberger, for example, musical perception proceeds from figural aspects to the more formal aspects of music. While most children (and untrained adults) perceive the figural aspects early in the course of musical development (attending to grouping of rhythmic or pitch elements that form musical phrases), the perception of the more formal aspects of music (e.g., representation of musical phrases in terms of tonal or metrical systems) appears possible only in conjunction with musical training. The final stages of musical development of the musically gifted, however, depend on the capacity to freely attend to, and shift focus among the more figural/intuitive and the more formal/metrical aspects embedded in rich musical phenomena (Bamberger, 1991).

From another point of view, developing an operational grasp of tonal materials is a particularly important step along the route to musical development. Young children, for example, may learn to imitate musical phrases easily but they are usually unable to represent their knowledge of the music in any other manner (e.g., in a new key, style, backwards, etc.). Here the ability to transform the music freely is a matter of further development. In both cases, we suggest that later stages of development are characterized by mixing modes of representation, a process by which tonal knowledge becomes increasingly articulated and internalized, and which does not occur without training.

We can now better appreciate Joachim's advice to the young Rubinstein. Joachim wanted Rubinstein's training to include opportunities for developing multiple representations of musical knowledge extending beyond the conditions and intensive support he was already receiving. Joachim felt this level of command was necessary to sustain Rubinstein's artistic career. Generalizing beyond this case, however, we need to ask how this development takes place for a broader population of musically gifted performers.

LOOKING BEYOND PERFORMANCE FOR EVIDENCE OF MUSICAL UNDERSTANDING

Knowledge of how to play a particular instrument, usually the entire focus of early musical training, is not enough to foster the kind of development expected of the musically gifted. That is, reciting memorized literature at auditions does not necessarily correlate well with a broad range of musical knowledge. For example, in a study conducted at several schools of music, including the New England Conservatory, approximately 80% of incoming students (American) were unable to notate accurately the well-known song "Happy Birthday" (Davidson, Scripp, & Welsh, 1989). Imagine, if you will, music students who easily sing and play the tune on their instrument, yet who cannot verify the accuracy of their notations without the use of an instrument.

What does this suggest about this population of gifted performers who have studied music privately and participated in ensembles for years? One view suggests that these students know very little about music. A more useful view suggests that these data indicate the nature of the educational challenge facing musically gifted students: how to form and coordinate multiple representations of their knowledge of music.

Correct Version

**Figure 7.1. Notations of the tune "Happy Birthday" by entering
conservatory students**

Analyzing the patterns of misunderstandings may reveal more
about the problems of coordinating diverse aspects of musical
knowledge. As we see from the example above, these students have
trouble reconciling particular (figural) features of the melody in
question with general (formal) assumptions about music. In this
case, entering conservatory students commonly presuppose that
simple songs conform to the pattern of four beats to the measure, or
that simple melodies begin and end with the same pitch (the tonic or
first note of the scale). Ignoring the rhythmic grouping or melodic
contour of the melody, these students distort the details of the tune
in relation to general assumptions about the music. Unfortunately,
they do not yet have the ability to verify their presumptions because
of a lack of coordination between performance knowledge and their

understanding of the notation system. However, it is precisely the integration between performance, internal aural perception, and representational skills which suggests the development of underlying musical cognition for the performing musician (Davidson & Scripp, 1992).

Assessing Mastery of the Symbol System Through Reading Skills

There is wide agreement that the mastery of symbol systems extends the range of thinking in a particular domain. Olson, for example, stresses the function of symbol systems as thinking tools: "Skillful use of a symbolic system involves the mastery of both its structure and its rules of transformation as modes of thought. Once mastered, these symbolic skills may be considered as forms of intelligence primarily because the range of their applicability is virtually limitless" (Olson, 1978, p. 63).

On the other hand, some question the necessity of performing artists mastering the conventional symbol system for music. For instance, while Gardner (1972) claims that the ability to use a symbol system skillfully and consistently implies operational knowledge of the symbolic elements in an artistic domain, he disclaims the importance of this skill for the musically gifted by adding that "the ability to read notations is a helpful, but not essential, adjunct for most performing artists" (p. 307).

The contradiction between these two views of symbol systems has direct bearing on our view of the musically gifted. While evidence from a variety of sources suggests that the musically gifted prosper in environments that support the coordination of multiple perspectives on cognitive skills in relation to the symbol system of the domain (Davidson & Scripp, 1992), it is clear that the integration of reading skills is not easily achieved with training. For example, gifted performers beginning their conservatory training can read simple unfamiliar tunes with their instrument but show relatively primitive understanding when asked to sing comparable tunes at sight. Again, despite a great deal of performance experience and years of private lessons in music, these students cannot transfer the ability to read music across two different modes of performance. As a result, entering conservatory students reading unfamiliar music often show little of the tonal understanding untrained children display while rendering and representing familiar songs (Davidson & Scripp, 1989, 1988a).

The examples below draw from a case study of a conservatory voice student, Jeanie, whose music reading skills are representative of many entering college-level music students. Although this vocal major easily sightreads a melody on the piano—an instrument on which she has had no formal training—her vocal rendition is full of errors. With her voice she can only match the broad outlines of the melodic contour, suggesting a relatively imprecise grasp of the symbol system. Comparing the sightsinging performance to the written music given suggests how disparate these skills can be.

Top Line: Melody to be Sung or Played at Sight

Bottom Line: Sightplay Performance
Semester One

Figure 7.2a. Sightreading with an instrument

Top Line: Melody to be Sung or Played at Sight

Bottom Line: Sightsinging Performance
Semester One

Figure 7.2b. Sightreading without an instrument

These examples further suggest instrumental performance effectively masks a far less sophisticated internal understanding of music: in this case, the ability to construct a coherent, tonal melody from notation without previous hearing or the use of an instrument.

Would Jeanie perform any differently if she took the time to learn the first few measures of the melody by rote first? In other words, once the tonality of the piece is established, can we then expect a more coherent rendition of the melody? The example in Figure 7.3 suggests otherwise. After learning to sing the first two measures of a melody through rote imitation, she is again unable to retain the previous tonal framework, let alone sustain the thread of the notated melody, without the support of piano accompaniment.

The inability of many incoming first-year students to perform music reliably without the use of a mechanical instrument suggests a crisis in the development of the gifted musician. Recognizing that

COMPLETE THE MELODY TASK

Top Line: Melody to be Sung at Sight after Rehearsing after Rehearsing the First Phrase

Bottom Line: Sightsing Performance

Figure 7.3. Complete the melody task

there may indeed be such a crisis in the making, the New England Conservatory sponsored a research agenda investigating how musical development occurs in relation to the skilled understanding of the symbol system.

THE NEW ENGLAND CONSERVATORY MUSIC READING PROJECT

Reported in this chapter are findings based on a small sample of data selected from a 2-year longitudinal research effort at the New England Conservatory of Music. Specifically, this research project investigated the relationship between *sightplaying* (unaccompanied sightreading with an instrument) and *sightsinging* skills (unaccompanied sightreading without an instrument). Analyses of the data collected in this study suggest a new way to look at the nature of performance knowledge and an expanded conception of musical development for the musically gifted.

The New England Conservatory supported this study because of the ongoing controversy among musicians concerning the appropriate focus of music education for the musically gifted in relation to music reading skills. Although previous research in music reading provides strong evidence for underlying music cognition when comparing expert with novice pianists in terms of eye movements (Bean, 1938), information processing models (Wolf, 1976), or sensitivity to musical structure (Sloboda, 1984), it provided little insight into the differences across modalities of music reading. Since previous research focused on the mechanical translation of symbol to sound, the more intrinsic aspects of reading processes remained mysterious to both the researchers and the participants. In short, the ability to anticipate sounds mentally was not explored as a measure of musical understanding in the reading process.

When mental imagery is stressed in past research, it usually takes the form of advice from an educator or personal introspection from psychologists of music. For example, some educators specify singing as an effective way of engaging musicians mentally while reading music—and later accommodating the technical demands of the instrument afterwards: "Control of pitch when singing is largely a mental process. Regular vocalizing during the instrumental class may result in the players' increased ability to relate musical notation to sounds rather than to specific fingerings or slide positions" (Mursell & Glenn, 1938, p. 308).

Psychologists of music stress the value of tonal imagery as the underlying basis for music cognition for the practicing musician. Seashore, for example, spotlights internal tonal imagery as the surest index of tonal understanding. For him the capacity to hear "concrete, faithful, and vivid tonal imagery" (1967, p. 5) through the mind's ear appears to be directly measurable in the task of sightsinging:

> . . . The power of concrete, faithful, and vivid tonal imagery. This capacity I should say, is the outstanding mark of a musical mind at the representation level—the capacity of living in a representative tonal world. This capacity brings the tonal material into the present; it colors and greatly enriches the actual hearing of musical sounds; it already determines the character and realism of the emotional experience; it is familiarity with these images which makes the cognitive memory for music realistic. Thus, tonal imagery is a condition for learning, for retention, for recall, for recognition, and for the anticipation of musical facts. Take out the image from the musical mind and you take out its very essence. (Seashore, 1967, pp. 5–6)

Still missing, however, is empirical evidence for the development of internal imagery in relation to music reading skills. Speculation that sightsinging skills are the link between internal tonal imagery and instrumental sightreading motivated earlier classroom studies in sightsinging development (Davidson & Scripp, 1988c, 1988d) at New England Conservatory. Although these studies identified levels of development in terms of classroom behaviors (reliance on cues, ability to resist miscues, degree of eye contact), little was learned about the impact of sightsinging skills in relation to instrumental reading skills.

The Pilot Study

Data analyzed from the initial pilot study ($N = 16$), however, strongly suggest that music reading skills vary considerably across modes of performance. Most NEC students are instrumental majors with little singing experience. Not surprisingly, overall measures of pitch accuracy (total errors scored in seven sightplaying and seven sightsinging items) show that these students are much more precise sight-readers on their instruments (3.3 errors average per seven short tonal melodies) than with their voice (68.1 errors average). Two results are surprising:

1. On average, vocal majors were no better at sightsinging than the instrumental majors.
2. Second-year students were not significantly better at sight-singing than first-year students.

The first finding strongly suggests that the ability to construct an accurate reading of the music without the support of a musical instrument is a skill expressed with the voice, but not acquired through voice or instrumental lessons. The second finding suggests the skill of sightsinging is not easily improved with instruction. Although accuracy does tend to improve with the second-year students, the improvement does not appear to be significant.

The pilot study also revealed sharp differences between primary dimensions of performance accuracy (of pitch and rhythm) in sight-singing and sightplaying. Differences in accuracy across the two performance conditions were much more pronounced in pitch than with rhythm inferring that these variables represent independent aspects of music reading skills. Specifically, pitch accuracy varies radically according to the mode of performance while rhythmic accuracy does not.

While these data suggest that rhythmic development is more stable than pitch development, we are left to speculate why this is so. One possible hypothesis is that the musically gifted are more extensively trained in rhythm. Another hypothesis is that the conditions of performance support the internalization of musical knowledge in different ways. While performance of pitch is externally defined on an instrument, rhythm is not. In other words, pressing the key of a piano has more to do with producing a unique pitch than a particular duration. Since there is no key to press for a specific durational value or rhythmic configuration on the piano, we can assume that rhythmic production relies more on internal representation.

Further analyses of these data support the differentiation of pitch and rhythmic accuracy in terms of the level of internalization of music reading skills. In other words, given comparable pieces to read, pitch accuracy depends on the mode of production. Accordingly, there is no significant correlation between sightplaying (SP) and sightsinging (SS) when considering pitch accuracy. In stark contrast, rhythmic accuracy shows strong positive and statistically significant correlations across the two conditions of performance (see numerous examples in Figure 7.4). This suggests that rhythmic reading skills are not specific to the mode of performance but rather the level of internal representation governing both modes of performance.

	SP pitch	SS pitch	SP rhythm	SS rhythm	SP overall	SS overall
SP pitch accuracy	+					
SS pitch accuracy	N.S.	+				
SP rhythmic accuracy	N.S.	N.S.	+			
SS rhythmic accuracy	N.S.	N.S.	.76 p<.001	+		
SP overall accuracy	N.S.	N.S.	.96 p<.0001	.70 p<.003	+	
SS overall accuracy	N.S.	.88 p<.0001	.61 p<.01	.70 p.<.003	.60 p<.02	+

[Pearson correlation coefficient r=.76, p<.001] between both SP (Sightplaying) and SS (Sightsinging) conditions.

Figure 7.4. Pearson Correlation Coefficients between measures of accuracy in sightreading [Pilot Study: Scripp, 1986]

Correlational analysis reveals trends that suggest producing pitch without the instrument (SS pitch accuracy) predicts accurate performance in sightsinging ($r = .88$, $p < .0001$). On the other hand, rhythmic accuracy in instrumental performance (SP rhythm) appears to be virtually synonymous with overall accuracy on the instrument (SP overall). This suggests that pitch in sightsinging is the crucial difference in expanding cross-modal reading skills.

The lack of correlation between producing correct pitches on the instrument and any other measure of sightreading accuracy implies that learning to "play the right notes" develops in isolation from the skills necessary for reading rhythm or producing pitch vocally. Put more starkly, more internalized reading skills do not necessarily develop with instrumental training. It appears that the development of sightsinging skills provides the basis for integrative music reading skills for the musically gifted.

The Longitudinal Sample

Although sightsinging skills appeared crucial to expanding and internalizing music reading skills, little was known as to how the stages of development might unfold. Accordingly, a commitment to a longitudinal research design was made in order to systematically observe changes in music reading skills at the individual level.

The participants ($N = 87$) were randomly selected from a population of students taking courses in sightsinging at New England Conservatory. These courses are required for all students regardless of background or instrumental major in virtually every college-level music degree program. Hence, the sample represents the range of background experience and performing skills of students typically found at any major conservatory of music in the United States.

Longitudinal data collection occurred four times over a 2-year period. The participants were given four different yet comparable versions of a sightreading test, the Watkins-Farnum Performance Scale (Watkins & Farnum, 1954), a widely used standardized test for sightreading on instruments. The examples were rewritten for appropriate vocal range and in clefs familiar to each student. In addition, error detection exercises and interview questions were given at each sampling point.

Evidence for Development

The data collected in this study consist of three fundamental aspects of musical knowledge in relation to music reading: production, perception, and reflection. Based on the guiding principles of assessment recently developed in arts programs (Gardner, 1989; Winner, Davidson, & Scripp, 1992), we can begin to understand the context of reading skills in these three dimensions. The experimental design, therefore, provides insight into performance knowledge in two modalities of performance (production), error detection (perception), and responses to questions, unsolicited comments, and introspective writing during the course of the study (reflection).

In the following case study, taken from the longitudinal study of New England Conservatory student reading skills, we see how a gifted student increasingly coordinates related facets of the reading process.

A Case Study: Jeanie's Music Reading Development

After Jeanie applied to New England Conservatory she learned she was admitted for two reasons: her extensive experience singing in semi-professional musical theater productions and the faculty's recognition of her potential to become a professional artist. Her gift is readily displayed in her singing, her performance demeanor, and her commitment to beginning professional training. At no time was she asked to sightread music in her audition—standard procedure for most applicants. The first steps toward artistic development, however, began with two years of music reading (solfege) classes (for a description of this curriculum see Davidson & Scripp, 1988b, 1988c) along with her lessons in vocal technique and repertoire.

Beginning with the disparity between instrumental reading skills and sightsinging skills revealed in our first examples, we trace Jeanie's progress over a 2-year period. She struggled to develop her performance and perceptual skills through sightsinging training. Happily, we can report that Jeanie mastered these skills through much hard work, completed her undergraduate studies and is now in graduate school. More significant in terms of the research, she reports that her musical development primarily involved integrating her newly acquired music reading skills with her gift as a performing artist.

Figure 7.5 is a quantitative survey of Jeanie's development in sightsinging. It requires considerable interpretation in order to see clearly the possible connections between these various skills and how, when taken together, they suggest qualitatively different levels of musical skills in performance.

Three different conditions of performance are considered in this survey:

SIGHTSINGING	semester 1	semester 2	semester 3	semester 4
pitch errors	54	34	15	14
pitch error recoveries	3	12	6	4
rhythm errors	9	17	20	3
rhythm error recoveries	0	0	0	2
use of reading strategies	3	15	10	1
COMPLETE THE MELODY TASK				
pitch errors	25	18	6	6
pitch error recoveries	5	5	4	1
rhythm errors	8	8	21	6
rhtyhm error recoveries	4	2	2	5
use of reading strategies	0	6	8	6
ERROR DETECTION				
undetected errors	8	4	4	3
falsely detected errors	2	2	1	1
detected errors	0	4	4	5

DEFINITION OF TERMS

errors: deviations from the notation given
recoveries: correct notes immediately following error
strategies: when notes are added or omitted in relation to the notation
undetected errors: inability to identify deviations from the notation
falsely detected errors: incorrectly identifying deviations from the notation
detected errors: ability to identify deviations from the notation

Figure 7.5. Evidence for development of sightsinging skills

1. Sightsinging melodies given a starting pitch,
2. Completing melodies (after rehearsing the opening phrase), and
3. Error detection (comparing a piano performance of melodies written in standard notation).

These conditions represent three different lenses on musical development: the ability to construct music from a single reference pitch ("from scratch"), the ability to complete a musical statement after learning the first phrase (resisting or employing musical inference as is appropriate), and the ability to perceive differences between the notation and a rendition of a simple melody (discrimination).

Two things are novel about this survey: scoring instances of recovery and employment of reading strategies in performance. Besides noting the cumulative amount of errors made in a reading session, the inclusion of instances of recovery suggest the development of tonal or rhythmic stability. Recovery encapsulates the ability to compensate for errors that occur. In other words, considerable expertise is demonstrated when, in performance, the sightreader perceives a discrepancy between the performance and the notation, and then spontaneously devises a way of compensating for the error in order to bring the melody back on pitch and/or at the proper time.

Reading strategies, on the other hand, suggest preventative measures taken to assure stable or accurate performance. Strategies such as elaboration (adding notes to the music in order to strengthen the connections between notes), reduction (substituting structurally important notes for less secure pitches or rhythms), and omission (leaving out notes that may undermine the performance) are strategies that emerge in live performance at sight. All three strategies imply the ability to anticipate problems in the performance and the willingness to employ coping mechanisms to bolster the structural integrity of the music.

Analyses of Jeanie's performance skills and her reflective writing during her two years of studying solfege suggest four distinct levels of music reading development common to many students, regardless of major area of study. Evidence for dramatic changes in tonal stability in performance and the appropriate use of reading strategies suggests sightsinging development as an important window into musical development. Although the levels are roughly synchronous with semesters of study, for many students this development may be severely delayed, or more quickly accomplished. Despite differences in previous experience, it appears a majority of these gifted young musicians all proceed through these stages as they are challenged to integrate their comprehension of the notation system with their instrumental or vocal performance skills.

Level one: Disorientation, guesswork. In the first semester, sightsinging tasks force students to encounter their level of coordination of reading skills. Although most instrumentalists read music regularly, it is their sightsinging performance which illuminates the disintegration of their musical perceptions or performances in relation to written music. Jeanie's earlier performance examples are typical of the errors that are made by many students at this level. What is striking is the incapacity to recover from errors or to employ reading strategies appropriate to the pitch or rhythmic difficulties encountered. Typically, at this stage, students like Jeanie cannot find errors in the piano performance, and are likely to indicate "false errors"—disparities she imagines that occur—instead.

SAMPLE ERROR DETECTION

Figure 7.6. Sample error detection

When asked to complete a melody, there are far fewer errors and far more recoveries from errors. This should be expected because the tonality and meter of the piece are clearly established in rehearsal and Jeanie is able to take advantage of the music to infer what is musically appropriate. However, over time, it appears that this condition of performance appears no more stable than the relatively unsupported condition—implying that eventually, a rehearsed phrase may have no more effect on stabilizing a performance than a single note taken as a reference. Precise decoding of the passage requires a more powerful tonal orientation.

Jeanie's reflective writing at the end of the first semester gives several additional clues to her understanding of the critical dimensions of performance when she reads music. She recalls confronting the concept of intonation in the context of performance and being unable to construct the frame of reference necessary to respond to criticism:.

> Since my arrival at NEC I've heard so much about intonation. I never realized the true complexity of the subject. In chorus or in lessons I would hear "The pitch is flat, can you sing it a little higher?" or "can you try to sing it in tune this time?" Remarks of this nature sounded so judgmental and vague to me. Often I would think to myself, "If I could keep it in tune, I would." Sometimes I didn't even know where the problems lie.

For a student who cannot identify errors in performance, criticism of intonation is arbitrary or inscrutable. Responding to the criticism systematically and meaningfully is impossible.

Level two: Developing tools for stable representation of the melody. The second level is characterized by the emergence of strategic thinking in performance. For Jeanie this means employing strategies such as elaboration almost indiscriminately in the performance (see Figure 7.7 below). But the use of strategies has measurable effects on the tonal stability of the rendition. Compared with the first-level performance, she is recovering on pitch after approximately 2.8 notes (34 errors/12 recoveries), whereas the first time the "span of recovery" was approximately 18 notes (54 errors/3 recoveries). This suggests that her strategies are working to help her anticipate difficulties, discover errors, and find her way back to the pitch despite short periods of disorientation.

As far as rhythm is concerned, however, these strategies may have an adverse effect on stability in performance. Whereas pitch is recovered 35% of the time (12 recoveries per 34 errors), in rhythm there are few or no recoveries to false entrances of pitch. Only in level four does she use strategies to coordinate both dimensions of performance across two modes of performance (sightsinging and sightplaying) consistently.

Significant progress in error detection, however, signals that perception is now increasingly in coordination with production skills. This is particularly clear in Jeanie's reflective writing as she becomes increasingly speculative about her work. Characterizing her past learning in terms of imitation, she now is more articulate about her reading problems and more interested in the development of inner hearing as a new way to approach or motivate her reading skill development.

> When I first arrived at NEC I knew little about reading music. I was a vocalist who needed to learn music by having someone play it for me. I never imagined how greatly I could benefit by learning to sightread with solfege (sightsinging). . . . In the beginning I experienced intonation problems. I had no idea of tonality and how notes were related to one other. . . . I've experienced a change in my own performance from my "imitation days" to my present level as a sightreader. Perhaps what I needed was a way in which we could hear the music before we performed it, not knowing a better way, we relied on imitation.

USE OF READING STRATEGIES IN PERFORMANCE

Figure 7.7. Use of reading strategies in performance

In addition, she is now able to identify tools for building new skills along with strategies and appropriate attitudes for putting these tools to work:

> We must begin very simply by looking for indications of what the piece's basic framework is—such as tempo, time signature and key. Knowing this, we will have enough information to at least keep a steady pulse and recover on the tonic. This is valuable. By keeping our place and by being able to recover we can find a new sense of confidence to trudge on ahead even though we are making errors. After all, errors are bound to be plentiful at first. . . . Learning to sightread is like learning a new language.

Level three: Internalizing performance knowledge. In level three, measures of accuracy and stability (span or proportion of recoveries) continue to improve. Jeanie is no longer dependent on the overt use of reading strategies while she focuses on pitch in performance. This suggests that either her reading strategies have increased in potency or that they are becoming increasingly internalized during performance.

Jeanie now reflects on her past incompetencies by observing the shortcomings of students new to the conservatory and begins to describe her reading processes in terms of systemic tonal understanding, rather than through specific strategies.

> Pitch is a tricky matter. Many freshmen entering NEC can't even sing scale degrees when asked. They are unaware of the relationship between notes and each other and the tonic. Therefore, the student must become acquainted with the scale before she can attempt to use it as a tonal reference in sight reading.

Besides stressing the importance of internalization, she characterizes strategies in terms of overarching qualities in the musical performance as well as the ability to think and work independently.

> Internalization plays a key role. Prior to this point a student may have experienced a need to vocalize aloud or to use grace [added elaborating] notes to help her keep in tune while sightreading. This process now becomes internalized. Modulation becomes a task handled smoothly and intelligently. Expressivity becomes a spontaneous and integral part of sightreading. Mistakes are often ignored, displaying true stability. The student can now "think on her feet". . . . The student assumes the role of teacher for herself. She eventually becomes the conductor or musical "problem solver."

Level four: Coordinating and applying reading skills.
Level four does not suggest complete mastery of the task. There are
still errors and occasional lapses into disorientation, and the ability
to find errors is still not completely developed. However, what becomes clear is that these skills are beginning to function in coordination with one another. Rhythmic and pitch recoveries increasingly occur in tandem. Reading strategies are used much more
judiciously and discreetly. And, from the student's point of view, the
application of these new skills is now of paramount interest.

Jeanie's understandings have been altered as a result of many
aspects of conservatory training, including fundamental changes in
her reading skills.

> I came to this school because I wanted to learn about opera. I thought
> it would more or less be an expansion upon what I was already doing,
> which was musical theater. I learned very quickly that it was a totally
> different ball game. . . . I refused to let my lack of experience distress
> me. In fact, I actually began to view being a singer as an advantage
> because I didn't have to spend 6 hours a day practicing like a pianist,
> so I could spend several hours of the day learning to read music. . . . I
> worked with Danhauser (sightsinging textbook) to learn how notes
> were organically related to each other. This was the first time I actually
> realized that I could teach myself a song without the use of a piano.
> The music was findable within myself. All I needed at first was a pitch
> and by singing grace notes from the tonic and other scale degrees I
> could sing any other note in the C major scale. Later I could achieve
> this phenomenon without being given even a pitch.

This transformation pervades her private studio lessons in vocal
repertoire as well by applying her reading skills toward a deeper
understanding of her performance goals.

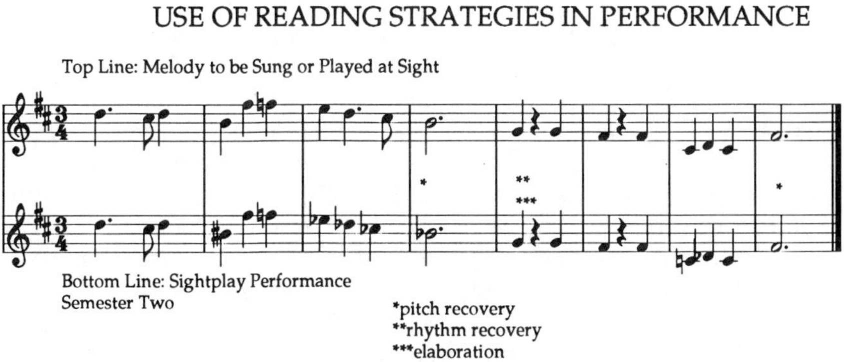

USE OF READING STRATEGIES IN PERFORMANCE

Top Line: Melody to be Sung or Played at Sight

Bottom Line: Sightplay Performance
Semester Two

*pitch recovery
**rhythm recovery
***elaboration

Figure 7.8. Use of reading strategies in performance

I remember on one occasion I was singing "Mandoline" by Fauré and was having trouble with a run. He [my teacher] kept having me solfege it, then sing it, then solfege it, then sing it and so on . . . until the feeling transferred into my singing. I found it much easier to sing the passage in tune with solfege syllables [sightsinging technique] because they gave me a sort of mental image of how the notes were related to one another tonally. . . . But, I know with patience, practice, and continued application of my solfege skills I will solve the problem, freeing myself to express more what I feel artistically.

Summarizing the Levels of Sightsinging Development

Clearly for Jeanie, and indeed for almost every gifted musician beginning professional training, the issue of music reading development is crucial for furthering artistic development. Although an experienced performer, she immediately finds music disorienting without prior rehearsal. Musical discrimination is, at best, uncertain, and suddenly common terms such as "intonation" become vague. However, after two years of work, considerable transformation takes place as she reports changing her mode of learning from imitation to self-construction. Through hard work developing her sightsinging skills, reflecting on this work as she progresses, and applying reading skills to her vocal repertoire, Jeanie eventually felt she was able to progress from being a "rote learner" to "becoming her own teacher."

Reviewing these four levels of reading development delineates a course of development that cannot solely be related to music reading classes. Again, conditions of support for the gifted include much more than simple exposure to instruction. It involves an understanding that includes substantive and authentic encounters with musical problems while building music reading skills, the development of tools or strategies for solving these problems, and the circumspection that comes with reflecting on one's own personal development during this period of growth.

Reviewing again the survey chart of Jeanie's sightsinging development, several points may be worth restating. Increased accuracy alone does not tell a very interesting story about musical development. An understanding of development requires looking at accuracy across a range of conditions as well as in interaction with several other measures of skill development such as error detection, ability to recover from errors, or use of reading strategies.

When looking across the data, several themes emerge: expression of tonal stability that is possible through recoveries from errors, fluctuating use of reading strategies in performance, eventual coordination of musical dimension of rhythm and pitch across a range of conditions, and the importance of looking at reflective writing to gain descriptive power. Without systematic collection of reflective writing over time, accounts of personal transformations cannot be inferred from evaluating performance alone.

Jeanie's example brings much of this to light. More than that, a longitudinal study of her sightsinging development also begins to clarify characteristic stages of skill development fundamental to artistic development: complex skills that have not previously been the focus of empirical studies.

JOYS AND PITFALLS OF LONGITUDINAL RESEARCH

Both the difficulties and the rewards of longitudinal research appeared to increase exponentially with each year of data collection. For starters, initially persuading students to participate in a research study extending over two years was not easily accomplished. Meeting for videotaped sessions at odd hours of the night is not every student's idea of a good way to spend time away from practicing one's repertoire. Furthermore, few incoming students expect to be accountable to any coursework over the 2-year period, much less a research study prying into sightsinging deficiencies. Perhaps for this reason, merely a quarter of the students completed the entire longitudinal sequence.

On the other hand, the joy of watching participating students' attitudes and interests in reading skill development radically change over the 2-year period was not anticipated either. Many participants not only developed great interest in observing their own skill levels change but also expressed great interest in speculating on the findings from the study as a whole. Perhaps relieved that reading skill coordination problems are shared by many students, several participants asked to view earlier videotaped performances to witness levels of development long since forgotten. Some of these students also participated in open discussions on levels of expertise as evidenced by videotaped individual performances over time.

Overall, while data collection proved more difficult than anticipated, the rewards of pursuing the study longitudinally became evident to researchers and teachers at the New England Conservatory through:

1. Greater opportunities for detailed observation by researchers and teachers of individual change along multiple dimensions over time,
2. New occasions for self-reflection by the student participants over time,
3. Changes in pedagogical practices at New England Conservatory engendered from the research study.

In the first case, keeping detailed accounts of sightreading performance tasks allows for much more variegated views of the kinds of errors made and strategies employed in coping with reading problems over time. A greater common understanding of changes in error types allows for a more shared view of what levels of development look like, and what problems can be expected by most gifted students as they become professional musicians.

Second, although much of the data collection involved experimental tasks, there were many opportunities for participants to reflect on or predict future changes in their skill development at any point in the 2-year study. As a result, many students began to write journals or papers reflecting deeper concerns for reading skill development. Also, some students involved in the study became interested in teaching assistantships focused on classes in reading skill development for first-year students.

Third, as a result of the longitudinal study, many faculty members became privy to experimental tasks designed for the study, preliminary findings, and follow-up tasks designed as the study progressed. Faculty members or teaching assistants not only incorporated experimental tasks into their own test designs, but also assessment procedures developed for the longitudinal study. Preliminary findings also proved provocative to the faculty. For example, since preliminary findings suggested a greater role for reflection in music reading development, more teachers now employ journal writing as a standard feature of their classroom activities and assessment practice. Follow-up classroom projects developed as the study progressed centering on novel ways of looking at skill integration across modalites of performance. Many of these approaches are now used regularly by students and faculty to explore a greater range of reading skill development throughout the initial years of conservatory studies.

THE VOICE AS THE MEDIUM FOR EXTENDING GIFTEDNESS

For professional musicians, that is, gifted instrumentalists who continue to develop artistic careers, vocal conception empowers and enriches instrumental performance. For Bernard Greenhouse, cellist with the Beaux Arts Trio, vocalization is internalized in performance, functioning as a guiding interpretive source independent of the instrument:

> The concentration should be on musical ideas rather than on the instrument as such. When I perform today, I find that I am not even aware of the cello in front of me. My concentration is entirely on something else. I sing the phrase before it is produced. I hear it in my mind and I get ideas for how to perform that phrase before it comes out of the instrument. (Delbanco, 1985, p. 62)

It is obvious from this passage that the development of musical gifts involves more than simply taking musical recitation on instruments as evidence for "knowing the music." Studying musical development based entirely on one representation of musical knowing—performance knowledge—belies the complexity of musical understanding. While Bamberger (1986) suggests that young gifted performers tend to have an "unusual capacity for representing musical elements and relations to themselves in multiple ways," she also expresses concern that they tend to "remain buried in the simultaneity that characterizes performance" (p. 408). Artistic development, therefore, relies on an understanding of music that is multidimensional as well as stable, and increasingly internalized to the point that the instrument itself is no longer the focus of musical performance. For Jeanie, our case study from the New England Conservatory reading study, it appears that sightsinging development is a powerful indicator that musical development is proceeding along these lines.

The assumption that gifted children become exceptional adults is taken for granted at the onset of professional training in musical performance. Almost all music students at a major conservatory can recall moments in childhood where they were seen as relatively gifted performers of music. But relying on a one-dimensional view of musical talent threatens further development. Ashima, the child described in the previous chapter, is distinguished more by her range of interests than for the singular nature of her giftedness. Formal instruction in piano does not fully represent her musical interest. Nor is the determination of giftedness readily apparent from instrumental performance alone. The wide range of spontaneous play of her early years becomes rooted in a range of musical activities supported by family, training, and community opportunities—performing with voice and instrument, composing silently and with the computer, learning accepted standard repertoire in classical music as well as interpreting musical theater or songs from popular culture. However, like Jeanie, her musical experiences in these early years will not likely be enough to sustain artistic development.

A closer look at this process reveals the conditions for fostering giftedness through an important set of challenges that are eventually posed in college/conservatory training. For Jeanie, taking responsibility for personal interpretive performance involves developing a deepening grasp and coordination of musical expression through sightsinging. This suggests that giftedness is catalyzed by a multiplicity of conditions supporting musical and personal growth. In this way children learn to cope with the expansive nature of their musical interests. An initial interest in a familiar piece becomes a problem of how to perform the piece flawlessly in public. Learning music reading skills becomes necessary for discovering new music and developing interpretive skills independent of coaching or rote learning. Reflecting on one's own course of musical development becomes a tool for deepening and coordinating these perceptions in relation to musical performance.

CONCLUSION

The challenge of building reading literacy skills in music is a promising window on musical development for the musically gifted. Gifted music students, like all children in early schooling, may find performing and understanding the language of music relatively unproblematic, whereas reading and notation skills may pose severe challenges. The kind of development that takes place in conjunction with natural or intuitive learning may seem wholly at odds with the more formal learning that is required for gifted musicians later in life. Accordingly, when students face novel music reading tasks they may find that sensorimotor intuition or rehearsed responses are no longer sufficient. On the other hand, reading notation for "correct answers" does not necessarily lead to appropriate artistic renditions. For this reason, Jeanie, like others in the longitudinal study, is particularly impressive when she displays categorical changes in her approach to the reading tasks. Music reading poses opportunities to select and employ a range of strategies for both decoding and exploring the meaning of the music.

A way of viewing the success or failure of education for the musically gifted can be seen through this study. By not stressing the coordination of skills necessary for supporting the musically gifted, music education fails to alert the student to the demands of the domain. Underscoring his view of education for understanding,

Gardner (1991) suggests: "Students must have the frequent opportunities to adopt multiple perspectives and stances with reference to the material in question. In the absence of such opportunities, students seem fated to maintain a one-dimensional view of the topic or material" (p. 237).

The education of the musically gifted, then, should reflect nothing less than a widening scope of opportunities for weaving together the various strands of musical knowledge that begin early in childhood and need to be reintegrated with skills that are learned later in life.

This study also illustrates a new way of portraying the evolution of musical understanding. Through related music reading tasks we can trace deepening musical development in terms of the eventual coordination of multiple representations in performance, perception, and reflective thinking (Davidson & Scripp, 1992). Only if musical understanding is stable across many different conditions, and is increasingly articulate and internalized with training, will early musical giftedness transform into mature artistry. In light of Bamberger's (1986) observations of musically gifted performers in rehearsal and in private lessons, Jeanie's stages of sightsinging development suggest how musical knowledge constructed from early childhood into adolescence is reexplored and deepened with professional training in music sightreading skills:

1. Although young gifted musicians display an unusual capacity for representing musical relations to themselves in multiple ways, it appears these relations are grasped all at once as a single network, with little reflection, and little understanding of the symbol system.
2. Later, often in conjunction with music reading experiences, multiple dimensions and their internal representations come apart spontaneously, reflecting the need to reflect, question, and analyze music in terms of standard notation.
3. The "all at once" imitation or "stimulus-response" learning process no longer integrates the functional relationships in performance and ceases to contribute to music reading skills.
4. The ability to coordinate multiple dimensions and their internal representations on a conscious level from music notation appears necessary in order to achieve "the thoughtful but still spontaneous artistic performance of the adult" (Bamberger, 1991, p. 89).

The music reading case study from the New England Conservatory longitudinal study supports this view. Describing assorted reading tasks across various modes of representation helps to illuminate the unfolding development of stable internal tonal imagery, strategies for the reduction or elaboration of musical information, and the growing links with musical perception and reflective thinking. The coordination of these skills through Jeanie's example illustrates how we can take notice of categorically different levels of performance integration and notational knowledge that will support gifted musicians as they progress from imitation toward independent artistic thinking in their subsequent professional careers.

REFERENCES

Bamberger, J. (1986). Cognitive issues in the development of musically gifted children. In R. Sternberg & J. Davidson (Eds.), *Conceptions of giftedness* (pp. 388–413). London: Cambridge University Press.

Bamberger, J. (1991). *The mind behind the musical ear.* Cambridge: Harvard University Press.

Bean, K. (1938). An experimental approach to the reading of music. *Psychological Monographs, 226,* 1–80.

Davidson, L., & Scripp, L. (1988a). Young children's musical representations: Windows on music cognition. In J. Sloboda (Ed.), *Generative processes in music* (pp. 195–230). Oxford: Oxford University Press.

Davidson, L., & Scripp, L. (1988b). Sightsinging at New England Conservatory of Music. *Journal of Music Theory Pedagogy, 2*(1), 51–68.

Davidson, L., & Scripp, L. (1988c). A developmental view of sightsinging: The internalization of tonal and temporal space. *Journal of Music Theory Pedagogy, 2*(1), 10–23.

Davidson, L., & Scripp, L. (1988d). Sightsinging ability: A quantitative and a qualitative point of view. *Journal of Music Theory Pedagogy, 2*(1), 51–68.

Davidson, L., & Scripp, L. (1989). Education and development in music from a cognitive perspective. In D.J. Hargreaves (Ed.), *Children and the arts: The psychology of creative development* (pp. 59–68). Leicester, UK: Open University Press.

Davidson, L., Scripp, L., & Welsh, P. (1989). "Happy Birthday": Evidence for conflicts of perceptual knowledge and conceptual understanding. *Journal of Art, Mind, and Education,* 65–74.

Davidson, L., & Scripp, L. (1992). Surveying the coordinates of cognitive skills in music. In R. Colwell (Ed.), *The handbook for research in music teaching and learning* (pp. 392–413). New York: Schirmer Books, Macmillan.

Delbanco, N. (1985). *The Beaux Arts Trio: A portrait.* New York: William Morris.

Gardner, H. (1972). *The Arts and human development: A psychological study of the artistic process.* New York: Wiley & Sons.

Gardner, H. (1989). Project Zero: An introduction to Arts PROPEL. *Journal of Art and Design Education, 8*(2), 167–182.

Gardner, H. (1991). *The unschooled mind.* New York: Basic Books.

Mursell, J. L., & Glenn, M. (1938). *The psychology of school music teaching.* New York: Silver Burdette.

Olson, D. R. (1978). The arts as basic skills: Three cognitive functions of symbols. In S. Madeja (Ed.), *The arts, cognition, and basic skills* (pp. 59–88). St. Louis: CEMBREL, Inc.

Rubinstein, A. (1973). *My young years.* New York: Alfred Knopf.

Seashore, C. (1967). *Psychology of music.* New York: Dover Books.

Sloboda, J. (1984). Experimental studies of music reading: A review. *Music Perception, 2*(2), 222–236.

Watkins, J., & Farnum, S. (1954). *The Watkins–Farnum Performance Scale.* Winona, MN: Leonard Music.

Winner, E., Davidson, L., & Scripp, L. (Eds.). (1992). *Arts PROPEL: A handbook for music, Harvard Project Zero.* Cambridge, MA: Harvard Project Zero.

Wolf, T. (1976). A cognitive model of musical sight–reading. *Journal of Psycholinguistic Research, 5*(2), 143–171.

8

Creative Thinking and Creative Performance in Adolescents as Predictors of Creative Attainments in Adults: A Follow-up Study After 18 Years

Roberta M. Milgram
Eunsook Hong

What do Boris Yeltsin, president of the Russian Republic, and Carol Pederson, a 23-year-old financial manager, have in common? As young people the abilities of both went unrecognized. Those talents could have been recognized if one knew where to look.

As a youngster, Yeltsin was merely average when it came to academic achievement. On the other hand, his outstanding leadership abilities were evidenced even in high school when he led a student protest strike against the administration to correct a perceived injustice. As you can imagine, he was not rewarded for this display of leadership, but was instead expelled from school. Carol Pederson also had school problems. Although she found mathematics quite difficult, this did not stop her from becoming a millionaire at age 22. She said, "I had trouble with numbers, but when you put a dollar sign in front of them, I understood perfectly." When other children played their usual games, Carol went to the race track, traded in penny stocks, and read the *Wall Street Journal*.

In this chapter we present a theoretical formulation and empirical evidence to support our position that the exclusive use of formal school-oriented predictors of intelligence and school grades forfeits the identification of a great deal of talent. Moreover, we suggest that examining out-of-school activities in children helps find hidden abilities and reduce talent loss. Milgram's 4 × 4 Model of the structure of giftedness provides the rationale for expecting that measures of creative thinking and creative leisure activities may be more valid predictors of remarkable life accomplishments than tested intelligence and school grades. In this chapter we present the results of an 18-year longitudinal study in which this prediction was investigated. Implications of the findings for the identification and enhancement of giftedness are discussed as well.

Much to the dismay of teachers and administrators committed to the value of special education for gifted learners, many children identified as gifted and given special educational opportunities to nurture their gifts do not attain notable life achievements. In fact, some children who were not identified as gifted or given special educational opportunities grow up to be eminent adults. Some researchers, teachers, and administrators attribute this problematic situation to a widely accepted but limited definition of giftedness (McClelland, 1973; Tannenbaum, 1983; Wallach & Wing, 1969). They support their position by citing the lack of evidence for the predictive validity of IQ and achievement test scores with reference to extraordinary behavior in adults.

Broadening the concept of giftedness allows for the recognition of a wide variety of abilities in addition to high general intelligence and school grades. The unidimensional definition of giftedness pioneered by Terman (1925) and Terman and Oden (1947, 1959) which dominated the field of giftedness for many years, has more recently given way to a multifaceted view. Definitions of giftedness proposed by Marland (1972), Gardner (1983), Guilford (1956, 1967), Sternberg and Davidson (1986), Tannenbaum (1983), and Torrance (1962, 1966, 1980), included creativity, leadership ability, and abilities in the performing and visual arts. Defining operationally abilities such as creative thinking, musical ability, leadership, and so forth, proved difficult, however. The psychometric tools are lacking.

Milgram's efforts to clarify and operationalize a broader view of giftedness resulted in her 4 × 4 Model of the structure of giftedness (1989b, 1990, 1991, 1993). In the 4 × 4 Model, giftedness is depicted in terms of (a) categories, two having to do with aspects of intelligence (general intellectual ability and specific intellectual ability) and two with aspects of original thinking (general original/creative thinking and specific creative talent); (b) four ability levels (profoundly gifted, moderately gifted, mildly gifted, and nongifted), hence the name 4 × 4; and (c) three learning environments (home, school, and community) embedded in a framework of individual differences. The 4 × 4 Model is described in detail elsewhere (Milgram, 1989b, 1990, 1991, 1993). However, in order to clarify the theoretical framework which guided the current 18-year follow-up

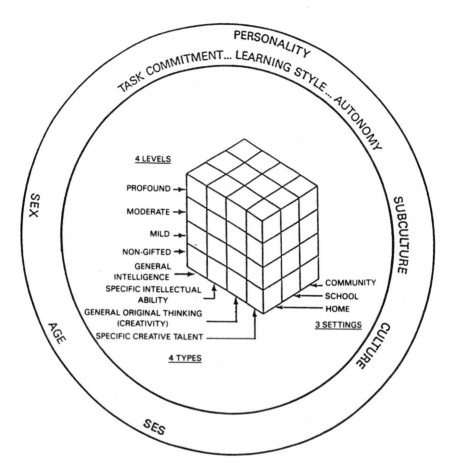

Figure 8.1. Milgram: 4 × 4 Model of the structure of giftedness

study, the four categories postulated in the 4 × 4 Model will be briefly summarized below.

The first category, general intellectual ability or overall general intelligence, refers to the ability to think abstractly and to solve problems logically and systematically. This ability is measured in adults and children by performance on psychometric tests and is most frequently reported as an IQ score.

The second category, specific intellectual ability, refers to a clear and distinct intellectual ability in a given area, such as mathematics, foreign language, music, or science. For example, in mathematics a person might demonstrate outstanding computational ability, knowledge of mathematical principles, or deep understanding of mathematical concepts. Artistic ability might be reflected in aesthetic appreciation and technical skill. Specific intellectual abilities are reflected in performance that may be highly competent, but not necessarily highly original. Specific intellectual abilities in children and adolescents are often, but not invariably, expressed in superior academic performance in school subjects as reflected in school grades and achievement tests.

The third category, general original/creative thinking, describes the process of generating solutions that are unusual and of high quality. Creative thinkers generate ideas that are imaginative, clever, elegant, or surprising. This ability is measured by tests of divergent thinking.

The fourth category, specific creative ability, refers to clear and distinct domain-specific creativity. Talent is manifested in both children and adults in socially valuable, novel products in science, mathematics, art, music, social leadership, business, politics, or any other human endeavor. One way to identify specific creative talent in children before these abilities become fully realized in one's vocation is by examining out-of-school leisure-time activities.

The approach to defining giftedness exemplified by the 4 × 4 Model and the tools developed based on the model may provide some help in improving procedures for the identification of gifted learners. If IQ and school grades are not valid predictors of gifted behavior in adults, we must consider alternative predictors. The 4 × 4 Model suggests that creative thinking and the performance of creative leisure-time activities in children and adolescents are alternatives worth considering.

CREATIVE THINKING

Taken together, findings that have accumulated over the years provide considerable empirical support for the construct validity of creative thinking formulated as ideational fluency, the ability to generate a large number of responses to a stimulus. General original/creative thinking and overall intelligence are empirically distinguishable (Wallach, 1970, 1971). There is a relationship between quantity and quality of ideational output, with high ideational production a precondition for quality responses (Milgram, Milgram, Rosenbloom, & Rabkin, 1978), and there is an order effect with popular responses (more conventional or stereotyped ideas) emitted earlier and more original ideas appearing later in the response sequence (Milgram & Rabkin, 1980). The ability to generate many ideas was found to predict the ability to generate many original solutions to laboratory problems in children at all age levels and in young adults (Hong & Milgram, 1991; Milgram, 1983; Milgram & Arad, 1981).

The validity of ideational fluency measures of creative thinking has not yet been resolved. In an extensive review of the literature, Barron and Harrington (1981) cited 70 studies in which a positive relationship was obtained between measures of ideational fluency and nontest real-world indices of creative behavior. On the other hand, Wallach (1985) questioned the validity of ideational fluency-based measures of original thinking and summarized the results of a number of concurrent studies indicating that general original/creative thinking is not significantly related to specific real-world creative performance. Torrance (1972a, 1972b, 1980) and Torrance and Wu (1981) reported evidence of long-term predictive validity of the Torrance Test of Creative Thinking. In this test, however, IQ and creative thinking are confounded (Wallach, 1970). Hence, the predictive validity of ideational fluency-based measures of creativity remained to be investigated.

Milgram and Milgram (1976a) reported moderate evidence of concurrent validity for the Tel-Aviv Creativity Test, with reference to the performance of creative activities in adolescents. The Tel-Aviv test is a measure of ideational fluency unconfounded with intelligence (Milgram & Milgram, 1976b). In the study described below we used creative thinking data generated by the Tel-Aviv test to examine the long-term predictive validity of creative thinking with reference to the criterion of real-world accomplishment in adults.

CREATIVE PERFORMANCE

Another approach to the assessment of creativity focuses on leisure-time activity. Children's leisure activities may be valid predictors of talent accomplishment in adults (Milgram, 1989b, 1990, 1991, 1993). Leisure activities are intrinsically motivated out-of-school hobbies and activities that young people do for their own enjoyment and by their own choice, and not in order to fulfill school requirements or to earn grades or credits. Although not related to school, they may still be highly intellectual endeavors (e.g., computer programming, working out mathematical solutions, conducting scientific experiments, composing music). The voluntary performance of unusual and high-quality leisure activities reflects not only intellectual abilities, but also task commitment, persistence, and other cognitive and personal-social attributes that strongly determine life outcomes. For these reasons one could argue that leisure activities in adolescents are stable and valid indicators of similarly unusual and high-quality accomplishments in adults.

A series of innovative studies of intrinsically motivated creative activities and accomplishments in adolescence was conducted by Holland and his associates (Holland, 1961, 1985; Holland & Austin, 1962; Holland & Nichols, 1964; Holland & Richards, 1965; Richards, Holland, & Lutz, 1967). They examined thousands of retrospective self-reports of college-age students and found creative attainments in high school to be associated with continuing creative activity in college. Wallach and Wing (1969; Wing & Wallach, 1971) adopted the Holland approach in their investigation of creative, intrinsically motivated activities in college students. On the basis of their findings they urged that creative activities be used in college student selection, claiming that the recommended procedure would succeed in selecting students who would later make outstanding contributions in the real world.

Building upon the work of Holland and his associates and that of Wallach and Wing cited above, Milgram developed the Tel-Aviv Activities Inventory. A major innovation of the new scale was to replace the general undifferentiated list of items tapping creative accomplishment with the following nine specific domains of creative performance: music, science, art, social, literature, community service, drama, sports, and dance. It has been used to investigate the out-of-school activities of children (Milgram, Yitzhak, & Milgram, 1977) and adolescents (Milgram & Milgram, 1976a). The instrument has been used in studies of individual differences in creative performance in children ranging in age from preschool through high school (Gorsky, 1990; Hong & Milgram, 1991; Kfir, 1989; Milgram, Dunn, & Price, in press; Milgram & Milgram, 1976a; Milgram, Yitzhak, & Milgram, 1977). Although some evidence for short-term predictive validity of measures of creative performance has been reported, the long-term predictive validity of measures of creative performance remains to be investigated.

In the current study we utilized data collected 18 years ago from the entire senior class ($N = 159$) of a Tel-Aviv high school. The data were measures of intelligence, school grades, divergent thinking, and out-of-school activities. The first wave of this study was described in detail by Milgram and Milgram (1976a). Here we compared the Activities Inventory protocols gathered 18 years ago from adolescents with current measures of accomplishment in five life areas: academic, vocational, community service, family, and leisure activities. Adult accomplishments were defined operationally as those activities that are unusual and of high quality. We developed a self-report questionnaire that consisted of items tapping adult attainments in each sphere. Each of the five areas consisted of items in ascending order of accomplishment, from relatively frequent activities of low quality to relatively rare items of high quality. For example, in the work area, a high score was obtained by subjects who reported that their duties carried a high level of responsibility, initiative, and independent decision making. Subjects who reported that their relationships to spouse and children were highly important sources of support, encouragement, and satisfaction and who reported exceptionally successful communication within the family and a wide variety of activities received high scores in the area. A list of diverse community and leisure-time activities were presented and the responses of subjects reflected the degree and quality of their participation.

We first examined the adult accomplishments of adolescents who had high scores on general leisure activities, that is, who reported a large number of leisure activities across a variety of different domains. We expected that scores on measures of general creative thinking and overall creative performance gathered in adolescence—but not IQ scores and school grades gathered at the same time—would be related to creative achievement in adults.

Remarkable career attainments in adults, with few exceptions, focus on a single domain of endeavor. It is reasonable to expect youngsters destined to become gifted adults to demonstrate early and intensive interest and ability in a specific domain. In addition to the predictor-criterion relationships cited above in which the total score for leisure activities was the predictor and the five life areas were the criteria, we examined the predictive validity of domain-specific leisure activities in adolescence with specific reference to adult vocational accomplishments. We expected (a) a relationship between the domain of leisure activity in adolescence and the domain of vocational activity in adulthood, and (b) a higher level of work accomplishment for those subjects whose adolescent leisure activities and adult occupations were matched. The study focusing on the role of domain-specific leisure activities in career guidance of gifted and talented adolescents is described in full detail elsewhere (Hong, Whiston, & Milgram, 1993).

METHOD

Subjects

Subjects were 67 of the 159 subjects who participated in a study of creative thinking and creative performance that was conducted 18 years ago. The database included the entire senior class of a high school in Tel Aviv, Israel and was described in detail by Milgram and Milgram (1976a). Subjects with missing values for one or more variables were eliminated from the analysis. The resulting sample size was 48 (20 men and 28 women). The subjects ranged in age from 34 to 36 years, with a mean of 35.02 years.

Instruments

Tel-Aviv Activities Inventory (Milgram, 1973). The current study utilized the Tel-Aviv Activities Inventory scores collected 18 years ago by Milgram and Milgram (1976a). The inventory consisted of 43 items that tap out-of-school activities in nine areas. The test yielded scores for nine areas of activity and a summed total score for overall leisure activity. The areas and the number of questions in each subscale (in parentheses) are as follows: Music (8), Science (4), Art (3), Social (6), Literature (6), Community Service (3), Drama (6), Sports (5), and Dance (2). Subjects indicated their out-of-school activities by marking "yes" or "no" to each of the items on an answer sheet. The dance category was not included in the current study because it consisted of only two items.

In order to investigate the relationship between the leisure activities in adolescence and adult work accomplishment, we computed four scores for each subject: Arts, Science, Social Activities, and Sports. The Arts score combined items in the Music, Art, Literature, and Drama areas of the Activities Inventory. The Social Activities score combined items from the Social and Community Services. The four scores were computed by summing the number of "yes" responses on each item of the respective scales for each individual. These scores measured in adolescence were used to predict adult occupations.

Inventory of Adult Accomplishment (Milgram, 1989a). The instrument consisted of 55 items tapping adult attainments in five life domains (i.e., Work, Academic, Family, Community, and Leisure Activities). Subjects answered "yes" or "no" to each item. In addition, subjects were given the opportunity to give details and elaborate on their answers.

The occupations reported by subjects on the Inventory of Adult Accomplishment (Milgram, 1989a) were classified according to the 12 occupational interest areas of the Guide for Occupational Exploration (GOE) (U.S. Department of Labor, 1979). The occupations reported by our subjects fell into seven interest areas: Artistic, Scientific, Mechanical, Industrial, Business Detail, Humanitarian, and

Leading-Influencing. Inspection of items of the Activity Inventory and GOE interest areas indicated that the Social items better matched the Leading-Influencing interest area, and the Community Service items in the predictor better matched the GOE Humanitarian area. Accordingly, we created a new area that combined the work interest areas of Humanitarian and Leading-Influencing and named it Social-Leadership.

There was only one subject whose adult occupation was in the Industrial area and two subjects in Business Detail. Accordingly, the two areas were combined and categorized as Other. Since the Activities Inventory administered in adolescence did not include any items that might have predicted the Mechanical area of occupation, it too was categorized as Other. Thus, four broad categories of occupational interest (i.e., Artistic, Scientific, Social-Leadership, and Other) were used as the criteria in examining the relationship between the focus of out-of-school activities in adolescence and the domain of vocational activity in adulthood.

In addition to classifying adult occupations, the Inventory of Adult Accomplishment also yielded a score for work accomplishment. It consisted of a total score that combined items tapping work responsibility and work accomplishment.

Creative thinking measures. An adapted version of the Wallach and Kogan (1965) measure of ideational fluency, consisting of four subtests (alternate uses, pattern meanings, similarities, and line meanings) with four items per subtest, was the measure of creative thinking. The test was scored for ideational fluency, the number of discrete responses given, and unusual or rare ideas, that is, responses given by 5% or less of the group.

Intellectual ability and scholastic achievement. The Milta (Ortar, 1966) group intelligence test was used. It consisted of five verbal subtests (sentence completion, vocabulary, verbal analogies, oddities, and arithmetic). The measure of scholastic achievement was a grade point average based on six major school subjects.

The Tel-Aviv Activities Inventory was group-administered in a single session in December 1973. In 1990, subjects were located and whenever possible contacted by telephone ahead of time in order to enlist their cooperation in the study. Following the phone contact, the Inventory of Adult Accomplishment was mailed to each subject. Strenuous efforts, including an additional mailing and follow-up telephone calls were made to maximize the number of questionnaires returned. Although 67 (42%) of the original 159 subjects returned the questionnaire, only 48 (30%) were usable. Among the

19 subjects eliminated from the analysis, 11 subjects did not specify their occupations, and eight subjects had missing information on their out-of-school activities reported 18 years ago.

COMPARISONS

We first examined the relationships between the four predictor measures (intelligence, school grades, creative thinking, and overall leisure activities) and the five criterion scores of adult accomplishment (work, academic, family, community service, and leisure activities). The total creative performance score was related to two criterion scores, work accomplishment ($r = .26$, $p < .05$) and family satisfaction ($r = .26$, $p < .05$). The general creative thinking score was related to adult leisure activities ($r = .37$, $p < .01$, $n = 46$). School grades in high school were related to later academic achievement ($r = .28$, $p < .05$, $n = 46$). Intelligence as measured in adolescence was not related to any one of the five criterion measures of adult accomplishment in simple correlations. The results reported above cannot be attributed to a restricted range of intelligence test scores in our subjects, as the subjects of the current study were an entire 12th-grade class representing a wide range of IQ scores.

We next examined the relationship of the specific domains of creative performance in adolescence to adult accomplishment in the work area. The activity domains upon which leisure activities in adolescence were focused were determined for each subject by computing the percentage of items in each domain to which the subject answered "yes." The leisure domain with the highest percentage was called the first-focus domain, and the one with the second highest percentage, the second-focus domain. Both first- and second-focus domains were used to determine the degree of match between leisure activities as reported in adolescence and adult occupations. Seven subjects did not have a discernible focus of leisure activity in adolescence.

We examined the relationship between the four domains of leisure activities in adolescence (Arts, Science, Social Activities, and Sports) and the four GOE areas of occupation in adulthood (Artistic, Scientific, Social-Leadership, and Other) described above. Means and standard deviations for the leisure activities subscale by GOE interest area are presented in Table 8.1. For 35% of the subjects (17 out of 48), adolescent leisure activities matched adult occupations 18 years after the initial assessment of leisure activities.

Table 8.1. Means and Standard Deviations for the Leisure Activities Inventory Subscale by GOE Interest Area

Leisure activities domain	GOE occupational interest area			
	Artistic (*n* = 7)	Scientific (*n* = 9)	Social-Leadership (*n* = 25)	Other (*n* = 7)
Arts	2.14	.88	1.00	1.00
	(.89)	(.78)	(.91)	(1.41)
Science	.14	.33	.12	0.00
	(.37)	(.50)	(.33)	(0.00)
Social Activities	.71	.44	.36	.28
	(.48)	(.52)	(.56)	(.48)
Sports	.43	.44	.40	.57
	(.53)	(.52)	(.50)	(.53)

Note: Standard deviations are in parentheses.

We compared the adult work accomplishment scores of subjects whose adolescent leisure activities and adult occupation were matched (n = 17) with those whose activities and occupations were not matched (n = 31). The mean work accomplishment score of the matched group was significantly greater than the mean score of the nonmatched group (t = 2.01, $p < .05$, n = 46). Means and standard deviations (in parentheses) of work accomplishment scores of the matched group and unmatched group were 8.65 (2.23) and 6.90 (3.15), respectively. Thus, subjects whose leisure activities in adolescence matched their adult occupation had more responsibility in their jobs and their work accomplishment level was higher.

DISCUSSION

The findings suggest that creative thinking and creative performance are better predictors of adult life accomplishment than intelligence or school grades. Creative thinking and creative performance were related to adult accomplishment in three important life areas. As might be expected, school grades in adolescence predicted academic achievement in adults. However, grades in school were unrelated to any accomplishments in adult life outside the academic area. Intelligence test scores did not predict adult life accomplishment in a single life area.

Creative thinking predicted the amount of overall leisure activity in adults. The relationship between measures of general creative thinking ability and indices of overall leisure activities in children and adolescents is frequently cited as evidence of the validity of the former measures (Barron & Harrington, 1981). Our findings provide support for this position by demonstrating not only concurrent but predictive validity for a divergent thinking measure.

Most of the subjects did not report much activity in the area of community service. This may have been because young adults in their early thirties are still focused on their own career and personal development. It may be that community service involvement will develop in the years to come.

The finding of a relationship between adolescent leisure activities and adult vocation was impressive. Leisure activities were related to later occupation in 35% of our subjects. Moreover, leisure activities related not only to vocational choice but to level of work accomplishments as well. The important contribution of personality characteristics to vocational choice is well recognized and frequently used in understanding career development and in vocational guidance (Osipow, 1983). Leisure activities as a tool in career counseling have, however, been largely ignored. Our findings indicate that participating in leisure activities may be as valid a predictor of occupational choice as personality typologies.

Numerous investigators have stressed the importance of expanding our view of giftedness, yet have not considered the role of out-of-school activities in the development of talent. Extraordinary accomplishment in adults is not simply a gift but an achievement, as an enormous amount of effort is required for the actualization of talent (Bloom, 1985). Terman (1925), the pioneer investigator of giftedness, reported a large number and wide variety of out-of-school activities for the intellectually gifted children whom he subsequently followed throughout their lives. He did not, however, examine the efficacy of these leisure activities as predictors of future eminent achievements. One reason was the lack of required psychometric tools. In an effort to provide a valid tool for early identification of gifted and talented children, Hong, Whiston, and Milgram (1993) analyzed the factor structure of the Tel-Aviv Activities Inventory and suggested ways to refine the instrument to make it a more precise predictor of vocational choice and thus more useful in the career guidance of adolescents. We are currently analyzing the Terman database with this probability in mind (Whiston, Milgram, & Hong, 1992).

JOYS AND PITFALLS OF LONGITUDINAL RESEARCH

There has been extraordinary satisfaction in conducting a study that spans 18 years. There have also been frustrations. The baseline data for this study were collected in the wake of the Yom Kippur War that took place in Israel beginning in October 1973. Data were collected in a period of ceasefire just after school had resumed meeting regularly, and Israel was not yet fully sure that the war was indeed over. Continuing to conduct research was viewed as a reflection of the determination of Israeli society to normalize daily life as much as possible in order to decrease the stress that inevitably accompanies such situations. While collecting data, it was obvious from the remarks of the students that it was difficult for them to understand why we were conducting such seemingly trivial research at such a time. Every one of them knew that after graduation they would be mobilized and serve three years in the military. We have often wondered what effect this timing of data collection had on the study and, of course, we will never know.

Collection of criterion data after 18 years was fraught with problems. We were not able to locate all of the subjects. We found some uncooperative, one in jail, one had committed suicide, and some no longer lived in Israel. Perhaps even more frustrating was the fact that some returned the criterion questionnaires in unusable condition. In the light of the small number of subjects, this was particularly aggravating. We would have preferred to utilize statistical techniques such as structural equation modeling rather than the correlational analysis that we employed. However, the small number of subjects available after 18 years and the large amount of missing data precluded our using such an approach.

Despite the pitfalls and frustrations cited above there has been enormous satisfaction in the project as well. We derived satisfaction from the quality of creative performance of the subjects in the study. Even though the number of subjects was small, they were not a sample but rather an entire senior class.

The greatest satisfaction derived from this study was the indication provided by the data that continued research on leisure activities as a predictor of adult attainment is warranted. This will require concerted efforts to refine the leisure activity inventory so that it can be used with greater precision and efficacy in the identification of talent in young people.

We return now to Boris Yeltsin and Carol Pederson, the examples that we discussed at the beginning of this chapter. Had we administered the Activities Inventory to these people when they were adolescents, we might have been impressed by their unusual responses. Further discussion of their unusual activities and interests might have lead to their receiving useful career guidance. However, despite the fact that they were not identified as gifted youngsters and did not benefit from special educational interventions, they did manage to actualize their potential abilities. These happy-ending stories serve to support the popular prejudice that gifted children will realize their talents without educational intervention, yet many gifted youngsters fail to realize their potential abilities (Tannenbaum, 1983). Marland (1972) reported, "disturbingly, research has confirmed that many gifted children perform far below their intellectual potential. We are increasingly being stripped of the notion that a bright mind will make its own way" (p.9). Some have estimated that as many as 15-30% of high school dropouts are gifted and talented. The results of the study reported in this chapter indicate that adding the dimension of leisure activities to identification procedures may contribute to solving this pressing problem.

REFERENCES

Barron, F., & Harrington, D. M. (1981). Creativity, intelligence and personality. *Annual Review of Psychology, 32,* 439–476.

Bloom, B. S. (1985). *Developing talent in young people.* New York: Ballantine Books.

Gardner, H. (1983). *Frames of mind: The theory of multiple intelligences.* New York: Basic Books.

Gorsky, H. (1990). *Creative thinking as a predictor of creative performance in elementary school students.* Unpublished master's thesis, Tel-Aviv University, Ramat-Aviv, Israel.

Guilford, J. P. (1956). The structure of intellect. *Psychological Bulletin, 53,* 267–293.

Guilford, J. P. (1967). *The nature of human intelligence.* New York: McGraw-Hill.

Holland, J. L. (1961). Creative and academic performance among talented adolescents. *Journal of Educational Psychology, 52,* 136–147.

Holland, J. L. (1985). *Making vocational choices: A theory of vocational personalities and work environments* (2nd ed.). Englewood Cliffs, NJ: Prentice-Hall.

Holland, J. L., & Austin, A. W. (1962). The prediction of the academic, artistic, scientific, and social achievement of undergraduates of superior scholastic aptitude. *Journal of Educational Psychology, 53,* 132–143.

Holland, J. L., & Nichols, R. C. (1964). Prediction of academic and extracurricular achievement in college. *Journal of Educational Psychology, 55,* 55–65.

Holland, J. L., & Richards, J. M. (1965). Academic and nonacademic accomplishments: Correlated or uncorrelated. *Journal of Educational Psychology, 56,* 165–174.

Hong, E., & Milgram, R. M. (1991). Original thinking in preschool children: A validation of ideational fluency measures. *Creativity Research Journal, 4,* 253–260.

Hong, E., Whiston, S. C., & Milgram, R. M. (1993). Leisure activities in career guidance for gifted and talented adolescents: A validation study of the Tel-Aviv Activities Inventory. *Gifted Child Quarterly, 37*, 65–68.

Kfir, B. (1989). *Creative thinking and creative performance as predictors of creative achievements in architecture.* Unpublished master's thesis, Tel-Aviv University, Ramat-Aviv, Israel.

Marland, S. P., Jr. (1972). *Education of the gifted and talented.* Washington, DC: U.S. Government Printing Office.

McClelland, D. C. (1973). Testing for competence rather than for "intelligence." *American Psychologist, 28*, 1–14.

Milgram, R. M. (1973). *Tel-Aviv Activities Inventory.* Ramat-Aviv, Israel: Tel-Aviv University, School of Education.

Milgram, R. M. (1983). A validation of ideational fluency measures of original thinking in children. *Journal of Educational Psychology, 75*, 619–624.

Milgram, R. M. (1989a). *Inventory of Adult Accomplishment.* Ramat-Aviv, Israel: Tel-Aviv University, School of Education.

Milgram, R.M. (Ed.). (1989b). *Teaching gifted and talented learners in regular classrooms: An impossible dream or a full-time solution for a full-time problem?* Springfield, IL: Charles C. Thomas.

Milgram, R. M. (1990). Creativity: An idea whose time has come and gone? In M. A. Runco & R. S. Albert (Eds.), *Theories of creativity* (pp. 215–233). Newbury Park, CA: Sage.

Milgram, R. M. (Ed.). (1991). *Counseling gifted and talented children; A guide for teachers, counselors, and parents.* Norwood, NJ: Ablex.

Milgram, R. M. (1993). Intrinsically motivated behavior in adolescence as a predictor of giftedness in adults. In S. G. Isaksen, M. M. Murdock, R. L. Firestien, & D. J. Treffinger (Eds.), *Understanding and recognizing creativity: The emergence of a discipline (Vol. 1).* Norwood, NJ: Ablex.

Milgram, R. M., & Arad, R. (1981). Ideational fluency as a predictor of original problem-solving. *Journal of Educational Psychology, 73*, 568–572.

Milgram, R. M., Dunn, R., & Price, G. S. (Eds.). (in press). *Teaching gifted and talented learners for learning style: An international perspective.* New York: Praeger.

Milgram, R. M., & Milgram, N. A. (1976a). Creative thinking and creative performance in Israeli children. *Journal of Educational Psychology, 68*, 255–259.

Milgram, R. M., & Milgram, N. A. (1976b). Group versus individual administration in the measurement of creative thinking in gifted and nongifted children. *Child Development, 47*, 563–565.

Milgram, R. M., Milgram, N. A., Rosenbloom, G., & Rabkin, L. (1978). Quantity and quality of creative thinking in children and adolescents. *Child Development, 49*, 385–388.

Milgram, R. M., & Rabkin, L. (1980). A developmental test of Mednick's associative hierarchies of original thinking. *Developmental Psychology, 16,* 157–158.

Milgram, R. M., Yitzhak, V., & Milgram, N. A. (1977). Creative activity and sex-role identity in elementary school children. *Perceptual and Motor Skills, 45,* 71–376.

Osipow, S. H. (1983). *Theories of career development* (3rd ed.). Englewood Cliffs, NJ: Prentice-Hall.

Ortar, G. (1966). *Milta intelligence scale.* Jerusalem: Hebrew University School of Education and Israel Ministry of Education.

Richards, J. M., Jr., Holland, J. L., & Lutz, S. W. (1967). The predictions of student accomplishment in college. *Journal of Educational Psychology, 58,* 343–355.

Sternberg, R. J., & Davidson, J. E. (Eds.). (1986). *Conceptions of giftedness.* New York: Cambridge University Press.

Tannenbaum, A. J. (1983). *Gifted children: Psychological and educational perspectives.* New York: Macmillan

Terman, L. M. (1925). *Genetic studies of genius: Mental and physical traits of a thousand gifted children.* Stanford, CA: Stanford University Press.

Terman, L. M., & Oden, M. H. (1947). *Genetic studies of genius: Vol. 4. The gifted child grows up: Twenty-five years' follow-up of a superior group.* Stanford, CA: Stanford University Press.

Terman, L. M., & Oden, M. H. (1959). *Genetic studies of genius: Vol. 4. The gifted child at mid-life: Thirty-five years' follow-up of the superior child.* Stanford, CA: Stanford University Press.

Torrance, E. P. (1962). *Guiding creative talent.* Englewood Cliffs, NJ: Prentice-Hall.

Torrance, E. P. (1966). *Torrance tests of creative thinking.* Bensenville, IL: Scholastic Testing Service.

Torrance, E. P. (1972a). Career patterns and peak creative achievements of creative high school students twelve years later. *Gifted Child Quarterly, 16,* 55–62.

Torrance, E. P. (1972b). Predictive validity of the Torrance Tests of Creative Thinking. *Journal of Creative Behavior, 3,* 236–252.

Torrance, E. P. (1980). Growing up creatively gifted: A 22-year longitudinal study. *Creative Child and Adult Quarterly, 5,* 148–159.

Torrance, E. P., & Wu, T. (1981). A comparative longitudinal study of the adult creative achievements of elementary school children identified as highly intelligent and highly creative. *Creative Child and Adult Quarterly, 6,* 71–76.

U.S. Department of Labor, Employment and Training Administration. (1979). *Guide for occupational exploration.* Washington, DC: U.S. Government Printing Office.

Wallach, M. A. (1970). Creativity. In P.H. Mussen (Ed.), *Carmichael's manual of child psychology* (Vol. 1, 3rd ed., pp. 1211–1272). New York: Wiley.

Wallach, M. A. (1971). *The intelligence/creativity distinction.* Morristown, NJ: General Learning Press.

Wallach, M. A. (1985). Creativity testing and giftedness. In F. D. Horowitz & M. O'Brien (Eds.), *The gifted and talented: Developmental perspectives* (pp. 99–123). Washington, DC: American Psychological Association.

Wallach, M. A., & Kogan, N. (1965). *Modes of thinking in young children: A study of the creativity-intelligence distinction.* New York: Holt, Rinehart & Winston.

Wallach, M. A., & Wing, C. W., Jr. (1969). *The talented student: A validation of the creativity-intelligence distinction.* New York: Holt, Rinehart & Winston.

Whiston, S. C., Milgram, R. M., & Hong, E. (1992). *Intrinsically motivated behavior in gifted and talented youth as predictors of adult occupational attainment.* Unpublished manuscript.

Wing, C. W., Jr., & Wallach, M. A. (1971). *College admissions and the psychology of talent.* New York: Holt, Rinehart & Winston.

9

The Torrance Tests of Creative Thinking: From Design Through Establishment of Predictive Validity

Bonnie Cramond

THE IMPETUS FOR CREATIVITY RESEARCH

In 1937, a young man in the dual role of counselor and high school teacher was struggling to reach some particularly challenging students in a rural Georgia school. In spite of the difficulties that he found in attempting to teach and counsel them, he "sensed that these young people possessed something very valuable and precious" (Torrance, 1990, p. 2). The teacher, E. Paul Torrance, went on to work for six years at Georgia Military College where he recognized that many of his students had been sent to boarding school because they were too full of ideas to be tolerated in their local schools. Yet, he noted that many of them went on to become successful in politics, business, the military, education, the arts, science, and other fields (Torrance, 1990).

Torrance's ideas about the special something that these students exhibited coalesced with the discovery of a book, *Square Pegs in Square Holes* by Margaret Broadley (1943). Broadley described the tests developed at the Human Engineering Laboratories by Johnson O'Connor (1945). The test that particularly caught Torrance's attention was the one entitled "Creative Imagination." It was designed to measure an aptitude which, "unless it is used and directed into the right channels, it is like a wild colt roaming the prairies, picturesque, perhaps, but little else. . . . Well-directed and developed, the aptitude can lead you into deeply satisfying creative work" (Broadley, 1943, p. 69). Reflecting upon O'Connor's words, Torrance developed the Mother Goose Test to assess the creativity of elementary school children.

As his teaching career was interrupted by a term of duty in the U.S. Army, Torrance's interest in creativity research incubated during the next few years as he worked as a counselor for disabled veterans at the University of Minnesota and Kansas State University. There he met yet more "wild colts" and continued to reflect upon the best way to identify and nurture their creativity (Torrance, 1990).

When he later went to work with Air Force Survival Training as a research psychologist, he made an important discovery. "I found that I was really training the men for creative behavior" (Torrance, 1989, personal communication). He also found that the jet aces were a group of very creative individuals. He recognized indications of "wild colts" from their biographical data, but these men had learned discipline and how to survive (Torrance, 1990). Torrance found further indications of creativity in their responses to the Rorschach and in their scores on the Risk-Taking Scale of a biographical inventory (Torrance, 1954). These findings, and almost seven years of experience in Air Force survival research, led him to conclude that, "whenever you encounter a situation or problem for which you have no learned or practiced solution, some creativity is required" (Torrance, 1989, personal communication).

THE RESEARCH PROGRAM AT THE UNIVERSITY OF MINNESOTA

In 1958, Torrance went to the University of Minnesota as Director of the Bureau of Educational Research. Not long after that, the Bureau's Faculty Advisory Board recommended establishing a 25-year program in research on giftedness. The Dean of the College of Education, Walter W. Cook, was interested in the pattern of abilities he had observed in test results at the University of Minnesota Laboratory School. He was convinced that students varied on the various ability, aptitude, and intelligence tests because the instruments were measuring different abilities; children could be gifted in some areas and not others. He recommended that the 25-year study attempt to explore the various kinds of giftedness (Torrance, 1990).

Because of his long-term interest in creativity, this was the area that Torrance chose to investigate first. "I decided to concentrate on creativity first, then go on to study other kinds of abilities. However, creativity was too overwhelming, so I never left it. I started to develop measures of creative potential" (Torrance, 1989, personal communication).

These initial investigations were three-pronged. Torrance continued to work on the biographical inventory that he had used with the pilots. He also decided to broaden the data pool of the inventory from the survivors of emergencies and extreme conditions to include creative scientists, inventors, and explorers. He and his research assistants looked at the characteristics which were theorized to be necessary for outstanding success in each field and then asked themselves what life experiences would give a person those characteristics and abilities (Torrance, 1990). Torrance and one of his research assistants developed an instrument and began refining it (Torrance & DeYoung, 1958). One validity study which yielded excellent results was completed before the project was abandoned (Dauw, 1965). "When I learned that Calvin Taylor and his associates were having such success with biographical inventories, I decided to give further development of our biographical inventories low priority. I regret this decision" (Torrance, 1990, p. 19).

The second area of investigation was motivation. Torrance and his assistants devised The Creative Motivation Scale (Torrance, 1959, 1963, 1985) based on Tumin's (1953) theories about motivational factors that are obstacles to creativity. The obstacles that Tumin listed—excessive quest for certainty, for power, meaning, and social relations, and pathological relations—were expanded and converted into scales with several items in each. Torrance recently recounted, "It has consistently been shown to have good reliability and validity over the years, but it has never been published commercially. I developed a form for children called What Makes Me Run, but the norms have not been completed" (Torrance, 1990, p. 18).

It was the third part of this research program that was to become the focus of Torrance's research over the next several years—the design and refinement of the Torrance Tests of Creative Thinking (Torrance, 1966, 1974). "I have always been interested in empowering children, releasing their creative potential. But first I had to measure that potential. So I have a reputation as a psychometrician, but all along I have worked with the development of creativity" (Torrance, 1989, personal communication). Those familiar with Torrance's work know that his establishment of the Future Problem Solving Program (Torrance, Bruch, & Torrance, 1976), development of the Incubation Model for creative teaching (Torrance & Safter, 1989), and founding of the Creative Scholars Network give testimony to these words (Frasier, 1990).

Although Torrance saw the development of the tests as a means to an end, these eponymous tests of creative thinking have gained worldwide attention. The Torrance Tests of Creative Thinking have been used in over 2,000 studies and have been translated into more than 32 languages (Frasier, 1990). It is the purpose of this chapter to summarize the development of the tests and the longitudinal studies that have been undertaken to investigate their predictive validity.

THE TORRANCE TESTS OF CREATIVE THINKING

Research Definition of Creativity

Prior to developing activities for the tests, Torrance had to find a research definition for creativity. He considered at least 50 before choosing a process definition. With process as the focus, "I could then ask what kind of person one must be to engage in the process successfully, what kinds of environments will facilitate it, and what kind of products will result from successful operation of the process" (Torrance, 1990, p. 6). Torrance defined creativity as

> a process of becoming sensitive to problems, deficiencies, gaps in knowledge, missing elements, disharmonies, and so on; identifying the difficulty; searching for solutions, making guesses, or formulating hypotheses about the deficiencies; testing and retesting these hypotheses and possibly modifying and retesting them; and finally communicating the results. (Torrance, 1974, p. 8)

He particularly liked this definition because it described creativity as a very natural process arising from a strong human need to resolve the tension experienced when something is sensed as missing or incomplete. This put creativity within the reach of everyday people in everyday life rather than in the realm of the highest creative accomplishment experienced by so few (Torrance, 1990). It was also possible at any age, and thus consistent with his goal of addressing creative development from preschool through graduate school and into professional development (Torrance, 1974).

Purpose and Rationale

In keeping with his stated interest of measuring creativity in order to develop it, Torrance (1966) delineated the following five purposes for using creativity tests: (a) to promote understanding of the human mind, its functioning and development; (b) to assist in the development of individualized instruction; (c) to provide additional information for remedial and psychotherapeutic programs; (d) to assess the differential effects of educational materials, programs, curricula, procedures, and so on; and (e) to point out potentialities that might otherwise go unnoticed—especially in children from culturally diverse and lower socioeconomic backgrounds.

Torrance argued the need for early recognition of creative abilities in order to provide the educational and guidance opportunities necessary to nurture them. In his words,

> We must consider what kind of creative potential we want to identify and predict. Do we want to identify only those potentialities that will flourish in spite of all efforts to thwart them? Or, do we want also to identify those potentialities that will be realized under intelligent guidance, more favorable learning conditions, and the like? (Torrance, 1966, p. 6)

His task of establishing predictive ability would have been easier with the former purpose; however, his interest in developing the creativity of children directed him to choose the latter.

Design and Structure

In designing the activities to measure creative thinking abilities, Torrance needed some criteria. Each task had to fit his chosen definition of creativity as a natural, everyday process. Tasks had to be suitable for students from kindergarten through graduate and professional school to enable the study of development and comparisons of age groups. Each activity had to be easy enough for the young or disabled to make a creative response, yet difficult enough to challenge the most able. Activities had to be unbiased with regard to gender and race, and open-ended to allow for responses from different experiential backgrounds. In addition, Torrance wanted the testing experience to be enjoyable (Torrance, 1966, 1974, 1990).

With these criteria in mind, Torrance reviewed past efforts at measuring creativity by individuals such as Barron (1957), Flanagan (1957), and Guilford (1956). He chose some well-known activities for testing and created others. All activities were personally screened by Torrance and administered to various groups so that he could observe the individuals' responses. Items such as Mother Goose prints, coat hangers, bicycles, the doctor's kit, and the nurse's kit were replaced by objects equally known to different races, socioeconomic groups, and genders (Torrance, 1990). (In 1977, Torrance published a review of 20 studies on the lack of racial or socioeconomic bias in the Torrance Tests of Creative Thinking.)

The chosen battery of activities was then administered to a sample of subjects in the fall and winter of 1959-1960. The activities that were retained for the tests (a) were the most different from one another as determined by factor analysis, (b) provided maximal sampling of the thinking involved in creative achievements in various domains, and (c) best elicited responses from both children and adults (Torrance, 1966, 1990). These batteries of activities were called the Minnesota Tests of Creative Thinking, the predecessors to the Torrance Tests of Creative Thinking (TTCT) that were developed after Torrance moved to the University of Georgia (Torrance, 1966, 1974).

Components of the Torrance Tests of Creative Thinking, Verbal

The TTCT verbal tests are available in two forms, A and B, each of which consists of five different types of activities: Ask-and-Guess, Product Improvement, Unusual Uses, Unusual Questions, and Just Suppose. The stimulus for each task consists of a picture to which individuals respond in writing (Torrance, 1966, 1974).

The first type of activity, Ask-and-Guess, is based on research linking curiosity to creativity, especially scientific creativity (Torrance, 1966, 1974). Individuals are asked to respond to three tasks involving a picture stimulus: (a) "Ask Questions," which elicits questions that cannot be directly answered by viewing the picture; (b) "Guess Causes," which encourages the individual to think speculatively about causes of events depicted; and (c) "Guess Consequences," which is designed to reveal the respondent's ability to hypothesize about possible effects of events depicted (Torrance, 1966, 1974).

The Product Improvement Activity and the Unusual Questions Activity have obvious links to the type of creative productivity where one is required to improve something or "make do" with commonplace materials (Torrance, 1966, 1974, 1990). According to Torrance, these activities have been two of the most dependable measures, and appeal to individuals of all ages and walks of life. He has observed that on these measures, economically disadvantaged individuals seem to have an advantage in responding (Torrance, 1990).

The Product Improvement Activity asks the respondent to improve a toy so that children will have more fun playing with it (Torrance, 1966, 1974). The Unusual Questions Activity requires respondents to generate unusual uses, and then unusual questions, about a commonplace object. This activity was based on Burkhart's

(1961) concept of "Divergent Power," a factor he considered essential for creativity in the classroom. The activity on the TTCT was adapted from one used on Burkhart and Bernheim's (1963) test which they found to correlate rather highly with their criteria for creativity in art (cited in Torrance, 1974).

The Just Suppose Activity is a variation of Guilford's (1959) Consequences test. Although Torrance believed that the Guilford task measured an important dimension of creativity, he was disappointed in the results of his first efforts with it because the respondents did not seem to enjoy the task. Therefore, the stimulus pictures of the Just Suppose Activity were designed to be more motivating, to elicit a higher degree of fantasy, and to be more effective with children than the Consequences task.

Torrance recalled that the psychologist Thurstone, a former assistant of Thomas Edison, used a similar task to select his graduate assistants. Thurstone is said to have posed an unusual idea or improbable conclusion to prospective students. Those who immediately dismissed the idea with logic were considered too incurious for graduate study (Torrance, 1966, 1974). Convinced of the importance of this type of activity for assessing an individual's tolerance and playfulness with unusual ideas, Torrance kept searching for more exciting stimuli (Torrance, 1966, 1974, 1990).

He found what he was looking for in Alastair Reid's (1960) *Supposing*. Elementary students and research assistants enjoyed "supposing" and produced some very exciting responses. Paul Henrickson, an artist and research assistant, quickly produced several "Just Suppose" situations and illustrated them. Torrance selected six for each of the two forms of the Just Suppose Test and began trying them out (Torrance, 1990).

Besides the stimuli used in the consequences type activity, there are other important differences between Torrance's tests and Guilford's. One difference is the way that the dimensions of fluency, flexibility, originality, and elaboration are assessed. Guilford used a different stimulus task for each of the different dimensions of divergent thinking, and Torrance scores each stimulus on several dimensions (Torrance, 1991, personal communication). Two other differences are in the instructions (Torrance, 1990). Guilford's instructions do not indicate what type of responses are desired, whereas the directions in the TTCT motivate the respondents for fluency, flexibility, and originality. The other key difference is that Guilford's test (1959) limited the number of responses that individuals were asked to give; Torrance found that test takers produce more original responses after their initial obvious answers are given (Phillips & Torrance, 1977). This is similar to Mednick's (1962) conclusion that the less probable, more remote responses that a person makes are more likely to be creative.

> Guilford and I discussed these differences, but we had both gone too far with our own approaches to change. Guilford did at least acknowledge that I had a point. When measuring jumping ability, you don't just go out and ask people to jump. You have to get them to want to jump if you want a valid measure. This is one reason my tests get a better prediction of creative ability than other tests. (Torrance, 1989, personal communication)

Components of the Torrance Tests of Creative Thinking, Figural

Contrary to what many people think, the figural tests of the TTCT are not simply nonverbal measures of the same creative abilities or tendencies as measured on the verbal tests. In fact, performance on the verbal and figural measures show very little correlation ($r = .06$). The three activities of the figural tests are designed to measure three different creative aspects or tendencies than the verbal tests measure (Torrance, 1990). As with the verbal measures, the instructions are designed to motivate the respondents to give unusual, detailed responses.

The Picture Construction Activity was designed to assess the tendency of creating meaning out of a seemingly meaningless object. Respondents are required to create a picture that includes a given shape as an integral part. A 10-minute time period for this activity allows the elaborators to add many details, or the original thinkers to incubate and produce an uncommon response (Torrance, 1966, 1974).

The Incomplete Figures Activity measures the tendency toward structuring and integrating. It is an adaptation of the Drawing Completion Test developed by Franck and used in studies by Barron (1957) and others. Based on principles of Gestalt psychology, it creates tension in the respondent to finish the picture quickly and in the easiest way possible. The more creative tendency is to resist the tension long enough to construct a less obvious response (Torrance, 1966, 1974).

The Repeated Figures Activity elicits the tendency to return to the same stimulus again and again, perceiving it in a new way each time. Individuals who give creative responses are required to disrupt structure in order to create something new (Torrance, 1990).

Scoring and Interpretation

Torrance tried several different scoring systems and rejected them because they were either ineffective, inefficient, or both. For example, one score that proved to be an effective predictor of creative productivity, the inventive level score (see Table 9.2), was based on a modification of the criteria used by the U.S. Patent Office in determining whether or not an invention should be patented (Torrance, 1959). Despite its effectiveness, the inventive level score was abandoned because it was too time-consuming for the scorers (Torrance, 1991, personal communication).

Because they were so well defined, Torrance decided to use Guilford's (1956) four divergent thinking factors as follows: (a) fluency —the number of relevant responses, (b) flexibility—the number of different categories or shifts in responses, (c) originality—the number of unusual yet relevant ideas as determined by statistical infrequency, and (d) elaboration—the number of details used to extend a response (Torrance, 1966, 1974, 1990).

Scoring varies according to the task. For example, fluency, flexibility, and originality are used to score all activities on the verbal tests (Torrance, 1990). Torrance does not encourage the use of an elaboration score on the verbal tests because it is difficult to get interrater reliability for untrained scorers (Torrance, 1966, 1974).

For the figural tests, the three activities are arranged in order of increasing complexity. In the first task, individuals are instructed to create an unusual picture with details that produce a more complete story—originality and elaboration are motivated. In the second activity, individuals are asked to give a variety of responses, adding flexibility to originality and elaboration. Fluency is a minor consideration because with only 10 figures, many of the respondents will complete them all in the time allotted. Fluency is added as an important dimension in the third task when respondents are given a number of repeated figures to complete originally, elaborately, and with flexibility (Torrance, 1966, 1974). Thus, individuals who use one part of the TTCT Figural, such as the Repeated Figures Activity, without using the others, do not allow the respondents the necessary warm-up for optimal performance.

What the scores mean. Because the TTCT are based on the belief that creativity is developmental and can be affected through specified experiences, Torrance dissuades interpretation of scores as a static measure of a person's ability (Torrance, 1966, 1974, 1979). Torrance is cognizant that the use of the full battery of the

TTCT, Verbal and Figural, is still not able to measure the essence of creativity.

> A high degree of these abilities (usually designated as fluency, flexibility, originality, and ability to sense deficiencies, elaborate, and redefine) does not guarantee that the possessor will behave in a highly creative manner. A high level of these abilities, however, increases a person's chances of behaving creatively. (Torrance, 1974, p. 9)

For most purposes, he has eschewed the use of a composite verbal or figural score and recommended that users base their interpretations on the separate subscores as indicators of specific strengths and areas in need of development (Torrance, 1966, 1974, 1979). He has, however, indicated that "such a score does seem to give a rather stable index of the total amount of creative energy a person has available or is willing to use" (Torrance, 1974, p. 56). It was the investigation of the predictive ability of this index that led to the longitudinal studies on the TTCT.

THE CHALLENGE OF ESTABLISHING PREDICTIVE VALIDITY

Whatever the theoretical construct on which a test is based, the value of that test is determined to a large extent by its ability to predict performance later in life. The premier example can be seen in the realm of intelligence testing, where the Binet test of intelligence, in spite of its lack of a theoretical basis and incapacity to measure more than a few human abilities, has weathered translations and updates. It has endured because of its predictive validity; children who score highly on the *Stanford-Binet Intelligence Scales* tend to do well in school.

However, the task of predicting so mercurial a quality as creativity presents special challenges. The fragile nature of creativity has been cited by researchers who have reviewed the deleterious effects that competition (Amabile, 1983), behavior of significant others (Feldman, 1988; Torrance, 1981a), historical events, the social milieu (Simonton, 1991), and a variety of other inner and outer forces can have on the creative productivity of an individual (Feldman, 1988; Gardner, 1988). In fact, Feldman speculated that there must be "hundreds of possible vectors of influence on development, including the centrally important specific physical, emotional, and intellectual qualities of the individual whose development we are trying to comprehend" (Feldman, 1988, p. 276). When given the additional hindrances of time and attempting to correlate paper-and-pencil test scores to real-life accomplishments, predicting creative behavior becomes quite demanding.

Torrance (1981a) realized that establishing adequate predictive validity for tests of creative thinking ability presented particular difficulties. During the initial 6-year period of testing in Minnesota elementary schools, he had seen many of the children in his sample "surrender" their creativity at an early age. He feared that a "fourth-grade slump" (Torrance, 1966, 1968) was indicative of this trend which would destroy the best predictions.

Torrance himself had misgivings when he considered the magnitude of the task. He realized that the typical problems inherent in longitudinal research would need to be resolved: maintaining contacts with subjects, storing the data, and obtaining financial support. He knew that the problem of maintaining contacts would be especially difficult with children because of their mobility and name changes that might take place as they grew up (Torrance, 1981a). However, he could not have foreseen a particular problem that would beset him in maintaining contact with these children—the onset and escalation of U.S. involvement in the Vietnam War. When he attempted after seven years to contact those who had been seniors in 1959, he found that some of the original subjects were deceased or were in combat in Vietnam (Torrance, 1969).

The lack of funding was a continuing problem; all of the TTCT studies have been entirely self-supporting. Torrance has blamed several events or factors for complicating the issue of receiving research support (Torrance, 1990, personal communication). First, the studies proved to be far more expensive than Torrance had anticipated. This delayed the work for a number of years as he struggled to finance the project himself. Then, the U.S. Office of Education pressured him to write a monograph on creativity. He originally declined, claiming he had to devote what time he had to the TTCT project. Secretary of Health, Education, and Welfare John Gardner increased the pressure until Torrance acceded. Torrance's work on the monograph further interrupted the longitudinal studies. By the time the commissioned manuscript was completed, however, Gardner had resigned his post and the Office of Education was no longer interested in creativity (Torrance, 1990, personal communication). The completed monograph, too long for a journal article, but too short for a book, was never published (Torrance, 1992, personal communication).

At about this time, Torrance moved to The University of Georgia as Chair of the Department of Educational Psychology, Research, and Measurement. This position was particularly demanding because two departments had been merged to create the new one, and two new graduate programs were added. Personnel, program, funding, and other administrative concerns so occupied him that he had to use the Christmas recess of 1967 to write the report on the longitudinal examination of the fourth-grade slump (Torrance, 1968). This work was interrupted by the death of his father on New Year's Eve. The fourth-grade slump study appeared on Senator Proxmire's list and was ridiculed in the *Reader's Digest*. These events exacerbated the problem of obtaining outside funding (Torrance, 1990).

Despite these problems, investigators have conducted at least six longitudinal studies on the predictive validity of the TTCT. These studies, outlined below, have attempted to answer the question of how well the *Torrance Tests of Creative Thinking* predict later creative productivity.

MEETING THE CHALLENGE

Preliminary Studies

The first study of the predictive validity of the TTCT, conducted by Torrance, Tan, and Allman (1970), was initiated in 1958 with 325 elementary education majors. The predictor instruments used were the earliest developed batteries of the *Torrance Tests of Creative Thinking*. Six-and-a-half years later, follow-up data were obtained from 114 of the individuals on a criterion instrument entitled "A Teacher's Self-Inventory," a check list developed to assess teachers' activity and achievement. Analyses comparing the responses of the upper and lower 27% on originality indicated that 69 of the 127 items significantly differentiated the high originals from the low originals ($p < .05$). These items were used to develop a composite index that correlated .62 with the originality score and .57 with the total creativity score. From this, the investigators concluded that the creativity test administered to teacher trainees in their junior year of college predicted classroom teaching behavior eight years later (Torrance, 1972b; Torrance, Tan, & Allman, 1970).

In 1964, Cropley administered a battery of six of Torrance's creativity tests to 111 seventh-grade students. Five years later he compared their creativity scores with their achievement in art, drama, literature, and music. The canonical correlations computed between the combined creativity test scores and the combined creativity criterion scores were in the order of .50, leading him to conclude that the creativity test scores were significant predictors of creative achievements (Cropley, 1971).

The year after Cropley's study was begun, Witt used three of the test tasks from the *Torrance Tests of Creative Thinking* in addition to his own *Favorite Group Games Test* to identify 16 creative second, third, and fourth graders from a group of about 200 economically disadvantaged black children. Twelve of those identified participated in a continuing program for creative, disadvantaged children that emphasized summer and after-school enrichment as well as family and school interventions. In the sixth year of the program's existence Witt wrote, "Of the twelve children, ten have revealed superior talent and have achieved at a high level in one or more art forms. Three of these ten children have demonstrated superior verbal creativity in science and other areas" (Witt, 1971).

The aforementioned investigations gave some credence to the *Torrance Tests of Creativity* as predictors of later creative productivity. However, the major body of longitudinal research was initiated by Torrance in two elementary schools and a high school in Minneapolis in the late 1950s (Torrance 1969, 1972a, 1972b, 1980, 1981a) .

The Minnesota Studies

Beginning in 1958 and continuing through 1964, all pupils enrolled in grades one to six in two elementary schools were administered various batteries of the TTCT each year. Beginning in September 1959, all students enrolled in grades 7-12 of the University of Minnesota High School also completed the tests. Three major points of data collection have been completed and reported (Torrance 1969, 1972a, 1972b, 1980, 1981a), and the fourth follow-up is in progress.

The seven-year follow-up of high school students. The first follow-up of this group was conducted in the spring of 1966 with the students who had been seniors in 1959. While still in high school, the students had been given the original version of the *Torrance Tests of Creative Thinking*. Responses were scored for fluency, flexibility, inventive level, and elaboration (Torrance, 1972b). Later, the tests were rescored on the basis of the 1966 published scoring guides and inventive level was replaced by originality (Torrance, 1969). In addition, scores were available for all of the students on the *Iowa Tests of Educational Achievement* and for most of them on the *Lorge-Thorndike* or the *Stanford-Binet Intelligence Scales*. Near the end of their senior year, the students were asked to complete a five-item peer nomination questionnaire. This sociometric questionnaire requested the students to nominate three of their classmates on the basis of the following criteria:

1. Who in your class comes up with the *most ideas?*
2. Who have the most *original* or *unusual ideas?*
3. If the situation changed or if a solution to a problem wouldn't work, who would be the *first ones to find a new way of meeting the problem?*
4. Who do the *most inventing and developing of new ideas, gadgets, and the like?*
5. Who are the *best at thinking of all the details involved* in working out a new idea and *thinking of all the consequences?* (Torrance, 1969, p. 224)

In all, the measures administered during high school yielded data on the students' intelligence, high school achievement, peer nominations of creativity, and creativity as measured by the TTCT in scores of fluency, flexibility, originality, and elaboration.

Criterion data were obtained for 46 of the original 69 subjects. In addition to biographical and demographic information, the follow-up questionnaire included a question about subjects' most creative achievements, a question about aspirations, and a check list of creative accomplishments. The creative accomplishments check list was comprised of items that assessed the type and degree of individual creative accomplishment. Besides achievement in the arts, the items included research, work innovations, inventions, and change in life philosophy (Torrance, 1969).

From this information, five trained judges derived three indices of creative achievement in the following way:

1. An index of quantity of creative achievements was obtained by first assigning a weight of one for every creative achievement attained once or twice and two for every achievement attained three or more times, and then summing the weighted scores.
2. An index of quality of creative achievement was obtained by rating the originality of the most creative achievements on a 10-point scale. The mean interrater reliability coefficient was .65.
3. Finally, an index of creative motivation was obtained by rating the degree of originality required to realize each student's vocational aspiration. The mean interrater reliability coefficient was .69 (Torrance, 1972a).

Product-moment correlation coefficients calculated to determine the degree of relationship between the predictor variables and the criterion variables are shown in Table 9.1 (Torrance, 1969, p. 226; 1972b, p. 247).

As indicated in Table 9.1, the four subtest scores of the Torrance Tests of Creativity (fluency, flexibility, originality, and elaboration) were better predictors of creative achievement than were intelligence, high school achievement, or peer nominations. When these four TTCT scores were entered into a stepwise regression equation, the following multiple correlation coefficients were obtained: (a) .50 with Creative Quality, (b) .46 with Creative Quantity, and (c) .51 with Creative Motivation. In other words, the four TTCT scores accounted for 25% of the variance noted in Creative Quality, 21% of the variance in Creative Quantity, and 26% of the variance in Creative Motivation.

These results indicated that the TTCT scores obtained when the students were seniors in high school were powerful predictors of their creative achievement and motivation seven years later. The 7-year interval between initial testing and follow-up was considered to be the shortest reasonable time for the group to complete their doctorates. "The 7-year followup was a mistake, but this was my last chance to collect data before leaving Minnesota, and I was afraid I would not get good cooperation after I relocated in Georgia. However, I have gotten good cooperation in both the elementary and high school subjects" (Torrance, 1990, personal communication).

Table 9.1.   Product Moment Correlation Coefficients Between Creativity Predictors Obtained in 1959 and the Three Indices of Creative Achievement Established in 1966

	Criterion Variables		
Predictors	Creative Quantity	Creative Quality	Creative Motivation
Intelligence Test	.22	.37*	.32
High School Achievement	.09	.20	.15
Peer Nominations on Creative Criteria	.13	.13	.18
Fluency (TTCT)	.44*	.39*	.34*
Flexibility (TTCT)	.44*	.48*	.46*
Originality (TTCT)	.40*	.43*	.42*
Elaboration (TTCT)	.37*	.32	.25

*p ≤ .01

The second follow-up of the high school students: 12th-year interval. Five years later, Torrance sent a questionnaire similar to the one he had used in the 1966 study to the entire 1959 University of Minnesota High School population ($N = 392$). By this time, even the freshmen who had been tested had had enough time to record some creative accomplishments. The response rate was approximately 60%, with 117 females and 119 males returning the completed questionnaire (Torrance, 1972b).

Once again, expert judges derived the three indices of creative achievement: Creative Quantity, Creative Quality, and Creative Motivation. The mean interrater reliability coefficient of the five judges was .91. The methods of obtaining these indices were refined slightly as follows:

1. The quantity of creative achievements was derived by adding the number of creative achievements checked or listed by each respondent.
2. The quality of highest creative achievements was based on the judges' ratings on a 10-point scale of the three most creative achievements reported by the respondents.
3. The measure of creative motivation was also based on 10-point ratings of the respondents' statements of what they would most like to do in the future, assuming the necessary talent, training, and opportunity.

Table 9.2 (Torrance, 1972b, p. 249) provides information on the correlations between the predictors and the criteria broken down by gender. All of the creativity predictors were significant at the .01 level. However, the correlations were generally lower for the females than for the males. This gender effect was even more profound when the IQ score from the *Lorge-Thorndike* test was used as a predictor of creative achievement. These results indicate that the creative achievements of females may be less predictable than those of the males, at least with the measures used in this study. This may be because of a greater impact of intervening variables, such as marriage and family, on females' creative achievements. To test this hypothesis Torrance, Bruch, and Morse (1973) studied the effect of using the Life Experience data derived from Taylor and Ellison's scoring (1967) with the women in the study. It did improve predictability.

For males, however, the creativity measures were consistently better predictors of quantity of creative achievements than was the IQ measure. For quality of creative achievements and creative aspi-

Table 9.2. **Product Moment Correlation Coefficients Between Creativity Predictors Obtained in 1959 and the Three Indices of Creative Achievement Established in 1971**

	Males (n = 119)			Females (n = 117)		
	Criterion Variables					
Predictors	Quantity	Quality	Aspiration	Quantity	Quality	Aspiration
IQ (Lorge-Thorndike)	.24*	.40*	.37*	.06	.29*	.18**
Fluency (TTCT)	.31*	.29*	.27*	.28*	.33*	.27*
Flexibility (TTCT)	.32*	.31*	.27*	.25*	.32*	.23*
Originality (TTCT)	.41*	.45*	.45*	.37*	.40*	.30*
Elaboration (TTCT)	.27*	.34*	.37*	.27*	.35*	.29*
Inventive level	.42*	.43*	.42*	.28*	.41*	.32*

*$p \leq .01$;**$p \leq .05$

rations, originality and inventive level were the only two creativity measures that were better predictors than the IQ score.

By combining the scores on the creativity test battery administered in 1959 into a total creativity score to predict the combined creativity criteria derived in 1971, a canonical correlation of .51 was obtained for the full sample. When looking at the genders separately, a canonical correlation of .59 was obtained for males and one of .46 for females.

This data collection point illustrated once again that creativity measures administered in high school were able to accurately predict individuals' adult creative accomplishments on three dimensions: Quantity of creative achievements, quality of creative achievements, and creative aspirations or motivation. A major question remained, namely how well could the TTCT administered in elementary school predict adult creative achievements?

The 22-year follow-up of elementary school students. In 1979-1980, a follow-up was conducted with the students who had been in the two Minneapolis test-site elementary schools between 1958-1964. During that 6-year testing period, participating students completed a variety of measures of creative thinking, including various forms of the *Torrance Tests of Creative Thinking*, a biographical inventory, creative writing samples, check lists of creative activities performed on their own, *Buck's House-Tree-Person Test*, and sociometric questionnaires. In addition, standardized intelligence and achievement test scores were available for most of the participants. In order to be included in the follow-up study, the individual had to have completed one or more batteries of creativity tests each year for at least three years. Of the 400 participants who met this criterion, approximately 70% were located and sent questionnaires. Of these, 211 (116 females and 95 males) returned the completed questionnaires (Torrance, 1980, 1981a).

A creativity index was calculated for the respondents using data collected over three years of creativity testing. It was derived, in part, by converting raw scores for all of the tests available for a specific school year to standard scores based on the national norms accumulated in the early 1960s. The mean creativity index of the respondents did not differ significantly from national norms. Nor did it differ significantly from the mean for students in the initial study. Therefore, it was concluded that the respondents were probably representative of the initial study sample (Torrance, 1981a).

Two questionnaires were used. The first elicited biographical and demographic information similar to that requested in the follow-up of the high school students (Torrance, 1972a, 1972b). Among many other questions, it asked about career ambitions and projections, high school creative achievements, post-high school creative achievements, and the achievements considered most creative by the students themselves. Those who returned the first questionnaire were sent a second questionnaire, designed specifically to generate responses about the individuals' "Creative Style of Life Achievements," those that are not ordinarily publicly recognized and acknowledged, such as organizing an action-oriented group (Torrance, 1981a).

Five indices of creative achievement were derived from the questionnaire responses to be used as criteria:

1. The number of high school creative achievements was based on a check list of 25 types of achievement in the sciences, visual and performing arts, language, leadership, and business, similar to the one used for many years by the National Merit Scholarship program and the studies of Wallach and Wing (1969).
2. The number of post-high school creative achievements was derived from the check list of creative accomplishments designed for the follow-up of the high school students and listed earlier (Torrance, 1969).
3. The number of "creative style of life" achievements was derived from a check list consisting of 22 categories of everyday creative achievements that are not publicly recognized. It includes

things such as unrecognized artistic and design creations, learning new skills, and so on.

4. The quality of highest creative achievements was based on the composite ratings of expert judges of the creative achievements described by the subjects as in the previous follow-up studies reported. Interrater reliabilities obtained using Cronbach's alpha for the three judges were .86 for male respondents and .83 for females.

5. Creativeness of future career image was also based on the ratings of the three judges. This index differed from the Creative Motivation Index used in the 1966 high school follow-up in that this time the respondents answered *two* questions that judges rated on the creativeness of the future career images. Whereas in the 1966 study respondents had been asked to indicate what they would most like to do in the future assuming the requisite talent, training, and opportunity, this time respondents were asked to project both realistic and fantasy-oriented future aspirations. The interrater reliabilities obtained using Cronbach's alpha were .81 for both male and female respondents (Torrance, 1981a).

To determine how well the creativity measures predicted future achievements, Pearson product-moment correlation coefficients were calculated between the creativity index derived from elementary school assessments and each of the five indices of creative achievement obtained 22 years later (Torrance, 1981a). As indicated in Table 9.3 (Torrance, 1981a, p. 60), all correlation coefficients were significant at the .001 level. A multiple correlation coefficient of .63 was obtained for the five criteria entered into a stepwise multiple regression equation.

The second analysis was undertaken to examine differences between the upper half and the lower half of the respondents as determined by a median split on the creativity index. Using t-tests to compare means and chi squares to check for other than an equal proportion of High and Low Creatives on each of the indices, Torrance concluded that the High Creatives and the Low Creatives were significantly different on the five indices of creative achievement ($p < .001$) (Torrance, 1981a).

These results demonstrated the power of the creativity measures, when combined in a battery, to assess some abilities which are related to later creative productivity. Other studies have investigated the predictive validity of subtests such as the bonus scoring on the Repeated Figures Test (Torrance, 1972c), unusual visual perspec-

Table 9.3. Product Moment Correlation Coefficients Between
the Creativity Index Obtained in 1958-64 and the Five Indices
of Creative Achievement Established in 1980

Criteria of Creative Achievement	Males ($n = 95$)	Females ($n = 116$)	Total ($n = 211$)
Number of High School Creative Achievements	.33	.44	.38
Number of Post-High School Creative Achievements	.57	.42	.46
Number of Creative Style of Living Achievements	.42	.48	.47
Quality of Highest Creative Achievements (Ratings)	.59	.57	.58
Quality of Future Career Image	.62	.54	.57

All coefficients of correlation are significant at the .001 level.

tive on the Repeated Figures Test (Torrance, 1972d), the criterion-referenced indicators from the TTCT, Figural, Streamlined (Torrance, 1981b), and the Just Suppose Test (Torrance & Safter, 1989). To date, the 22-year study of the predictive validity of the Torrance Tests of Creative Thinking has been the most comprehensive and persistent investigation into the skills, motivation, and opportunities related to creative accomplishment.

CONCLUSIONS FROM THE LONGITUDINAL STUDIES

The results of the longitudinal studies provide strong evidence of the predictive validity of the *Torrance Tests of Creative Thinking*. It is apparent that such measures of creative thinking administered in childhood can be good predictors of later adult creative achievements. Overall, the correlation coefficients may be considered of moderate magnitude for the social sciences (Cohen, 1988). However, when one takes into account that these correlations were obtained after a 7- to 22-year time lapse, and by correlating pencil-and-paper measures with real-life accomplishments, they are impressive.

As remarkable as the results in Table 9.4 (Torrance, 1981a, p. 61) may seem, factors other than those assessed through creativity tests have value in predicting creative achievement. As discussed earlier,

**Table 9.4. Selected Correlates of Adult Creative Achievement
of Total Sample**

Variable	N	No. HS Ach.	No. Post HS Ach.	Style Life	Quality Cr. Ach.	Quality Fut. Image
Creativity Index	211	.38**	.46**	.47**	.58**	.57**
Future Career Image	206	.29**	.33**	.33**	.42**	.44**
HTP IQ (Buck)	181	.16*	.19*	.06	.21**	.13
S-B/WISC/CMM IQ Adj.	156	.15	.18*	−.02	.34**	.32**
Foreign Experience	211	.22**	.15*	.21*	.23**	.26**
Time Out	211	.00	.11	.31**	.14	.12
Mentor	211	.23**	.23**	.24**	.33**	.23**
Age	211	−.08	.00	.00	−.07	−.07
Marital Status	211	.03	.03	.07	.03	−.05
Age Married	211	.13	.02	.14	.18*	.19*
Number of Children	211	−.09	−.11	−.08	−.14*	−.14*

*$p \leq .05$; **$p \leq .001$

Torrance and others are only too aware of the fragile nature of childhood creativity. Therefore, Torrance (1980), in the 22-year follow-up, also obtained information from the respondents about spurs and obstacles to their creative achievement. From this information he concluded that there are critical correlates in addition to creative ability evidenced in childhood. The most important of these appeared to be having an enduring childhood future career image and a mentor at some time. These two variables were related to all five criteria of adult creative achievement (Torrance 1980, 1981a).

An enduring future career image is the term Torrance has used to describe the tendency of the high creatives to "fall in love" with something in elementary school that later became central to their future career image (Torrance, 1981a). This is illustrated by the case of a child who was writing science fiction stories and space age dramas in third grade. In high school he founded a state science fiction society with an amateur magazine and a yearly convention that is still an annual event. This individual is now a successful science fiction novelist (Torrance, 1980).

Most of the mentors who made a difference in these individuals' lives have been teachers, often in elementary school. The vivid memories that many of the most creative individuals have of their mentors provide testimony to the lasting impact these early contacts have had on their lives. One respondent, who is a successful author and illustrator of children's books, recalled a fourth-grade experience:

In response to a creative writing assignment . . . I began my first book. Actually, I only got 30-some pages into it. Never finished. But Mr. Myers was most encouraging. He had me read what I was writing in installments. Later that year I began writing and illustrating another book outside of class. Mr. Myers took an active interest in it. Without such encouragement, I may not have had the confidence to sit down last summer and write the first in a series of children's books. (Torrance, 1981a, p. 56)

Having an enduring future career image and a mentor may have been easier for boys growing up in the 1950s and early 1960s than it was for girls. Many girls would not have aspired to a career or sought a mentor for their creative pursuits. Therefore, the prominence of these variables may provide a partial explanation for the observed gender differences in the predictability of adult creative achievements (see Table 9.2).

Two other variables that served as predictors were measures of intelligence and having had experience in foreign living and study. Intelligence test measures, however, did not correlate as highly as measures of creative thinking, and were especially poor in predicting "Creative Style of Life Achievements." It appears that having taken time out from formal education and work is significantly related to the Style of Life criterion, but only to that (Torrance, 1981a).

THE CONTINUING CHALLENGE

The amount of data collected for the 22-year follow-up was so vast that there are additional quantitative and qualitative analyses to be conducted (Torrance, 1981a). There are unanswered questions about whether the results found with the Minnesota group would be generalizable to other samples. As Torrance (1972a) pointed out, the majority of the students in the Minnesota studies were the offspring of professional and business people. The mean IQ of the elementary group as assessed by Buck's *House-Tree-Person Test* was 134, and 121 as assessed by tests such as the *Stanford-Binet, Wechsler, and California Test of Mental Maturity*. It has been noted elsewhere that divergent thinking tests are more reliable and valid in the gifted than the nongifted population (Runco, 1986).

It is uncertain how the results would differ with other, less advantaged populations. However, the lowered predictability of the creative achievements of females as compared to males may give some indication of the bleak results that might be expected with a group less likely to have to freedom to pursue their creative potential. The everyday struggle to survive doesn't leave much time for creative accomplishments. "In both schools many of the children lived in Federal housing developments and were from definitely disadvantaged backgrounds. They were difficult to locate 22 years later. We did locate enough of them to get some notion of how poverty influenced the chances of creative achievement. They just don't have a chance (Torrance, 1990, personal communication)."

Also of consequence is the fact that the respondents in the studies were in their 20s and 30s. It may be that their most creative achievements had not been completed, or even started. Or, perhaps great creative works had been completed, but had not yet gained recognition. As one respondent explained, "I wish Dr. Torrance would contact me again. Since I completed the questionnaire, I started my own business. It has been successful enough to allow me the time to pursue my real love—art."

Another data collection point could be even more challenging than the ones already conducted. Torrance and one of his graduate students, Chris Nelson, are in the process of collecting and analyzing the data from the 30-year follow-up. No doubt there will be more attrition from the respondent group as people could not be contacted for various reasons. However, more time has passed for individuals, especially those who took time out to go to Vietnam, to achieve their childhood creative potential. Torrance is especially interested in examining the predictive validity of the sociometric questionnaires that had the students rate their classmates on creative criteria (Torrance, 1991, personal communication). The study is ongoing.

Perhaps most interesting to individuals contemplating longitudinal research is the question, "Why?" Why does someone persevere in the face of personal setbacks, criticisms, financial crises, or methodological problems with longitudinal studies? The answer, in this case, may be suggested in a little sign above the door in Torrance's study: "Innovate or vegetate."

REFERENCES

Amabile, T. M. (1983). *The social psychology of creativity.* New York: Springer-Verlag.

Barron, F. (1957). The psychology of imagination. *Scientific American,* 199, 151–166.

Broadley, M. (1943). *Square pegs in square holes,* Garden City, NY: Doubleday.

Burkhart, R. C. (1961). *Four creativity personality factors in art and teacher education.* Unpublished manuscript.

Burkhart, R. C., & Bernheim, G. (1963). *Object Question test manual.* University Park, PA: Pennsylvania State University, Department of Art Education.

Chassell, L. M. (1916). Tests of originality. *Journal of Educational Psychology, 7,* 317–328.

Cohen, J. (1988). *Statistical power analysis for behavioral sciences.* Hillsdale, NJ: Erlbaum.

Cropley, A. J. (1971). Some Canadian creativity research. *Journal of Research and Development in Education, 4*(3), 113–115.

Dauw, D. C. (1965). *Life experiences, vocational needs and choices of original thinkers and good elaborators.* Unpublished doctoral dissertation, University of Minnesota, Minneapolis.

Feldman, D. H. (1988). *Creativity: Dreams, insights, and transformations.* In R. J. Sternberg (Ed.), *The nature of creativity* (pp. 271–297). New York: Cambridge University Press.

Flanagan, J. C. (1957). *Flanagan classification test 16A, Ingenuity.* Chicago, IL: Science Research Associates.

Frasier, M. M. (1990). *Torrance verbal and figural tests: Measuring general creative thinking processes.* Paper presented at Annual Meeting of the American Educational Research Association, San Francisco, CA.

Gardner, H. (1988). Creative lives and creative works: A synthetic scientific approach. In R. J. Sternberg (Ed.), *The nature of creativity* (pp. 298–321). New York: Cambridge University Press.

Guilford, J. P. (1956). Structure of intellect. *Psychological Review, 53,* 267–293.

McCloy, W. (1939). Creative imagination in children and adults. *Psychological Monographs, 51*(5), 88–102.

Mednick, S. A. (1962). The associative basis of the creative process. *Psychological Review, 69,* 220–227, 232.

O'Connor, J. (1945). *Ideaphoria.* New York: Johnson O'Connor Research Foundation.

Phillips, V. K., & Torrance, E. P. (1977). Levels of originality at earlier and later stages of creativity test tasks. *Journal of Creative Behavior, 11,* 146.

Runco, M. A. (1986). Predicting children's creative performance. *Psychological Reports, 59,* 1247–1254.

Simonton, D. K. (1991). Personality correlates of exceptional personal influence: A note on Thorndike's (1950) creators and leaders. *Creativity Research Journal, 4*(1), 67–78.

Simpson, R. M. (1922). Creative imagination. *American Journal of Psychology, 33,* 234–243.

Taylor, C. W., & Ellison, R. L. (1967). Biographical predictors of scientific performance. *Science, 155,* 1075–1080.

Torrance, E. P. (1954). *The development of a preliminary Life Experience Inventory for the study of fighter interceptor pilot combat effective-*

ness. San Antonio, TX: Air Force Personnel and Training Research Center, Lackland AFB.

Torrance, E. P. (1959). Current research on the nature of creative talent. *Journal of Counseling Psychology, 6,* 309–316.

Torrance, E.P. (1959, 1963, 1985). *Creative motivation scale: Norms technical manual.* Athens, GA: Georgia Studies of Creative Behavior.

Torrance, E. P. (1966). *Torrance tests of creative thinking: Norms-technical manual* (Research ed.). Princeton, NJ: Personnel Press.

Torrance, E. P. (1968). A longitudinal examination of the fourth grade slump in creativity. *Gifted Child Quarterly, 12,* 195–199.

Torrance, E. P. (1969). Prediction of adult creative achievement among high school seniors. *Gifted Child Quarterly, 13,* 223–229.

Torrance, E. P. (1972a). Career patterns and peak creative achievements of creative high school students twelve years later. *Gifted Child Quarterly, 16,* 75–88.

Torrance, E. P. (1972b). Predictive validity of the *Torrance Tests of Creative Thinking. Journal of Creative Behavior, 6,* 236–252.

Torrance, E. P. (1972c). Predictive validity of "bonus" scoring for combinations on repeated figures tests of creative thinking. *Journal of Psychology, 81,* 167–171.

Torrance, E. P. (1972d). Tendency to produce unusual visual perspective as a predictor of creative achievement. *Perceptual and Motor Skills, 34,* 911–915.

Torrance, E. P. (1974). *Norms-technical manual: Torrance Tests of Creative Thinking.* Lexington, MA: Ginn.

Torrance, E. P. (1977). *Discovery and nurturance of giftedness in the culturally different.* Reston, VA: Council on Exceptional Children.

Torrance, E. P. (1980). Growing up creatively gifted: A 22-year longitudinal study. *Creative Child and Adult Quarterly, 5,* 148–158, 170.

Torrance, E. P. (1981a). Predicting the creativity of elementary school children (1958-80)—and the teacher who "made a difference." *Gifted Child Quarterly, 25,* 55–62.

Torrance, E. P. (1981b). Empirical validation of criterion-referenced indicators of creative ability through a longitudinal study. *Creative Child and Adult Quarterly, 6,* 136–140.

Torrance, E. P. (in press). *Experiences in developing creativity measures: Insights, discoveries, decisions.* In J.C. Houtz (Ed.), *The educational psychology of creativity.* New York: Fordham University Press.

Torrance, E. P., Bruch, C. B., & Morse, J. A. (1973). Improving predictions of the adult creative achievement of gifted girls by using autobiographical information. *Gifted Child Quarterly, 17,* 91–95.

Torrance, E. P., Bruch, C. B., & Torrance, J. P. (1976). Interscholastic futuristic creative problem-solving. *Journal of Creative Behavior, 10,* 117–125.

Torrance, E. P., & DeYoung, K. (1958). *Life experience inventory: Creativity form.* Minneapolis: University of Minnesota, Bureau of Educational Research.

Torrance, E. P., & Safter, H. T. (1989). The long range predictive validity of the Just Suppose Test. *Journal of Creative Behavior, 23,* 219–223.

Torrance, E. P., Tan, C. A., & Allman, T. (1970). Verbal originality and teacher behavior: A predictive validity study. *Journal of Teacher Education, 21,* 335–341.

Tumin, M. (1953). Obstacles to creativity. *ETC, 11,* 261–271.

Wallach, M. A., & Wing, C. W., Jr. (1969). *The talented student: A validation of the creativity-intelligence distinction.* New York: Holt, Rinehart.

Witt, G. (1971). The life enrichment activity program, Inc.: A continuing program for creative, disadvantaged children. *Journal of Research and Development in Education,* 4(3), 14–22.

10

The Study of Mathematically Precocious Youth: The First Three Decades of a Planned 50-Year Study of Intellectual Talent*

David Lubinski
Camilla Persson Benbow

Our increasingly technological society requires many well-trained scientists. Yet decreasing numbers of college students are choosing engineering, mathematics, and physical science majors (National Science Board, 1982; Office of Technology Assessment, 1988; Turner & Bowen, 1990). For example, between 1966 and 1988, the number of college freshmen majoring in mathematics and science decreased by 50% (Green, 1989). This trend has generated concern among several leaders in the physical sciences, a concern that is amplified by the marked underrepresentation of women in engineering and physical sciences, especially at advanced educational levels and among faculty in math/science departments. Many educational and vocational psychologists have embraced these concerns. Some have been moved to ask: Within our student population, are there measurable psychological attributes that are predictive of individuals who will maintain a commitment to and achieve career excellence in math/science disciplines (and are these attributes gender-differentiating)? Whatever psychologists do to address the mounting concern over our future technological capabilities, addressing both components of the aforementioned question (i.e., maintaining a commitment and achieving excellence) is critical. After all, simply enhancing the number of individuals who ulti-

*Address correspondence to either Camilla P. Benbow or David Lubinski, Co-Directors of the Study of Mathematically Precocious Youth (SMPY), Department of Psychology, Iowa State University, Ames, IA 50011-3180. Support was provided by a grant from the National Science Foundation (MDR 8855625).

mately earn advanced degrees in engineering or the physical sciences would be counterproductive if these individuals ultimately found themselves either occupationally unfulfilled or unable to work competently in engineering and physical science careers.

In this chapter, we will describe the planned 50-year longitudinal study that is being conducted by the Study of Mathematically Precocious Youth (SMPY), a study that is now in its third decade. To enrich this description, we will illustrate how this data bank can be used to address the aforementioned student problem that currently has attracted much attention among educators within the math/science pipeline and educational and vocational psychologists outside of it. Specifically, we will present data from SMPY and the psychological literature that have relevance for identifying the early psychological antecedents of competence and satisfaction at all points along the math/science pipeline, from selecting a college major to earning a doctorate in a technical discipline. Factors especially conducive to exceptional achievements will be given particular attention, as will special influences that contribute to the optimal educational and vocational development of the nascent physical scientist; possible influences related to gender differences in achievement will be stressed throughout. The chapter begins, therefore, with a description of SMPY itself, which is followed by a brief outline of the theoretical model guiding our research and employed to organize the study's empirical findings.

THE STUDY OF MATHEMATICALLY PRECOCIOUS YOUTH (SMPY)

SMPY was founded by Julian C. Stanley in September 1971 at Johns Hopkins University. The practical premise guiding the work of SMPY is and has been to conduct research through service to intellectually gifted adolescents with a special emphasis on the mathematically talented. By providing innovative educational programs and educational guidance, SMPY's aim is to facilitate individual development toward academic achievement from the early identification of exceptional intellectual talent (Stanley, 1977; Stanley & Benbow, 1986). In the process, SMPY attempts to discover the optimal mechanisms that promote both intellectual and social well-being among the gifted. To facilitate meeting these goals, SMPY established a 50-year longitudinal study, which currently includes about 5,000 mathematically and/or verbally talented individuals identified over a 20-year period. Through this study, SMPY is trying to develop a better understanding of the processes whereby precocious forms of intellectual talent, identified during childhood, develop into noteworthy products of adult achievement and creativity.

The Conception of Mathematical and Verbal Precocity Embedded in SMPY's Selection Procedures

SMPY's conception of mathematical and verbal precocity is the manifestation of exceptional mathematical/verbal reasoning abilities at a very early age. Subjects are selected for our longitudinal study around ages 12 to 13, in the seventh or eighth grade. These students must have earned scores in the top 3% on conventional standardized tests administered in their schools (e.g., Iowa Tests of Basic Skills). This intellectually select group of students is then given the opportunity to take the College Board Scholastic Aptitude Test (SAT) through a "talent search" (a concept developed by SMPY to identify exceptionally able students, cf. Keating & Stanley, 1972).[1] The SAT was designed for above-average high school juniors and seniors to assess mathematical and verbal reasoning abilities critical for university course work (Donlon, 1984). Because talent search participants are four to five years younger than the population of college-going high school seniors for whom the SAT was designed, and because few adolescents have received formal training in algebra or beyond (Benbow, 1992a; Benbow & Stanley, 1982a, 1982b, 1983a), this form of assessment is known as out-of-level testing.

SAT score distributions of 12- to 13 year-olds in the top 3% for their grade level are consistently indistinguishable from those typically observed among high school students (Benbow, 1988). These scores are especially spectacular for the mathematics component of the SAT, inasmuch as without formal training, many of these students score above the cutoff for the most elite universities. Moreover, given the abstract nature of the SAT and the sheer novelty of the problems, it suggests that this instrument functions for these students at a far more analytical reasoning level than it does for high school students who have been exposed explicitly to the specific content of the SAT through high school course work (Benbow, 1983, 1992b; Benbow & Stanley, 1980, 1981, 1983b; Stanley & Benbow, 1986).

For these youngsters, such intellectually abstract problems as those found on the SAT are ideal for revealing systematic sources of intellectual differences among the gifted that are obscured by ceiling effects in conventional instruments. Even among educational researchers, the realization that one-third of the IQ range is found in the top 1% is frequently underappreciated. Assuming an IQ standard deviation of 16, the cut-off score for the top 1% is somewhere

---

[1] Talent search programs have recently expanded, allowing gifted students the opportunity to take the ACT.

around 137, but IQs extend beyond 200. In addition, the individual differences found in that range are psychologically meaningful and important to differentiate. The differences in educational accomplishments and career achievements among individuals in the top and bottom quartiles of the top 1% are truly remarkable (Benbow, 1992b). It is clearly useful to differentiate the able from the highly able in upper ability ranges, as well as to structure educational opportunities and acceleration accordingly (Lubinski, Benbow, & Sanders, in press). (For detailed discussions of the SAT's predictive validity within this upper third of the IQ distribution [following 10-year temporal gaps, age 13 to 23] see Benbow [1992b] and Lubinski & Dawis [1992].)

Longitudinal Design of SMPY

A time-line for the longitudinal study is shown in Figure 10.1. There are five cohorts in all: Four were assembled through talent searches, while a fifth cohort is composed of graduate students in top U.S. mathematics and physical science departments. (Each cohort is separated by a few years.) Combined, the cohorts span 20 years, with findings from each cohort serving in part as a replication for similar analyses conducted in other time frames.

Cohort	N	When Identified	Age at Identified	SAT Criteria	Ability Level
1	2188	1972 -1974	12 -13	Verb. $\geq$ 370 or Math $\geq$ 390	1%
2	778	1976 -1979	12	Top 1/3 of Talent Search Participants	0.5%
3	423	1980 - 1983		Math $\geq$ 700 Verb. $\geq$ 630	0.01%
Comparison Group		1983	12	SAT-M + SAT-V $\geq$ 540	5%
		1982	12	500 - 590 Math 600 - 690 Verb.	0.5%
4 $\geq$ 1000		1987 -	12	Math $\geq$ 500 or Verb. $\geq$ 430	0.5%

Projected time-line for the Study of Mathematically Precocious Youth's (SMPY'S) planned 50-year longitudinal study.

Figure 10.1. The SMPY Longitudinal Study: Its Cohorts of Subjects

Because the students in the first four cohorts were identified over a 20-year period using the same criteria, the study allows for a reasonable assessment of historical effects. Lack of ability to know and measure the extent to which specific historical periods influenced participants' development is a problem associated with most longitudinal studies. For example, we do not know how being a young adult during the Great Depression affected the development and achievement of participants in the *Genetic Studies of Genius* (Terman, 1925-1957). Similar data collected across multiple time points allow some degree of control of such historical influences in the SMPY study. SMPY will be able to ask, for example, what difference it makes, in terms of ultimate achievement, to have been a gifted adolescent in the early 1970s versus the 1990s.

Another unique aspect of the SMPY design is the ability to modify and add new assessment materials. Cohort 4 grows by approximately 400 participants each year, allowing us to ask questions not pertinent to 1972 participants. For example, we are currently assessing the relationship between family climate and giftedness, using the Moos and Moos Family Environment Scale (Moos & Moos, 1986), which was not available in 1972. The currency of the study is, therefore, maintained. A retrospective/longitudinal study of graduate students in the nation's top engineering, mathematics, and physical science departments has been initiated (Cohort 5) to ascertain whether such students differ in substantive ways from students identified via the talent search.

Cohorts

The first four SMPY cohorts were formed using different ability cutoffs on the SAT. The first three cohorts are successively more able, while the fourth, consisting of primarily Midwestern residents who are being identified through the Office of Precollegiate Programs for Talented and Gifted (OPPTAG) at Iowa State University, represents the same ability level as Cohort 2. A detailing of each cohort outlined in Figure 10.1 is given below.

Cohort 1 was identified in SMPY's March 1972, January 1973, and January 1974 Talent Searches as seventh or eighth graders scoring at least 390 on the SAT-M or 370 on the SAT-V. Those cutoff scores were selected because they represented the average performance of a random sample of high school females on the SAT. Students were drawn primarily from the state of Maryland, with a heavy concentration from the greater Baltimore area. Cohort 2 is comprised of at least the top third of seventh-grade students from SMPY's December 1976, January 1978, and January 1979 Talent

Searches (using cutoff scores at or above the top .5% in ability nationally). These students were drawn from the Mid-Atlantic states. It should be noted that these first two cohorts are separated by at least three years. About 60% of the participants are male.

Cohort 3 is comprised of three groups and is national in its representation. It consists of approximately 300 students who scored at least 700 on SAT-M before age 13 between November 1980 and November 1983.[2] It also includes more than 150 students scoring at or above 630 on SAT-V before age 13. (These scores represent the top 1 in 10,000 for mathematical and verbal reasoning abilities, respectively.) Finally, for comparison purposes, Cohort 3 includes 100 seventh-grade students scoring at chance on SAT (i.e., SAT-M + SAT-V 540) in the 1983 Talent Search conducted by the Center for Talented Youth (CTY) at Johns Hopkins University. Because chance performance tends to imply low ability, it is important to keep in mind that this last group's ability level is still in the top 3-5% on national norms (only students in the top 3-5% in ability can enter a Talent Search); thus, by most definitions they too would be considered modestly gifted.

Cohort 4 consists of 1,000 students, primarily Midwesterners, scoring before age 13 at least 500 on SAT-M, 430 on SAT-V, *or* at least 20 on an ACT subtest/composite. Like Cohort 2, they represent the top .5% in ability. Students in Cohort 4 had enrolled in Iowa State's summer program for intellectually talented youth. At present, several comparison groups also are being formed from the Iowa Talent Search, which screens students with abilities in the top 3% in the nation, as well as from students in the normative ability range.

Finally, Cohort 5 contains over 750 individuals from various engineering, mathematics, and physical science disciplines who are currently enrolled in the United States' top graduate programs. Approximately 50% of the sample consists of females. In 1991, we secured permission from the Chairs of 48 of a subset of this country's best engineering, mathematics, and physical science graduate training programs to survey their graduate students on a number of the key variables used in our research on Talent Search participants. This sample was surveyed in the spring of 1992, with a response rate of 93%.

Collectively, the five cohorts of SMPY comprise approximately 5,000 highly able students. This number will soon increase to about 6,000. All of the students in the five cohorts are being surveyed at critical junctures throughout their youth and adult lives, as can be

---

[2]Some of the examples provided may not involve actual Cohort 3 members, but individuals identified by Julian Stanley using the same criteria.

seen in the timeline in Figure 10.1. Each cohort, moreover, will be surveyed at the same ages to ensure comparability of findings across cohorts.

Status of Longitudinal Study

To date, we have surveyed Cohort 1 at age 13, 18, 23, and 33 (in progress). Cohort 2 also has been surveyed at ages 13, 18, and 23, with the last survey just being completed. Cohort 3 has been surveyed at ages 13, 18, and 23 (in progress). Cohort 4 has been surveyed at age 13 and 18 (in progress). Cohort 5 has been surveyed at age 23 only, but that survey included much retrospective information. Response rates to our several follow-up surveys range from 75% to well over 90%. Respondents do not differ from nonrespondents on key variables including ability, family background, and college attendance (Benbow & Arjmand, 1990; Benbow & Stanley, 1982a). We now turn to a presentation of the theoretical model that guides our work.

THEORETICAL MODEL

What information is most profitable to collect from the SMPY participants and how is this information best organized? Data we collect correspond to the central components of the Theory of Work Adjustment (TWA). TWA was initially developed to conceptualize the critical determinants of adjustment to work (Dawis & Lofquist, 1984; Lofquist & Dawis, 1969, 1991). The predictive utility of TWA is revealed in its capacity to forecast the length of time an individual is likely to stay in a given occupation or career track. This model is appropriate for SMPY because it addresses the determinants of vocational pathways, such as being more attracted to academic versus vocational/technical coursework in high school or choosing a college major. It also is useful for better understanding the amount of coursework students are likely to desire in various disciplines as a function of their abilities and preferences. A schematic representation of TWA is found in Figure 10.2.

According to TWA, two critical dimensions of correspondence operate in concert to structure educational and career development, *satisfaction* and *satisfactoriness*. Satisfaction is a subjective parameter estimated by the student or employee; it has to do with how the person feels in a particular learning or occupational environment (determined by the extent to which an individual's needs correspond to the educational/occupational reinforcers or reward structures); satisfactoriness is an objective parameter estimated by data collected by educators and employers (determined by the extent to which an

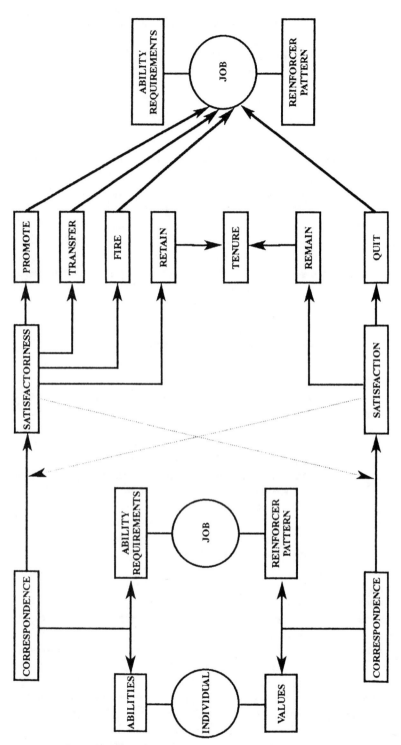

Figure 2.

A depiction of the theory of work adjustment. (Adapted from Dawis and Lofquist, 1984.) The dotted lines serve to illustrate how satisfaction and satisfactoriness function jointly to determine educational/career tenure. When an individual is not satisfactory the environment is motivated to transfer or fire the individual, whereas if the individual is not satisfied, the person is motivated to leave.

individual's abilities correspond to the educational/occupational requirements). Satisfaction is predictive of how motivated an individual is likely to be in pursuing a particular educational/vocational path, whereas satisfactoriness predicts how highly an educational program or career track will value an individual.

Put another way, individuals are motivated to meet their needs or to attain reinforcers. To secure these commodities, they will exercise their abilities. Work environments also have needs, needs for individuals with certain abilities. To attract these people, work environments offer certain reinforcers. Therefore, in ideal settings, a mutual correspondence is established and defines a special kind of ("ideal") person/environment interaction, which, in occupational environments, is called *vocational adjustment*. This theory places equal emphasis on assessing the individual and the environment. Educational and work environments are assessed for their ability requirements and reward structure, while individuals are assessed for their ability levels and specific needs or preferences.

Intellectual Abilities

There are many different kinds of human abilities (cognitive, perceptual, psychomotor) predictive of educational and vocational excellence and success. But, clearly, intellectual abilities are most central to securing advanced educational credentials and achieving excellence in the sciences. The psychological literature reveals considerable consensus about how intellectual abilities are organized (Ackerman, 1987, 1988; Carroll, 1985; Humphreys, 1979; Lubinski & Dawis, 1992; Snow et al., 1984). There are basically three broad categories of human intellectual abilities predictive of educational and vocational performance criteria. All three categories are defined by distinct representational or symbolic systems: verbal/linguistic, numerical/quantitative, and spatial/mechanical. All three classes share appreciable communality, what is typically referred to as general intelligence or the general factor (g) cutting across all types of cognitive tests. Individual differences in one's facility with these three representational/symbolic systems hold different implications for channeling development and forecasting competence in contrasting educational/vocational paths (Gottfredson, 1986, 1988; Humphreys, Lubinski, & Yao, 1993; Lubinski & Dawis, 1992). Assessing individual differences in these three content domains of talent (plus the general factor defined by their communality) provides ideal information for educational, personnel, and vocational psychologists.

With respect to the substantive focus of this chapter, where engineering and the physical sciences are at center stage, being facile at mathematical reasoning is at premium. But evidence is mounting to suggest that spatial abilities are of secondary importance and perhaps of even greater importance than verbal abilities (Humphreys et al., 1993). This is certainly the case for most engineering occupations. Nevertheless, all three systems of content are important in any mathematics or science career. We highlight spatial abilities because although academic and applied psychologists have keenly appreciated the importance of both verbal and quantitative abilities for achieving advanced educational credentials, many have tended to underestimate the critical importance of spatial abilities for math/science disciplines. Tests of mechanical reasoning and spatial visualization are typically restricted to use in regard to nonprofessional technical careers. Yet many graduate degrees in the technical disciplines require appreciable levels of spatial visualization (Humphreys et al., 1993). Because we have relatively comprehensive assessments of our Talent Search participants' quantitative and verbal abilities (they take the SAT to qualify for our educational programs for the gifted), we administer a number of spatial and mechanical reasoning tests to assess their status on these abilities as well. All three classes of abilities are assessed by SMPY in its work with intellectually talented students.

Preferences (Interests and Values)

For years, psychologists have known that vocational interests and values are among the most critical determinants of contrasting educational paths and vocational choices (Benbow & Lubinski, in press; Dawis, 1991). Two of the most well-known systems and measures for assessing these attributes are Holland's Hexagon (Holland, 1985) and the Allport, Vernon, and Lindzey (1970) Study of Values (SOV). Interestingly, both instruments consist of six major preference dimensions or evaluative attitudes; in addition, they share appreciable overlap. Holland's Hexagon consists of the following General Interest Themes (with prototypic careers of individuals with high standing given in parentheses): Realistic (Agriculture, Mechanical/Technical), Investigative (Physicist, Professor), Artistic (Writer, Artist), Social (Counselor, Social Worker, Teacher), Enterprising (Executive, Marketing/Sales), and Conventional (Office Support Staff). The dimensions of the SOV correspond to and correlate highly with Holland's Themes: Political, Theoretical, Aesthetic, Social, Economic, and Religious, respectively.

Using these two systems, physical scientists tend to be distinguished by their high investigative qualities followed secondarily by high realistic scores, plus relatively low normative standing on the social dimension. Similarly, on the SOV, engineers and physical scientists have markedly high theoretical values (preference for working with ideas) and relatively low social values (preference for working with people). This pattern corresponds to a "people versus things" dimension dating at least back to Thorndike (1911), one of the most prominent preference dimensions found in the psychology of individual differences. This dimension also manifests marked gender differences, both in normative samples and among the gifted, as will be discussed below.

THE DATA

Contemporary data collected at Iowa State University (ISU) over the last five years (1988-1992) in our programs for the gifted exemplify how we assess abilities beyond those tapped by the SAT as well as critical preferences relevant to educational/vocational development. During the summer, we now profile approximately 400 mathematically and verbally talented youth on a variety of specific abilities and major preference dimensions. Since we are concerned here with engineering and physical science talent, Tables 10.1 and 10.2 contain data from participants at or above the top 2% in mathematical talent (SAT-M 350 at age 13). Students who qualified for our summer programs primarily via their verbal abilities (i.e., their SAT-M was under 350) were omitted. This, in turn, gives a better picture of the gender differences in specific abilities and preferences for individuals who are indeed in possession of at least a minimal amount of quantitative talent for achieving educational and vocational excellence in the physical sciences. Such gender differences, although not central to the study originally, have captured much of SMPY's attention due to their implications and robustness, and are of particular concern in this chapter.

The ability profiles in Table 10.1 reveal that whether the participants are male or female, their specific abilities tend to be highly developed. Moreover, for those meeting the 350 SAT-M cutoff score (or the top 2% in mathematical reasoning ability for 13-year-olds), gender differences in verbal ability (SAT-V) and Advanced Raven's are essentially nonexistent. On a number of key specific abilities, however, including mathematical reasoning ability, pronounced gender differences emerge even at this superior level. For the mathematical reasoning abilities assessed by the SAT, consistent effect sizes favoring males are approximately .50. On tests of three-dimensional spatial visualization and mechanical reasoning, gender differences are even more pronounced (with effect sizes of approximately .80). Clearly, among the mathematically gifted, marked gender differences exist on the two major classes of specific abilities

Table 10.1. Ability Profiles of Mathematically Gifted Students Attending a Summer Academic Program Across Five Separate Years by Gender

YEAR	GENDER		N	AGE-ADJUSTED SAT-M X̄	SD	SAT-V X̄	SD	ADVANCED RAVEN'S N	X̄	SD	MENTAL ROTATION TEST N	X̄	SD	BENNETT MECHANICAL REASONING N	X̄	SD
1992	M	★	72	494	93	398	91	72	24.6	4.1	72	31.3	7.7	72	49.8	7.1
1992	F	★	45	458	66	396	82	45	24.3	4.4	45	23.7	8.8	45	45.3	5.2
1992	M	■	84	486	91	395	88	85	24.4	4.2	83	31.6	7.5	83	49.9	7.0
1992	F	■	49	465	76	404	90	47	24.6	4.5	48	24.1	8.9	49	45.6	5.2
1991	M	★	68	532	101	426	78	68	25.1	3.9	68	29.9	8.1			
1991	F	★	51	480	87	418	87	51	25.8	4.3	51	25.1	10.2			
1991	M	■	107	579	101	413	81	92	25.2	4.2	95	30.0	8.1			
1991	F	■	67	472	85	418	80	58	25.9	4.2	63	24.1	10.0			
1990	M	★	69	537	100	415	79	69	24.5	6.5	69	29.2	9.1			
1990	F	★	48	487	74	422	76	48	25.3	4.4	48	22.5	9.7			
1990	M	■	87	545	96	415	79	82	24.6	6.8	80	29.8	8.8			
1990	F	■	61	487	71	419	80	57	25.1	4.1	56	21.6	9.4			
1989	M	★	20	585	86	441	98	20	27.3	4.4	20	24.9	9.9	20	40.2	9.4
1989	F	★	11	505	80	449	96	11	24.7	5.1	11	17.8	4.1	11	35.6	8.0
1989	M	■	43	593	95	446	78	21	27.0	4.4	40	23.8	9.7	42	42.2	10.0
1989	F	■	34	514	82	455	79	11	24.7	5.1	34	21.8	7.9	32	35.2	9.4
1988	M	★	57	562	81	435	59	57	26.6	3.8						
1988	F	★	32	491	65	424	80	32	25.1	5.3						
1988	M	■	72	571	85	440	62	66	26.8	3.7				8	39.3	6.5
1988	F	■	39	500	64	425	76	36	25.3	5.3				9	29.0	7.2

★ Students who took all of the tests

■ All students who took any one test

All subjects were identified by a talent search at age 13 and subsequently enrolled in a summer academic program for the gifted at Iowa State University (ISU). Students qualified for this program if, as seventh graders, they earned scores of at least 500 on the mathematics SAT (SAT-M) or 430 on the verbal SAT (SAT-V). Only students with SAT-M $\geq$ 350 (roughly the top 2% in mathematical reasoning ability) are included here. (Note that the group of students who took all of the tests is also included in the group who took at least one test.) ISU's Talent Search is particularly noteworthy because it has the highest participation rate in the nation (more than 75% of all eligible students) and the highest ability scores. Students in these programs tend to be (personally) motivated and (family) supported: Except for limited-income families, parents pay for them to attend. Tests: College Board Scholastic Aptitude Test (mathematics = SAT-M, verbal = SAT-V; for participants beyond the seventh grade, SAT scores were adjusted downward 4 points/month); Raven's Progressive Matrices (Advanced), a nonverbal measure of general intelligence; Vandenberg Test of Mental Rotations, a test designed to assess the ability to conceptualize and manipulate 3-dimensional objects mentally; Bennett Mechanical Comprehension Test (Form AA), a test designed to assess inferences based on primitive kinds of physical mechanisms (gears, pulleys, springs, etc.); Allport, Vernon, and Lindzey (1970) Study of Values, a measure designed to assess the relative intensity of six "evaluative attitudes" used to approach life: theoretical, aesthetic, social, economic, religious, and political.

Table 10.2. Preference Profiles of Mathematically Gifted Students Attending a Summer Academic Program Across Five Separate Years by Gender

STUDY OF VALUES

YEAR	GENDER		N	THEORETICAL		SOCIAL		ECONOMIC		AESTHETIC		POLITICAL		RELIGIOUS	
				X̄	SD	X̄	SD	X̄	SD	X̄	SD	X̄	SD	X̄	SD
1992	M	★	72	46.7	7.1	35.7	6.8	43.7	7.1	36.7	7.1	44.0	6.7	33.2	10.9
	F	■	45	41.5	8.2	44.0	7.4	39.3	6.7	43.6	6.7	37.4	5.9	34.2	10.0
	M	★	73	46.7	7.1	35.7	6.8	43.6	7.1	36.6	7.1	44.0	6.7	33.5	11.0
	F	■	45	41.5	8.2	44.0	7.4	39.3	6.7	43.6	6.7	37.4	5.9	34.2	10.0
1991	M	★	68	47.7	7.0	37.1	7.3	41.6	7.2	36.4	8.2	42.9	6.6	34.2	10.4
	F	■	51	42.0	6.8	43.2	8.1	37.8	6.9	42.6	7.1	39.0	7.2	35.4	10.2
	M	★	77	47.6	6.9	37.1	7.0	41.8	6.9	36.5	8.3	43.1	6.8	33.8	10.1
	F	■	57	41.7	7.0	43.8	8.3	37.5	7.0	42.8	7.5	38.7	7.0	35.6	10.3
1990	M	★	69	46.6	8.8	38.4	7.8	40.4	8.2	38.4	8.4	42.5	6.9	33.4	11.4
	F	■	48	40.3	8.0	44.0	8.0	35.8	7.1	42.1	6.4	40.1	6.7	37.5	8.1
	M	★	73	46.6	8.7	38.3	7.6	40.4	8.1	37.8	8.7	42.7	6.8	33.9	11.3
	F	■	51	40.7	8.0	43.6	8.1	35.3	7.2	42.8	7.1	40.1	6.6	37.1	8.4
1989	M	★	20	49.3	7.4	35.4	5.9	40.3	9.4	37.3	8.0	45.0	7.8	30.8	11.1
	F	■	11	39.0	9.1	42.3	9.1	41.1	9.6	40.6	5.2	40.4	9.3	36.6	12.5
	M	★	43	50.0	6.8	34.8	7.5	42.2	8.2	37.0	7.7	44.1	8.2	30.9	10.7
	F	■	34	41.8	7.4	41.2	8.3	39.6	7.7	43.9	8.2	39.2	7.2	34.3	10.9
1988	M	★	57	48.0	8.5	34.4	7.8	44.9	7.6	35.3	8.1	45.2	8.2	32.4	12.8
	F	■	32	42.3	7.5	40.7	8.0	38.2	7.5	43.6	8.4	40.1	6.2	34.9	10.3
	M	★	61	48.3	8.5	34.5	7.6	44.7	7.4	35.0	8.0	44.8	8.3	32.9	12.7
	F	■	33	42.5	7.4	40.9	8.0	38.0	7.5	43.4	8.4	40.0	6.2	35.2	10.2

★ Students who took all of the tests

■ All students who took any one test

268

critical for engineering and physical science achievement and excellence. These differences in specific abilities contribute to the well-known gender differences at all points on the math/science pipeline, but other factors combine with specific abilities to increase the disparity between the genders.

Table 10.2 contains preference data on the same mathematically gifted subjects. Mathematically gifted males possess a tenacious commitment to a theoretical point of view. Gifted females, on the other hand, possess a more balanced value profile; they value social and aesthetic pursuits more highly than the theoretical sentiment so indicative of their male counterparts (although the theoretical scores are elevated for the females relative to their gender). Similar conclusions emerge from the interest pattern of mathematically gifted subjects. Table 10.3 provides data from Cohort 2 on the six Holland themes. The females, again, are relatively evenly distributed across artistic, investigative, and social interests, whereas the males are centrally focused on the investigative interest and (secondarily) on realistic interests for working with things.

The above gender-related patterns have been observed over decades in both normative (Stanley et al., 1992) and gifted samples (Lubinski & Humphreys, 1990a)—including all four SMPY cohorts over the past 20 years. From these profiles, gifted females would be anticipated to be relatively equally committed to educational and career tracks involving aesthetic (forms of self-expression), social (interpersonal contact), and theoretical (scientific/technical) domains. In contrast, the males should be expected to be inordinately represented all along the math/science pipeline. Interestingly, both males and females are comparatively low in their religious orientation, which is typical for scientists in general.

Table 10.3. Holland's Themes of Mathematically Precocious 13 Year-Olds, by Gender

	N	Realistic	Investigative	Artistic	Social	Enterprising	Conventional
Females	83	45.7	53.0	50.8	45.1	44.5	49.2
Males	202	49.8	54.0	42.0	41.1	47.0	51.3

$7.5 < S.D. < 8.5$

Male/female profiles of Holland's themes of vocational interests compiled from subjects in Cohort 2.

Longitudinal Data

The following data relate to some critical educational and vocational covariates of the aforementioned ability/preference personal attributes. Table 10.4 provides longitudinal data from Cohort 1 on the educational achievements and aspirations of our mathematically talented subjects collected at age 23. Although males and females are equally likely to have earned or aspire to advanced degrees, males far outnumber the females in engineering and physical science areas, particularly at the doctoral level. Among our mathematically gifted subjects, eight times as many males as females are choosing to earn doctorates in engineering, mathematics, or physical science (cf. Lubinski & Benbow, 1992). Similar longitudinal data were obtained in our more able samples, Cohorts 2 and 3 (Benbow & Lubinski, 1992). Among students in Cohort 2 (individuals with mathematical abilities in at least the top .5% of the ability range), 12% of the females compared to 27% of the males were pursuing doctorates in mathematics, engineering, or physical science. Moreover, the results of the age 18 survey of Cohort 3 indicated that 77% of males and 47% of females who had earned at least a 700 on SAT-M before age 13 (top 1% in 10,000 in mathematical reasoning ability) were pursuing bachelor degrees in those areas.

Table 10.4 seems to indicate as well that it is not the scientific aspect of the physical sciences that turns off females (they are well represented in biology and medicine), but rather, as one would infer from their profile of interests and values, it is the inorganic nature of the physical sciences that they appear to find less appealing. Gifted females, like females in general, apparently prefer educational subject matter and vocational settings where the content is organic. The "people versus things" dimension that Thorndike (1911) initially described might be more centrally defined as an "organic versus inorganic" gender differentiating parameter of educational/vocational interests (Benbow & Lubinski, in press). Interestingly, the antecedents to these career choices are manifested in contemporary samples of gifted adolescents, our Cohort 4. In our summer programs for the gifted, mathematically gifted females are divided equally between math/science courses and English/foreign language courses. Males, in contrast, are six times more likely to enroll in math/science than English or foreign languages. These data indicate that gender differences in interests and values (well in place at age 13; Lubinski & Benbow, 1992; Lubinski, Benbow, & Sanders, 1993) influence course selection when multiple choices are made available.

In conclusion, highly able males and females, when considered as

Table 10.4. Longitudinal Data for Mathematically Talented Students (Top 1%), Identified by a SMPY Talent Search at Age 13. Percentages Reflect Students' Current Level of Educational Attainment or Pursuit (at age 23) by Gender.

Highest Degree / Major	Bachelor		Advanced Less than Doctorate		Doctorate		Total Across Degrees	
	Males	Females	Males	Females	Males	Females	Males	Females
Math and Science								
Mathematics	3.4	3.5	0.3	0.7	0.5	0.0	4.2	4.2
Engineering	16.2	7.6	7.9	3.0	3.4	0.7	27.5	11.3
Physical Science	2.2	1.5	0.5	0.4	3.7	0.2	6.4	2.1
Biology	2.2	5.4	0.3	0.4	1.1	1.5	3.6	7.3
Medicine					8.7	5.9	8.7	5.9
Social Science	4.8	6.1	0.4	2.0	1.9	0.9	7.1	9.0
Humanities	2.5	5.0	0.1	2.4	0.8	1.7	3.4	9.1
Law					6.4	4.1	6.4	4.1
Business	7.1	11.1	4.5	5.0	0.8	0.7	12.4	16.8
Total All Majors	42	52	15	17	28	17	85	86
Math/Science Majors	24	18	9	5	18	9	51	32

Longitudinal data on achieved or intended educational credentials compiled 10-years following Cohort 1's identification at age 13.

a group, have differing ability and preference profiles. When evaluating these differences in the light of the Theory of Work Adjustment, the data inevitably lead to the prediction that highly able males and females will find personal fulfillment in differing career tracks. The psychological profiles of mathematically talented males are more congruent with studying physical science than are those of mathematically gifted females. These predictions were borne out by the longitudinal data collected by SMPY. As adults, mathematically talented males are more heavily represented in the sciences, especially the inorganic sciences, and at the highest educational levels, than their female peers.

CASE HISTORIES

In the above section we tried to accomplish two goals, to outline (a) the types of data that SMPY collects and their uses, and (b) how SMPY's theoretical model guides its investigations. To furnish a richer understanding of the achievements of mathematically talented students and how they can be understood in terms of our theoretical model, it might be useful to attach some ideographic content to the aforementioned normative statistics and trends by pulling a few case histories from our files. This will serve to exemplify how the above attributes operate within individuals.

Case 1

One 12-year-old female in Cohort 2 scored 610 on the SAT-M and 520 on SAT-V in seventh grade. Results of subsequent assessments revealed that she had high spatial and mechanical reasoning abilities (the Differential Aptitude Tests [DAT] Space Relations was 49, the DAT Mechanical Reasoning was 52), while her strongest evaluative attitude was theoretical on the SOV (Theoretical = 59 and Social = 28). The Strong Interest Inventory revealed that her Investigative theme, particularly in science and mathematics, was very high (I = 56, Science = 68, Mathematics = 65).[3] These scores would lead one to predict that she would find personal fulfillment in a scientific career. Indeed, consistent with her ability/preference

---

[3]Means and standard deviations for Holland's General Occupational Themes in normative samples follow (these were taken from Campbell, 1977, p. 33): Realistic (females = 45.5, 9.9; males = 54.5, 10.1), Investigative (females = 48.5, 10.1; males = 51.5 9.9), Artistic (females = 53.2, 8.9; males = 46.8, 11.0), Social (female = 51.3, 9.0; male = 48.7, 10.9), Enterprising (female = 48.1, 8.8; male = 51.9, 11.1), and Conventional (females = 50.1, 10.2; males = 49.9, 9.8).

profile, the following summer she attended SMPY's special fast-paced mathematics program, being driven by her parents a long distance each week to allow her to participate. She performed well (although not extraordinarily well) in this high-level class for mathematically gifted students. Then, at age 14, she entered Carnegie-Mellon to pursue her interests in cosmology; she wanted to prove that God did exist. Because she was so young and had not adequately sampled Advanced Placement (AP) courses or college courses on a part-time basis, the staff of SMPY registered some concern regarding her readiness for college. Despite this reasonable concern, she performed admirably at Carnegie-Mellon, graduating with six academic honors. With her earlier career goals still intact, she went on to graduate school at the University of Chicago to study astrophysics and, currently, at age 25, is pursuing postdoctoral work in that area. Although newly out of graduate school, she had authored three publications in the premier journal of her field, the *Journal of Astrophysics*. Clearly, this student confirmed the predictions forecast by TWA (based on her personal attributes) in terms of career choice.

Case 2

A second SMPY female was a 13-year-old in the early 1970s (Cohort 1) with a SAT-M score of 590 at age 13. Her DAT mechanical reasoning and space relations scores were also high, 55 on both. Her interests were found to lie in the investigative and realistic sectors of Holland's hexagon, while her strongest evaluative attitude was theoretical (T = 53) followed by political and social (P = 46, S = 45). This ability/preference profile would suggest that she would choose a quantitatively oriented career that involved some people contact. At that time (early 1970s) she was one of the most able females SMPY had identified and certainly one of the most motivated in mathematics. She participated in SMPY's first fast-paced mathematics class and completed 3.5 years of precalculus mathematics in 12 months. Subsequently, she enrolled in SMPY's special calculus class and again performed extremely well. She earned the highest score in the class on the AP Calculus BC exam administered at the end of the program, scoring 192 points out of a possible 210. She reported loving applied math and dreamed of one day entering MIT. At age 17, however, she entered the University of Michigan to pursue a degree in computer science, a degree which she readily completed. She subsequently married and, shortly thereafter, obtained a master's degree in computer science, earned by attending night school. A few years later she returned to school to obtain a MBA, and is currently working for a financial service company in her hometown. This choice of a career allowed her to fulfill her need to work with numbers and with people, needs which became evident at age 13 when SMPY tested her preferences.

Case 3

An exceptional boy was brought to our attention at age 9, at about the same time we were working with the female noted above. He had been tested by a school psychologist, using the 1937 Stanford-Binet Intelligence Scale (which is appropriate for this high ability level), and earned an IQ of 190. Two years later, at age 11, he took the Preliminary Scholastic Aptitude Test (PSAT); his PSAT score was 75 on Math and 53 on Verbal. (Note: it has been our observation that verbal ability, as assessed by the SAT/PSAT, develops more slowly than mathematical reasoning ability, with few high scores earned by young children.) At age 10, he completed the Holland's Occupational Checklist, showing interest in investigative followed by artistic careers. His strongest evaluative attitude on the SOV was theoretical (T = 54) followed by political (P = 47). Given his exceptional level of general intellectual ability, the staff of SMPY created the very first fast-paced mathematics class, called "Wolfson I" in honor of its capable instructor, in an attempt to meet this gifted child's educational needs. After making all of the arrangements for setting up the class, he decided that he did not want to attend. Subsequently, however, he did decide to enroll in our second fast-paced mathematics class, which started 1 year later. He performed well in that class and then went on to attend SMPY's special calculus class. At age 11, upon completion of the calculus class, he took the AP Calculus BC exam and earned a score of 4, which is comparable to having earned an A in a 1-year college calculus course. At age 12 he entered an academically rigorous and selective private high school. Although young, he performed well and graduated 30th in his class of 90 students. He then came to Johns Hopkins at age 14 and had a bad start. In his first course, freshman chemistry, he earned a D. The instructor saw him as far too bright for such a grade and made him retake the course, which he did successfully. Thereafter, things seem to proceed more smoothly and he graduated, Phi Beta Kappa, at age 18 with a major in the humanities. The following fall he entered the University of California-Berkeley Law School, from which he graduated first in his class at age 21. He then went to Stockholm on a 1-year Fulbright award, where he studied International Law and again graduated first in his class. At this point in his career, he felt that some applied experiences might be useful. Thus, he became a clerk for a Circuit Court Judge in Washington, DC for one year. Since he was still only 24 when his clerkship ended, he was eligible for a Marshall scholarship. As a Marshall scholar, he studied philosophy at Jesus College in Oxford, England. While working toward his D. Phil., he taught British Constitutional Law full time at Oxford University. At age 28 he should be completing his degree there. He now wishes to join a Law School faculty and eventually to become a Supreme Court Judge. Reflecting upon this exceptional young man's profile, one can readily comprehend how his educational/career choices are in correspondence with his abilities and preferences. At age 10 he liked to deal with abstract content involving political themes, and his verbal abilities are highly developed.

Case 4

At the same time that we were working with the last two students, another came to our attention. This young man also had an extremely high IQ, a score of 212 on the 1937 Stanford-Binet Intelligence Scale. At age 11, he earned an SAT-M of 730 and an SAT-Verbal of 440. One year earlier, at age 10, he scored a 53 on the DAT Mechanical Reasoning test and 43 on the DAT Spatial Relations test. When he completed the Strong, his primary theme was conventional (65), while on the Study of Values his highest score was for theoretical (51), followed by social and economic (45 and 44, respectively). This is not a typical preference profile for our gifted subjects, particularly the high conventional score. These results would predict some difficulty in the career decision-making process for this young man. There are few conventional careers, his primary career interest theme, that this young man would find challenging. He enrolled in our first fast-paced mathematics class and successfully completed 4.5 years of mathematics in 14 months. After this initial success, however, things did not proceed so well. Although he enrolled in a night class in calculus at Johns Hopkins, he earned a D in the class, partly because he traveled with his father for one month during the semester. Moreover, even though this young man graduated from a parochial high school at age 14, he did not perform academically anywhere near his potential. Apparently, the well-meaning faculty at the high school were so impressed by the boy, whom they considered a genius, that they allowed him to slack off (Julian C. Stanley, 1991, personal communication). Unfortunately, this newly acquired behavior did not change. He entered Johns Hopkins at age 14, but left during his third year. He would not do any work or attend classes. He subsequently transferred to a much less selective school and changed his major from economics to geography. After college graduation, he worked as a paralegal and attended law school at night. At age 28 he completed law school and subsequently joined a good law firm. Again, the pattern of choices, although not the level of achievement, was congruent with this young man's ability/preference profile.

Detailing the individual case histories not only provides a richer appreciation of the nature of intellectual giftedness, it also reveals the unique paths that the gifted choose to traverse. Such students tend to achieve highly (Benbow, 1992; Lubinski & Benbow, 1992; Lubinski & Humphreys, 1990a; Swiatek & Benbow, 1991a, 1991b), but not necessarily in a smooth or normatively sequenced fashion. Each chooses to develop his or her high potential in different ways. Intentions and plans are implemented and terminated in idiosyncratic developmental trajectories containing an appreciable component of chance (Lubinski, Benbow, & Sanders, 1993; Tannenbaum, 1983). It appears that many gifted students (not unlike their less able peers) frequently try many disciplines (educational/ vocational tracks) before their abilities and preferences hit upon an environmental ecology whose response requirements and reward structure is of sufficient correspondence to motivate the kind of commitment necessary for truly remarkable academic achievements. More often than not, however, the final career choices seem to be in correspondence with abilities and preferences.

IMPLICATIONS: STEPPING BACK

Among Terman's (1925-1957) most noteworthy contributions to the field of intellectual giftedness was his documentation of the central importance of *general intelligence* ("*g*"), or the communality cutting across all forms of cognitive tests. In another context, Schmidt and Hunter (1992; Schmidt, Ones, & Hunter, 1992) have convincingly revealed that general intelligence accounts for approximately 50% of the variance in a variety of work-performance criterion behaviors. But it was not until the 1980s that our methodological sophistication was such that artifacts could be controlled to reveal just how psychologically significant the construct of general intelligence actually is. In the words of Meehl (1990): "Almost all human performance (work competence) dispositions, if carefully studied, are saturated to some extent with the general intelligence factor *g*, which for psychodynamic and ideological reasons has been somewhat neglected in recent years but is due for a comeback [cf. Gottfredson (1986)]" (p. 125).

The construct of general intelligence was never underappreciated by Stanley (1977) when he assembled the edifice of SMPY. But

Stanley did stand on Terman's shoulders. The core of general intelligence is profitably assessed by the communality running through verbal/linguistic, numerical/quantitative, and spatial/mechanical tests. Stanley wondered if tests concentrating on each symbolic/representational system might have differential validity for scientific achievement among the gifted. He focused on mathematical reasoning ability and, over the past 20 years, documented that, even in gifted samples, it is indeed useful to conduct more differentiated assessments of the intellectual repertoire than those conducted by Terman. Among the gifted, marked discrepancies in verbal abilities over quantitative abilities result in highly verbal educational and subsequent career tracks (e.g., law, philosophy, journalism), whereas the inverse pattern is more typical of engineers and physical scientists (Benbow, 1992b; Humphreys et al., 1993). Whatever innovations future longitudinal researchers bring to the area of giftedness, they would do well to model Stanley.

Stanley did not reject the power of the construct of general intelligence, he appreciated it, assimilated it, and measured his innovations against what Terman had achieved. This is how his contribution was measured. And his out-of-level assessments conducted through SMPY and now nationally in other research programs are appreciably more sophisticated and systematic than Terman's earlier work. He did not "bash" Terman, he refined him. Future researchers seeking to uncover other kinds of intellectual talent or measures of known aspects of intellectual talent would do well to measure their creations against existing techniques. In this way, the precise magnitude of new contributions can be appraised in the clearest possible light. Paradigm shifts are best accomplished by those who understand the strengths and weaknesses of the normal paradigms that, currently, best explain the variance that we are interested in. Our suggestion for where to look next is within the context of normal science, but, while not wholly innovative, should hold substantial dividends for future researchers.

The SMPY model has systematically selected participants for longitudinal tracking based on their quantitative and/or verbal precocity. Spatial/mechanical reasoning abilities have not been used for identification. Moreover, such abilities are correlated in the low .60s with mathematical reasoning abilities (Lubinski & Humphreys, 1990b) and in the low .50s for verbal ability. For individuals in the top 1% of spatial/mechanical reasoning abilities, approximately half will be below 93% in mathematical reasoning ability and thus missed by talent searches following the SMPY model. Many more than half will be below this value in verbal ability. One of our greatest untapped resources for the math/science pipeline, students with high spatial/mechanical reasoning abilities, are often disqualified

for advanced training in the physical sciences because of their relatively low levels of mathematical or verbal ability. Such students
might be especially intriguing to follow longitudinally. They might
also be difficult to aggregate for assessment, inasmuch as they tend
to be rather inconspicuous personologically and come from lower
SES levels relative to the mathematically and verbally gifted.

CONCLUSION

In summary, the Study of Mathematically Precocious Youth (SMPY)
is a planned 50-year longitudinal study, which is currently in its
third decade. A theoretical model for guiding and organizing our
educational and vocational longitudinal research, the Theory of
Work Adjustment (TWA), was elaborated. To supply some context for
these descriptions, data were provided, based on inferences drawn
from TWA, which speak to the discrepant male/female ratio of
achieved educational credentials in engineering and the physical
sciences, and which appraise the verisimilitude of this model. It was
suggested that contemporary researchers assimilate what is known
about the nature and organization of human abilities when evaluating the conservation, development, and optimal utilization of different kinds of precocious talent.

REFERENCES

Ackerman, P. L. (1987). Individual differences in skill learning: An integration of psychometric and information processing perspectives. *Psychological Bulletin, 102,* 3–27.
Ackerman, P. L. (1988). Determinants of individual differences during skill
  acquisition: A theory of cognitive abilities and information processing. *Journal of Experimental Psychology: General, 117,* 299–329.
Allport, G. W., Vernon, P. E., & Lindzey, G. (1970). *Manual for the study of
  values.* Boston, MA: Houghton-Mifflin.
Benbow, C. P. (1983). Adolescence of the mathematically precocious: A five-
  year longitudinal study. In C.P. Benbow & J.C. Stanley (Eds.), *Academic precocity: Aspects of its development* (pp. 9–37). Baltimore,
  MD: Johns Hopkins University Press.
Benbow, C. P. (1988). Sex differences in mathematical reasoning ability in
  intellectually talented preadolescents: Their nature, effects, and possible causes. *Behavioral and Brain Sciences, 11,* 169–232.
Benbow, C. P. (1992a). Mathematical talent: Its origins and consequences.
  In N. Colangelo, S.G. Assouline, & D.L. Ambroson (Eds.), *Talent
  development: Proceedings from the 1991 Henry B. and Jocelyn Wal-*

lace *National Symposium on Talent Development* (pp. 95–123). Unionville, NY: Trillium Press.

Benbow, C. P. (1992b). Academic achievement in math and science over a decade: Are there differences among students in the top one percent of ability? *Journal of Educational Psychology, 84*, 51–61.

Benbow, C. P., & Arjmand, O. (1990). Predictors of high academic achievement in mathematics and science by mathematically talented students: A longitudinal study. *Journal of Educational Psychology, 82*, 430–441.

Benbow, C. P., & Lubinski, D. (1992, June). *Gender differences among intellectually-gifted adolescents: Implications for the math/science pipeline.* Invited address at the annual convention of the American Psychological Society, San Diego, CA.

Benbow, C. P., & Lubinski, D. (1993). Consequences of gender differences in mathematical reasoning ability: Some biological linkages. In M. Haug, R. E. Whalen, C. Aron, & K. L. Olsen (Eds.), *The development of sex differences and similarities in behaviour* (pp. 87–109). London: Kluwer Academic Publishers in the NATO Series.

Benbow, C. P., & Stanley, J. C. (1980). Sex differences in mathematical ability: Fact or artifact. *Science, 210*, 1262–1264.

Benbow, C. P., & Stanley, J. C. (1981). Mathematical ability: Is sex a factor? *Science, 212*, 118–119.

Benbow, C. P., & Stanley, J. C. (1982a). Consequences in high school and college of sex differences in mathematical reasoning ability: A longitudinal perspective. *American Educational Research Journal, 19*, 598–622.

Benbow, C. P., & Stanley, J. C. (1982b). Intellectually talented boys and girls: Educational profiles. *Gifted Child Quarterly, 26*, 82–88.

Benbow, C. P., & Stanley, J. C. (1983a). *Academic precocity: Aspects of its development.* Baltimore, MD: Johns Hopkins University.

Benbow, C. P., & Stanley, J. C. (1983b). Sex differences in mathematical reasoning ability: More facts. *Science, 222*, 1029–1031.

Carroll, J. B. (1985). Exploratory factor analysis: A tutorial. In D. K. Detterman (Ed.), *Current topics in human intelligence: Vol 1., Research methodology* (pp. 25–58). Norwood, NJ: Ablex.

Campbell, D. P. (1977). *Manual for the SVIB-SCII* (2nd ed.). Stanford, CA: Stanford University Press.

Dawis, R. V. (1991). Vocational interests, values, and preferences. In M. Dunnette & L. Hough (Eds.), *Handbook of industrial and organizational psychology* (Vol. 2, 2nd ed.; pp. 833–871). Palo Alto, CA: Consulting Psychologist Press.

Dawis, R. V., & Lofquist, L. H. (1984). *A psychological theory of work adjustment: An individual differences model and its application.* Minneapolis, MN: University of Minnesota Press.

Donlon, T. F. (1984). *The College Board technical handbook for the Scholastic Aptitude Test and Achievement Tests.* New York: College Entrance Examination Board.

Gottfredson, L. (Ed.). (1986). The g factor in employment [Special issue]. *Journal of Vocational Behavior, 29*(3).

Gottfredson, L. (Ed.). (1988). Bias in testing [Special issue]. *Journal of Vocational Behavior, 31*(3).

Green, K. C. (1989). A profile of undergraduates in the sciences. *American Scientist, 77*, 475–480.

Holland, J. C. (1985). *Making vocational choices: A theory of vocational personalities and work environments* (2nd ed.). Englewood Cliffs, NJ: Prentice-Hall.

Humphreys, L. G. (1979). The construct of general intelligence. *Intelligence, 3*, 105–120.

Humphreys, L. G., Lubinski, D., & Yao, G. (1993). Utility of predicting group membership: Exemplified by the role of spatial visualization in becoming an engineer, physical scientist, or artist. *Journal of Applied Psychology, 78*, 250–261.

Keating, D. P., & Stanley, J. C. (1972). Extreme measures for the exceptionally gifted in mathematics and science. *Educational Researcher, 1*, 3–7.

Lofquist, L. H., & Dawis, R. V. (1969). *Adjustment to work.* New York: Appleton-Century-Crofts.

Lofquist, L. H., & Dawis, R. V. (1991). *Essentials of person environment correspondence counseling.* Minneapolis: University of Minnesota Press.

Lubinski, D., & Benbow, C. P. (1992). Gender differences in abilities and preferences among the gifted: Implications for the math/science pipeline. *Current Directions in Psychological Science, 1*, 61–66.

Lubinski, D., Benbow, C. P., & Sanders, C. E. (1993). Reconceptualizing gender differences in achievement among the gifted: An outcome of contrasting attributes for personal fulfillment in the world of work. In K. A. Heller, F. J. Monks, & A. H. Passow (Eds.), *International handbook for research on giftedness and talent* (pp. 693–708). Oxford, UK: Pergamon Press.

Lubinski, D., & Dawis, R. V. (1992). Aptitudes, skills, and proficiency. In M. Dunnette & L.M. Hough (Eds.), *The handbook of industrial/organizational psychology* (Vol. 3, 2nd ed.) (pp. 1–59). Palo Alto, CA: Consulting Psychologists Press.

Lubinski, D., & Humphreys, L. G. (1990a). A broadly based analysis of mathematical giftedness. *Intelligence, 14*, 327–355.

Lubinski, D., & Humphreys, L. G. (1990b). Assessing spurious "moderator effects": Illustrated substantively with the hypothesized ("synergistic") relation between spatial visualization and mathematical ability. *Psychological Bulletin, 107*, 385–393.

Lubinski, D., & Thompson, T. (1986). Functional units of human behavior and their integration: A dispositional analysis. In T. Thompson & M. Zeiler (Eds.), *Analysis and integration of behavioral units* (pp. 275–314) Hillsdale, NJ: Erlbaum.

Meehl, P. E. (1990). Appraising and amending theories: The strategy of

Lakatosian defense and two principles that warrant using it. *Psychological Inquiry, 1,* 108–141.

Moos, R. H., & Moos, B. S. (1986). *The manual for the family environment scale* (2nd ed.). Palo Alto, CA: Consulting Psychologist Press.

National Science Board. (1982). *Today's problems, tomorrow's crises.* Washington, DC: National Science Foundation.

Office of Technology Assessment (1988). *Educating scientists and engineers: Grade school to grad school.* Washington, DC: U.S. Government Printing Office.

Schmidt, F. L., & Hunter, J. E. (1992). Development of causal model of processes determining job performance. *Current Directions in Psychological Science, 1,* 89–92.

Schmidt, F. L., Ones, D. S., & Hunter, J. E. (1992). Personnel selection. *Annual Review of Psychology, 43,* 627–670.

Snow, R. E., Kyllonen, P. C., & Marshalek, B. (1984). The topography of ability and learning correlations. In R. J. Sternberg (Ed.), *Advances in the psychology of human intelligence* (Vol. 2, pp. 47–104). Hillsdale, NJ: Erlbaum.

Stanley, J. C. (1977). Rationale of the Study of Mathematically Precocious Youth (SMPY) during its first five years of promoting educational acceleration. In J. C. Stanley, W. C. George, & C. H. Solano (Eds.), *The gifted and the creative: A fifty-year perspective* (pp. 73–112). Baltimore, MD: Johns Hopkins University Press.

Stanley, J. C., & Benbow, C. P. (1986). Youths who reason exceptionally well mathematically. In R. J. Sternberg & J. E. Davidson (Eds.), *Conceptions of giftedness* (pp. 361–387). New York: Cambridge University Press.

Stanley, J. C., Benbow, C. P., Brody, L. E., Dauber, S., & Lupkowski, A. E. (1992). Gender differences on eighty-six nationally standardized aptitude and achievement tests. In N. Colangelo, S. G. Assouline, & D. L. Ambroson (Eds.), *Talent development* (pp. 42–65). Unionville, NY: Trillium Press.

Stanley, J. C., Keating, D. P., & Fox, L. H. (Eds.). (1974). *Mathematical talent: Discovery description and development.* Baltimore, MD: Johns Hopkins University Press.

Swiatek, M. A., & Benbow, C. P. (1991a). A ten-year longitudinal follow-up of participants in a fast-paced mathematics course. *Journal for Research in Mathematics Education, 22,* 138–150.

Swiatek, M. A., & Benbow, C. P. (1991b). A comparison of gifted accelerates with ability-matched nonaccelerates. *Journal of Educational Psychology, 83,* 528–538.

Tannenbaum, A. J. (1983). *Gifted children: Psychological and educational perspectives.* New York: Macmillan.

Terman, L. M., et al. (1925–1957). *Genetic studies of genius* (Vols. I-V). Stanford, CA: Stanford University Press.

Thorndike, E. L. (1911). *Individuality.* Cambridge, MA: Riverside Press.

Turner, S. A., & Bowen, W. G. (1990). The flight from the arts and sciences: Trends in degrees conferred. *Science, 250,* 517–521.

11

The Achievement of Eminence: A Longitudinal Study of Exceptionally Gifted Boys and Their Families*

Robert S. Albert

So long as we trace development from its final outcome backwards, the chaining of events appears to be continuous, and we feel we have gained an insight which is completely satisfactory or even exhaustive. But if we proceed in the reverse way, if we start from the premises inferred . . . and try to follow these up to the final result, then we no longer get the impression of an inevitable sequence of events which could not have been otherwise determined. . . . Hence the chain of causation can always be recognized with certainty if we follow the line of analysis (i.e., reconstruction), whereas to predict it . . . is impossible.

—Freud, 1955, pp. 167–168

BACKGROUND

From a developmental perspective, the attainment of eminence must involve family members, close mentors (often peers), and educators, within at least two major transformations: The first is both cognitive and personality based and helps convert early giftedness into creative potential. An important experience in this transformation is the early identification by others and the self-discovery and use of one's giftedness. This is often an outgrowth of other general experiences within the family, but central to it are an appreciation of the specifics of one's gifts (e.g., I am a poet, the young T.S. Eliot discovers), confidence in one's ability, and initiative in family expe-

*I wish to thank Pitzer College, the Robert Sterling Clark Foundation, and the Catherine T. MacArthur Foundation for their financial support through the lifetime of the project; a special thanks goes to Mark A. Runco, who has been a friend and hardworking coworker over many years.

riences with a growing sense of autonomy (Albert, 1992; Ochse, 1990). This transformation usually occurs within the first four Eriksonian developmental stages in which, on balance, the child acquires workable capacities for trust, autonomy, initiative, and industry. Critical experiences generally include responding to and exploring novelty, setting goals for oneself, and being able to stand and meet comparisons with others—family and peers—without feeling overly competitive or inadequate, acts which help in gaining self-confidence through one's own efforts. (One of the clearest depictions of these processes is Eudora Welty's, 1984.)

Even among the exceptionally creative a second transformation is apparently necessary during adolescence and early adulthood. This transformation appears to be more critical and more permanent in its influence on creativity than the first because it comes during a time of ego and personality stabilization (Conley, 1985; Hauser, 1991). It is during these years that one can begin to predict the possibilities for real-life creative behavior. One must see a well-balanced set of cognitive skills, increasing focus on one's own interests, the presence of aesthetic values, and problem-oriented critical personality dispositions (especially for autonomy and calculated exploration and risk taking). Energized by moderately strong ambition and achievement motivations, this constellation can lead to a highly committed, socially responsible, and intrinsically motivated individual with high abilities focused on a specific area of interest (Albert, 1990; Bloom, 1985).

Although these developments occur over a broad span of time and in multiple settings, evidence for them most often appears first within the family, and then eventually outside of it. Eminence is rarely, if ever, achieved through a dependence on conventional thinking in defining and solving significant problems (Campbell, 1960; Gruber, 1986; Howe, 1982; Lumsden & Wilson, 1981; Nicholls, 1983). It has become increasingly evident that one salient characteristic of healthy development and eminent careers is the ability to think and work in a recognizably individualized (but not bizarre) manner. This capacity can be learned over a lifetime as a product of experience and becomes part of one's adult identity (Albert, 1991; Holton, 1973; MacKinnon, 1962; Wallingford, 1988). Moreover, once in place this part of one's identity becomes consolidated and operates over long periods of time, influencing both the quality and persistence of one's creative behavior (Dudek & Hall, 1992).

Over the years empirical work has demonstrated several conspicuous features about eminent persons. In spite of their differences, they can be adequately described by standard psychological concepts and measures (Ochse, 1990). Although distinctive in some aspects of their development and their careers, persons achieving eminence are continuous with the general population in much of their development and behavior—an observation stressed by both Galton and Freud (Albert, 1975). However they are generally more cognitively gifted or talented in some domain(s) and become career oriented earlier and for longer periods than their childhood cohorts (Ceci, 1990; Simonton, 1984; Terman, 1954, 1955; Zuckerman, 1977). Further, their early family experiences also differ when compared to their contemporaries (Albert, 1971, 1980; Gilmore, 1974; Goertzel & Goertzel, 1962; MacKinnon, 1962, 1983; Roe, 1952; Simonton, 1987). These individuals often hold a "special" place and role within their family which makes their presence and giftedness even more apparent and significant to the family dynamics (Albert, 1971, 1992; Eisenstadt, 1978). Furthermore, most eminent persons, regardless of their field of interest, are similar to one another in the focus of their motivations, inordinate work drive, orientation toward locating and solving difficult problems, values they honor and express through their work, and probably as important as anything else, in their motivation to maintain their identities as actively creative persons. Some of these differences can be observed early in adolescence (Getzels & Jackson, 1962; Vienstein & Hogan, 1975).

RATIONALE

My main interest over the years has been in giftedness as potential for the achievement of eminence. Not only is such achievement important, but it is rare; the means and processes through which it occurs are neither fully understood nor highly predictable in spite of a tremendous recent expansion in related research. When this project was conceived in the late 1960s, most of what was understood about the attainment of eminence had come from and been limited to the study of eminent adults (usually dead); moreoever, predominately white Western males. Even if one were to take into account the restrictive cultural biases in the data, much of the work involved two problems. The most obvious is retrospective selectivity in the recall and placement of crucial events, factors, and persons in the eminent person's early development whether by the person themself or the researcher-biographer. The second problem, the one Freud described, is the occurrence of unpredicted events (Albert, 1980;

Elder, 1974) that can knock the most gifted development off course. But there is another deficit to this literature which is that it usually tells little or nothing about the conditions of "failure," and who or what specifically might have impeded the development of giftedness into eminence. (Two notable exceptions are Montour's 1977 study of the prodigy William James Sidis, and Keniston's *The Uncommitted*, 1965.) Like many clinical and detailed case studies, such investigations may suggest hypotheses concerning insights into persons and experiences operating in a bright person's formative years (e.g., Keniston, 1965). Often enough, these hypotheses held up to more rigorous empirical observations (e.g., Harrington, Block, & Block, 1980; Helson, 1985, 1987; MacKinnon, 1983).

Through the late 1960s and early 1970s, most of the interest in the area of giftedness was centered upon demographic and psychometric characteristics of gifted children and their parents. Little research addressed the achievement of eminence. Early in the 1970s, this project was designed to investigate the "development over time" of two groups of boys who were clearly exceptionally gifted in two different domains—math/science and general IQ. The design included boys' families as integral parts of the research. Twenty-six subjects were selected from the Johns Hopkins Study of Mathematically Precocious Youth (Stanley, George, & Solano, 1977) whose performances on a set of standardized mathematics and science assessments placed them in the 99th percentile. The second sample consisted of 28 boys who were selected from the Mentally Gifted Minors programs in four California school districts. All of these subjects had IQs in excess of 150. Through the years, nominally gifted and ungifted children have been periodically used in the project as control groups (Albert & Runco, 1989; Runco & Albert, 1986). In addition to the longitudinal investigation of achievement, different levels and domains of giftedness are being compared as they develop and interact with family variables and other processes.

RESEARCH DESIGN

One may choose from several longitudinal designs, depending on one's purpose, which in turn is set by one's questions and interests. Theoretical questions drive the project from inception to conclusion. Potentially, longitudinal studies end only when the participants are no longer able or available to continue (e.g., Dudek & Hall, 1992). The research procedures and the flow of data are organic and lifelong, as we see in Block, Block, and Keyes (1988), Helson's (1985), and Vaillant's (1977, 1983) ongoing work.

This project's earliest and sustained goal has been to find, test, and document the developmental continuities and discontinuities between and within two groups of exceptionally gifted boys, focusing on cognitive and personality developments that influence participants' education, career choices, and career achievement. The most important analyses are comparisons. The project was initially designed to maximize the clarity of these comparisons. The present research's significance comes from several of its salient characteristics, including its longitudinal time span, the diversity of measurement instruments used, and the variety and different levels of data generated through the participation of both parents and their gifted child on tests and through extensive interviews. The initial research issue raised in this project had to do with the effect of cognitive giftedness, family dynamics, and experiences on children of different levels and types of giftedness (Albert, 1969).

Soon several other important questions followed which implicated the role of temperament/environment interactions (Scarr & McCartney, 1983). Can early intrafamily factors be altered or enhanced by later variables such as educational opportunity, mentors, career opportunities and choices? If so, how? In short, how locked in are exceptionally gifted boys to their early personality and family characteristics and domains of giftedness? And implied here is the question: Can creativity be deliberately enhanced or even taught after childhood?

The guiding hypothesis of the project is the view of giftedness as exceptionality (Albert, 1980), operating as an organizer (biological and psychosocial in nature), whose influences are both cumulative and epigenetic. Anna Freud's concept of developmental line describes this broadband sequence of influences as do early attachment behaviors (Tyson & Tyson, 1990). Organizers influence the child's own sensitivities to and choices of environmental exchanges, as well as determining many of the interpersonal responses the child experiences in the course of his or her development. Another interest concerns the development of psychological health from preadolescence and its possible linkage with noteworthy creative ability (cf. Ludwig, 1992; MacKinnon, 1983; Richards, 1990).

Creative potential was explored with both samples, first as independent variables then, in the context of family structure and interactions, as dependent variables, and also as predictors. An equally critical issue is whether parents themselves also show high degrees of creative potential. How did childrearing evidenced by the parents influence the development of creative potential, independence, and ambitions of their exceptionally gifted sons? This information, which was derived from questionnaires and interviews, was used to determine not only if there were significant early cognitive and motivational differences among the families, but to explore why some families were more successful than others in facilitating their son's early creative potential.

To be confident of their ability to measure and hopefully predict later behaviors, all of the personality and cognitive measures used in this project were standard, extensively researched instruments being tested in this project for their predictive power in terms of adult eminence.

Sample

Because most personality and cognitive developmental trends show little stability until age 10 (Kagan & Moss, 1962), and different personality traits, factors, and styles may contribute positively to academic achievement at one age but negatively at another (Cattell, 1971), only exceptionally gifted boys within the range of 11-14 years were selected for this longitudinal research. Moreover, Stanley, Keating, and Fox's (1974) data had shown that at least among mathematically precocious youth, early adolescence may be too early to observe the "classic pattern" of high theoretical and aesthetic values and distinctively low(er) social, religious, and political values frequently found among creative adults. Most likely these value patterns require extensive periods of family modeling and encouragement, along with specific educational and avocational experiences, in order to develop (Monsaas & Englehard, 1990; Roe, 1952; Zuckerman, 1977). Observing our exceptionally gifted subjects longitudinally should make it possible to replicate some of these observations and observe how values impact on career choices and behavior.

Because most of the serious investigations on creativity and achievement of the time (circa 1960-1970) were male-centered, only male subjects were used. To have added an equivalent number of females would be to study a sample whose size and complexity would have been beyond the capacity of this project's resources, and in the case of equally exceptionally gifted Math/Science girls, extremely difficult to locate (cf. Stanley & Benbow, 1981-1982). Third, Helson was undertaking her own longitudinal investigation of creative and noncreative college women (Helson & Moane, 1987). Although not focused directly on eminence, this project was and has remained focused on women's career choices and developments. In fact, although unintended, the interested reader will find both conceptual and empirical complementarity between this project and Helson's (cf. Helson, 1985, 1987). Lastly, the author was the father of two gifted boys who showed striking differences, raising the question of how it was possible for full brothers, one year apart in age, to be gifted in different domains.

With all this in mind, the project was designed as a straightforward two-sample longitudinal study in which two closely matched cohorts, differing primarily in one basic cognitive ability, were measured repeatedly with the same instruments at the same age after the same length of elapsed time. Within this time span, now 18 years, two follow-up studies have taken place—when subjects were in high school and four years later in their early adulthood. A third follow-up is planned for 1992-93 now that the subjects are at an age when many eminent careers appear to take off (Albert, 1975, 1992; Raskin, 1936; Simonton, 1984).

Methodology

For all its power, there are standard problems involved in a longitudinal study, such as the attrition of subjects over time, the high level of commitment necessary on the part of the participants, the sampling biases introduced in selection of samples, and the effects of being assessed repeatedly, whether or not the same instruments are used time and again. We were prepared for some of these problems, and in other ways we have simply been fortunate.

Potential problems have been met in the following ways. First, to minimize bias in selection, specific psychometric and age criteria were set before any subject was contacted. The selection of all 54 subjects was by persons other than the principal researcher. For example, in 1977 the first step in contacting the 26 families of our math-science subjects was through the Johns Hopkins University Study of Mathematically Precocious Youth (SMPY). All families of boys in the top 99th percentile on the SAT-M were sent a detailed description of the research, its basic rationale and general goals, a statement of the principal researcher's credentials and publications, accompanied by a covering letter from SMPY's director Julian Stanley confirming this information. At this time, the families were sent letters of consent to sign if they wished to participate and a postal card directing me to contact them for further information. All subsequent meetings were with the permission of the families and at their convenience.

The same procedure was used in 1978 in the Southern California area to select the second sample of 28 exceptionally high-IQ boys. The same information about the project, letters of consent, and postal cards were sent by the directors of Mentally Gifted Minors programs in four school districts to all of the families within their district who had 12-year-old sons meeting the criterion of a 150+ IQ. Again the basic decision to participate or not was made by, and has remained with, the participants.

Because all participants are volunteers, a high level of interest in and motivation to participate in the project was virtually assured. Nonetheless, a problem of bias in the samples was introduced through the self-selection of subjects. An important reason for family participation was that at the onset they were told that the initial observations and interviews would be the most time consuming and personally demanding of all assessments. This was especially so for the parents. But by the same token, it was the intensive and personal nature of these interviews that allowed a deeper relationship to form between almost all of the participants and the investigator. In the process of getting to know the parents, we found that they were usually quite interested in the education and development of their gifted children. A number of families were familiar with the popular literature on giftedness. Clearly they were motivated to learn from the interviews and the project.

Because there would be long intervals between meetings, personal contact has been maintained with all families through seasonal cards, telephone calls, and some visits. As it was stressed initially by the interviewer and specifically in the letter of consent, all participants were (and have been) free to leave the project for whatever reason(s) without an explanation. Forcing them to remain when they no longer wished to could engender feelings of resentment and constraint, and therefore bias whatever data were being gathered.

Instruments and Procedure

Two major considerations guided the selection of instruments and procedures. First, all instruments had to have demonstrated high levels of reliability and validity. They were standard instruments well established in the research literature on giftedness, creativity, and personality assessment (e.g., Runco, 1991; Wallach 1983, 1985; Wallach & Kogan, 1965). Just as critical to the project, two complementary sources of data were used: A psychometric measure was paired with either in-depth interviews or observable behavior and independent reports (e.g., G.P.A., academic progress, awards, etc). There are two reasons for using the complementary forms of data collection. One was to assure that data on important variables were acquired through at least two independent sources. Just as important, we would be able to compare the predictive validity of the various sources of data in the achievement of eminence. The measures used and most of the questions asked of parents and subjects were the same, allowing for a number of comparisons between parents and child.

Initial data collection (1977-1979). This consisted of two extensive open-ended interviews, one with both parents together and a later one with each parent alone. (Both interviews had been extensively pretested on families with an exceptionally gifted son the same age as the prospective subjects.) The interview with parents together consisted of questions developed by Albert and from Marjoribank's (1979) semistructured interview. The instrument covered the parents', grandparents', and siblings' early and contemporary demographics, educational and occupational history, as well as measuring the families' presses for Achievement, Activity, Intellectual interests, Independence, and each parents' involvement in the child's development (Marjoribank, 1979; see Table 11.1.) The parent-alone interview covered each parent's early family history, educational experiences, and aspirations, recalling when the parent was the same age as their son. This interview covered parents' description of their own parents (the indexed child's grandparents), their aspirations, and involvement with the parent as a child and adolescent. Also investigated were each parent's present sense of the son's future personal and social development, especially as these pertained to career goals and achievement. Lastly, each parent was asked to make a descriptive prediction of his or her son's future, occupationally and in general. All interviews were tape recorded except in two cases in which a parent requested no taping. One important consequence and a benefit from having all interviews conducted only by the principal investigator is that a high level of consistency in style, emphasis, and interpersonal relationship was established.

After the first parent-together interview, a separate self-addressed, packet of standard psychological measures was left for each participant. Participants were instructed to fill them out independently, and when completed, to mail them back to the principal investigator. All were returned. The reason for leaving the packages

Table 11.1.   The Environmental Forces and Their Related Environmental Characteristics Used in the Interview Schedule: Learning Environment in the Home*

Environmental Force	Reliability	Environmental Characteristics
1. Press for Achievement	.94	1a. Parental expectations for the education of their child
		1b. Social press
		1c. Parents' own aspirations
		1d. Preparation and planning for child's education
		1e. Knowledge of child's educational progress
		1f. Parental interest
		1g. Valuing educational accomplishments
2. Press for Activeness	.80	2a. Extent and content of indoor activities
		2b. Extent and content of outdoor activities
		2c. Extent and purpose of the use of T.V. and other media
3. Press for Intellectuality	.88	3a. Number of thought-provoking activities engaged in by children
		3b. Opportunities made available for thought-provoking discussions and thinking
		3c. Use of books, periodicals, and other literature
4. Press for Independence	.71	4a. Freedom and encouragement to explore the environment
		4b. Stress on early independence
5. Mother Dominance	.66	5a. Mother's involvement in child's activities
		5b. Mother's role in family decision making
6. Father Dominance	.67	6a. Father's involvement in child's activities
		6b. Father's role in family decision making

*Adapted from Majoribanks (1979)

at this time was to allow participants an opportunity to become familiar with the measures and, if necessary, to discuss them with the interviewer before he returned to California. During this first stage, no formal interviewing of the gifted child was conducted, although the purpose of the researcher's visit was explained to each subject, who was also required to sign a letter of consent. In the subsequent 4-year follow-ups, almost all of the questions asked earlier of parents about their childhood, educational and career aspirations, and experiences were now posed to the subject. This matching of parents' and children's interviews was designed for comparisons between the two sets of data, and to determine whether or not there are significant antecedent relationships related to crucial developmental outcomes. For example, both the parents and the subject were asked identical questions regarding independence training and practices. The results were published by Albert and Runco (1989).

All interviews were subsequently transcribed and analyzed by two professionals, each with extensive clinical and research experience in family processes and individual interviewing; the Loevinger *Sentence Completion* tests (Loevinger & Wessler, 1970) were scored by other persons trained specifically on that measure.

Overview of Empirical Findings

Over the years, the project's conceptualization and empirical results have been closely linked. This has had the benefit of allowing readers to follow the progress of the project and to see how "new" questions may arise and lead to new and revised thinking (e.g., the recent appearance of crossovers and noncrossovers which will be discussed below).

From the beginning, the data and analyses have been organized into three main areas: Subjects' and parents' personalities separately and together, how these compare with one another and their relationships to sons' and parents' creative potential; the identification of creative potential among youth of different levels and kinds of giftedness. More recently, subjects' and parents' ego development have become a focus of analyses along with their early adult personalities, creative development and career decisions.

Demographic Characteristics of the Parents

In keeping with earlier research on gifted children, the exceptionally gifted boys' parents attained considerably more education than their national cohorts and with only one exception, they were clearly members of the middle to upper-middle socioeconomic classes. On these indices and race and religion the two samples were closely matched (Albert, 1980). Mothers averaged 16 years of education, and 65% of them were college graduates. Fathers averaged just over 17 years of education, and 90% were college graduates. Equally important, parents came from families in which formal education had been valued and pursued for several generations, a finding that supports the evidence of a good many biographies of persons eminent in a number of fields. Nineteen of the math-science boys' and eight of the exceptionally high-IQ boys' maternal grandparents were college graduates. Among their paternal grandparents, the figures were six and seven, respectively, and all but three were high school graduates. Another example of the remarkably high level of education among the families are the 16 postgraduates among the grandparents. This is impressive when one considers the depression years and the more restricted opportunities available to them. In spite of these being extremely well-educated families, one interesting difference exists between the two samples: Many more of the exceptionally high-IQ group parents than the math-science group parents were the first college graduate in their families. The significance of this for sons' educational career choices have been reported in Albert and Runco (1987) and gives added weight for taking an intergenerational perspective on the transmission of parental influences (cf. Van Ijzendoorn, 1992, for a review of studies pertaining to this).

Birth Order and Special Family Position

Over the years social science literature (Altus, 1966; Schacter, 1963; Wagner & Schubert, 1979) has addressed the question of birth order as it may influence achievements. The premise is that one's birth order, like gender, predisposes both parents and the child to specific parent-child interactions and socialization practices. In several cases, this tends to be true, leading to regularly developmental outcomes such as accelerated academic performances of first sons and only children when compared to the other birth orders (Altus, 1966; Wagner & Schubert,1979). This outcome appears even more evident for gifted and talented children. One way to conceptualize this phenomenon among eminent persons has been to narrow the general category of birth order to a more specific type of family position which constantly occurs among eminent-to-be and eminent persons. I have designated this as a "special" family position (Albert, 1983). Both samples in this project had closely matched distributions of birth orders. Combined samples included 3 only children, 24 oldest children, 11 middle children, and 16 youngest children. The finding that first-born boys were the largest group in the sample supports the expectation that most gifted children will be either the oldest or only child in their families.

In addition to "specialness" there is another way of examining birth order, which is to look for parent-child birth order similarities and differences. It is assumed that a similar birth order for parents (especially fathers) and sons would influence dynamics within the families. In this regard I found a large difference between the two samples. Among the exceptionally high-IQ boys, eight mother-son pairs and nine father-son pairs had matching birth order. A statistically significant difference from the exceptionally high-IQ sample are the three mother-son matchings and 12 father-son matchings in the math-science sample. Other research shows that among scientists, father-son (and less clearly daughter) relationships appear more salient and influential in sons' educations and career achievements than mother-son relationships (Eidnuson, 1962; Roe, 1952; Terman,1955). Just as important, the opposite appears in the case of adult artists, politicians, and socially committed college students (Albert, 1980; Barber, 1985; Goertzel & Goertzel, 1962; Keniston, 1965, 1968). Research shows that early father-son relations, as well as father absence (Storfer, 1990) can have a distinct bearing on a son's mathematical aptitudes (Howe, 1990). Looking at our samples, we find that among the math-science sample's 26 fathers, 17 had mathematically related degrees and careers, which suggests that one basis for the initial greater father-son similarity among math-science boys may be the interaction between their genetic similarity in mathematical aptitude and their similar birth orders (cf. Stanley et al., 1977, for an interesting discussion of this possibility, and Grotevant, Scarr, & Weinberg, 1978, for empirical evidence). It appears also that the more bases for father-son similarities, the earlier the identification of the son's particular giftedness (Albert, unpublished data) and the more likely there will be behavioral similarities leading to subsequent reinforcements. However, growing similarities and modeling may tightly bind the father and son, limiting the son's later explorations of self and development of interests and identity.

Another developmentally significant fact found among many eminents is the exceptionally high rate of early parental death experienced before age 16 (Albert, 1971, 1980; Bennington, 1983; Eisenstadt, 1978). Approximately 33% of American Presidents, British Prime Ministers, Cox's historical geniuses, and Roe's eminent American scientists underwent this exceptional experience. So far, no parental deaths have occurred among the samples. But there is one finding appearing during the second follow-up that highlights the developmental significance father-son relationships can have in sons' educations and careers. Eight sons who, as of the 1987-88 follow-ups, had absent fathers due to divorce and separation, were functioning educationally very much below their exceptionally gifted cohorts. This is important not only because of its profound developmental implications regarding father-son relationships, but because, according to research (Conley, 1985; Costa & McCrae, 1980; Rutter, 1989; Whitbourne, 1986), one's personality is very stable from early adulthood on. If so, these young men have much to overcome.

Analyses Using IQ and Achievement Tests

The relevance of intelligence (IQ) for creative potential has been examined many times (Runco & Albert, 1986; Wallach & Kogan, 1965). The present data offered an excellent opportunity to test what is referred to as the threshold hypothesis. This holds that creativity and IQ are correlated significantly only in the lower and moderate ranges (e.g., IQ between 95-120). Other researchers (Barron, 1969) have found indirect evidence for this relationship, but the results have been anything but consistent, especially when gifted IQ measured by the Stanford Binet is the measure of intelligence (ranging from 146-165). The creative potential of subjects measured by Wallach and Wing's (1969) test of divergent thinking and their exceptionally high IQs were found to be negatively correlated on five different measures of creative potential (two divergent thinking tests, scored for fluency and originality, as well as with ratings from the Teachers' Evaluation of Students' Creativity; Runco, 1984). Correlations between moderately gifted IQs (between 121-130 and 131-145) and these measures of creative potential were small but positive and significant. There are three points to note here: (a) there are modest correlations in the opposite direction predicted by the threshold hypothesis for exceptionally high IQs; (b) these correlations are considerably higher than those for subjects in the 95-120 IQ range, which the threshold hypothesis would predict having large, positive correlation between IQ and creativity; (c) when using subjects' achievement test scores as the measure of intelligence, the results are opposite from those obtained when IQ is used (Runco & Albert, 1986). Among subjects in the top quartile of achievement scores, there were highly significant positive correlations between all of the creativity measurements and the achievement scores. (The opposite was the case for IQs.) Among the lower quartile groupings of achievement scores, however, achievement and creativity measures were not significantly correlated. Clearly, within particular ranges of IQ and achievement test scores, IQ scores and achievement scores relate inconsistently to creative potential, and quite often in opposite directions from one another. Neither set of data supports the threshold hypothesis, but they do support research by Chauncey and Hilton (1983), Nicholls (1983), and Stanley et al. (1977) showing that achievement tests are more reliable and accurate than IQ tests as estimates of "real-life" giftedness.

Other Creativity Assessments

Among the project's exceptionally gifted boys there were no significant correlations between the Biographical Inventory of Creativity (BIC) and Wallach and Wing's divergent thinking scores. Given their reliabilities and the evidence for their validity, one can feel confident that these are distinctly different measures of creative potential. The BIC taps a subject's vocational and avocational behaviors, preferences, and active interests. The Wallach and Wing test measures production of responses—the quantity and originality of a subject's divergent thinking in figural and verbal modes. Both samples of exceptionally gifted boys are significantly higher in creative potential when compared to same-age average junior high and high school boys (Albert, 1980), as assessed with both the BIC (Schaefer & Anastasi, 1968) and the Wallach-Wing (1969) divergent thinking instruments.

The same holds for their parents. Not only are the parents significantly better educated than their national cohorts, but their creative potential scores surpass both their sons' and large groups of Duke University male and female students', many of whom are exceptional in their own right. On all Wallach and Kogan (1965) divergent thinking scores—figural, verbal, and total—both samples' fathers scored significantly higher than male students from Duke University. Furthermore, with only the exception of the math-science mothers' figural subtest scores, all subjects' mothers' divergent thinking scores were higher than the Duke University students, male and female. To the degree that these parental paper-and-pencil performances have a bearing in the real world, we believe that these parents are modeling creative skills and at the same time are encouraging similar interests and modes of thought for their gifted sons. Moreover, extensive parental education has been found to positively influence early IQ scores *and* adult achievement (Ceci, 1990). When this is linked to differences in the complexity and style of causal reasoning ability between children and adults and among lay adults, lawyers, and psychologists (who also differ from one another; Kuhn, Amsel, & O'Laughlin, 1988), there is strong reason for believing that parents' own levels of education and creative potential will be powerful influences, not only in their sons' educational ambitions but in their reasoning styles and eventual levels of achievement. Supporting this possibility is MacKinnon's (1962) evidence that the families of creative subjects show a significantly greater preference for complex, asymmetrical patterns over conventional line drawings on the Barron-Walsh Art test than did the families of noncreative subjects. Using different measures, a similar difference also appears in Weisberg and Springer's (1961) study.

Personality and Family Variables

Although "family" is defined in various ways in the social sciences, this project focuses on three components of each subject's family: the parents' personality dispositions as measured by the CPI and interviews, their creative potential, and the family presses (measured by Marjoribanks' Family Inventory, 1979, and interviews). Along with teaching the child what is essential information for becoming an acceptable family and societal member, families model and quite often explicitly voice their main values, customs, and goals (e.g., Monsass & Englehard, 1992). From among these family variables, I have selected those that may have a direct bearing on long-term achievement, intellectuality, and creative behavior (cf. Bloom, 1985; Getzels & Jackson, 1962; Howe, 1990; Ochse, 1990; Oden, 1968, for evidence of such family influences). The assumption is that parental behaviors operating early in a child's development can have an enduring influence on their developmental pathways (Rutter, 1989), facilitating a gifted child's becoming first a potentially creative person and, possibly, an eminent one. Certainly more complex than it appears, this assumption has considerable validity (Bloom, 1985; Howe, 1990) and appears to be also transcultural.

It has been clear from the start that both samples' scores on a variety of measures of creative potential had quite different patterns of interrelationships (Runco & Albert, 1986). The math-science boys' creative potential scores are specific to the particular measure used and the domain tapped; no two measures are significantly intercorrelated. The opposite holds for the exceptionally high-IQ boys' scores. All of their creative potential scores were significantly and positively intercorrelated. In general, creativity scores were independent of SAT and IQ scores, the exception being a moderate ($p = .05$) correlation between IQ and verbal divergent thinking. This suggests that giftedness in different domains is associated with different patterns and types of creative potential as early as age 12, and this in turn tells us that each sample goes into its teens with its own pattern of creative potential. Throughout the project, the math-science sample has been found to be far less influenced by their family and social environments than the exceptionally high-IQ sample. This was first mentioned by Albert and Runco (1986, 1987) and

Runco and Albert (1987), and will be further documented in several papers now in preparation related to parents and subjects' CPI profiles. The developmental consequence is that each sample's families is "working" with a distinct pattern and degree of developmental "openness."

This, in turn, leads to an important developmental issue: whether and to what degree creativity can be taught, and for whom, in what domains, and through what types of interventions and experiences (Brinkman, 1981; Howe, 1990, Ch. 2). For example, there is a significant positive correlation between parents' and sons' divergent thinking ($r = .55; p = .02$; Runco & Albert, 1986). One might expect this considering the long-standing claim of parent-child similarities in both talent and interest among eminent persons, beginning with Galton (1869; Goertzel & Goertzel, 1962; Grotevant, Scarr, & Weinberg, 1977; MacKinnon, 1962, 1983). But the data raise questions about this intrafamily similarity because the two samples' creativity scores related differently to their parents' scores. Math-science boys' divergent thinking test scores were significantly correlated *only* with their mothers' divergent thinking scores. This is particularly notable in light of the literature that holds that mathematical aptitude is more male-based and father-centered, and verbal aptitude is more female-based (e.g., the higher verbal and lower mathematic aptitudes often observed among father-absent sons). Yet among the exceptionally high-IQ sons one finds that their divergent thinking scores are significantly correlated with both parents' divergent thinking scores, making for another striking difference between the two samples. The relationship between parents' and childrens' divergent thinking may therefore be partly a function of the level of sons' and parents' cognitive ability as well as the domain of giftedness.

Other data underscore and confirm these domain differences on the Bond-Vaillant Defense Questionnaire, The California Psychological Inventory, and to a lesser degree, The Loevinger Sentence Completion Test. (These results are being prepared for publication.) In almost all analyses at age 12, the exceptionally high-IQ boys' personalities, defensive styles, and stages of ego development are clearly more similar to their parents—both parents—than are those of the math-science boys and their parents. A simple conclusion is that the exceptionally high-IQ boys are much more susceptible, or "open," to parental influences up through early adolescence than are the math-science boys. This is no simple matter but quite likely reflects a mix of heredity, selective identification differences in parental styles and modeling, and the influences of differing reinforcing contexts. Nor are these the only intrafamilial cognitive differences between the two samples. Exceptionally high-IQ parents' (especially fathers') divergent thinking scores were highly significantly correlated with the sons' IQs. This is all the more important given that the boys' own divergent thinking scores are statistically independent of any index of their own cognitive ability.

California Psychological Inventory

Personalities are influential in how persons at any age think of themselves, and how they interact with others. Self-images and personality dispositions determine an individual's consistency within a variety of situations (Albert, 1992, p. 265; Conley, 1985) and interpersonal consistencies in everyday life (Conley, 1985). Because parents of gifted children have been found to have rather distinctive personality styles of their own (Southern & Plant, 1968; Viernstein & Hogan, 1975; Viernstein, McGinn, & Hogan, 1977), investigating the influences of parents' personalities may be one way of merging Galton's emphasis on heredity in the attainment of eminence with Freud's emphasis on dynamic experiential forces in the genesis of the personality traits and motivations that underlie the creative drives that result in eminence (Albert, 1975; Simonton, 1991).

The California Psychological Inventory (CPI) was chosen for its neutrality regarding intrapersonal pathology and its validity with a variety of populations including a number of specifically creative groups (Gough, 1987). We will first describe the parents' personalities, because they form part of the background for a family's dynamic influence on parents' perceptions, interactions, specific teaching strategies, and support for their sons' development.

There are two important ways in which the CPI profiles of the two samples of parents of the exceptionally gifted boys differ. First, the profiles of the exceptionally high-IQ mothers and fathers are significantly more similar to one another than those of the math-science parents. In fact, there is only one significant CPI difference among the exceptionally high-IQ parents: Mothers had higher Psychological Mindedness scores, as one would expect. Among the math-science parents, however, there were consistent parental differences. These fathers were significantly higher than the mothers on the CPI scales for Dominance, Self-Acceptance, Good-Impression, Intellectual-Efficience, Achievement through Conformance, and Well-Being. In general, the exceptionally high-IQ parents appear on the CPI to be more alike and more sociable, confident, and self-accepting than the math-science parents. They, in turn, are more interested in their own Achievement through Independence, and more self-controlled then exceptionally high-IQ parents. These findings are consistent with results from studies of adult scientists (Chambers, 1964; Cox, 1926; Rushton, Murray, & Paunonen, 1983; Simonton, 1987; Terman, 1955) and with our two samples' family presses reported below.

Both samples' fathers' CPI profiles resemble those of creative architects and writers with their high need for Achievement through Independence, high degrees of Psychological Mindedness, Flexibility, and Femininity (Barron, 1969; MacKinnon, 1962). Somewhat surprisingly, and again a domain difference, the exceptionally high-IQ mothers' CPIs (but not, as one would expect, those of the math-science mothers) closely matched creative women mathematicians. The math-science mothers closely resembled female MENSA members (the high-IQ organization) in their CPI profiles. These results are counterintuitive insofar as one would expect either that the mothers would match MENSA females or that the math-science mothers would resemble women mathematicians.

At age 12, it was difficult to say if these results predicted the creative futures of the boys, although as we will report below, they did relate to age 12 creative potential. One unexpected family predictor of early creative potential was the degree of CPI intrafamilial similarity. Psychoanalysis postulates and data from Getzels and Jackson (1962), Goertzel and Goertzel (1962), MacKinnon (1983), and Weisberg and Springer (1961) suggest that parents' disagreements and their personality dissimilarity are sources of stress among families of creative children and eminent persons. On 11 of the 18 total CPI scales, exceptionally high-IQ parents' scores were more similar—that is, less a potential source of intrafamily stress—than the math-science parents. Math-science parents, in turn, were more similar to one another on only 5 of the 18 CPI scores. (These 5 scales are different from the 11 scales on which exceptionally high-IQ parents were matched.) Lastly, the two samples of parents' CPI profiles differed significantly on five scales: Dominance, Sociability, and Good Impression, on which the exceptionally high-IQ parents' scores were almost identical, and Responsibility and Achievement through Independence on which the math-science parents' scores were more similar (Albert & Runco, 1986).

Examined separately, the two samples again show domain differences. Low parental similarity is associated with high *general* creative potential among the exceptionally high-IQ boys, and high divergent thinking test scores among the math-science boys. Furthermore, there are three other significant (conceptually and statistically) relationships between parents' CPI profiles and their sons' creative potential. First the parental CPI scale Capacity for Status was consistently negatively correlated with all boys' creative potential scores. This scale (Gough, 1987) is an index of parental ambitiousness and status seeking and indicates a high degree of concern for one's social acceptance. High scorers would tolerate very little deviance in their children without being anxious and vigilant. Other studies point to a strong relationship between high concern (worry) for conventional status and authoritarian parenting, and this has recently been found to be a detriment to academic achievement among adolescents (Steinberg, Dornbusch, & Brown, 1992). High parental similarity on the CPI Tolerance scale among the exceptionally high-IQ parents and high parental similarity on the CPI Achievement through Conformance scale among the math-science parents each correlated with the sons' lower than cohort's creativity scores. When taken together, these results indicate that among exceptionally gifted 12-year-old boys, parental differences and intrafamilial stress have a greater capacity for potentiating a gifted boy's creativeness than parental trait similarity or high degrees of tolerance, acceptance, and conformity.

Early Family Environmental Presses

The concept and measurement of family environmental presses is drawn from Marjoribanks' (1979) *Family Environment Inventory*. Presses can be viewed as parents' internal motivations and, from the perspective of the child, environmental pressures. The implication, borne out by Marjoribanks (1979) and this study, is that families' parenting goals and efforts are far from random, instead pushing and guiding parent-child interactions along specific paths toward specific ends.

One very important way in which families can influence their gifted child's achievement is through an early awareness of the child's particular giftedness. Early identification, certainly no later than elementary school (Albert, 1978; Bloom, 1985; Robinson, 1981), can lead to early specialized interest and instruction, capitalizing on the child's own cognitive giftedness and identification with parents. Because it takes years of immersion for even the most gifted child to acquire the necessary levels of skill and knowledge to excel (Albert, 1992; Hayes, 1981; Walters & Gardner, 1986) early identification can be an asset to the child if he or she is not pushed by unreasonable parental demands (Montour, 1977). Giftedness, especially exceptional giftedness, contributes to the selectivity of early experiences (Montour, 1977; Walmsley & Margolis, 1987). To the extent that our exceptionally gifted boys' families differ in key areas of personality values, emphases, and birth orders, it is likely that the early family lessons taught and the early experiences encouraged will also differ.

Two brief examples follow. The exceptionally high-IQ families—mothers and fathers—were significantly more involved with their sons on an everyday activities level. (As reported, these boys' test performances were much more open to their parents' influences than those of the math-science boys.) This high parental involvement was manifested in two ways—from the interview content and parents' higher scores on the presses for Activity, Independence, and Father and Mother Involvement. Families that stress activity emphasize involvement in such extracurricular pursuits as music, sports, languages, reading, and so on. The exceptionally high-IQ boys' parents were also significantly more involved with their sons' recreational activities, and equally important, they themselves took more courses outside of the home than did the math-science families.

Although the math-science parents were not as clearly involved in their sons' daily activities (and the sons recognized this to some extent, Runco & Albert, 1987), neither were they indifferent to their sons' potential. These families emphasized their sons' independence significantly more than the exceptionally high-IQ families did (Albert & Runco, 1989). Along with their strong press for independence, math-science families also emphasized their sons' achievement more than the exceptionally high-IQ families.

Certainly, these differences affect sons' creative potential, but only for the exceptionally high-IQ sample in which there were significant positive correlations between family presses and sons' BIC creativity scores and divergent thinking test scores. In contrast, there were *no* significant relationships among the math-science families' presses and their sons' creativity scores.

These family domain differences show up even more clearly in multiple regression analyses. Only 19.8% of the variance of the math-science boys' divergent thinking scores was associated with their family presses (Independence, Mother Involvement, and Father Involvement) but 55.1% of the variance in the exceptionally high-IQ boys' divergent thinking test scores was accounted for by their family presses (Intellectuality, Mother Involvement, and Achievement). The same clear domain differences hold true on the second measure of creative potential. A mere 9.8% of the variance for math-science boys' BIC total scores (Art/Writing and Math/Science scales) is accounted for by their families' presses (Independence, Intellectuality and Father Involvement) compared to 50.3% for the exceptionally high-IQ boys' BIC score total scores (Father Involvement, Activity, and again Intellectuality). Not everything about these two samples of families differs, however: The presses of Father Involvement and Intellectuality contributed to both samples' creative potential, indicating that both groups' fathers were positively influencing their exceptionally gifted sons' intellectual efforts at a very strategic developmental stage.

In summary, one can say that the creative potential of the exceptionally high-IQ boys was more influenced than the math-science boys' by their families' presses for Intellectuality, Activity which implies initiative, Father Involvement, and by their fathers' own creativity measured by tests of divergent thinking. In the case of the math-science boys, the family presses for Independence and both parents' involvement along with their mothers' own creativity contributes to their early creative potential. Involvement of the father relates to creative potential in both samples at age 12.

Longitudinal Results

For all the questions raised and data collected at the beginning of the project, there were some unanticipated developments (Albert & Spangler, 1992). The first follow-up was conducted when the subjects were 16 years old. They were all asked many of the same questions as in the first data collection point about schooling, aspirations, potential careers, and the sources of important lessons for life. Many answers can be categorized as extremely concrete (e.g., "I like being at Hopkins") or extremely vague (e.g., "I guess I'll be a businessman." "I haven't thought much about it this year; I have exams coming up."). The item was useless in eliciting information, leading me to believe I was never going to learn much from these adolescents.

Four years later, however, I discovered that close to one-third of the young men in each sample had made educational and career decisions that were not predicted or even considered at the onset of the study. Even more surprising, these "crossovers" had changed, in their personalities and career aspirations, to now closely resemble the majority of boys in the other sample to which they crossed, for example, a shift from math-science to community medicine; from a business career to graduating from California Technological Institute. In college these boys had selected courses and careers that were much more aligned with and expressive of their age 22 personalities and interest than those at age 12.

In order to give the reader an appreciation of these unanticipated developments, we present some data regarding the crossovers and noncrossovers. As one might expect, it is easier to observe the crossovers among the math-science sample than those among the exceptionally high-IQ sample. Educational and career meandering and switches are far more common, accepted, and encouraged among liberal arts students. An equally gifted boy in mathematics, physics, or engineering usually experiences more curricular guidance and has more specific career choices put before him. To exit this track he must radically change. Inspection of the early test scores of crossovers shows that they were as gifted and creative as the rest of their sample who did not cross over. Therefore, it was not because a lack of cognitive or creative potential that they changed.

For most gifted persons, creativity, identity, and career choice come together during their late teens or early 20s, and these two samples are no exceptions. It was after the second (1988-1990) follow-up study that the changes appeared. Analyses focused on the subjects' age 22 "Adjective Check List" personality profiles, their age 12 and 22 ego developments according to the Loevinger Sentence Completion Test, and their parents' when their sons were age 12, Vaillant's Early Childhood Environment Scales, and their Bond-Vaillant Defense Style Questionnaire results. Only results on the personality profiles of crossovers and noncrossovers and their early home environments will be presented. More details can be found in Albert and Spangler (1992).

Once the crossover/noncrossover phenomenon was discovered, and before the data were coded and analyzed, Albert and Spangler (1992) derived some hypotheses regarding them. In each sample, the personalities of crossovers differed significantly from that of noncrossovers. Although these changes took place within a 10-year period, one would expect that it is probably a more difficult change for math-science boys to crossover than for the exceptionally high-IQ boys. We see evidence of this in the tables. Math-science crossovers are significantly more dominant, attracted to novelty and change, autonomous and self-willed, assertive, and more of a free child. Not only do the math-science crossovers show more of a creative personality (ACL scale 25), but they indicated more self-assertion and intrinsic motivation than the exceptionally high-IQ crossovers.

Regardless of other considerations at this time, these are substantial personality differences, and they raise questions about their

Table 11.2.   Adjective Check List Scales Applied to Hypotheses with Major Descriptors

Behavior Style

(Dom) Dominance	"behaves in an assertive fashion," "emphasizes being with others; gregarious," "Is power-oriented; values power in self or others."
(End) Endurance	not "conservative"; "persist in any task undertaken," is "curious."
(Ord) Order	emphasizes "neatness," "organization," "routine," "conventional."
(Cha) Change	emphasizes "seeks novelty of experience and avoid routine"; "characteristically pushes and tries to stretch limits."
(CPS) Creative Personality Scale	"adventurous," "genuinely values intellectual and cognitive matters," "interests wide"; not "timed."
(A-2) High Origence High Intelligence	"high value placed on both affect (origence) and rationality (intellectence). High scores suggest versatility, unconventionality and individuality."

Motivational Needs

(Ach) Achievement	"ambitious," ". . . determined to do well and usually does."
(Int) Intraception	"Genuinely values intellectual and cognitive matters," does not "give up and withdraw where possible in the face of frustration and adversity."
(Aut) Autonomy	"egotistical," "independent and autonomous but also assertive and self-willed."

Self-Image Reported

(S-Cfd) Self Confidence	"behaves in an assertive fashion," "has a high aspiration level for self."
(P-Adj) Personal Adjustment	"energetic," "self-confident"; not "apathetic," not "timid" or "withdrawn."
(Iss) Ideal Self Scale	"Has a wide range of interests," "Is productive," ". . . elements of narcissistic ego inflations."
(Mas) Masculine Attributes Scale	"forceful," not "submissive," "self-confident," "initiative."
(Fem) Feminine Attributes Scale	"adaptable," "appreciative," not "defensive" or "fault-finding."

Transactional Analysis Scales: Predominate Child

(FCS) Free Child Scale	"daring," "enterprising," "pleasure-seeking," "versatile."
(ACS) Adapted Child Scale	"experiences great difficulty in setting aside subordinate childhood roles"; is "very dutiful" is not "argumentative" and "determined."

Note: All descriptions are drawn from either *The Adjective Check List Manual* (1983) or *The Adjective Check List* of standard scales. Categories are Albert and Runco's.

Table 11.3. Hypotheses, Means, Standard Deviations, and t-values: *Math-Science* **Crossovers and Non-Crossovers On Specific Adjective Check List (ACL)**

	Math/Science Crossovers		Math/Science Noncrossovers		
	M	S.D.	M	S.D.	t-value
Behavioral Style					
Dom	58.33	(5.29)	45.86	(11.25)	3.10*
End	45.78	(7.29)	48.33	(9.10)	.71
Ord	44.44	(8.68)	48.73	(9.72)	1.09
Cha	57.89	(7.91)	50.33	(10.97)	1.80*
CPS	64.67	(5.45)	54.13	(10.58)	2.75**
A-2	55.33	(7.14)	51.93	(10.53)	.85
Motivational Needs					
Ach	52.44	(6.77)	47.73	(9.97)	1.25
Int	51.22	(8.70)	52.60	(8.77)	.37
Aut	59.89	(7.01)	51.67	(10.61)	2.13*
Self-Image Reported					
S-Cfd	58.56	(5.15)	47.13	(10.11)	3.14**
P-Adj	51.78	(6.24)	48.67	(10.03)	.83A
Iss	56.56	(9.81)	48.40	(11.14)	1.81*
Mas	53.55	(5.46)	48.20	(12.15)	1.24A
Fem	44.11	(9.88)	49.07	(9.36)	1.23
Predominant Child					
FC	62.00	(10.98)	47.87	(10.71)	3.10**
AC	44.56	(5.08)	50.53	(10.25)	1.62

Note: All significant mean difference are in hypothesized direction
A = Difference not significant, hypothesis confirmed.
*1 - tail p-value ≤ .05 **1-tail p-value ≤ .01
Adapted from Albert & Spangler, 1992.

Table 11.4. Hypotheses, Means, Standard Deviations, and t-values: *Exceptionally High-IQ* **Crossovers and Noncrossovers on Specific ACL Scales**

	Expt-High IQ Crossovers		Expt-High IQ Noncrossovers		
	M	S.D.	M	S.D.	t-value
Dom	47.00	(5.43)	50.80	(14.08)	.56A
End	54.00	(4.06)	37.40	(6.39)	4.90**
Ord	54.20	(5.93)	37.80	(6.76)	4.08**
Cha	45.00	(6.82)	62.60	(6.07)	4.31B
CPS	53.60	(9.40)	60.40	(9.13)	1.16A
A-2	56.60	(10.43)	61.60	(4.04)	1.00
Ach	48.60	(3.58)	44.20	(9.83)	.94A
Int	49.60	(13.24)	45.40	(5.13)	.66
Aut	48.80	(12.66)	60.80	(6.38)	1.89*

Table 11.5. Hypotheses, Means, Standard Deviations, and T-values Between *Two Samples'* Crossovers on Specific Adjective Check List (ACL) Scales Crossovers

ACL Scale	Hypotheses Tested	Math-Science M	S.D.	Excpt. High IQ M	S.D.	t-value
Dom	Math-Science *higher* than Excpt. High IQ	58.33	(5.29)	47.00	(5.43)	3.81**
End	Excpt. High IQ *higher* than Math-Science	45.78	(7.29)	54.00	(4.06)	2.30*
Ord	Excpt. High IQ *higher* than Math-Science	44.44	(8.68)	54.20	(5.93)	2.22*
Cha	*No* difference between the subgroups	57.89	(7.91)	45.00	(6.82)	3.05**B
CPS	*No* difference between the subgroups	64.67	(5.45)	53.60	(.40)	2.83*B
A.2	*No* difference between the subgroups	55.33	(7.14)	56.60	(10.43)	.27A
Motivational Needs						
Ach	*No* difference between the subgroups	52.44	(6.77)	48.60	(3.58)	1.17A
Int	*No* difference between the subgroups	51.22	(8.70)	49.60	(13.24)	.28A
Aut	Math-Science *higher* than excpt. High IQ	59.89	(7.01)	48.80	(12.66)	2.14*
Self Image						
S-cfd	Math-Science *higher* than Excpt. High IQ	58.56	(5.15)	44.80	(4.55)	4.97**
P-adj	*No* difference between the subgroups	51.78	(6.24)	42.80	(12.03)	1.87A
ISS	*No* difference between the subgroups	56.56	(9.81)	55.60	(10.78)	.17A
MAS	*No* difference between the subgroups	53.55	(5.46)	48.20	(7.12)	1.58A
Fem	*No* difference between the subgroups	44.11	(9.88)	45.40	(11.78)	.22A
Predominate Child						
FC	Math-Science *higher* than Excpt High IQ	62.00	(10.98)	45.00	(5.24)	3.22**
AC	Excpt. High IQ *higher* than Math-Science	44.56	(5.08)	50.20	(7.43)	1.70

antecedents. Looking at their age 12 data, the crossovers' ego development and early home environments are congruent with these changes. Their age 12-22 ego development was much greater and toward more independence than that for their noncrossover cohorts. At age 12 there was no significant difference between the ego development stages of the two groups, both being between a highly conformist stage and one in which there is a sense of one's self as independent of others. (See Hauser, 1991; Loevinger & Wessler, 1970, for some of the behavioral and developmental ramifications of these stages.) When parents' levels of ego development were examined, as one would expect, they were significantly higher (more developed) than their sons' (p = .03), but there were no significant differences between the two samples of mothers or fathers. It is the magnitude of the math-science crossovers' ego development over the 10 years that is most striking.

Just how much the math-science crossovers had changed can be seen when they are compared to the change of exceptionally high-IQ crossovers and noncrossovers. At age 12, the math-science crossovers' level of ego development was lower than either of the exceptionally high-IQ subgroups (p = < .05). But by age 22, the math-science crossovers had moved from being primarily self-protective and wary of other persons' blame and control to an individualistic stage in which the self is the guide and decision maker (p = .02); their level of ego development was now equal to that of the exceptionally high-IQ crossovers, who also had moved up in their ego development. What makes these changes thought-provoking, is that noncrossovers in both samples showed hardly any change in their levels of ego development between the ages of 12 and 22. This makes sense. These boys had to change little in order to stay on their early career paths. Whatever in their development had put them there in the early years was still sufficient and applicable at age 22.

Needless to say, the data have shown that the subjects' families are involved. There are significant linkages between parents' own levels of ego development and the degree of early home environmental support given to the son and his subsequent development. Both have significant positive bearings on a son's own continued development.

CONCLUSION

To some extent, two of the project's early questions have been answered: There are definitely domain differences in exceptional giftedness; early cognitive giftedness is at best a necessary but far from sufficient agent in subsequent personal development and career choice among exceptionally gifted boys. What is also clear is that much of their early ego development, creative potential, and later personality changes are related to their parents' personalities, levels of creative potential, and ego development, and the specific family presses these boys had experienced.

By using standard measures of personality, ego development, family presses, cognitive and creative performances over time, the project has demonstrated that it is possible to locate, distinguish, and document developmentally significant differences within and between two samples of exceptionally gifted boys and their parents. Equally important, is the evidence (both direct and indirect) that the degree of intrafamily stress, the presence of parental differences, and the quality of father-son relationships are important in potentiating these boys' creative and educational potential. Furthermore, the high degree of creativity that other research has reported in families of eminence-achieving persons occurs within these families as well. This is evidence that these exceptionally gifted boys did not start at ground zero in their own creative potential or efforts. Families are not only launching pads but can fuel their sons' later creativeness. This should alert and encourage parents and educators to their own contributions to the development of potential. Neither a high-IQ nor a talented math-science boy is a better candidate for eminence, because it is the "fit" between the candidate and his career that matters (Albert, 1992).

What Is It About Longitudinal Research That Is So Gripping?

The power, the problems—many logistical—and the risks of longitudinal research have become increasingly evident as time goes by. Many are spelled out in this volume. But there is one aspect not often discussed that is highly influential in longitudinal research—perhaps more than in other designs. This has to do with the fit that must exist between the investigators and the primary content and goals of their projects. Possibly more than any other type of research design, longitudinal research is a statement of the researcher's own sense of self, career purpose, and intellectual passion. How else could anyone devote so much of his or her lifetime to one set of people, purposes, and questions? My own experiences tell me that longitudinal research is a professional statement that over time becomes a personal definition. Sooner or later longitudinal research is as much an act of personal commitment as it is of pure science, fulfilling one basic requirement for a creative life which is the meshing of knowledge, purpose, and emotion in the individual making the effort. Once in, never out; and once underway, the project and those personal relationships that make it up, and upon which its continuance relies, can take on lives of their own. Naturally, they change, as most enduring relationships do. But it is critical for anyone who anticipates designing and conducting longitudinal research to consider their own motivations and interests, because there is a degree of private and interpersonal commitment, engagement, and responsibility that is not always present in other research designs.

Some time ago it was reported that the participants were far from set in their ways (Albert & Runco, 1986). Now we see developmental changes and variety within and between the samples. Whatever these young men's subsequent and final destinations, it should be underscored that much of the data and outcomes emerged from the project's longitudinal perspective and multifaceted methodology. The third follow-up began Fall 1992, when according to other evidence (Albert, 1975; Cox, 1926; Raskin, 1936; Simonton, 1984) signs of eminence should appear.

REFERENCES

Albert, R. S. (1969). The concept of genius and its implications for the study of creativity and giftedness. *American Psychologist, 24,* 743–745.

Albert, R. S. (1971). Cognitive development and parental loss among the gifted, the exceptionally gifted and the creative. *Psychological Reports, 29,* 19–26.

Albert, R. S. (1975). Toward a behavioral definition of genius. *American Psychologist, 30,* 140–151.

Albert, R. S. (1978). Observations and suggestions regarding giftedness, familial influence, and the achievement of eminence. *Gifted Child Quarterly, 22,* 201–211.

Albert, R. S. (1980). Exceptionally gifted boys and their parents. *Gifted Child Quarterly, 24,* 174–179.

Albert, R. S. (1983). Family positions and the attainment of eminence. In R. S. Albert (Ed.), *Genius and eminence: The social psychology of creativity and exceptional achievement* (pp. 141–154). Oxford, UK: Pergamon Press.

Albert, R. S. (1990). Identity, experience, and career choice among the exceptionally gifted and eminent. In M. A. Runco & R. S. Albert (Eds.), *Theories of creativity* (pp. 13–34). Newbury Park, CA: Sage.

Albert, R. S. (1991). People, processes, and developmental paths to eminence: A developmental-interactional model. In R. M. Milgram (Ed.), *Counseling gifted and talented children* (pp. 75–93). Norwood, NJ: Ablex.

Albert, R. S. (1992, August). *Sensitive periods in a developmental model of achievement of eminence.* Paper presented at the American Psychological Association Centennial Convention, Washington, DC.

Albert, R. S., & Runco, M. A. (1987, April). *Educational and family perceptions of exceptionally gifted and non-gifted pre-adolescent boys.* Paper presented at the Biennial meeting, Society for Research in Child Development, Baltimore, MD.

Albert, R. S., & Runco, M. A. (1989). Independence and the creative potential of gifted and exceptionally gifted boys. *Journal of Youth and Adolescence, 18,* 221–230.

Albert, R. S., & Spangler, D. (1992). Giftedness, creative efforts, and identity: Their relationships to one another. In J. Carlson (Ed.), *Advances in cognition and educational practice* (Vol. 1, pp. 181–205). Greenwich, CT: JAI Press.

Altus, W. D. (1966). Birth order and its sequelae. *Science, 151,* 44–49.

Barber, J. D. (1985). *The Presidential character: Predicting performance in the White House* (3rd ed.). Englewood Cliffs, NJ: Prentice-Hall.

Barron, F. S. (1969). *Creative person and creative process.* New York: Holt, Rinehart and Winston.

Bennington, H. (1983). Prime ministers and the search for love. In R. Albert (Ed.), *Genius and eminence: The social psychology of creativity and exceptional achievement* (pp. 358–373). Oxford, UK: Pergamon Press.

Block, J., Block, J., & Keyes, S. (1988). Longitudinally foretelling drug usage in adolescence: Early childhood personality and environmental precursors. *Child Development, 59,* 336–355.

Bloom, B. S. (Ed.). (1985). *Developing talent in young people.* New York: Ballantine Books.

Brinkman, L. (1981). Creative product and creative process in science and art. In D. Dutton & M. Krantz (Eds.), *The concept of creativity in science and art* (pp. 129–156). The Hague: Montinus Nijhoff.

Campbell, D. T. (1960). Blind variation and selective retention in creative thought as in other knowledge processes. *Psychological Review, 67,* 380–400.

Cattell, R. B. (1971). *Abilities and their structure, growth and action.* Boston, MA: Houghton Mifflin.

Ceci, S. J. (1990). *On intelligence—more or less: A bio-ecological treatise on intellectual development.* Englewood Cliffs, NJ: Prentice-Hall.

Chambers, J. A. (1964). Relative personality and biographical factors to scientific creativity. *Psychological Monographs, 78* (7, Whole No. 584).

Chauncey, H., & Hilton, T. L. (1983). Are aptitude tests valid for the highly able? In R.S. Albert (Ed.), *Genius and eminence: The social psychology of creativity and exceptional achievement* (pp. 85–98). Oxford, UK: Pergamon Press.

Conley, J. J. (1985). Longitudinal stability of personality traits. *Journal of Personality and Social Psychology, 49,* 1266–1282.

Costa, P. T., Jr., & McCrae, R. R. (1980). Still stable after all these years: Personality as a key to some issues in adulthood and old age. In P. B.

Baltes & O. G. Brim, Jr. (Eds.), *Life-span development and behavior* (Vol. 3, pp. 65–102). New York: Academic.

Cox, C. M. (1926). *Genetic studies of genius, Vol. 2: The early mental traits of three hundred geniuses.* Stanford, CA: Stanford University Press.

Dudek, S. Z., & Hall, W. (1992). Personality consistency: Eminent architects 25 years later. In R.S. Albert (Ed.), *Genius and eminence* (2nd ed., pp. 303–314). Oxford, UK: Pergamon Press.

Eidnuson, B. T. (1962). *Scientists: Their psychological world.* New York: Basic Books.

Eisenstadt, J. M. (1978). Parental loss and genius. *American Psychologist, 33*, 211–223.

Elder, G. H., Jr. (1974). *Children of the great depression: Social change in life experience.* Chicago, IL: University of Chicago Press.

Freud, S. (1955). *Beyond the pleasure principle* (Standard ed.). London: Hogarth Press.

Galton, F. (1869). *Hereditary genius.* New York: Macmillan.

Getzels, J. W., & Jackson, P. W. (1962). *Creativity and intelligence: Explorations with gifted students.* New York: Wiley.

Gilmore, J. V. (1974). *The productive personality.* San Francisco, CA: Albion.

Goertzel, V., & Goertzel, M. G. (1962). *Cradles of eminence.* London: Constable.

Gough, H. G. (1987). *Manual for the California Psychological Inventory.* Palo Alto, CA: Consulting Psychologists Press.

Grotevant, H. D., Scarr, S., & Weinberg, R. A. (1978, March). Are career interests inheritable? *Psychology Today, 13*, 88–90.

Gruber, H. E. (1986). The self-construction of the extraordinary. In R. J. Sternberg & J. Davidson (Eds.), *Conceptions of giftedness* (pp. 247–263). New York: Cambridge University Press.

Harrington, D. M., Block, J., & Block, J. (1987). Testing aspects of Carl Roger's theory of creative environments: Child-rearing antecedents of creative potential in young adolescents. *Journal of Personality and Social Psychology, 52*, 851–856.

Hauser, S. T. (1991). *Adolescents and their families: Paths of ego development.* New York: The Free Press.

Hayes, J. R. (1981). *The complete problem solver.* Philadelphia, PA: Franklin Institute Press.

Helson, R. (1985). Which of those young women with creative potential became productive? Personality in college and characteristics of parents. *Perspectives in personality* (Vol. 1, pp. 49–80). Greenwich, CT: JAI Press.

Helson, R., & Moane, G. (1987). Personality changes in women from college to midlife. *Journal of Personality and Social Psychology, 53*, 176–186.

Holton, G. J. (1973). *Thematic origins of scientific thought: Kepler to Einstein.* Cambridge, MA: Harvard University Press.

Howe, J. A. (1990). *The origins of exceptional abilities.* Oxford, UK: Basil Blackwell.

Howe, M. J. (1982). Biographical evidence and the development of outstanding individuals. *American Psychologist, 37*, 1071–1081.

Keniston, K. (1965). *The uncommitted.* New York: Dell.

Keniston, K. (1968). *Young radicals.* New York: Harcourt, Brace.

Kagan, J., & Moss, H. A. (1962). *Birth to maturity: A study in psychological development.* New York: Wiley.

Kuhn, D., Amsel, E., & O'Laughlin, M. (1988). *The development of scientific thinking skills.* New York: Academic.

Loevinger, J., & Wessler, R. (1970). *Measuring ego development: Construction and use of a sentence completion test.* San Francisco, CA: Jossey-Bass.

Ludwig, A. M. (1992). Creative achievement and psychopathology: Comparison among professions. *American Journal of Psychotherapy, 46*(3), 330–356.

Lumsden, C. J., & Wilson, E. O. (1981). *Genes, mind and culture.* Cambridge, MA: Harvard University Press.

MacKinnon, D. W. (1962). The nature and nurture of creative talent. *American Psychologist, 17*, 484–495.

MacKinnon, D. W. (1983). The highly effective individual. In R.S. Albert (Ed.), *Genius and eminence: The social psychology of creativity and exceptional achievement* (pp. 114–127). Oxford, UK: Pergamon Press.

Marjoribanks, K. (1979). *Families and their learning environment: An empirical study.* London: Routledge & Kegan Paul.

Monsaas, J. A., & Englehard, G., Jr. (1990). Home environment and competitiveness of highly accomplished individuals in four talent fields. *Developmental Psychology, 26*, 264–268.

Montour, K. M. (1977). William James Sidis: The broken twig. *American Psychologist, 32*, 265–279.

Nicholls, J. G. (1983). Creativity in the person who will never produce anything original or useful. In R.S. Albert (Ed.), *Genius and eminence: The social psychology of creativity and exceptional achievement* (pp. 265–279). Oxford, UK: Pergamon Press.

Ochse, R. (1990). *Before the gates of excellence: The determinants of creative genius.* New York: Cambridge University Press.

Oden, M. (1968). A 40-year follow-up of giftedness: Fulfillment and unfulfillment. *Genetic Psychology Monographs, 77*, 71–86.

Raskin, E. A. (1936). Comparison of scientific and literary ability: A biological study of eminent scientists and men of letters of the nineteenth century. *Journal of Abnormal and Social Psychology, 31*, 20–35.

Richards, R. (1990). Everyday creativity, eminent creativity, and health. *Creativity Research Journal, 3*, 300–326.

Robinson, H. B. (1981). The uncommonly bright child. In M. Lewis & L. Rosenbaum (Eds.), *The uncommon child* (pp. 57–81). New York: Plenum.

Roe, A. (1952). *The making of a scientist.* New York: Dodd, Mead.

Runco, M. A. (1991). *Divergent thinking.* Norwood, NJ: Ablex.

Runco, M. A. (1984). Teachers' judgements of creativity and social validation of divergent thinking lists. *Perceptual and Motor Skills, 59,* 711–717.

Runco, M. A., & Albert, R. S. (1986). The threshold hypothesis regarding creativity and intelligence in gifted, talented, and non-gifted children: An empirical test. *Creative Child and Adult, 11,* 212–218.

Runco, M. A., & Albert, R. S. (1987, April). *Exceptionally gifted children's personality dispositions and their relationship to parental personality and the family environment.* Paper presented at the meeting of The Society for Research in Child Development, Baltimore, MD.

Rushton, J. P., Murray, H. G., & Paunonen, S. V. (1983). Personality, research creativity and teaching effectiveness in university professors. *Scientometrics, 5*(2), 93–116.

Rutter, M. (1989). Pathways from childhood to adult life. *Journal of Child Psychology and Psychiatry, 30,* 25–51.

Scarr, S., & McCartney, K. (1983). How people make their environments: A theory of genotype-environment effects. *Child Development, 54,* 424–435.

Schacter, S. (1963). Birth-order, eminence, and higher education. *American Sociological Review, 28,* 757–768.

Schaefer, C., & Anastasi, A. (1968). A biographical inventory for identifying creativity in adolescent boys. *Journal of Applied Psychology, 52,* 42–48.

Simonton, D. K. (1984). *Genius, creativity, and leadership.* Cambridge, MA: Harvard University Press.

Simonton, D. K. (1987). Developmental antecedents of achieved eminence. *Annals of Child Development, 4,* 131–169.

Simonton, D. K. (1991). Latent-variable models of posthumous reputation: A guest for Galton's *g. Journal of Personality and Social Psychology, 60,* 607–619.

Southern, M. L., & Plant, W. T. (1968). Personality characteristics of very bright adults. *The Journal of Social Psychology, 75,* 119–126.

Stanley, J. C., & Benbow, C. P. (1981–1982, Winter). Using the SAT to find intellectually talented seventh graders. *The College Board Review, 122,* 26–27.

Stanley, J. C., George, W. C., & Solano, C. H. (1977). *The gifted and the creative.* Baltimore, MD: Johns Hopkins University Press.

Stanley, J. C., Keating, D. P., & Fox, L. H. (1974). *Mathematical talent: Discovery, description and development.* Baltimore, MD: The Johns Hopkins University Press.

Steinberg, L., Dornbusch, S. M., & Brown, B. B. (1992). Ethnic differences in adolescent achievement. *American Psychologist, 47,* 723–729.

Storfer, M. D. (1990). *Intelligence and giftedness: The contributions of heredity and early environment.* San Francisco, CA: Jossey-Bass.

Terman, L. M. (1954). The discovery and encouragement of exceptional talent. *American Psychologist, 9,* 221–230.

Terman, L. M. (1955, January). Are scientists different? *Scientific American, 437.*

Tyson, P., & Tyson, R. L. (1990). *Psychoanalytic theories of development: An integration.* New Haven, CT: Yale University Press.

Vaillant, G. E. (1977). *Adaptation to life.* Boston, MA: Little, Brown.

Vaillant, G. E. (1983). *The national history of alcoholism.* Cambridge, MA: Harvard University Press.

Van Ijzendoom, M. H. (1992). Intergenerational transmission of parenting: A review of studies in nonclinical populations. *Developmental Review, 12,* 76–99.

Viernstein, M. C., & Hogan, R. (1975). Parental personality factors and achievement motivation in talented adolescents. *Journal of Youth and Adolescence, 4,* 183–190.

Viernstein, M. C., McGinn, P. V., & Hogan, R. (1977). The personality correlates of differential verbal and mathematical ability in talented adolescents. *Journal of Youth and Adolescence, 6,* 169–178.

Wagner, M. E., & Schubert, H. J. (1979). Sibship-constellation effects on psychosocial development, creativity and health. In H. W. Reese & L. P. Lipsitt (Eds.), *Advances in child development and behavior* (Vol. 14, pp. 57–128). New York: Academic.

Wallach, M. A. (1983). What do tests tell us about talents? In R. S. Albert (Ed.), *Genius and eminence: The social psychology of creativity and exceptional achievement* (pp. 99–113). Oxford, UK: Pergamon Press.

Wallach, M. A. (1985). Creativity testing and giftedness. In F. D. Horowitz & M. O'Brien (Eds.), *The gifted and talented: Developmental perspectives* (pp. 99–123). Washington, DC: American Psychological Association.

Wallach, M. A., & Kogan, N. (1965). *Modes of thinking in young children.* New York: Holt, Rinehart and Winston.

Wallach, M. A., & Wing, C. W., Jr. (1969). *The talented student: A validation of the creativity-intelligence distinction.* New York: Holt, Rinehart & Winston.

Wallingford, K. (1988). *Robert Lowell's language of the self.* Chapel Hill: University of North Carolina Press.

Walmsley, J., & Margolis, J. (1987). *Hot house people: Can we create super human beings?* London: Pan Books.

Walters, J., & Gardner, H. (1986). The crystallizing experience: Discovering an intellectual gift. In R. J. Sternberg & J. E. Davidson (Eds.), *Conceptions of giftedness* (pp. 306–331). New York: Cambridge University Press.

Weisberg, P. S., & Springer, K. (1961). Environmental factors in creative function. *Archives of General Psychiatry, 5,* 64–75.

Welty, E. (1984). *One writer's beginnings.* Cambridge, MA: Harvard University Press.

Whitbourne, S. K. (1986). *The me I know: A study of adult identity.* New York: Springer-Verlag.

Zuckerman, H. (1977). *Scientific elite: Nobel laureates in the United States.* New York: Free Press.

12

Project Choice: A Longitudinal Study of the Career Development of Gifted and Talented Young Women

Elyse S. Fleming
Constance L. Hollinger

OVERVIEW AND BACKGROUND OF THE STUDY

The enactment of the Women's Educational Equity Act by Congress in the late 1970s provided for innovative new programs expressly designed to overcome internal and external barriers to fulfillment of the potential of diverse groups of women. Funding availability for previously neglected target groups of women also provided the opportunity for undertaking fundamental research in areas such as the career development of gifted young women. The Women's Educational Equity Act Grants competition was seen as a particularly exciting outlet for accomplishing two important purposes: (a) learning more about the lifespan of gifted and talented young women, and (b) developing and field testing a career development package for dissemination to school guidance and counseling personnel. The awarding of the grant to the authors in 1975 underwrote the development and validation of a diagnostic-prescriptive model program to provide special career-based services to talented young women diverse in cultural, ethnic, and socioeconomic backgrounds. Equally important, it provided the longitudinal framework and initial database for the continuing study of gifted women's lives.

Initial Objectives of Project CHOICE

The primary objectives of Project CHOICE (Creating Her Options in Career Exploration) were (a) to develop procedures for identifying barriers that might interfere with the fulfillment of the potential of gifted and talented high school girls from diverse racial and family backgrounds in a variety of settings, (b) to design and use strategies for removing those identified internal and external barriers, and (c) to evaluate the effectiveness of the interventions.

Talent Definition and Identification Procedures

The creation of a team of program developers representing specialists in gifted education, the psychology of women, career development, adolescent development, clinical psychology, and guidance and counseling, provided a platform for an innovative program design. The investigators adopted the then-current federal definition of gifted and talented (Marland, 1972) utilizing three separate data sources: standardized test scores, teacher grades, and student self-report, such as biographical data (Fleming & Hollinger, 1981).

Fourteen talent categories were created utilizing quantitative data collected from six urban, midwestern high schools: two public coed, two all-female parochial, and two all-female private. Talent information was provided by the young women themselves on a biographical inventory designed especially for this study. These talent categories included: academic aptitude (IQ), English achievement test scores, math achievement test scores, English grades, math grades, leadership, home-related accomplishments (landscaping, gourmet cooking), athletics, community involvement, employment history, literary arts, visual arts, co-curricular activities (eg., debating, science fair), and performing arts. Criteria were established for each of the categories such that a talent score from 0 to 5 could theoretically be assigned for each young woman on each dimension. All protocols were scored by two persons and coded with reconciliation of scorer differences when encountered (Fleming & Hollinger, 1981). The records of 1,141 sophomore women from the six schools were thus screened through a blind review in order to identify those eligible for participation.

All students who had attained a rating of 4 or 5 on any one of the 14 academic or nonacademic talent dimensions were flagged. The mean number of separate talents for this group was 3.5 but 13 students had as many as eight or nine high ratings each. Ninety percent, or 286 of the 318 gifted and talented young women identified through the blind review process accepted the invitation to participate in the career development project. In fact, only six young women refused to participate, mostly because of schedule conflicts.

The characteristics of the identified group paralleled the features of the schools from which they came (see Table 12.1), but sharply contrasting socioeconomic differences emerged. For example, in the

Table 12.1. Educational Level, Work Status, and Occupational Level of Parents of Program Cohort by School In Percentages

	Parochial I (n = 67) F	M	Parochial II (n = 39) F	M	Private I (n = 22) F	M	Private II (n = 14) F	M	Public I (n = 82) F	M	Public II (n = 94) F	M
Educational Level:												
1. Graduate or Professional Degree	9.3	5.3	11.1	0.0	75.0	27.3	50.0	9.1	42.5	24.7	56.3	19.3
2. Master's Degree	11.1	8.8	3.7	5.9	15.0	59.1	50.0	45.5	20.5	27.4	31.3	42.2
3. Bachelor's Degree	18.5	15.8	14.8	17.6	0.0	0.0	0.0	27.3	13.7	17.8	3.8	26.5
4. One to three years of college	11.1	5.3	11.1	11.8	0.0	9.1	0.0	9.1	5.5	5.5	2.5	3.6
5. Associate Degree	38.9	59.6	25.9	44.1	10.0	4.5	0.0	9.1	13.7	21.9	5.0	8.4
6. Technical or Trade School Certificate	11.1	5.3	33.3	17.6	0.0	0.0	0.0	0.0	2.7	1.4	1.3	0.0
7. High School Diploma	0.0	0.0	0.0	2.9	0.0	0.0	0.0	0.0	1.4	1.4	0.0	0.0
Work Status:												
1. Full-time	90.9	34.5	96.4	31.3	94.7	27.3	91.7	0.0	87.8	43.5	91.1	42.0
2. Part-time	1.8	18.2	0.0	9.4	5.3	4.5	0.0	9.1	4.1	18.8	3.8	16.0
3. Volunteer (unpaid)	1.8	10.9	0.0	6.2	0.0	0.0	18.2	1.4	8.6	0.0	16.0	0.0
4. No work outside home	0.0	5.5	3.6	21.9	0.0	9.1	0.0	63.6	0.0	2.9	0.0	9.9
5. Previous, but not current work outside home	1.8	21.8	0.0	28.1	0.0	9.1	8.3	9.1	2.7	14.5	2.5	8.6
6. Full-time and volunteer	3.6	1.8	0.0	3.1	0.0	0.0	0.0	0.0	4.1	1.4	2.5	1.2
7. Part-time and volunteer	0.0	3.6	0.0	0.0	0.0	0.0	0.0	0.0	0.0	5.8	0.0	4.9
8. Former worked; volunteer	0.0	3.6	0.0	0.0	0.0	18.2	0.0	0.0	0.0	4.3	0.0	1.0
Occupational Level:												
1. Higher Executive/Major Professional	5.6	0.0	0.0	0.0	80.0	4.5	72.7	0.0	31.1	2.7	57.5	3.7
2. Managerial/Lesser Professional	22.2	7.0	17.9	9.4	10.0	13.6	9.1	8.3	18.9	21.9	20.0	34.6
3. Administrative Semi-Professional	25.9	8.8	7.1	6.3	5.0	4.5	18.2	0.0	24.3	15.1	15.0	11.1
4. Clerical/Sales	9.3	28.1	7.1	12.5	0.0	0.0	0.0	8.3	5.4	23.3	7.5	13.6
5. Skilled Manual	25.9	1.8	28.6	6.3	0.0	0.0	0.0	0.0	13.5	6.8	0.0	0.0
6. Semi-Skilled Manual	11.1	12.3	28.6	6.3	0.0	4.5	0.0	4.1	0.0	0.0	1.2	0.0
7. Unskilled Workers	0.0	1.8	10.7	9.4	5.0	0.0	0.0	0.0	1.4	0.0	0.0	0.0
8. Full-time Houseperson	0.0	40.4	0.0	50.0	0.0	72.7	0.0	83.3	1.4	30.1	0.0	35.8

F = Father
M = Mother

independent school sample, between 50% and 75% of the fathers possessed graduate and professional degrees, compared to only 9%-11% of the fathers in the two parochial schools. School membership became a variable not only for family background differences, but for patterns of talent. Only talents in leadership and performing arts were not significantly correlated with school membership.

After identifying the target young women, the next major task became one of assessing their special needs in career education and the presence of internal and external barriers to fulfillment of potential. A battery of instruments was administered to determine which factors might be operating in each case. Included were Spence, Helmreich, and Stapp's (1974) *Personal Attributes Questionnaire* (PAQ); Helmreich and Spence's (1974) *Work and Family Orientation Questionnaire* (WOFO); and Helmreich, Stapp, and Ervin's (1974) *Texas Social Behavior Inventory* (TSBI), designed to measure social self-esteem. Subscales comprising the *PAQ* include: *Masculinity* (M) or instrumental, agentic characteristics; *Femininity* (F) or expressive, communal attributes; and *Masculinity-Femininity* (M-F) consisting of items tapping aggressiveness and dominance, and a second cluster of items tapping emotional vulnerability and the need for emotional support. The WOFO consists of four scales designed to measure *Work Orientation* (W), *Mastery* (M), *Competitiveness* (C), and *Personal Unconcern* (PUN), purporting to tap a lack of concern for the opinions of others regarding one's achievement (Fleming & Hollinger, 1979). Three modified Horner cues (1972) were also added to measure Fear of Success (FOS) along with Holland's (1977) *Self-Directed Search*, a career development measure. Project-developed scales designed to assess sensitivity to external barriers to career attainment were also administered: the *Problems Checklist* and the *Sex Discrimination Checklist*. The questionnaire included other items designed to determine the young women's career and lifestyle aspirations, their perceptions of family aspirations for them, and their confidence in attaining educational and occupational goals (Fleming & Hollinger, 1979).

Demographic Descriptions Of Project CHOICE Sample Through Time

Early characteristics. As illustrated in Table 12.1, the six schools represented quite different background patterns of educational and occupational status within and between sites. For this reason, many analyses were conducted separately for each school. For example, within the private sector, one school had no mothers employed full time outside of the home, while in another, over 27% of the mothers were working full time. Most of the Project CHOICE young women came from quite traditional homes even for the 1970s, with only 43.5% of the mothers employed full time as compared to a national average of 60% during that same period. Nearly 82% of the sample lived with their biological parents, 12% lived with mother only, 1.4% with father only, 3.1 % with mother and stepfather, 1% with father and stepmother, and less than 1% resided with a guardian. The racial distribution was as follows: 85.5% white; 13.2% Black; 1% Asian; and .3% Hispanic.

Program Features

When all the instruments were scored and recorded, an individual profile was created including a multimodal-multidimensional diagnostic-prescriptive formula. The predominant internal and external barriers were identified, as well as needs for career exploration and planning experiences, or help with setting more realistic career goals. Each prescription was formulated in accordance with the individual's talents, aspirations, and background characteristics. Some needed to deal with issues concerning multipotentiality; others needed help in raising their career expectations as, for example, our aspiring cosmetologists with 99th percentile profile ratings on the Differential Aptitude battery subtests. A specific example is Tara, whose father was a construction worker and whose mother was a homemaker. She was selected on the basis of high academic achievement both in standardized tests, with a 98th percentile score in mathematics, and almost straight As in the freshman year of high school, although group indices of cognitive ability were in the high-average range. Tara's aspirations and lifestyle preference were to be a homemaker, working from time to time as a dental assistant or hygienist. With respect to internal barriers, there was strong evidence of fear of success. External barriers included no role model and lack of financial resources. Her prescription included exploration of the medical continuum, identifying a mentor, and membership in a weekly group that focused on internal barriers resulting from gender socialization. She was encouraged to attend, with her parents, our Sunday afternoon workshop on financing a postsecondary education. Tara currently is a pediatrician with aspirations to enter academic medicine, and at the time of the latest follow-up she was engaged to be married.

A career development program model drawn from the work of Holland (1973) and Super (1963) was designed. It included components providing for understanding issues in female socialization;

acquiring a realistic assessment of one's interests, abilities, and values; gathering information regarding the requirements and rewards of appealing occupations; engaging in reality testing, decision making, and life-planning activities. Intervention strategies were implemented by randomly assigning the participants to one of 16 groups for 14 weeks. These groups varied in composition: (a) homogeneous internal barrier emphasis (i.e., all low self-esteem young women, all low achievement motivation, all low assertiveness, all fear of success, or those with multiple problems); (b) no identified internal barriers; or (c) heterogeneous barriers or career exploration needs. Structured experiences were designed, including planned exercises and exposure to occupational resource materials in career information labs.

Sunday meetings provided opportunities for the young women and their families to learn more about postsecondary academic, vocational, and financial opportunities. A career workshop including approximately 100 women professionals from aeronautical engineer to zoologist, as well as homemakers and community volunteers, was held so that participants could interact and mentorships could be established. Special mentorships were created for those students who wanted more intensive experiences in specific career fields (e.g. psychiatry, marine biology, security analysis). Some of these relationships were long-term and sustained, others were quite brief and fleeting.

Due to the insistence of the schools, all young women who wanted to participate in the program were included, which prevented the creation of randomly selected control groups. While the preferred experimental design could not be implemented, this arrangement did allow for more young women to participate. However, the extreme weather conditions of Winter 1977-1978 provided naturally occurring control groups. A series of blizzards which made local travel extraordinarily difficult resulted in the formation of no-, low-, and high-participation groups providing the means, after all, for examining program effectiveness. Thirty-nine subjects did not participate at all; 82 were defined as low participants attending four or fewer sessions; and 81 attended five or more sessions and were defined as high participants. A comparable gifted sample from the class of 1978 from the same high schools was selected for posttest comparison.

Early Outcomes

At the conclusion of the program in 1978, posttesting with the original battery was completed. Clinical assessments were made for each individual in terms of their growth in overcoming any internal barriers and advancement in career maturity. Statistically significant improvement on the clinical assessment was strongly related to degree of participation, but was less influenced by whether the young woman was homogeneously or heterogeneously placed in her group assignment. Conscientious efforts by group leaders to individualize the program for each participant in terms of her special needs helped to account for the lack of significance of these grouping effects. The personality measures also showed few statistically significant changes as a function of program attendance. This was not surprising in view of a short 14-week intervention. Additional contact was not made until five years later, during the subjects' senior year in college. The most recent follow-up was undertaken shortly after the participants' 10-year high school reunions, in 1990.

CONTEXT OF THE LITERATURE

Theories of Women's Career Development

Prior to 1980, career development theories were almost exclusively derived from the study of men. In his most recent text on career development theory, Osipow (1983) stated, "For many years, questions of career development concerning women were ignored or given cursory treatment, partly out of a lack of social interest and partly because the confusing nature of career development in women made the topic difficult to study" (p. 254). Such "difficulty" was affirmed earlier by Ginzberg (1966) who concluded that the career development of women was substantially more complex than that of men. In the absence of a comprehensive theory of women's career development, research and intervention efforts focused on identifying, understanding, and "overcoming" the internal and external barriers that thwarted women in their attempts to realize their potential. Low self-esteem, fear of success, lack of assertiveness, and achievement motivation issues were but a few of the identified internal barriers. Sex-role stereotyping, salary and wage discrepancies, job discrimination, educational inequities, and home and family responsibilities were identified in the literature as representative of the many external barriers confronting women (see Blaubergs, 1978; Helson, 1990; Horner, 1972; Osipow, 1973).

By the late 1970s and mid-1980s, a number of researchers began the formulation of career development theories sufficiently comprehensive to account for the career development of women. By recognizing and incorporating sociopsychological and sociostructural dimensions, researchers such as Astin (1985), Farmer (1985), Gottfredson (1981) and Tittle (1983) set forth career development theories which more closely approximated women's life experiences. Of the "traditional" career development theorists, Super (1980) revised his Self-Concept Theory of Vocational Choice. Common to these theorists is a recognition that career development, especially with respect to women, can not be viewed in isolation, but rather must be viewed in relation to other life spheres. In reformulating career development theory, these researchers drew attention to the interrelatedness and interdependence of multiple life roles and the impact of those roles on career decision making and development.

Consonant with the work of Belenky, Clinchy, Goldberger, and Tarule (1986), Gilligan (1982, 1988), Josselson (1987), and others who have argued on behalf of women's different "voice" or world view, Marshall (1989) called for a "revisioning" of career development theory. In such revision, the stereotypically masculine, linear formulation of career development would be abandoned in recognition that women's career development is best characterized as cyclic. From this revisionist perspective, separate theories are required for understanding women's career development, a position with which Harmon (1985), Mednick (1989), and others have disagreed, arguing that this view instead serves only to perpetuate societal stereotypes and the gender inequities characteristic of the status quo. Furthermore, the sociological realities of the workplace which gifted young women do and will continue to encounter, at least for the foreseeable future, are simply incongruent with the revisionist perspective. While the "reformist-revisionist" debate is far from being resolved, the theoretical advances that have been made since the inception of Project CHOICE have contributed significantly to an understanding of the diverse life pathways chosen by gifted women.

Longitudinal Studies of Career Development of the Gifted

Much of what is known about the career development of gifted individuals comes indirectly from cross-sectional research conducted primarily with samples of white males and above-average abilities from middle- to upper-class families. Indeed, Horowitz and O'Brien (1985) concluded that, "one of the most evident gaps in the research literature on giftedness comes from the failure of most investigators to assume a developmental perspective" (p. 450). As a result, relatively little is known about the actual development of the careers of gifted individuals in general, and gifted women in particular.

Longitudinal research on the gifted has focused primarily on the realization of potential and has done so, almost exclusively, from a "societal loss" perspective. By examining outcome variables such as educational attainment, career level and status, income and awards received, longitudinal research has sought to identify what gifted individuals achieve over the course of the lifespan and to understand the reasons for the differential achievement observed among those identified a priori as gifted. In general, the literature documents achievements recognized by society that characterize the lives of gifted individuals.

Multipotentiality, perfectionistic expectations for self, expectations of others, and insufficient career education are but a few of the obstacles or barriers to achieving Terman's "promise of youth" (Fleming, 1985). At present, a number of challenges to the longitudinal study of the gifted exist. First, consensus has not been reached regarding the standards for evaluating and determining whether potential has indeed been achieved. Although Sternberg and Davidson (1985) discussed the accomplishments of Terman's sample as "quite extraordinary" (p. 59), Wallace (1985) concluded that Terman's sample "has not produced a single truly illustrious individual" (p. 362). Identifying evaluation standards for areas of artistic talent, for example, is an even more complex challenge, especially considering the all-too-common posthumous nature of societal recognition. A second and related challenge is that of determining a lifespan timetable for predicting accomplishments. Particularly for gifted women, current research suggests that a linear timetable would be inappropriate. Third, evaluating accomplishments against standards and a lifespan timetable must consider the sociohistorical and individual life contexts within which the accomplishments were achieved (Wallace, 1985). As yet little is known about the giftedness-context interactions that may thwart or facilitate the realization of potential. Finally, questions surround the issue of multipotentiality. Which "potential" is to be realized? Should gifts and talents of highest societal priority be considered first and foremost? Have some talents been overlooked in unidimensional identification and selection approaches such that an individual, selected for intellectual precocity, is viewed as not realizing his or her potential while he or she struggles to "break through" in the visual arts?

For the most part, longitudinal research is merely a series of "snap-shots" heavily dependent on when the "picture was taken." Quite simply, determinations of the realization of potential are not easily made (Tannenbaum, 1983).

The Special Case of Career Development Patterns in Gifted Women

Women's career development is, beyond question, substantially more complex than that of their male counterparts, and the complexity is exacerbated by the expectations elicited by the label of "gifted," expectations held by others as well as by the gifted young woman herself. Expectations arising from sex-role stereotypes may directly contradict those derived from the "gifted" label, compounded by young women's socioeconomic status, racial or ethnic heritage, religious upbringing, or idiographic circumstance, as well as historic era. The gifted young woman finds herself amidst strong and frequently conflicting messages of what she "should," "ought," or "must" be. While much has been written about the presses and stressors of biculturalism, less has been written, and still less understood, about the presses and stressors of what amounts to multiculturalism.

With the exception of Terman (1959), few investigators have conducted longitudinal studies of gifted and talented women. Consonant with Sears and Barbee's (1977) findings for Terman's gifted women, Arnold (1993), Kerr (1985), Rodenstein and Glickauf-Hughes (1979), Kaufman (1981), Subotnik, Karp, and Morgan (1989), and others have documented the "failure" of gifted women to achieve at levels commensurate either with their ability or comparable to their male counterparts. Indeed, in their recent review, Reis and Callahan (1989) concluded that "bright women are clearly adult underachievers" (p. 102).

In assessing the realization of potential by women, issues discussed above appear even more salient for the Project CHOICE sample. With respect to the standards used to evaluate adult achievements, outcome variables such as educational level, career status, and income will inevitably be lower among those gifted women choosing traditionally "feminine" careers such as nursing, teaching, or the arts. Where requirements for formal education do not include advanced degrees, remuneration is less than that for the "major" professions and societal awards and recognition are infrequent. "Snapshots" of life achievements taken according to a linear, chronological-age timeline will reflect lesser achievements among those women choosing to take time out for marriage and family. Examining accomplishments in isolation fails to identify the role of sociohistorical and personal contexts as they differentially obstruct or facilitate women's career achievements. Finally, for those women with multipotentiality, choosing to realize a stereotypically feminine talent or ability rather than a stereotypically masculine one will, in the current societal context, lead to conclusions of lesser achievement. The identification of these issues in evaluating the realization of potential is not meant to suggest that gifted women currently achieve in accordance with their giftedness, but rather to highlight the need for a careful and cautious approach to evaluating what they have indeed achieved. To the extent that the standards and processes for making the determinations are grounded in a stereotypic reality, the societal contributions made by gifted women will invariably be depressed and devalued.

FIVE- AND TEN-YEAR FOLLOW-UPS

Five-Year Wave: Sample

During the 1982-83 academic year, an effort was made to contact the original Project CHOICE sample. Many of the families had moved after their daughters had graduated from high school, and current addresses were difficult, and in some cases impossible to obtain.

Nonetheless, 120 usable responses were received after a second request. This represented a 45% response rate for participants for whom pre-post test data were available. Comparability of this group of respondents to the original sample with respect to race, socio-economic status, level of occupational aspiration, and degree of crystallization of career aspiration was established. Proportional representation by school sector was also maintained.

Five-Year Wave: Instrumentation and Procedures

The original questionnaire was modified to determine the educational status and projected plans of the participants, the type of schools they were attending or had attended, their expected date of graduation, college major, employment and marital histories, future educational and occupational goals, confidence in attaining these goals, and a rating of overall life satisfaction (Fleming & Hollinger, 1986). Also included in the battery were the Personal Attributes

Questionnaire (PAQ; Spence, Helmreich & Stapp, 1974), the Texas Social Behavior Inventory (TSBI; Helmreich, Stapp, & Ervin, 1974), and the Work and Family Orientation Questionnaire (WOFO; Helmreich & Spence, 1974), which had been administered twice during the high school years (Hollinger & Fleming, 1988).

Ten-Year Wave: Sample

In 1990, the fortuitous occasion of 10-year reunion celebrations facilitated the updating of mailing lists. With the cooperation of alumni offices, it was possible to determine the whereabouts of a number of young women who might have otherwise been lost due to name changes, relocations, and in many cases the departure of their families from the immediate geographic area.

Responses were received from 126 of the original Project CHOICE subjects. They ranged in age from 27 to 29 years old. This represented 47% of those retested as high school juniors. The most dramatic differences occurred among school categories: public, parochial, or independent. Analyses were thus conducted using school category as the independent variable. As was the case with the earlier follow-up, the heterogeneity of the original sample with respect to socioeconomic status, ethnicity, and other background features was retained.

Ten-Year Wave: Instrumentation and Procedures

Each individual who could be located was sent a 12-page questionnaire containing many of the same items and scales used in the 1976-1977 identification/assessment battery and in the 1984 follow-up. New items, some of which were open-ended, were added to assess aspects of the young women's lives that reflected their current developmental stage, including perceptions of greatest achievements and greatest sources of satisfaction.

RESULTS

First Follow-up: Five Years Later

At the time of the 1983-1984 follow-up, 93% of the cohort was attending a postsecondary institution with 81% enrolled in 4-year programs. Only 7% and 5% respectively were attending community colleges or proprietary schools. Most were following the traditional time schedule anticipating college graduation four years after high school completion. Five percent were married, 3% had children, and only 2% described themselves as full-time homemakers. The vast majority were full-time students, one-quarter of whom also held part-time employment.

A review of the reported college majors showed that the majority (51%) were majoring in traditional feminine areas, including education, nursing, the social sciences, and the arts. Nontraditional majors were reported as follows: business (14%), math/science (12%), engineering (8%), and premedicine (1%) (Fleming & Hollinger, 1986).

Second Follow-up: Ten Years Later

By 1990, 48% remained in the original metropolitan area, and an additional 20% remained in the Midwest. This reflects a rather high degree of geographic stability. Of course, the probability of receiving and returning responses was higher for those within the proximate geographic area. There was a scattering of individuals residing in the South and West, but 17% lived in the eastern part of the country. Two of the respondents resided in Europe, one is a Peace Corps volunteer in Central America, and one is employed in Hawaii.

Educational accomplishments appear to be quite remarkable (see Table 12.2). All private school attendees completed a bachelor's level degree and all but 8% of the public sector women had done so as well. However, 32.4% of the parochial women either had not gone on to postsecondary programs or their work was still in progress. When viewed another way, the pursuit of postsecondary education has been extraordinarily high when contrasted with national statistics which reveal that only 19.2% of women graduating from high school in 1980 had completed Bachelor degrees by 1989 (Statistical Abstract, 1990). The contrast is even more dramatic when compared with Ohio data which suggest that only 13.9% of Ohio women have earned the Bachelor degree (Statistical Abstract, 1990). Further, the Project CHOICE young women were selected for a wide variety of talents and gifts, not exclusively academic. High percentages are pursuing advanced graduate degrees; as Table 12.2 indicates, 57% of the private sector alumni and 53% of the public school alumni report that graduate and professional degrees are either completed or in progress (Fleming & Hollinger, 1990).

When their educational aspirations expressed at age 15 were contrasted with their educational attainment at age 29, 48.4%, or

**Table 12.2. Project CHOICE: 10-Year Follow-Up
Highest Educational Level by School Category**

No Post Secondary Education

School	Freq.	%
Parochial	6	16.2
Private	0	0.0
Public	2	2.7
Total	8	6.3

		Completed		In Progress	
	School	**Freq.**	**%**	**Freq.**	**%**
Bachelors					
	Parochial	11	29.7	4	10.8
	Private	6	42.9	0	—
	Public	27	36.5	2	2.7
	Total	44	35.2	6	4.8
Masters					
	Parochial	4	10.8	2	5.4
	Private	5	35.7	0	—
	Public	15	20.2	7	9.5
	Total	24	19.2	9	7.2
Ph.D.					
	Parochial	1	2.7	0	—
	Private	0	—	1	7.1
	Public	1	1.4	5	6.8
	Total	2	1.6	6	4.8
M.D.; D.D.S.					
	Parochial	2	5.4	0	—
	Private	1	7.1	0	—
	Public	5	6.8	2	2.7
	Total	8	6.4	2	1.6
Law					
	Parochial	1	2.7	0	—
	Private	1	7.1	0	—
	Public	2	2.7	2	2.7
	Total	4	3.2	2	1.6

*Some Non-Degree Coursework: Parochial 3 (8%); Public 3 (4%); Total = 4.8%.
Associate Degree: Parochial 3 (8%); Public 1 (1%); Total = 3.2%.

60 of the women equaled or surpassed their adolescent expectation. Nearly 52%, or 64 young women, had not yet achieved the level projected as sophomores in high school. A strong relationship continued to remain between those early educational aspirations and current educational status, $r = .46$ ($p < .0001$; Hollinger & Fleming, 1991).

Data on marital status reveal that 48% of the sample were married 10 years after high school graduation, but the rate varied remarkably from 65% of the parochial women to 29% of the private school women. Approximately one-third of the public school women had married, with another 17% of this group either engaged or living with a significant other. Eight percent of the total group members were living with a significant other, while 3.2% were divorced. Indications from the interview material suggest that several others were seriously contemplating divorce action at the time of the mailing. Comments in response to a question about what they expected to happen in five years with respect to their marriages made it clear that dissolution was a strong possibility (Fleming & Hollinger, 1990).

To place these data into a national perspective, the median age of marriage for U.S. women is 22.8 years (Statistical Abstract, 1990). This suggests that, for the gifted women in our sample from the private and public school sectors, there was a tendency to delay marriage. At age 28 only 29% of the independent and 48% of the public school graduates were, in fact, married.

Thirty-eight percent of the parochial, 14% of the private school graduates, and 24% of the public school graduates were mothers. Expressed another way, the majority, 73%, did not have children at this time, but the interview materials suggest that many plan to start a family within the next five years. National data reveal that in 1988, only 4.5% of women between 25-29 were expecting to be childless while 51.1% expected to have two children, 24.3% expected three children, and 9% expected four or more (Statistical Abstract, 1990).

Patterns of Career Development and Choice

Pretest data. Given the rather wide socioeconomic differences across schools, it was hypothesized that these differences would be reflected in the pretest personality and career aspiration measures (Time 1; see Table 12.3). Surprisingly, few statistically significant differences emerged. School differences were demonstrated on Femininity, Fear of Success and on the third occupational daydream from the *Self-Directed Search*, with the parochial schools showing higher Femininity scores, greater Fear of Success, and lower career aspirations. The meaning of differences on the third occupational daydreams item is not at all clear. It was also the only place where socioeconomic differences surfaced, and may simply be indicative of an experiential or historical factor in occupational daydream consistency for these then-15-year-old women. Only the Competitiveness

Table 12.3. Distribution of Internal Barrier for Program Cohort by School (Percentages)

	Total Cohort	Parochial I	Parochial II	Private I	Private II	Public I	Public II
1. Non-Assertiveness	11.9	12.3	20.0	13.6	25.0	6.6	10.7
2. Fear of Success	17.5	21.1	5.7	27.3	8.3	11.8	23.8
3. Low Self-Esteem	25.5	21.1	25.7	22.7	25.0	26.3	28.6
4. Low Achievement Motivation	11.2	5.3	28.6	9.1	16.7	6.6	11.9
5. Multiple Barriers	4.2	3.5	8.6	4.5	0.0	2.6	4.8
6. No Internal Barrier	29.7	36.8	11.4	22.7	25.0	46.1	20.2

factor on the WOFO differentiated between the black and white sophomores, with higher scores for the young black women competing in majority white schools (Fleming & Hollinger, 1979).

Sharper differences were reflected in the diagnosis and prescription of career information needs. Forty-two percent of the Parochial School I gifted and talented students were diagnosed as needing assistance in raising their aspirations; no student in Private School II and less than 4% of Public School II young women evidenced such a need. A large number of young parochial school women with outstanding grades and test scores believed that their highest imaginable level of adult achievement would be hairdresser, bookkeeper, or retail sales person. One of the young black women for whom we believe the program was most helpful initially believed that computer operator would represent her highest career accomplishment. A successful engineer today, she commented, "I often remember my group sessions fondly. They were, after all, the very essence of my professional self."

In contrast, nearly 32% of Private School I students and only 8% of Public School I students were assessed as requiring guidance in exploring back-up alternatives to their career choices, as exemplified by our budding neurosurgeon, who expected to take 20 years off between medical school and residency to raise her family, or our aspiring nuclear scientist with ordinary math and science scores though remarkable creative writing ability. School differences also were apparent in what was revealed about the level of sophistication regarding careers, the diffuseness of thinking, and the progress toward crystallization of career decision making. The effort on the part of staff was directed not at striving for premature closure but in broadening horizons or clarifying options already expressed. Overall, in Parochial School II, nearly 81% of the students were believed to need help in broadening horizons whereas in Private School II,

42% seemed in need of elaboration and exploration. Twenty-five percent of this group seemed to need more specific career focus, such as: "What kinds of medical specialties are there out there?" as contrasted with only 6.5% of Parochial School II subjects.

Differential diagnoses of internal barriers by schools were also startling (see Table 12.3). Nonassertiveness varied between a low of 6.6% in one public school to a high of 25% in one of the independent schools. Similar contrasts among the schools by sector were evident for achievement motivation as well as for the group identified as having no identified internal barriers at all, ranging from a low of 46.1% in one of the public schools to 11.4% in one of the two parochial schools. In sum, influences were exerted at both the individual school and school type.

Five-year follow-up. At the time of the 5-year follow-up, fully 93% were attending postsecondary programs, anticipating that graduation would occur at the traditional time. Further, 89% reported well-defined future educational goals including graduate school (40%), MBA (15%), Law degree (6%), MD (5%), and a variety of other educational alternatives.

An examination of change in educational aspirations over the 5-year period revealed that, while initial aspirations fell between a Master's and a Bachelor's degree, women's aspirations had increased in five years to nearly the Master's degree level. A review of the expressed educational goals at this period reveals that 29.5% maintained their earlier educational aspiration level, 18.9% decreased their level, and 51.6% increased their level from the sophomore year in high school to young adulthood. In fact, 35% raised their level of educational aspiration to a Level 1 or decided to seek a graduate or professional degree. When combined with those originally aspiring to graduate or professional degrees, fully 52% of the respondents had gone beyond their earlier aspirations (Fleming & Hollinger, 1986). These levels are all the more surprising in view of the broadened talent definition originally employed.

More detailed analyses of levels of career aspirations over the 6-year period showed no statistically significant change in career aspirations from the initially high ones set as high school sophomores. However, examination of changes in Holland codes over this same period reveals that 27.5% of the young women who had no specific career aspirations as high school sophomores had defined one over the six intervening years, 21% remained stable over the period, and 38% changed. These changes occurred in a surprising direction: 41% changed from a traditional Holland classification

(Social, such as elementary teacher; Artistic, such as musician; Conventional, such as bank teller) to a nontraditional classification (Investigative, such as chemist; Enterprising, such as sales manager; Realistic, such as fish and game warden). Project CHOICE women's occupational codes are dramatically different from Holland's (1985) college women norms. Only 21% are classified as Social as compared to 62% of the normative group, 21% of the Project CHOICE women classify as Enterprising whereas 2% of the normative group is so categorized, and finally, 15% of the normative group fell into the Investigative category while over 24% of the Project CHOICE sample does.

Ten-year follow-up. The distribution of current occupations classified by Hollingshead Level (Hollingshead & Redlich, 1958) indicates that over 20% of the young women are employed at the higher executive or major professional levels. Over 57% of the public and private school alumna are working at the business manager or lesser professional classifications (i.e., Level 2), as compared with only 30% of the parochial school graduates. Forty-one percent of parochial school alumni are employed as minor professionals in comparison with only 13% of the public school graduates (Level 3). No private school graduate is employed in clerical or sales (Level 4), whereas 8% of the parochial and 5% of the public school sector young women are. Three percent of the parochial students, one percent of the public, and no private school alumna were classified as full-time homemakers. The bare numerical classifications fail to capture the richness of the positions which are being held by a number of the sample members including law partners, physicians, project managers in public and private engineering firms, film/TV producers, concert musicians, systems/policy analysts, philosophers, neuroscientists, graphic and fine artists, horticulturists, and actresses. As high school sophomores, most wanted to be either cosmetologists or veterinarians, yet there is only one of each at this time (Fleming & Hollinger, 1990).

When current careers were compared with career aspirations expressed as high school sophomores, 46% or 58 of the respondents had already equaled or surpassed those levels at age 29, while 34% were currently functioning at a level that was lower than earlier aspirations would have suggested. For 25 women with no specific career aspirations as adolescents, 18 were already working at Level I or II careers (Hollinger & Fleming, 1991). Many credited Project CHOICE with opening doors that might have otherwise been closed. The mathematically talented young black woman mentioned earlier who aspired to a computer operator job is project manager at a major government aerospace agency, married to another engineer, and active in a number of service organizations. A daughter of a single immigrant parent employed as a seamstress was uncertain about future career possibilities in high school, but is now completing her residency in a medical specialty.

Not all of the young women are faring so well. One is totally disabled from an accident, and several are struggling with drug and alcohol issues, financial problems, or dysfunctional family situations.

The Role of Self-Perception in Career Development

Although Super's (1963) original theory is, in retrospect, insufficient for understanding the career development of Project CHOICE participants, his emphasis on the central role of self-concept has been validated consistently over time. Examination of self-concept, or more specifically, self-perceptions (Eccles, 1983; Gottfredson, 1981) has consistently contributed to a better understanding of the career choices and development of these gifted young women.

During the high school years, participants' self-perceptions of agency (or instrumentality) emerged as a primary contributor to social self-esteem, followed by self-perceptions of expressiveness such that androgynous individuals (high instrumental and high expressive) reported significantly higher social self-esteem (Hollinger, 1983). More central to career development was the finding that those evidencing no internal barriers to the realization of potential reported significantly higher self-perceptions of agency (attributes central to the protection, maintenance, and enhancement of the individual's self) than three of five groups characterized by identified internal barriers to the realization of potential (Hollinger & Fleming, 1984). Furthermore, participant responses on the *Self-Directed Search* were found to vary as a function of self-perceptions of instrumentality and expressiveness (Hollinger, 1984) as did self-perceptions of ability (Hollinger, 1985a). Self-perceptions of ability in turn were found to play a central role in discriminating those math-talented women aspiring to nontraditional mathematics and science careers from their counterparts who, despite comparable math ability, were aspiring to traditional mathematics and science careers or to stereotypically feminine non-math/science careers (Hollinger, 1983, 1985b).

Five-year wave. As in adolescence, self-perceptions of instrumentality were predictive of social self-esteem as were self-perceptions of expressiveness, though to a lesser degree (Hollinger, 1985c). Perceiving oneself to be agentic or instrumental was, in young adulthood, a significant correlate of confidence in ultimately achieving one's occupational goals and of general satisfaction with one's life (Hollinger & Fleming, 1988).

Ten-year wave. As participants approach the third decade of life, self-perceptions of instrumental and expressive attributes continue to predict participants' social self-esteem. Instrumental self-perceptions correlate significantly not only with such career relevant issues as mastery, orientation to work, and job satisfaction, but also with their satisfaction with relationships and family. Of equal, if not greater, interest are the nonsignificant correlations of such self-perceptions with actual educational and career level accomplishments. At initial glance, it would appear that perceiving oneself as agentic—captain of one's own fate—operates in accordance with idiographic definitions of goals. Agentic attributes may be manifested in managing a home and family, organizing a charity fund-raising event, or leading a surgical team in the operating theater. While some of our gifted young women may well have drawn on their agentic qualities to realize their educational and occupational goals, others may draw upon these same qualities to realize their individual goals for their families or their own personal or spiritual growth. In contrast, self-perceptions of expressiveness hold fewer "surprises" in that they correlate significantly with relational aspects of the participants' lives. Those perceiving themselves as possessing such expressive attributes as "gentle" and "helpful to others" report high degrees of satisfaction derived from their relationships with spouses, significant others, family, and friends.

Influence of Socioeconomic and Familial Antecedents on Goals and Aspirations

Initial expectations on the part of the investigators included a hypothesis that significant differences would occur among school categories, and that the two schools in each sector could be safely combined for analyses. To everyone's surprise, each school had its own special character and personality. The young women and their families had chosen to be enrolled in that particular building. The public schools were selected because of residential patterns, the parochial and independent schools through a careful decision-making process.

Families recognized similarities in the values promulgated by the schools they had chosen, which were expected to provide the most compatible academic environments for their daughters. Thus, while school control has served as a marker for socioeconomic status, other differentiating contextual features among and between schools have also emerged. Although the two private schools each drew from an affluent clientele, one attracted a higher number of professional families, where more mothers were employed. Daughters from this school (see Table 12.1, Private School I) had more scientific and professional interests as contrasted with those of Private School II where more subjects with aesthetic interests attended.

It seems choice of school was determined by a host of factors including shared values, cost, location, religious affiliation, size, program availability, disciplinary philosophy, and a variety of other socioeconomic and cultural characteristics. Families clearly placed different emphases on different constellations of features.

Particularly poignant were conversations with mothers of young women from the parochial schools. Many were employed in assembly line jobs, and recognized the need for their daughters to obtain educational opportunities they themselves had missed. These mothers would express concern if their daughters were not attending Project CHOICE sessions regularly. While their daughters had far exceeded their mothers in educational attainment by age 29 (see Table 12.2), these young women are more heavily represented in Hollingshead Level 3 jobs, administrative and minor professional titles, than the young women from the public and private sectors. They do continue to represent the more traditional values their families and schools sought to inculcate in terms of marriage and parenthood.

Life Satisfactions and Dissatisfactions

Five-year wave. One of the scales that has been repeated in the adult follow-ups measures whether these young women are satisfied with the way life is going for them at their particular stage of adult development. During the 5-year follow-up, the question was posed in a general way, whereas an expansion during the 1990 study helped to pinpoint particular areas of contentment and discontent. When questioned at age 21, 72% reported being either satisfied or very satisfied with the ways things were currently going with their

Table 12.4 Life Satisfaction Means & Standard Deviations for
Total Group and School Type

Variable	Parochial	Private	Public	Total
Post Secondary Ed.	3.39	4.14	3.96	3.82
	(1.17)	(.95)	(1.01)	(1.08)
Career	4.03	4.00	4.23	4.14
	(.96)	(1.04)	(.85)	(.90)
Family	4.41	3.57	3.86	3.99
	(.96)	(1.34)	(1.14)	(1.14)
Spouse	4.61	3.73	4.26	4.30
	(.74)	(1.35)	(1.16)	(1.09)
Significant Other	4.23	3.71	4.39	4.25
	(1.09)	(1.38)	(.74)	(.96)
Friendship	3.76	4.21	4.08	4.00
	(1.06)	(.89)	(.84)	(.92)
Personal Growth	3.76	4.21	4.10	4.01
	(.98)	(.98)	(.60)	(.79)
Work	3.64	3.77	3.65	3.66
	(.83)	(1.09)	(1.10)	(1.02)
Health	3.89	4.43	4.11	4.08
	(1.02)	(.85)	(1.01)	(1.00)
Money	3.41	3.57	3.11	3.25
	(1.32)	(1.45)	(1.14)	(1.24)
Spiritual	3.65	3.54	3.54	3.57
	(1.14)	(.88)	(.87)	(.96)
Leisure	2.83	2.71	3.07	2.96
	(.97)	(1.27)	(1.25)	(1.18)
Total Life				
Satisfaction	4.22	4.14	4.09	4.14
	(.75)	(.95)	(.72)	(.76)

lives, 20% were neutral, and 8% were dissatisfied or very dissatisfied.

Ten-year wave. By 1990, a fuller differentiation of sources of satisfaction and dissatisfaction was provided (Table 12.4). The mean life satisfaction rating on a 5-point scale was 4.14. This reflects the general level of optimism that characterizes our respondents. Most of the categories including career, family, spouse or significant other, friendships, personal growth, and health, attained ratings around the 4-point mark or "satisfied." There were some exceptions such as the leisure category with a total group mean rating of 2.96, documenting busy lives that permit fewer recreational opportunities than preferred. Financial struggles exist also, particularly for those still in school or with young, growing families (Fleming & Hollinger, 1990).

As has consistently been the case, there are marked differences among the school sectors in several categories. The private school graduates are very satisfied with their postsecondary education (4.14); the parochial graduates are not so pleased (3.39), and indeed they have had a good deal less of it. The public school alumnae assigned a mean rating of 3.96 on this issue, also indicating a rather high degree of satisfaction. The parochial school graduates were less satisfied with their personal growth (3.76) than were either the private (4.21) or public sector (4.10) respondents. Similarly with their health, parochial graduates assigned a rating of 3.89, and private school graduates gave a rating of 4.43. On the other hand, the private school graduates rated satisfaction with family, spouse, or significant other much lower. Family was rated 3.6 by the private school graduates but 4.4 by the parochial alumnae; satisfaction with spouse was rated 4.6 by the parochial school respondents and 3.7 by the private sector young women. It should be remembered that the rate of divorce was highest among the small private school group, 7% as compared with 2.7% for both the public and the parochial school sectors.

IMPLICATIONS

Career Development of Gifted Women: Implications for Theory and Practice

Throughout the course of Project CHOICE, there has been the consistent, recurring theme of diversity: diverse talents and abilities, educational and occupational aspirations, internal and external barriers, coping strategies, life choices, and ultimately the satisfaction derived from those choices. Each follow-up examination of the lives of these gifted and talented young women contributes additional confirmation of the project's initial individual differences approach. Despite common sociohistorical community, school, and family contexts shared by many within the subsamples, these gifted young women have chosen life pathways as richly diverse as the individual ability, interest, value, and attribute profiles that characterized them as adolescents. From a theoretical standpoint, these differences may ultimately parallel Josselson's (1987) pathways to identity formation, validate Astin's (1985) emphasis on structural opportunities, and confirm the need for Marshall's (1989) "revisioning" of career development theory. At present, however, the clearest theoretical certainty is that, regardless of commonality either of context or person, the filter of individual perception and interpretation of both context and the self plays a central role in the life decisions made by gifted young women. The great value some gifted women place upon interpersonal relationships might at least partially explain the greater complexity of their career development than is observed among their male counterparts. In practice, this observation emphasizes the need for counselors who are capable of counseling for diverse life choices, and more importantly, willing to take the time to understand fully how each gifted young woman sees and interprets her world.

Although we are beginning to understand young women's perceptions, we know much less about their current personal, familial, and work environments. Astin's (1985) emphasis on "structures of opportunity" is a first step, one that focuses on access to opportunities for realizing one's potential. Gottfredson's (1991) work with Holland in assessing career environments may ultimately enable identification of elements in the work environment that facilitate or obstruct women's realization of potential. In addition, however, a theoretical framework for exploring relational dimensions is needed. Marshall (1989) stated that women are not free to make career decisions independent of relational considerations. At present, we know little about the significant others, family, or interpersonal constellations and professional relational systems that may significantly influence the gifted young woman and her efforts to realize her potential. At best, current career development theory postulates a two-way interaction between the person and the work environment. For gifted women, recognition of a three-way interaction of person, work environment, and relational context may be needed. In practice, we must expand our focus beyond the gifted woman in isolation to the gifted woman in relational context, a focus which suggests the need for a systems approach. In the process, we must work much more with gifted boys and young men if we expect them to accept, support, and encourage their gifted spouses or significant others. Nor have we worked sufficiently with parents of gifted women whose influence may extend well beyond the time of deciding whether or not to take advanced math and science coursework. Bell's (1989) very important message to gifted girls that "there's something wrong here and it's not me" must also be heard and understood by the significant others in women's lives.

The Multidimensionality of Giftedness

The history of the study of giftedness is fraught with recurrent definitional arguments between adherents of very circumscribed and narrow psychometric parameters and those advocating much broader and all-inclusive conceptions (Sternberg & Davidson, 1986). Project CHOICE was developed during a period when the broadest of definitions was in vogue, as exemplified by the Marland Report (1972) which guided and directed programming throughout the states in the 1970s. Although components were subsequently eliminated by federal and state governmental agencies through the 1980s, the 14-factor definition employed by Project CHOICE has in its breadth turned out to have been a fortuitous decision after all.

Although some writers have expressed disappointment with the career outcomes of those selected solely on the basis of grade point averages or intelligence test scores (see Arnold, this volume; Wallace, 1985), the broader net cast by Project CHOICE has resulted in a richer array of occupational choices than might have ordinarily been expected. To be sure, there are more than a fair share of nurses, teachers, and social workers in the traditional feminine categories. There are also a number of nontraditional careers, including fields with relatively low incidences of female representation: engineer, physician, and lawyer. Some of these individuals, particularly in scientific fields may, in fact, have been identified originally because of their special abilities in mathematics rather than because of their remarkable general intellectual or overall academic performance. The major difference in this sample as compared with most, we believe, is the inclusion of those who excelled early on in the visual and performing arts and have continued to pursue these objectives through the intervening years. One young woman, a public school enrollee, had a clearly defined plan at age 15 to be, as her first choice, a concert soloist or next, a musician in a major orchestra, or at least a music teacher if the other goals did not materialize. This woman is currently a violinist in a prestigious European orchestra and a member of a small international touring ensemble during the off-season. A graduate of a distinguished American institute of music, she recently married a member of the orchestra. While she undoubtedly would have been identified for her academic giftedness, her musical ability is her unique characteristic in this context. A second young woman from the more artistically oriented of the independent schools took more time than average to complete a series of experiences at various art schools before receiving her degree. She currently has her own studio where she experiments with a unique art form using special materials. She has already been offered commissions for several of her major works by prominent decorators. Other Project CHOICE young women are producing films and TV shows, acting professionally, and concertizing. Some have embarked on successful business enterprises. In any case, the effort to codify accomplishments at age 15 such that a broad range of talents could be identified appears to have paid off handsomely in allowing us to follow more diverse accomplishments in adulthood than academic ones alone would have predicted. We believe this more inclusive definition has important implications for schools that counter current trends toward greater exclusivity. Without the broad net, many talents would have escaped detection. Further, the longitudinal design was crucial in the documentation of talent and the magnitude of those talents which were in only very embryonic stages at age 15. Achievements in new fine and graphic art forms emerged in the college and early adult years in individuals who might have appeared academically unremarkable as high school sophomores.

Counseling and Support Services for Gifted Females: Families and Schools

As described, the Project CHOICE program detailed a series of intervention strategies in the high school years for expanding the career horizons of gifted and talented young women. A series of structured group experiences enabled each participant to define herself and her abilities and interests, learn more about career possibilities, and begin to plan for the future. The set of experiences was placed in the general sociohistorical context for women in the mid-1970s by providing help in confronting the personal and real-world demons each individual faced at that time. For many, dealing with these weighty issues appeared to be overwhelming and seemingly premature. Overscheduling of activities and commitments from special-interest clubs to sports leagues seemed to be an effective way of avoiding the painful business of having to deal with the future now. For some, gender role socialization and career issues in general were of limited relevance because they were simply not developmentally ready to wrestle with future concerns when the intervention was scheduled. Others had a very limited view of what the world had to offer, a view provided only by versions depicted in films and television. These were but a few of the kinds of problems the program sought to help the young women address during their junior year in high school.

In retrospect, as we examine reported outcomes and listen to the comments of our respondents in adulthood, a series of difficult questions emerge. Some of our young women express regret about roads not taken, such as failing to pursue higher education options immediately after high school. Others express the isolation they have felt in pursuing nontraditional careers. Still others voice concerns about unsuccessful relationships or unacceptably high prices for living life "in the fast lane." For every phase and every unique constellation of factors and life choices thus far experienced, struggles and concerns are articulated by our young women. To be sure, these kinds of introspective reviews are developmentally appropriate. However, for those committed to improving the lives of gifted and talented women, there is frustration in not having ready answers to some important issues.

How can a helpful set of experiences be provided early enough and often enough to build the necessary skills and level of sophistication that young women growing up in the 1990s clearly will require for making wise career and lifestyle choices? In these times of financial retrenchment for schools, how can sufficient resources, human and material, be allocated to provide the sustained, nurturing guidance and counseling functions required? How can educators assist parents to join in partnership with schools in supporting their daughters' choices and capitalizing on educational and career opportunities as they develop? How can we assist skilled counselors to discover and build repertoires of experiences that capture the complexities of women's lives, choices, opportunities, constraints, and varied tempos? How early should these efforts begin?

Lifework Planning in the Adult Years

While Project CHOICE's intervention in the adolescent years might be viewed by some as being too late, the axiom "it is never too late" is, from our experience, valid. In fact, our intervention was actually too early for many. In adolescence, barriers to goals and dreams did not yet exist. As early as the 5-year follow-up, however, some participants were asking the question, "Where are you (Project CHOICE) when I need you?" Others were recalling sessions with a cognitive awareness that they had not been ready to hear at the time. In reality, a comprehensive examination of the life pathways, options, and decisions available to gifted women throughout the lifespan constitutes more than a single program can address and, more importantly, communicates much more than an individual can process and assimilate at a given developmental stage. More essential is the availability of knowledgeable counselors, programs, and support groups throughout the lifespan and particularly for the transition periods in life. As Noble (1989) observed, even "those who do reach maturity with their giftedness intact are still faced with what for some may be insurmountable obstacles" (p. 132). The chronic stress of "multiculturalism" (i.e., coping with a multitude of diverse and frequently conflicting cultural expectations or the "Superwoman

Syndrome") may lead to chemical dependency, eating disorders, and suicide while adult years of chronic underemployment and under-utilization of talents and abilities can be equally destructive. The adult gifted woman appeared no less likely to find herself in lose-lose situations than her adolescent counterpart. The neurosurgeon coping with the stressors of multiculturalism and the housewife with five children wrestling with the spectre of unrealized potential are in equal need of continued support.

At present, Project CHOICE participants are on the verge of entering the settling-down period of the second adult life phase (Bardwick, 1980). According to Gallos (1989), those achieving professional success at the expense of all other life spheres or having lived the "superwoman" life may curtail or abandon completely their career investments. Two of our young women appear to have done so already. One reported "making it as a hot shot attorney in Manhattan (and having the good sense to walk away from it)" and another commented about "escaping the big city rat race/money chase" as one of their three greatest life achievements. However, the majority of our successful professionals appear quite satisfied with their careers and accomplishments to date and are beginning to become cognizant of the need for balance in their lives. As one environmental engineer on the verge of matrimony reports, "sometime in the next five years, I'll be taking some time off to have a couple of kids. At this point I don't know how much time. Although I want to keep moving forward with my career, I don't want to sacrifice quality of life for advancement. I want a balanced personal life, and you can't have that *and* a job that demands 80–90-hour work weeks."

The literature contains little guidance for predicting decisions during the second adult phase for those who have already "settled down" to home and family in their twenties. While these young women currently report substantial satisfaction derived from personal and relational life spheres, might we not predict a similar shift in investment toward their comparatively less fulfilled life spheres of education and career? What this developmental transition period will hold for our young women is as yet unknown.

LONGITUDINAL RESEARCH FOR GIFTED WOMEN

Throughout the longitudinal period of Project CHOICE, much has changed with respect to theory, construct definition, methodology, and sociohistorical context. The Project's original theoretical bases was derived from Super (1963) and Holland (1973), and are no long-

er viewed as sufficient for understanding women's career development. Instrumentation such as the Personal Attributes Questionnaire (Spence & Helmreich, 1974), used originally to assess
"masculinity/femininity" has since evolved to a measure of "instrumentality and expressiveness." General perspectives have ranged
from reformist in the 1970s to revisionist in the 1980s. When reviewing the sociohistorical changes of the time period encompass-
ing Project CHOICE, the changes and associated challenges of the
period for the young women themselves become apparent. The peak
of the women's movement occurred during the participants' adolescence. They graduated from college during a major recession and
began their careers amidst a decade of political conservatism (see
Bardwick, 1990). They have lived through reformism and revision-
ism, from "fear of success" to "missed opportunities of a relational
nature." New theories, instruments, interpretations of instruments,
and differing perspectives all characterize the changing lens
through which their accomplishments and Project CHOICE itself
must be viewed. We will watch with great interest—and some trepi-
dation—the stories the next decade will tell.

REFERENCES

Arnold, K. D. (1993). The Illinois Valedictorian Project: Academically talented women in the 1980s. In K. Hulbert & D. Shuster (Eds.), *Wom-
en's voices through time* (pp. 393–414). San Francisco, CA: Jossey-
Bass.
Astin, H. S. (1985). The meaning of work in women's lives: A sociopsychological model of career choice and work behavior. *The Counsel-
ing Psychologist, 12*(4), 117–126.
Bardwick, J. M. (1990). Where we are and what we want: A psychological
model. In R. A. Nemiroff & C. A. Colarusso (Eds.), *New dimensions in
adult development* (pp. 186–211). New York: Basic Books.
Bardwick, J. M. (1980). The seasons of a woman's life. In D. McGuigan
(Ed.), *Women's lives: New theory, research and policy* (pp. 35–57).
Ann Arbor: University of Michigan Center for Continuing Education of
Women.
Belenky, M. F., Clinchy, B. M., Goldberger, N. R., & Tarule, J. M. (1986).
*Women's ways of knowing: The development of self, voice and
mind.* New York: Basic Books.
Bell, L. A. (1989). Something's wrong here and it's not me: Challenging the
dilemmas that block girls' success. *Journal for the Education of the
Gifted, 12*(1), 118–130.
Blaubergs, M. (1978). Personal studies of gifted females: An overview and
commentary. *Gifted Child Quarterly, 22*(4), 539–547.

Eccles, J. (1983). Expectancies, values and academic behaviors. In J. T. Spence (Ed.), *Achievement and achievement motives* (pp. 75–146). San Francisco, CA: W. H. Freeman.

Eccles, J. (1986). Gender roles and women's achievement. *Educational Researcher, 15*(6), 15–19.

Eccles, J. S. (1987). Gender roles and women's achievement-related decisions. *Psychology of Women Quarterly, 11*, 135–172.

Farmer, H. S. (1985). Model of career and achievement motivation for women and men. *Journal of Counseling Psychology, 32*, 363–390.

Fleming, E. S. (1985). Career preparation. In R. Swassing (Ed.), *Teaching gifted children and adolescents* (pp. 340–374). Columbus, OH: Merrill Publishing.

Fleming, E. S., & Hollinger, C. L. (1979). *Realizing the promise of female adolescents: A diagnostic-prescriptive model.* Final report to the Office of Education, Department of Health, Education and Welfare (W.E.E.A.P. # G00760497).

Fleming, E. S., & Hollinger, C. L. (1979). *Project CHOICE: Creating her options in career exploration.* Boston, MA: Educational Development Corporation.

Fleming, E. S., & Hollinger, C. L. (1981). The multidimensionality of talent in adolescent young women. *Journal for the Education of the Gifted, 4*, 188–198.

Fleming, E. S., & Hollinger, C.L. (1986). *Gifted and talented female adolescents: A six-year longitudinal study of life choices.* Paper presented at the annual meeting of the American Educational Research Association, San Francisco, CA.

Fleming, E. S., & Hollinger, C. L. (1990). *Project CHOICE: Gifted young women ten years later.* Paper presented at the National Association for Gifted Children Convention, Little Rock, AR.

Gallos, J. V. (1989). Exploring women's development: Implications for career theory, practice and research. In M. B. Arthur, D. T. Hall, & B. S. Lawrence (Eds.), *Handbook of career theory* (pp. 110–132). London: Cambridge University Press.

Gilligan, C. (1982). *In a different voice: Psychological theory and women's development.* Cambridge, MA: Harvard University Press.

Gilligan, C. (1988). Remapping the moral domain: New images of self in relationship. In C. Gilligan, J. V. Ward, & J. M. Taylor (Eds.), *Mapping the moral domain* (pp. 3–19). Cambridge, MA: Harvard University Press.

Ginzberg, E. (1966). *Lifestyles of educated women.* New York: Columbia University Press.

Gottfredson, G. D. (1991, April). *Using the Holland Occupational-Environmental Classification in research and practice.* Invited address presented at the American Educational Research Association Annual Meeting, Chicago, IL.

Gottfredson, L. S. (1981). Circumscription and compromise: A developmental theory of occupational aspirations. *Journal of Counseling Psychology, 28*(6), 545–579.

Harmon, L. W. (1985). What's new? A response to Astin. *The Counseling Psychologist, 12*(4), 127–128.

Hardesty, S., & Jacobs, N. (1986). *Success and betrayal: The crisis of women in corporate America.* New York: Franklin Watts.

Helmreich, R. L., & Spence, J. T. (1974). The work and family orientation questionnaire: An objective instrument to assess components of achievement motivation and attitudes toward family and career. *JSAS: Catalog of Selected Documents in Psychology, 4.*

Helmreich, R., Stapp, J., & Ervin, C. (1974). The Texas Social Behavior Inventory (TSBI): An objective measure of self-esteem or social competence. *Journal Supplement Abstract Service Catalog of Selected Documents in Psychology, 1974* 4(79). (Ms. No. 681).

Hennig, M., & Jardim, A. (1978). *The managerial woman.* London: Boyars.

Holland, J. L. (1973). *Making vocational choices.* Englewood Cliffs, NJ: Prentice-Hall.

Holland, J. L. (1977). *The self-directed search.* Palo Alto, CA: Consulting Psychologists Press.

Holland, J. L. (1985). *The self-directed search: Professional manual.* Odessa, FL: Psychological Assessment Resources, Inc.

Hollinger, C. L. (1983). Counseling the gifted and talented female adolescent: The relationship between social self esteem and traits of instrumentality and expressiveness. *Gifted Child Quarterly, 27*(4), 157–161.

Hollinger, C. L. (1984). The impact of gender schematic processing on the Self-Directed Search responses of gifted and talented female adolescents. *Journal of Vocational Behavior, 24,* 15–27.

Hollinger, C. L. (1985a). Understanding the female adolescent's self perceptions of ability. *Journal for the Education of the Gifted, 9*(1), 59–80.

Hollinger, C. L. (1985b). Self-perceptions of ability of mathematically talented female adolescents. *Psychology of Women Quarterly, 9*(3), 323–336.

Hollinger, C. L. (1985c). The stability of self-perceptions of instrumental and expressive traits and social self esteem among gifted and talented female adolescents. *Journal for the Education of the Gifted, 8*(1), 107–126.

Hollinger, C. L., & Fleming, E. S. (1984). Internal barriers to the realization of potential among gifted and talented female adolescents. *Gifted Child Quarterly, 28*(3), 135–139.

Hollinger, C. L., & Fleming, E. S. (1988). Gifted and talented young women: Antecedents and correlates of life satisfaction. *Gifted Child Quarterly, 32*(2), 254–259.

Hollinger, C. L., & Fleming, E. S. (1991, April). *Gifted and talented young women: A longitudinal examination of life choices.* Paper presented at the American Educational Research Association Annual Conference, Chicago, IL.

Hollingshead, A. B., & Redlich, F. (1958). *Social class and mental illness.* New York: Wiley.

Horner, M. S. (1972). Toward an understanding of achievement related conflicts in women. *Journal of Social Issues, 28,* 157–175.

Horowitz, F. D., & O'Brien, M. (1985). Perspectives on research and development. In F.D. Horowitz & M. O'Brien (Eds.), *The gifted and talented: Developmental perspectives* (pp. 437–454). Washington, DC: American Psychological Association.

Josselson, R. (1987). *Finding herself: Pathways to identity development in women.* San Francisco, CA: Jossey-Bass.

Kaufman, F. A. (1981). The 1964–1968 Presidential Scholars: A follow-up study. *Exceptional Children, 48*(2), 164–169.

Kerr, B. A. (1985). *Smart girls, gifted women.* Columbus, OH: Ohio Psychology Publishing.

Marland, S. P., Jr. (1972). *Education of the gifted and talented.* Washington, DC: U.S. Government Printing Office.

Marshall, J. (1989). Re-visioning career concepts: A feminist invitation. In M.B. Arthur, D.T. Hall, & B.S. Lawrence (Eds.), *Handbook of career theory* (pp. 275–291). London: Cambridge University Press.

Mednick, M. T. (1989). On the politics of psychological constructs: Stop the bandwagon, I want to get off. *American Psychologist, 44*(8), 1118–1123.

Noble, K. D. (1989). Living out the promise of high potential: Perceptions of 100 gifted women. *Development Journal, 1,* 57–75.

Osipow, S. H. (1973). *Theories of career development* (2nd ed.). Englewood Cliffs, NJ: Prentice-Hall.

Osipow, S. H. (1983). *Theories of career development* (3rd ed.). Englewood Cliffs, NJ: Prentice-Hall.

Reis, S. M., & Callahan, C. M. (1989). Gifted females: They've come a long way—or have they? *Journal for the Education of the Gifted, 12*(2), 99–117.

Rodenstein, J. M., & Glickauf-Hughes, C. (1979). Career and life-style determinants of gifted women. In N. Colangelo & R. T. Zaffrann (Eds.), *New voices in counseling the gifted* (pp. 370–381). Dubuque, IA: Kendall/Hunt.

Sears, P. S., & Barbee, A. H. (1977). Career and life satisfactions among Terman's gifted women. In J. C. Stanley, W. W. George, & C. H. Solano (Eds.), *The gifted and the creative: A fifty year perspective* (pp. 28–65). Baltimore, MD: Johns Hopkins University Press.

Spence, J. T., Helmreich, R., & Stapp, J. (1974). The Personal Attributes Questionnaire: A measure of sex role stereotypes and masculinity-femininity. *Journal Supplement Abstract Service Catalog of Selected Documents in Psychology, 4*(43). (Ms. No. 617).

Statistical Abstract of the U.S. (1990). Washington, DC: Government Printing Office.

Sternberg, R. J., & Davidson, J. E. (1985). Cognitive development in the gifted and talented. In F.D. Horowitz & M. O'Brien (Eds.), *The gifted and talented: Developmental perspectives* (pp. 37–74). Washington, DC: American Psychological Association.

Sternberg, R. J., & Davidson, J. E. (Eds.). (1986). *Conceptions of gifted-ness.* New York: Cambridge University Press.

Subotnik, R. F., Karp, D. E., & Morgan, E. R. (1989). High IQ children at midlife: An investigation into the generalizability of Terman's genetic studies of genius. *Roeper Review, 11*(3), 139–144.

Super, D. E. (1963). Self-concepts in vocational development. In D. E. Super, R. Starishevsky, N. Matlin, & J. P. Jordaan (Eds.), *Career development: Self-concept theory* (Research Monograph No. 4, pp. 1–16). New York: College Entrance Examination Board.

Super, D. E. (1980). Life span, life space approach to career development. *Journal of Vocational Behavior, 16,* 282–298.

Tannenbaum, A. J. (1983). *Gifted children: Psychological and educational perspectives.* New York: Macmillan.

Terman, L. M. (1959). The gifted group at mid-life. *Genetic studies of genius* (Vol. 5). Stanford, CA: Stanford University Press.

Tittle, C. K. (1983). Studies of the effects of career interest inventories: Expanding outcome criteria to include women's experiences. *Journal of Vocational Behavior, 22,* 148–158.

Wallace, D. B. (1985). Giftedness and the construction of a creative life. In F. D. Horowitz & M. O'Brien (Eds.), *The gifted and talented: Developmental perspectives* (pp. 361–385). Washington, DC: American Psychological Association.

13

A Generation of Leaders in Gifted Education

Rose A. Rudnitski

How does a field produce a generation of leaders committed to its development? That question was raised in gifted education after the *Marland Report* (1972) noted a lack of focus in goals and programming and a need for leadership in the field. The Graduate Leadership Education Project on the Gifted/Talented (GLEP) was funded by the U.S. Office of Education to be the vehicle for producing the next generation of leaders.

This chapter describes a retrospective study of 54 Fellows of the Graduate Leadership Education Project and presents their views of the program's effect on their careers and professional lives. The 38 participants in this study were former GLEP Fellows who studied in five cohorts at Teachers College, Columbia University, the University of Kansas, the University of Georgia, the University of Connecticut at Storrs, Purdue University, and the University of Virginia between 1977 and 1981. Now in their late 30s to late 50s, with a mean age of 43, many of the GLEP Fellows have indeed fulfilled their leadership potential.

HISTORICAL CONTEXT

Interest in the education of the gifted has been subject to cycles in the United States, especially in the latter half of this century. After World War II and into the early 1950s, though some programs for the gifted existed, there was little thrust toward their development and expansion. With the launching of Sputnik in 1957, however, gifted programs began to proliferate. This response to perceived Soviet scientific, technical, and military superiority did not last long, as U.S. domestic and social problems took precedence in the 1960s. In 1970, a renewed interest in the education of the gifted was reflected in the addition, by Congress, of Section 806, "Provisions related to

Gifted and Talented Children" to the 1969 Amendments to the Elementary and Secondary Education Act (ESEA). Section 806 added gifted students to the population aided by Titles II and V of the ESEA, and called for research on services provided. One major finding of this research was that

> Since there was no federal or national focus on leadership within the area of gifted and talented children and youth, state and local programs targeted at that population had tended to function in isolation from one another. This had resulted in the lack of an effective means of sharing new knowledge to foster a more concerted national program development for gifted and talented children and youth. (Little, Inc., 1971, pp. 5–6)

Many developments in the education of the gifted emanated from the *Marland Report* (1972), including an ERIC Clearinghouse on gifted education, grants for research, demonstration projects and training programs, and an influential, comprehensive definition of giftedness. The Graduate Leadership Education Project was conceived in this context to identify and develop the leadership potential of a talented group in order to sustain strong leadership and forge new directions for the field.

CONCEPTIONS OF LEADERSHIP

Situational Leadership

The theory of situational leadership defines leadership as a process by which a leader surfaces when that individual is perceived by a group as having or controlling the means to identify or attain group or individual goals (Foster & Silverman, 1988; Passow, 1978). GLEP exposed the Fellows to many situations in which they could develop leadership skills specific to the field. The GLEP curriculum was an addition to the regular graduate program at each Fellow's university and served to augment and enrich that program significantly.

Leadership and Gifted Education

In his psychosocial approach to giftedness, Tannenbaum (1983) states that there are five factors which must mesh in order to produce gifted performance: superior general intellect, distinctive special aptitudes, noncognitive traits, a challenging and nurturing environment, and good fortune or chance factors. Tannenbaum asserted that leadership is a talent in the social domain and that there is a positive relationship between social leadership and intelligence. In the GLEP selection process described below, it is evident that aptitude as measured by GRE, MAT scores, and academic records was a factor in identification. Because much of a leader's behavior involves some kind of cognitive problem solving, Tannenbaum also maintained that for leadership talent to develop, general intelligence must be combined with special aptitudes and skills. The following description of the GLEP identification process and program experiences highlights the aptitudes and skills, and the situations in which the Fellows were placed that helped to develop the expertise necessary for effective leadership.

THE GLEP PROGRAM

Program Goals

The general mission of the Graduate Leadership Education Project was to "help break the spirit of faddism that had traditionally characterized popular interest in the education of the ablest" (Tannenbaum, 1982). This was to be accomplished through identifying a group of potential leaders early in their careers and providing them with funding for intensive graduate study in the education of the gifted. The field-specific studies would build advocacy skills and commitment to the field in several crucial areas: the supervision and administration of programs; college teaching, with emphasis on teacher education; curriculum innovation, with emphasis on the design of enrichment programs; and educational research, with emphasis on basic and applied studies of giftedness and talent (Tannenbaum, 1982).

The goals were to be accomplished through the graduate programs at the collaborating universities, and GLEP activities organized by the Director, Abraham J. Tannenbaum, and Co-Director, A. Harry Passow, of Teachers College, Columbia University. Each of the seven GLEP universities had a doctoral program and at least one major figure in gifted education on its faculty. This individual served as the institutional representative to the program and participated in the design and implementation of GLEP activities for the Fellows. The institutional representatives met each year from 1976 to 1979, when funding ran out and the program was limited to Teachers College. They served as mentors for the Fellows, guiding their studies in the graduate programs at their respective universities. Their influence was later found to have been profound and long-lasting, making it somewhat difficult for the Fellows to separate the influence of GLEP from the mentor or the graduate program in which the mentor was a key figure.

Identification of the GLEP Fellows

The identification process designed by Tannenbaum was rigorous and comprehensive. The Graduate Leadership Education Project was open to masters and doctoral level students at the seven universities cited above, with higher standards for the doctoral students. Applications were reviewed by an independent panel of individuals chosen by Tannenbaum, comprised of people who were not involved in the education of the gifted, but who Tannenbaum described as being gifted themselves. Panelists focused on the following criteria when reviewing the applications:

1. academic record and potential, as demonstrated by transcripts, test scores, and recommendations
2. field experience and performance, such as experience teaching gifted children and directing or designing programs
3. scholarly and professional promise, as demonstrated by academic record, publications, or research projects
4. productivity demonstrated by the applicant's record of products, projects, and performances
5. nonacademic attributes such as leadership in professional and social groups, initiation of projects or programs, or artistic ability
6. career objectives, as described in a personal goals statement (Tannenbaum, 1976, p. 4)

In the spring of 1977, eight students were selected as GLEP Fellows from a pool of 45 applicants. The eight members of the First Wave chose to attend five of the cooperating institutions. Twelve students, the Second Wave, entered the program in Fall 1977, and 15 students, the Third Wave, in Fall 1978. Four Fellows were selected to begin their studies in Fall 1979, but funds were not sufficient to support them fully. These Fellows, the Fourth Wave, attended Teachers College, and received funding only for one course. In 1980, seven students were selected to receive half-fellowships, while others were designated "honorary fellows." Even without financial support, this designation later proved to be a significant influence on some of this group.

Programmatic Augmentation

GLEP program experiences were planned by the directors and institutional representatives to augment the knowledge and expertise gained by the Fellows in their regular graduate studies. According to the Fellows, the most influential GLEP experiences were the annual Summer Institutes. These institutes were held from 1977 through 1981 at Teachers College and attended by all of the Fellows as well as by many of the leaders of the field. The Fellows felt that the exposure afforded them at the Summer Institutes was invaluable, not only in terms of the recognition they received, but also in boosting their confidence in their own abilities and skills.

The Fellows of the first three waves received additional funding to attend conferences on gifted education. They were encouraged to write proposals and to present as well as to attend sessions. This experience served to enhance their knowledge of the field as well as to strengthen their proposal writing and presenting skills. GLEP Fellows often arranged formal and informal meetings and discussions for themselves at the conferences, using them as vehicles to build a sense of belonging to a group larger than the one at each home university.

Most of the Fellows also participated in off-campus field experiences. These included consulting with state departments of education and school districts to help develop programs for the gifted. Several Fellows served as interns in the U.S. Office of Education as well.

Program Evaluation

In the spring of 1979, Tannenbaum distributed a questionnaire to those Fellows who had, up to that time, participated in GLEP. Of the 34 Fellows, 21 (68%) responded to the questionnaire. In his account of the evaluation findings, Tannenbaum reported that the Fellows had been either moderately or highly satisfied with the relevance, and extent of GLEP activities associated with their graduate programs of study. Some respondents attached notes to the questionnaires to point out that financial support and the support of the project director to students on other campuses were highly effective as well.

In 1979, the Fellows rated the field experiences highly in terms of relevance, availability, and quality. Some Fellows indicated that the field experience had been part of the regular program of study at their institutions and could not be attributed to GLEP. When asked to list other experiences in which they had participated, almost all of the respondents cited the Summer Institutes at Teachers College as being influential. Many also cited GLEP support for attendance at national, regional, state, and local conferences. The effectiveness of these experiences was not indicated in the survey report.

Fellows also reported being either moderately or highly satisfied with the extent and availability of opportunities for leadership activities in the field as part of their training. They had participated in presentations, organization of programs, curriculum development, and advocacy activities. The only opportunity the Fellows rated as being inadequate was the opportunity to teach at the university level.

When asked to comment on the program and its effects, the Fellows most frequently cited internships, publication and editing, and the collegiality they experienced with other Fellows as being particularly satisfying. They also mentioned financial assistance they had received and the career advancement GLEP had afforded them. They felt that GLEP had served as a key to opening doors to career opportunities.

> They felt, in general, that GLEP would help open doors to the future for them in education of the gifted and talented. They appreciated being identified as leadership potential and meeting possible leaders of the field for the future. In some cases, they indicated it was difficult to separate out GLEP contributions from the normal opportunities provided by their university. (Tannenbaum, 1982, p. 25)

SIMILAR PROGRAMS

There have been three programs which were somewhat similar to the Graduate Leadership Education Project. The Teaching the Talented (TTT) Program, conducted at the University of Connecticut since 1969, was the most similar. Open to applicants from across the nation, it was designed to prepare personnel who could "identify and nurture the creative and academic talent of youngsters from disadvantaged backgrounds" (Gear, 1974, p. 8).

Applications to the TTT program consisted of the traditional measures of academic aptitude stipulated by the University of Connecticut's Graduate School of Education and a 5-page questionnaire designed by the TTT staff. The questionnaires were designed to ascertain each candidate's commitment, perceptions, strengths and weaknesses, learning styles, and values. They were reviewed by a selection committee composed of TTT staff members the first year, with the addition of representative TTT Fellows in subsequent years (Gear, 1974).

During the first five years of the program, 46 Fellows representing all regions of the continental United States participated in the Teaching the Talented Program for periods of one to three years. One-half of the Fellows were members of minority groups and about one-half were female. Most of the TTT Fellows were under 36 years of age, had Masters degrees, and had worked in education for more than 10 years, many with minority or disadvantaged students.

The program design for the TTT Fellows included theoretical, practical, and integrative experiences. The theoretical component was the regular graduate program in the education of the gifted at the University of Connecticut at Storrs. The practical component was the internship which was linked to a variety of integrative experiences. The program was designed for flexibility to adapt to the needs, goals, and interests of the individual Fellows (Gear, 1974). Many former TTT Fellows are active leaders in the field, teaching at colleges and conducting workshops and staff development programs throughout the nation. Three members of the 24-member Board of Directors of the National Association for Gifted Children are former Teaching the Talented Fellows.

The other programs that were similar to GLEP were the Illinois Graduate Leadership Training Program on the Gifted, and the Minnesota Gifted Education Masters Program. Each comprised a university graduate program, at least one practicum experience, opportunities for participants to interact, summer sessions, and a guest speaker series with leaders in the field.

A unique feature of the Illinois program was the provision for directed independent study as an integral part of the program. It was viewed as essential to provide this avenue for the students to explore problems and special interests. James J. Gallagher, the Illinois Program Director, stated, "Just as we stress the necessity for greater independence in the gifted students, we must, in our own training program, allow these persons the necessary freedom for exploration of their own. For that reason, time was set aside for independent study" (1966, p. 6).

Although the programs had many features in common, the Graduate Leadership Education Project was the most comprehensive and probably had the most wide-ranging impact on the field. The graduate study, the practicum experiences, and the internships in GLEP were conducted all over the United States, thus helping to create a national focus.

JOYS AND PITFALLS OF LONGITUDINAL
RESEARCH

When one follows a group over time, relationships can develop between the researcher and the subjects, especially when they are virtually peers and share professional and personal concerns on many levels. Some of the friendships formed can be long-lasting and deep, and enrich the life of the researcher. The same relationships, however, pose several problems. How can one be objective about people one has grown to care for in very personal ways? How does one separate the subjects from the friends; the findings from the emotion-laden life experiences; the conclusions from the concerns? These questions raise many ethical and methodological issues that are not the focus of this chapter, but which, nevertheless, are important to any discussion of longitudinal research. They are especially important to gifted education, where longitudinal studies are central to understanding the needs and development of the gifted and the influence of programs designed to accommodate them.

Along those lines, longitudinal studies of the gifted are likely to be conducted by persons who have an interest or a stake in the field. It would be very difficult for someone with a strong commitment to the education of the gifted to report findings that might reflect negatively on the field or the gifted individuals who might benefit from services and programs. Yet those without strong interest in the field will be unlikely to conduct the necessary research.

PROBLEMS AND PROMISES OF THIS
LONGITUDINAL STUDY

Some unique problems were encountered in conducting this study due to the long passage of time. The Director had retired and had discarded the Fellows' application materials. As the respondents had mentioned the application process as being comprehensive and unique, and as many had also reported a sense of pride in their essays and responses, the missing files were a source of disappointment.

Another difficulty for the researcher was that many of the GLEP Fellows found it difficult to distinguish standard graduate school experiences from the GLEP program experiences. As students, they had participated in the *whole* curriculum at all levels: the intended, the enacted, and the hidden. Each Fellow, and to some extent the directors, emphasized aspects of the whole curriculum that were most important to them. It was difficult for the researcher to decide which had the highest priority: the most frequent responses, the most intense responses, or the responses with the broadest implications.

It was difficult to locate some of the Fellows, especially since no effort had been made to track them as they graduated and moved into their first professional positions. The program evaluation in 1979 had been their last contact with the program and with their identification as GLEP Fellows. NAGC and TAG programs dating back to the 1970s were consulted to no avail. Some Fellows simply could not be found.

THE 1989 RETROSPECTIVE STUDY

In 1989, 10 years after the evaluation conducted by Tannenbaum, the first follow-up of the GLEP Fellows was undertaken after they had completed their studies and were established in their careers. The GLEP archives were analyzed and interviews of the GLEP Co-Director were conducted to elicit the history and structure of the program, and background information.

The Questionnaire

A self-rating, autobiographical questionnaire was constructed and sent to all GLEP Fellows for whom addresses were available. Items on the questionnaire asked if Fellows felt that they could be characterized as leaders in the field, and what characteristics or traits the respondents felt that they possessed which helped them to become leaders. The questionnaire was autobiographical in that the Fellows were asked to describe their career development since participating in the program (or enclose a curriculum vitae), and whether or not they felt that the program had contributed to their professional and personal development. The questionnaire also served as a lead-in to the interviews.

The Interview

The interview was designed to draw upon recollections from the Fellows and to provide further information on their perceptions of the program and its influence on their lives. In addition to the semistructured interview schedule, the Fellows were also asked to comment freely on GLEP, its participants, and its influences. Some interviews were in person, while others were by phone.

The GLEP Project Director, Co-Director, and Associate Director were also interviewed and presented with findings of this follow-up so their insights and additional perspectives could be included. They also provided information that was not available in the archives of the Graduate Leadership Education Project.

There were two mailings of the questionnaire. After an initial response of approximately 30 Fellows (60%), 8 were located with the help of other Fellows who knew their addresses or places of employment. The 38 respondents comprised 70% of the Fellows who had participated in the program in the five cohorts or waves. The respondents were distributed across the waves in direct proportion to the distribution of Fellows in the corresponding waves, an indication that this was a representative sample (see Table 13.1).

Of the 17 nonrespondents, current addresses for 8 could not be located. Others whose whereabouts were known, but who elected not to respond, include a professor, a state director of gifted education, a teacher in a school for the gifted, and the owner/director of an educational consulting firm. Another Fellow who refused to cooperate with this study is the founder of an agency which places youths from historically underrepresented populations in private preparatory schools. The fact that many of the nonrespondents are indeed in positions of leadership suggests that the response was not the result of a "reunion effect." Some Fellows who were successful according to the program goals did not respond while others who were not so successful by those standards did.

RESULTS

Thirty-three of the 38 Fellows who responded to the questionnaire were also interviewed. Ten years after their initial participation in GLEP, most of the Fellows had entered early- to late- middle age, and were settled with families. Most had reached the career path in which they thought they would remain. All of the respondents reported a high degree of satisfaction with their present careers and positions, with the majority citing "being in charge" as the primary source of satisfaction.

What follows is based on the responses of the 38 Fellows who answered the questionnaire and participated in an interview. The

Table 13.1. Profiles of Responding GLEP Fellows

Wave	Degrees		Institution Attended		Current Professions			
					Gifted Ed.		General Ed.	
I	PHD	7	TC, Columbia	3	Professor	4	State Curriculum Director	1
	EDD	1	U Conn	1	Administration	1	Assistant Superintendent	1
			U of Georgia	1			Administration	1
			U of Kansas	2				
			U of Virginia	1				
II	PHD	4	TC, Columbia	4	Professor	3	College Administration	1
	EDD	3	U Conn	1	State Director	1	Professor/ Consultant	1
	ABD	1	U of Georgia	2	Administration	1	Administration	1
			Purdue U	1				
III	PHD	4	TC, Columbia	5	Professor	3	Consultant	1
	EDD	5	U Conn	1	Administration	1	Publishing	1
			U of Georgia	1			Administration	1
			Purdue U	1			Teacher	1
			U of Kansas	1				
IV	EdM	2	TC, Columbia	3			Administration	1
	EDD	1					Teacher/Parent	2
V	PHD	3	TC, Columbia	10	Professor	3		
	EDD	5			Adjunct Professor	2	(Semi-Retired)	
					Administration	3		
	ABD	2			Consultant	1		
					Teacher	1		

information gathered through the questionnaires and interviews is combined to facilitate the reporting of the accomplishments and percepions of the Fellows.

Achievements

Did the Graduate Leadership Education Project on the Gifted/ Talented succeed in producing leaders in gifted education in the four areas delineated in the project goals?

Degrees. Thirty-one of the 38 respondents have earned doctoral degrees. Sixteen have earned the PhD and 15, the EdD. Two have MAs, one an EdM, and three classified themselves as ABD. One of the respondents with a masters degree has since earned the EdD, and the other is a doctoral candidate being advised by a Wave I GLEP Fellow who is on the faculty of her university.

Current professional positions. The Graduate Leadership Education Project delineated activities which would operationalize leadership in the field:

1. A leadership position or role
2. Membership or leadership in a professional organization
3. The development of curriculum materials
4. Publication and presentation
5. Consulting (Tannenbaum, 1982)

Professional organizations. At the time of the study, 14 of the respondents held positions of leadership in the field at the local or regional level. They were coordinators of programs for the gifted and led advocacy and parent groups in their communities. Thirty-three of the 38 respondents were members of professional organizations in gifted education. Five of the members of the Board of Directors of the National Association for Gifted Children were GLEP Fellows at the time of the study. Two Fellows were on the Board of AGATE, the New York State advocacy group, and Fellows were represented on boards of state associations for the gifted in Arizona, Arkansas, Georgia, Kansas, Louisiana, New Jersey, and Texas.

Leadership positions. Twenty-three respondents are involved in administration or consulting; 21 in college teaching either full time or as adjuncts, 12 in curriculum development and innovation, and 15 in educational research. Of the 23 Fellows who are working in administration or consulting, 11 are directly involved in gifted education. They are program coordinators for school districts, state departments, and universities. Most reported that they still feel a strong commitment to the field even if they are not working directly or solely with the gifted. Four elementary principals and an assistant superintendent view gifted education as an important part of their jobs, but not as their primary function.

The 21 Fellows who are involved in college teaching are relatively equally distributed in education and educational psychology. Fourteen of those teaching at the university level are offering courses in gifted education, nine full-time. Most of those who are involved in curriculum development and innovation are designing curriculum for gifted students.

Eleven of the 15 Fellows who are conducting educational research are primarily involved in research on the gifted. Seventeen of the respondents have received national grants, and nine have received grants from local sources for work in the field. Two have received Javits grants and two have been involved in initiatives with the National Science Foundation and the National Research Center on the Gifted/Talented.

Eighteen GLEP Fellows have helped to develop or direct state programs, and 32 have participated in these activities at the regional level. Five of the respondents reported media appearances in which they spoke on the education of the gifted, some in other countries, including Canada, Italy, and the United Kingdom.

Thirty-four of the 38 respondents felt that the Graduate Leadership Education Project on the Gifted/Talented helped to prepare them for leadership positions. Attaining a leadership position did not necessarily mean maintaining a commitment to the gifted, however. One Fellow who reported that her commitment to gifted education is not as strong as it once was, but who is a national leader in education, said that GLEP strongly influenced her career. She stated, "GLEP was a milestone. It was a turning point for me." Several Fellows made similar statements about the program's influence. This influence was due, they said, to the interaction with other Fellows and leaders in the field, designation as a Fellow, and a mentor relationship.

Publications and presentations. Almost all of the GLEP Fellows have published books, book chapters, articles, and curriculum materials on the education of the gifted. Fifteen of the Fellows have made presentations on the gifted, and eight have consulted in the field internationally. The respondents have also made many local and regional presentations on gifted education. Some of the Fellows commented that the large numbers of presentations may partially be a result of their experiences presenting at the Summer Institutes.

All but three of the respondents felt that the Graduate Leadership Education Project helped them to develop skills needed for proposal writing and presentations. The three who felt that it did not help them thought that they would have presented as much as they do now without the program.

Interactions with Fellows and leaders in the field. There was a strong sense of comraderie reported by the Fellows of the first three cohorts. They felt as though they were "special" after successfully completing the rigorous selection process and seminar activities. The stronger feeling of fellowship among the early, generally younger Fellows was probably due to the fact that they were purposely selected at the beginning of their careers for full-time graduate study. The later Fellows, all Teachers College students, were commuters who tended to be more settled, with reasonably high-paying jobs. As the Associate Director of GLEP stated in his interview, "Only more mature people could afford to be in it at T.C. The students were generally women whose husbands had substantial incomes." These students had less time to spend at GLEP meetings and less of a need for group affiliation. Most of the Fourth and Fifth Wave GLEP's remained in the professional positions that they held as Fellows. These tended to be local educational leadership positions in gifted education and curriculum.

The Summer Institutes, held every year from 1977 through 1981, were by far the most frequently mentioned program activity in reference to influence on Fellows' careers. At the Institutes, participants learned a great deal from interaction with leaders in the field and from interacting with other Fellows. Though improved presentation skills were an important effect of the Summer Institutes, friendships were formed and fostered at those summer meetings as well. Much of the intercohort and interuniversity activity occurred at the Summer Institutes. This is where they got a sense of being a "national" rather than a single university group. One Fellow said:

> I met people, particularly bright women, who were interested and interesting. The nicest part of GLEP is that it operated as a network across institutions and as a network on my own campus. Although I can cite no particulars, what I remember most is the intellectual excitement when we met as graduate students at conferences and at the T.C. Summer Institutes.

The effects of the peer interaction were apparently long-lasting. The Fellows reinforced the confidence and professional self-esteem of one another, and many still maintain contact. Several said that they call each other for professional advice and that they would hire a former GLEP Fellow before they would hire a comparable non-GLEP candidate.

Designation as a Fellow. The next most frequently mentioned influence of GLEP was the effect of being labeled as a future leader. The effect of the designation was apparently strongly felt by most Fellows. As one participant put it, " I felt quite honored to be a

GLEP Fellow. I felt I had been given a gift and could do things I wouldn't be able to do otherwise." Another said, "In all honesty, there was probably some 'halo effect' resulting from the GLEP Fellow label." It seems to have made no difference whether the designation came with funds as it did in Waves One, Two, and Three, or whether it was an "honorary" one or partially funded as it was for Waves Four and Five. A Fellow from the fifth wave said, "Money was never a thought to me. The designation was payment."

The Fellows also felt that the introduction to current leaders as potential leaders dramatically boosted their self-confidence as well as their exposure in the field. There was again little difference between cohorts in terms of degree and type of response. The opportunity to meet with "the greats" and speak with them about their own ideas helped their careers in two ways: by bolstering their own confidence, and by helping them to network and become known. One Fellow said, "The most significant aspect of my connection with it, however, was meeting the people in the field. Knowing [these people] personally is essential if you are to be a leader in the arena. It gave us a head start. There is an advantage to being known by persons in power."

Mentors. The third most frequently mentioned variable was the relationship with a mentor. Kaufman, Harrel, Milam, Woolverton, & Miller (1986) reported that the most significant number of mentors in the Presidential Scholars' lives was found in graduate school. Kaufman and her associates found that the most frequently mentioned function of the mentors was that of role model. Other behaviors which influenced the Scholars were the mentors' support and encouragement, and their guidance in professional socialization. Many of the GLEP Fellows mentioned having had no idea of the scholarly activities of academe and the tough work schedules of its leaders until they encountered their mentors, the institutional representatives at the participating universities.

The range of comments of the GLEP Fellows on mentor relationships was large. At one extreme, a Fellow said, "I can't say that anyone was a mentor. My own personal mentors came much earlier in life." At the other extreme, came this comment:

> [Mentor] turned my entire life around. All the words I want to use sound very dramatic. He gave me life. He provided me with professional opportunities in line with what I needed. He put me through school out of his own pocket and basically took me in as his daughter almost. He took me for who I was and not who I should be. His main philoso-

phy is to go with your strengths. I have very strong weaknesses. I could have been a stronger academician. He stood by me with my own unique strengths.

The mentors served as role models and influenced the Fellows in many ways. The following quotations exemplify the responses of the Fellows when speaking of the mentors: "I found myself blessed with a wonderful mentor whose prodigious work habits and impeccable professionalism have shaped my life. I cannot express how his tutelage and personal interest have enriched my life." "[He] caused me to view myself in a different way. I saw myself as a scholar." "[He] helped me and was extremely supportive. That was a key factor and influence. I think that the mentor relationship is really important."

Perceptions of Leadership

The Fellows were asked whether they thought of themselves as leaders, and why. All of the respondents perceived themselves as being leaders in some way, and most attributed their leadership to their own personal characteristics in combination with their professional expertise and training. One half of the Fellows who responded said that they were leaders because they had the necessary skills to act as catalysts for change. As one Fellow put it,

> I am a leader because I have been able to design, implement, and sustain a gifted program for the past 10 years. I am creative, insightful, persistent, a strategic planner and an excellent problem solver. I am curious and flexible and I can really get things done. I work well with people and have created a positive environment for students, teachers, and parents. As you can see by the long paragraph, I am not modest. I also possess a good sense of humor.

Other abilities, leadership behaviors, and characteristics mentioned by the Fellows as contributing to their own leadership were, in order of frequency of response: creativity, risk taking, interpersonal communication skills, and intellectual ability.

Commitment to the field. All of those who responded that they are still committed to the field said that the GLEP program had to some extent fostered their commitment. One Fellow said that GLEP had "reaffirmed a sense of efficacy in gifted education—that I belonged and could make a contribution."

They also felt that GLEP helped to produce leaders in the field. Typical responses on the subject of a cadre of leaders were exemplified by these three statements: "It helped to launch many who have today become leaders in gifted education." "I think it created a strong core of people who maintained an interest even when the Office of Gifted Education was closed under the Reagan administration." "The face of gifted education was influenced by the GLEP program."

Peer Leadership

The interaction of the Fellows as a group enabled the early Fellows to serve as mentors for those who succeeded them. Two Fellows at one institution were consistently and frequently named by Fellows as having been mentors for them. Each of these two peer leaders also mentioned the other as a strong influence. Both are now on the same faculty, one full-time, and one as an adjunct. Many Fellows in later cohorts spoke of this pair as mentors who sent them to consulting jobs and helped them with their careers. They viewed these two as the "luminaries," as two Fellows called them. They seemed, according to the other respondents, to have emerged as leaders at the beginning of the program.

The first peer mentor, called John for the purposes of this study, felt that the GLEP program contributed to his professional and personal development primarily through funding his doctoral studies.

> I don't mean this cynically; this was crucial. My coursework and the other opportunities afforded me . . . were invaluable in my development, professionally and personally. Without this funding, I might have had to settle for a lesser school. . . . What the fellowship provided was the critical mass of students that didn't exist before; [sic] prior to the GLEP program, I was the only doctoral student in the gifted program [there].

John had published and presented extensively, and served as consultant to many school districts and state and national departments of education around the globe. He felt that he was a leader because,

> My publications have had some influence in affecting practice and thinking, if in a small way. My students have begun to assume positions of leadership in the field, thus extending my (second-hand) influence. I have consulted extensively, allowing me to affect practice directly in some settings. I serve on some advisory boards in which capacity I am expected to exercise leadership. And, of course, since I

am an advisor to doctoral and masters students at a university, my students are compelled to acknowledge my leadership, at least while they are matriculated.

John was very satisfied with his present position. He viewed his university as "the pinnacle" and himself as his mentor's "protégé—his fair-haired boy." He felt that he learned "quite a bit" from his mentor "outside of class. I probably would have had this advantage even if the fellowship had not existed."

For Helena, as the other Fellow is referred to here, the Graduate Leadership Education Project was very influential. She stated, "GLEP gave me a mission—a seriousness of purpose—to take what these people did and make a field." She spoke of the writing she did in conjunction with the application for a GLEP fellowship as work of which she is still proud. "It showed that I had both an inner life and a public side and showed that I was capable of being a strong leader. [The Director] encouraged me to take a big risk in writing that story." In the beginning, the Director was her mentor, encouraging her to apply for the program, "but then it was [The Co-Director]. [The Co-Director] is my dominant mentor. He has been politically helpful. [John] has been a peer mentor. We complement each other. We have a great working relationship. We had the chance [through GLEP] to try out ideas and we wrote about them later."

Recently, she edited a seminal book on a current issue in curriculum for a major national curriculum organization. She viewed that issue, one in which she had been interested for her entire career, as the core of her life's work in education. She was not as focused on gifted education, viewing the entire field as being in need of change and new leadership. She no longer felt the same deep level of commitment to gifted education that she once felt. "There are bigger, harder questions in education now: restructuring, curriculum options. Schools are not working. . . . Many things that were once the exclusive domain of the gifted are now, and I believe this, good for all populations."

She also had an extensive, successful consulting practice. "I love teaching teachers. I love my consulting practice. I have achieved an expert level of skill. I like what I'm doing and don't want to be a full-time professor. I function better when I'm not burdened by bureaucracy."

Other Fellows mentioned each other, especially if they attended the same institution, as being supportive of each other and as having established close friendships. The difference between these two Fellows and the others seemed to be that they served as models for later waves. They also seemed to have helped their peers with their careers more than any others through actual placement and recommendation for jobs rather than just through providing the "usual" peer emotional support.

Chance factors. In his psychosocial definition of giftedness, Tannenbaum (1983) included chance as a factor in the realization of potential. Although the field of gifted education, with its foundation in the behavioral and social sciences, focuses on influences that are measurable, observable, and, perhaps, more valued by society, Tannenbaum thought that the effects of chance or luck on the development of potential could not be ignored. He wrote, "It is true that we cannot characterize luck and its essential ingredients, but our lack of attention to it should not obscure the fact that it has a powerful influence on achievement" (Tannenbaum, 1983, p. 205).

Many of the Fellows mentioned being grateful for having been in the right place at the right time in winning the GLEP Fellowship. Although most of the Fellows reported feeling "lucky" for having been chosen as Fellows, a few reported that life experiences which befell them by chance, at the wrong time in their development, hindered the development of their careers. One Fellow did not complete her dissertation for seven years after her participation in the program because she lost her data files in a house fire and because she had to care for her mother who became ill immediately afterward. Another reported that she had not responded to the questionnaire for this study in a timely manner because she had been having domestic difficulties and was not living at home at the time. She had left the field, but was now returning as a teacher in a gifted program and was going to complete the doctorate that she had started during GLEP.

For the most part, the reports of this rather successful group focused on good luck and chance factors that affected them positively. Their stories were essentially ones of success and fulfillment, expressing a high degree of satisfaction with their careers and personal lives. Even when they spoke of negative events, they indicated that overall, they had been fortunate to be chosen as GLEP Fellows.

The Directors

One interview was conducted with the Associate Director of GLEP, and a series of interviews, both formal and informal, were conducted with the Director. The Co-Director provided a great deal of information and served as a consultant to the follow-up study.

The Associate Director. The Associate Director came to the program in 1978-79, and left when funding ended in 1980. He thought that the program had an effect on the lives of the Fellows and the field.

> I think that if these people had not been in the program, they wouldn't have published or presented at all. Practitioners don't see themselves as writers. They don't have the confidence. It's not that they don't have the time. . . . Presenting and publishing are skills. In 1978 there was a weekly seminar. Many volunteered to make presentations to the group. They were presenting at NAGC and TAG before they finished.
>
> The networking effect and the reinforcement among them were very important. They formed an in group when they were there. They met at TAG and NAGC. They formed a group that reinforced each other. If they had only experienced their graduate programs, they wouldn't have formed the personal ties, especially at T.C., where it's not residential. They would have had the same experiences I had there as a student.

Parallel to the Fellows, the Associate Director feels that the most effective aspects of GLEP were the peer interaction, the networking with the leaders, the designation as leaders, and the characteristics of the individual Fellows. Although he had no idea of the exact responses of any of the Fellows involved in the study, he echoed much of what they said.

> The major characteristic of the Fellows, I think, was a *drive*. These people had goals and were working toward them with energy. They weren't going to be ABD's. The fact that they had the membership in the program gave them an introduction to people—like a calling card; the sense that they were special.
>
> The interaction among the Fellows was very important. The Summer Institutes gave them the opportunity to meet leaders in the field. The gifted thing is an attenuated field. There weren't that many opportunities.
>
> I think that this would be a valuable program in all areas of education. The major values come from pointing toward leadership and networking among institutions. This de-parochializes graduate education.

The Director. The Director of the Graduate Leadership Education Project could be characterized as a visionary, although he would not describe himself as such. A scholar and teacher who was consistently characterized by the Fellows as encouraging, and a builder of confidence and self-esteem, he believed that GLEP produced a cadre of leaders who may or may not have ended the cyclical nature of interest in the field. He believed that they will certainly have an effect on it. When asked about the success of the program, the Director said that the major contributors to the program's effectiveness were the Fellows, not funding, not the experiences, and not the graduate programs.

> When funding ran out it snowballed in the sense that the Fellows made the program so desirable. The quality of the *students* really made it; not the faculty. They attracted other good people who were interested in gifted education. I chose the fourth and fifth waves myself and was quite selective in the choosing.

On the goals of the program and the design of the experiences, the Director said:

> The original design of the program was to get people to make a commitment. We wanted to produce leaders in education and advocates for gifted education. Much of the leadership we have in gifted education comes from lay groups. We have professional groups which are not being replenished by younger generations. There were many leadership opportunities: practica, courses, internships in schools, research. The four areas of focus came from our doctoral program here. The exposure of the Fellows was also calculated.

Enrichment Parallels

The Graduate Leadership Education Project on the Gifted and Talented had many elements in common with enrichment programs in gifted education:

1. The process of identification used to select participants in GLEP was separate from their own selection process for graduate study at their university.
2. GLEP experiences were provided in addition to the regular programs at the participating universities.
3. GLEP participants were grouped together for some of their program activities and with other students in their regular programs.
4. GLEP Fellows felt specially selected for a specific reason.
5. The students formed mentor relationships with their teachers.
6. It was difficult to separate the influences of GLEP from regular graduate study programs and from the experiences and abilities of the participants.

An enrichment program provides a richer, broader, in-depth experience. In most instances, GLEP seems to have provided this, but the depth and breadth of the enrichment was perceived by the Fellows as being greater when they were away from their home campuses at conferences, seminars, and at the Summer Institutes. These were activities which could not be duplicated in their regular doctoral programs because it was not customary in this field for students, or the leaders, who were all professors, to visit other institutions. Though it may have been customary for institutional representatives to conduct seminars with their students, the inter-institutional gathering of leaders in the field was unusual and was perceived as unique. This networking among institutions is much more common in gifted programs than it is in regular ones. This is another element of GLEP which is common to enrichment programs in education.

From their recollections and record of accomplishments, it seems that when they are successfully identified, gifted students, even on the doctoral level, feel that they benefit significantly from an enrichment program which exceeds the requirements of their regular courses of study. The Fellows and the Director frequently mentioned the identification process as having successfully identified a group of potential leaders. These students were placed together and provided with opportunities, resources, and enrichment (Renzulli, 1989) that they normally would not have received. Fellows attributed much of their professional success to that help.

IMPLICATIONS FOR THE FIELD

The actual achievements of the GLEP Fellows are academic in focus and in line with the program goals. The thrust of the program was to produce committed leaders who had the skill to communicate that commitment through writing, speaking to practitioners and professional groups, teaching gifted students, and at the college and graduate level, teaching about gifted students. The commitment would also be demonstrated through consulting with school districts and state and national departments of education. A large number of the Fellows are in leadership positions and exercising those skills. In that sense, the program was a success.

Policymaking

Only two Fellows have left the field of education. All other respondents were working directly in the four areas of the program goals.

GLEP produced few policy makers or analysts. Although knowledge of the "governmental structures which affect the education of the gifted and talented" was included in the objectives for the Summer Institutes, the thrust of the program was scholarly or practitioner oriented. Although two GLEP Fellows were working in state education departments, no GLEP Fellows were working in the newly reestablished Office of Gifted Education in the United States Department of Education at the time of this study. It would seem that a program of GLEP's magnitude would have produced generalists in the national educational policy-making arena, and specialists in gifted education policy. Gifted education was facing a need for advocates with skills in policy making as much as in higher education and practice in the schools. The omission of policy making or analysis as a target area may have hindered the ability of GLEP to have an effect on the cycles of interest in the field. Indeed, most of the respondents thought that GLEP had had no effect in smoothing out the waves of interest in the education of the gifted.

Inclusion

The Fellows seemed to be representative of the field in general, with few Fellows from historically underrepresented groups. One respondent was African-American, and one was Hispanic. There was no place on the application or reference forms for the candidates to indicate race or ethnicity. From the archives available, it was apparently not a purpose of GLEP to provide a cadre of leaders from underrepresented groups, and little was done to improve their representation. The Fellows made no reference to this subject in answering a lengthy questionnaire and in their one to two and-a-half hour interviews. This omission is notable and may portend serious problems for gifted education. The inclusion of all groups is essential to the success, indeed, survival of any field of endeavor. Gifted education, a field often accused of elitism, could not afford to produce what was essentially another generation of white leaders.

Moral Dimensions of Leadership

The Graduate Leadership Education Project was designed to identify persons with leadership potential through a process that was separate from the graduate program selection process at their universities. It was also designed to develop and exercise skills necessary for leadership in gifted education. The heavy emphasis on skills development in professional leadership situations was apparently accompanied by lighter treatment of the affective side of leadership. The explicit articulation of affective goals could have changed the character of the program and the leaders it produced at a time when the United States was clamoring for higher ethical and moral standards for its leadership.

Personal Influences

A report on the Graduate Leadership Education Project would not be complete without mentioning the influence of its Director. Abraham Tannenbaum designed and directed the GLEP program experiences. He devised a comprehensive method of identifying gifted graduate students, especially those with high leadership ability, and he personally invited many of the applicants to apply for the Fellowships. He was referred to in almost every respondent's questionnaire or interview as encouraging the Fellows in all of their endeavors. Tannenbaum was also responsible for individually selecting the last two cohorts of Fellows. His judgment had an effect on the program, the individual lives of the Fellows, and on the field of gifted education. Tannenbaum's personal touch in encouraging the Fellows was evident even in relation to the field experiences. "Abe said that there was travel money and that we should 'use it or lose it,' so I went." These little personal threads of Tannenbaum's encouragement were woven throughout the Fellows' descriptions of their "tapestry of experiences."

In his own writing, Tannenbaum (1986) cautioned against provisions as opposed to programs in the field. Often what we call programs are really provisions which rely on transient elements such as the personality of the teacher. Although GLEP was an excellently designed and articulated program, Tannenbaum's personality ran through every aspect of it, and was essential to its nature. The Graduate Leadership Education Project would have been a very different program if it had been designed and directed by someone else.

Program Implications

Elements of GLEP incorporated into or offered as enrichment to teacher education programs might help to produce the leaders so essential to the professionalization of the field. A skill necessary for leadership in teaching is the ability to articulate what happens in the classroom and share it with other professionals. The presentations made by the GLEP Fellows in practicing leadership skills could be replicated in teacher education programs to afford participants similar opportunities. Many participants felt there is a need for a current GLEP-type program in the field of general education. More specifically, the GLEP Fellows felt that there is a need for another national leadership program in gifted education, and many said that they would enthusiastically participate in its development.

There is also a need for leadership on the international level. Though it is difficult to orchestrate international programs, especially in terms of funding, the possibility should be investigated. The gifted field has traditionally served as education's "proving ground" where the newest ideas have been tried and improved before dissemination to general education. The seeds of the current trends of interdisciplinary planning, portfolio assessment, and creative problem solving began in gifted education more than a decade ago. Gifted education would be a good place to initiate an international educational collaboration to produce new leaders.

Perhaps the involvement of this "generation of leaders" in the development of the planning of a program for "the second generation of leaders" would produce an even more effective combination of experiences. This generation of GLEP Fellows viewed themselves as risk takers and creative change agents. They were ready to meet the challenge of sustaining and improving any endeavor they pursued, especially the education of the gifted and talented. On that count, the Graduate Leadership Education Project has achieved its mission.

REFERENCES

Foster, W. H., & Silverman, L. (1988). Leadership curriculum for the gifted. In J. Van Tassel-Baska, et al. (Eds.), *Comprehensive curriculum for gifted learners* (pp. 356–381). Boston, MA: Allyn & Bacon.

Gallagher, J. J., et al. (1966). *Educational problems and planning for gifted students: Selected papers from the graduate leadership training program on the gifted* (ERIC Document No. ED020590). Springfield, IL: Illinois State Office of Program Planning for the Gifted.

Gear, G. H. (1974). *Teaching the talented program: A progress report* (ERIC Document No. ED102765). Storrs, CT: School of Education, University of Connecticut.

House, P. A. (1978). *Minnesota gifted education masters' program: Evaluation report* (ERIC Document No. ED166260). St. Paul: Minnesota State Department of Education.

Kaufman, F., Harrel, G., Milam, C. P., Woolverton, N., & Miller, J. (1986).

The nature, role, and influence of mentors in the lives of gifted adults. *Journal of Counseling and Development, 64,* 576–578.

Little, A. D., Inc. (1971). *Assessment of present United States office of education delivery system to gifted and talented children and youth* (Rep. No. 73529). Washington, DC: U.S. Office of Education.

Marland, S. P., Jr. (1972). *Education of the gifted and talented.* Washington, DC: U.S. Government Printing Office.

Passow, A. H. (1978). Styles of leadership training. *Gifted Child Today, 1*(5), 9–12.

Renzulli, J. S. (1989). *The enrichment triad.* Presentation at the Sheraton Center, Syracuse, NY.

Stogdill, R. M. (1974). *Handbook of leadership: A survey of theory and research.* New York: The Free Press.

Tannenbaum, A. J. (1976, October). *Proposed revised design: Graduate leadership education project/gifted and talented.* Proposal submitted to the U.S. Office of Education by Teachers College, Columbia University, New York.

Tannenbaum, A. J. (1977, April). *Graduate leadership education project on the gifted and talented.* Project Proposal submitted to the U.S. Office of Education by Teachers College, Columbia University, New York.

Tannenbaum, A. J. (1982). *Final technical report: Graduate leadership education project, gifted and talented.* New York: Teachers College, Columbia University.

Tannenbaum, A. J. (1983). *Gifted children: Psychological and educational perspectives.* New York: Macmillan.

14

The Program for Academic and Creative Enrichment (PACE): A Follow-up Study Ten Years Later

Sidney M. Moon
John F. Feldhusen

OVERVIEW AND BACKGROUND OF THE STUDY

During the past two decades, many school districts have implemented programs for educating gifted children based on numerous models. What are the long-term effects of these programs? Do children identified as gifted and enrolled in such programs show evidence of superior performance as they progress through school and later life? Thus far, there has been little empirical evidence available to answer these questions (Fox & Washington, 1985; Heller, 1991; Passow, 1989; Urban, 1991).

Purpose of the Study

In a recent national study, 75% of surveyed elementary programs for gifted children employed the pullout model (Cox & Daniel, 1984; Cox, Daniel, & Boston, 1985). A pullout program is one in which identified gifted students leave their regular classroom to attend a class designed to meet their special intellectual and academic needs. Although most pullout programs are taught by specially trained teachers, there is great variation in what is offered to students in the pullout format. Some programs provide little more than a hodge-podge of unrelated "enrichment" activities while others have clear goals and provide a well-designed sequence of learning experiences. Some pullout programs are offered for 2 hours once a week, others for one full day a week, others for 1 hour every day of the week, and so on.

The value of pullout programs has been vigorously debated within the field of gifted education (Belcastro, 1987). Strengths of the model include instruction by specialized teachers, freedom to implement a differentiated curriculum in a differentiated learning environment, and the opportunity for interaction with other gifted children (Cox & Daniel, 1984; Renzulli, 1987a, 1987b). Weaknesses include fragmentation, disruption of regular classroom routines, and the need for the children to make up the work missed in the regular classroom (Belcastro, 1987; Cox & Daniel, 1984; Van Tassel-Baska, 1987a, 1987b). In spite of the prominence of the model, few researchers have investigated its effectiveness.

In 1978, Feldhusen and Kolloff began developing a pullout enrichment program called the Program for Academic and Creative Enrichment (PACE) based on the curricular framework of the Purdue Three-Stage Model (Feldhusen & Kolloff, 1979, 1986; Kolloff & Feldhusen, 1981). In order to explore the effectiveness of PACE in developing talent among participating children, a 10-year PACE follow-up study was established to gather information about the accomplishments and future plans of former PACE students.

The Longitudinal Design

A combined longitudinal and retrospective multiple-case study design was employed in order to meet these objectives. A longitudinal study follows one or more individuals forward into time, collecting data at prescribed intervals. A retrospective study asks individuals to look back over a specific time period and relate perceptions of their experiences during that time period. A multiple-case study analyzes and compares findings from several cases in order to develop and test theoretical propositions (Moon, 1991a; Yin, 1989).

The longitudinal component of the PACE follow-up study was designed to investigate the accomplishments and future plans of secondary students who had been identified as gifted in elementary school by a broad-based identification procedure (Feldhusen & Kolloff, 1986), and who had participated in the PACE program for at least three years. The purpose of the retrospective component of the PACE follow-up study was to investigate the perceptions of 12th-grade students and their families of PACE's effectiveness in developing participating students' talent. From these perceptions, grounded theory (Glaser & Strauss, 1967; Strauss & Corbin, 1990) was developed about the strengths and weaknesses of the PACE program as a model of educational intervention for gifted children.

Asking high school seniors, their parents, and their families about experiences with an elementary gifted program provided valuable information about perceived short- and long-term effects of the program. By the end of high school, six years had elapsed—enough time to provide perspective, but not so much time that former students might have forgotten their experiences.

A study that examines a single cohort in a single setting is vulnerable to the interaction of treatment with setting and history (Cook & Campbell, 1979). In other words, the setting for the study may be so unique that generalization to other settings is not possible. Similarly, the sociohistorical context surrounding the cohort may render the results inapplicable to gifted children in a similar program at a different time. However, the PACE follow-up study was conducted within the qualitative research paradigm. Case study research often examines single cases intensively in order to generalize to theory rather than to populations (Gardner & Nemirovsky, 1991; Yin, 1989). The validity of such research is enhanced by reporting rich descriptions of the context and participants that allow readers to make informed judgments about the generalizability of the findings (Goetz & LeCompte, 1984; Lincoln & Guba, 1985). Thus, intensive study of one cohort of former PACE students in a single school corporation may yield information about talent development processes that will be relevant to other gifted youth in other times and settings.

A developmental perspective was introduced into the retrospective portion of the current study by asking participants to share their perceptions of both the short- and long-term effects of the PACE program. Seeking information about different time periods in a retrospective study allows comparison of participants' perceptions of the effects of an educational intervention during different periods of their lives.

RELATED RESEARCH

Follow-Up Studies of Gifted Programs

Although a number of scholars have investigated issues related to the development of giftedness, few have focused on the long-term impact of public school gifted programs on gifted students and their families. The Astor program 10-year follow-up (Ehrlich, 1978, 1984) was one of the first such attempts. The Astor Program, a special program for young high-IQ (140+) gifted children in New York City, developed a differentiated curriculum designed to teach both basic skills and thinking skills to maximize each child's capacities. Social and civic responsibility and the joy of learning were also stressed.

Ample time was allowed for encouraging the special talents, interests, and skills of each individual student. In 1984, 10 years after the inception of the program, a retrospective, qualitative follow-up study was conducted. The results of the study indicated that both parents and students felt that a number of long-lasting benefits had accrued to the Astor program participants (Ehrlich, 1984). These benefits were grouped into nine categories including curriculum, work habits, relationships with intellectual peers, interpersonal skills, and self-confidence. The study did not have a control group and measured effects only indirectly through the retrospective perceptions of participants.

Humes and Campbell (1980) reported a 15-year longitudinal follow-up of an interest-based, one-day a week, enrichment program for gifted students in the Greenwich, Connecticut public schools. The subjects were 100 high school graduates who had participated in the gifted program while in grades 4 through 6 over a 10-year period (1961-1970). The majority of the respondents evaluated the program positively on dimensions such as opportunity for interaction with other gifted students, encouragement of interests, and fulfillment of needs at the time of participation. Responses were mixed on the usefulness of field trips and guest speakers, the degree to which the program helped the students accept their giftedness, and the contribution of the program to improving attitudes toward learning. Again, this was a qualitative, retrospective evaluation by participants rather than an outcomes assessment study.

The federally funded Lighthouse project began in 1974 in Racine, Wisconsin (LeRose, 1986; Smith, LeRose, & Clasen, 1991). The project identified students by conducting an annual, broad-based screening of all incoming kindergarten students using the Stanford-Binet IQ test, deliberately including proportionate numbers of white and minority children in the experimental study. The top 9% of each major ethnic group (white, black, Hispanic, and other) were identified as gifted and randomly assigned to either a gifted treatment or control (no treatment) group. Preliminary results indicated that Lighthouse seventh graders scored significantly higher than accelerated seventh graders on the Engine Test of Creativity and that minority ninth graders who had participated in the gifted program had considerably higher grade point averages than controls (LeRose, 1986). A follow-up study was conducted 12 years after the inception of the project, when the original cohort of Lighthouse students were in their senior year of high school. Findings indicated that participation in the gifted program drastically reduced high school dropout rates among gifted minority students (Smith, LeRose, & Clasen, 1991).

Pullout Programs

Two curricular models for the design of pullout programs have been advanced by scholars in the field of gifted education: the Schoolwide Enrichment Model developed by Renzulli and his colleagues (Delcourt, this volume; Renzulli, 1977; Renzulli & Reis, 1985, 1986; Renzulli, Reis, & Smith, 1981) and the Purdue-Three Stage/PACE Model (Feldhusen & Kolloff, 1979, 1986; Feldhusen, Kolloff, Cole, & Moon, 1988). Both models employ broad-based identification procedures. Both attempt to develop higher level thinking skills and creativity in identified gifted children. Both provide guided learning experiences in complex problem solving, independent learning, and creative productivity.

Although there are many similarities between the two models, they also differ in subtle but important ways. PACE emphasizes intellectual and creative skill development. The Triad model emphasizes the development of creative productive behaviors. PACE places primary emphasis on identifying and nurturing intellectual talent, while Triad focuses on identifying and nurturing creative talent. Children revolve in and out of participation in a Triad program as they become more or less interested in developing a creative project. In the PACE program identified gifted students attend PACE classes on a regular basis regardless of fluctuations in their levels of motivation. PACE places slightly more emphasis than the Triad model on providing opportunities for intellectually stimulating interactions with gifted peers and slightly less on sophisticated independent project work.

Neither program has been extensively evaluated. Indeed, the debate about the efficacy of pullout programs has proceeded in an environment largely devoid of substantial comparative outcome research. Renzulli (1987a) claimed that: "There is no comprehensive study in existence that has compared various administrative patterns of organization under controlled conditions. . . . Causal comparative studies are totally absent in the literature" (p. 247).

Although causal *comparative* studies of various program models seem to be absent from the literature, a handful of controlled studies have been conducted to determine if a pullout program is better than no program at all. In a recent meta-analysis of the experimental research on pullout programs, Vaughn, Feldhusen, and Asher (1991) found that pullout programs had significant positive effects on the creative thinking skills (effect size = .32), critical thinking skills (effect size = .44), and reading achievement (effect size = .65) of participating students. The overall effect size of pullout programs on self-concept (effect size = .11) was not significant.

In the *Technical Report of Research Studies Related to the Revolving Door Identification Model* (Renzulli, 1988), eight investigations of pullout programs were described. The studies examine questions such as the social acceptability of students in an RDIM program (Skaught, 1988) and the effect that the Schoolwide Enrichment Model has on a total school system (Olenchak & Renzulli, 1989). Some of the studies examine the influence of educational enrichment on specific outcome variables like self-efficacy, interest levels, and creative productivity (Burns, 1988; Schack, 1988; Starko, 1988; Stednitz, 1988). Starko's study (1988) is one of the best extant evaluations of a theoretically driven pullout program. She examined the effects of the Revolving Door Identification Model on creative productivity by selecting subjects that had participated in a Revolving Door Identification Model (RDIM) program for at least four years and compared those students with similar students who had received no RDIM services. Starko found that participation in an RDIM program was a significant predictor of creative productivity outside of school.

In the earliest years of PACE a quasiexperiment was conducted to evaluate the effectiveness of the program (Kolloff & Feldhusen, 1984). No significant differences were found between the PACE students and controls on either of the two instruments used to measure self-concept. However, differences were found on some of the creativity measures. PACE students were significantly superior to control group members in verbal and figural originality.

Families of the Gifted

Interactions between giftedness and family systems have been studied from several perspectives. Most of the studies have been descriptive, investigating the characteristics of families that have one or more gifted children (Cornell, 1984; Cornell & Grossberg, 1987; Green, Fine, & Tollefson, 1988; Olszewski, Kulieke, & Buescher, 1987; Rimm & Lowe, 1988). A second group of studies has focused on the role of the family in developing talent in gifted individuals (Albert & Runco, 1986; Bloom, 1985a; Feldman, 1986; Goertzel & Goertzel, 1962). These studies indicate that the family has a tremendous influence on the gifted child, and may in fact be a major determinant of whether potential giftedness matures into high level achievement in a specific talent area.

Only a handful of studies have examined the influence of giftedness on family systems (Hackney, 1981). It appears that the presence of a gifted child can create unique problems for families (Colangelo & Dettman, 1983; Keirouz, 1989). This is especially true if the gifted child is underachieving in school (Rimm, 1986). There is also some research to suggest that labeling a child as gifted can have a significant impact on the family (Cornell, 1983; Cornell & Grossberg, 1986) and that long-term effects of labeling may be quite different from short-term effects (Colangelo & Brower, 1987).

THE RESEARCH DESIGN

This investigation was a retrospective, qualitative, multiple-case study conducted in two phases six years after students had graduated from the PACE program. The participants were 23 students who had been identified as gifted during elementary school and who had participated in the PACE program for at least three years. Families of the students were also included in the study.

The Site

Criterion-based selection procedures were used to choose the site for the study. The most important criterion was that the selected district had a PACE program in existence for 10 years. Consequently, students who participated in the program in elementary school would now be high school seniors. Second, it was important to locate a school district where the PACE program matched as closely as possible the theoretical design reported in the literature. Finally, the school district had to be large enough to contain some variation in the types of elementary schools that housed the PACE program and some diversity in the student population that participated in PACE so as to enhance the generalizability of the results.

The selected district, the Tippecanoe School Corporation (TSC), Lafayette, Indiana, met all of these criteria. It was the only district in the state of Indiana with a PACE program in existence for 10 years. Since the PACE program had been developed in and disseminated from this district over a 10-year period, it seemed logical to conclude that this site would represent as pure an implementation of the PACE model as possible. This conclusion was verified by informal discussions with the past and current directors of the PACE program and by the first author's firsthand knowledge of PACE in TSC over a 7-year period prior to the study.

The selected district also exhibited fairly wide variation in elementary schools and student population. At the time that the TSC participants were in PACE (Fall 1980-Spring 1985), the district encompassed farms, small towns, suburban developments, trailer court parks, and university housing. The elementary schools in the district reflected this variety, ranging in size from 100 to 700 students. The largest school was quite close to the university and contained a large population of students whose parents were affiliated with the university. The second largest elementary school was located near two city hospitals and contained a number of students whose parents were medical professionals. The two smallest schools in the district were isolated rural schools that seemed quite different in climate from the larger schools. By studying perceptions of PACE in this district, it was possible to see how PACE affected students in both large suburban schools and small rural ones. With the exception of inner-city schools, most of the types of schools represented in the state of Indiana existed within this one district.

Although most of the students in the district were white and middle class, there were a few students from ethnic minorities and number of rural students in the PACE population. Populations that were not well-represented in the selected district included inner-city, economically disadvantaged, and black students.

The PACE Program

Program goals. PACE is a pullout enrichment program for moderately to highly gifted elementary students that was designed to provide systematic and theoretically defensible enrichment education (Feldhusen & Kolloff, 1979, 1986; Feldhusen et al., 1988). The goals of PACE are:

1. To develop gifted students' basic thinking abilities
2. To help gifted students develop more adequate self-concepts by providing small group interaction with other gifted children
3. To help gifted students develop their intellectual and creative abilities through challenging instructional activities
4. To help gifted students become more independent and effective as learners (Feldhusen & Kolloff, 1979).

Cognitive objectives of the PACE program included production of multiple ideas for various cognitive tasks (Stage I), using effective techniques in solving closed (single-solution) and open (multiple-solution) problems (Stage II), and synthesizing ideas in independent and small group creative projects (Stage III) (Feldhusen & Kolloff, 1979, 1986).

Identification procedures. The screening phase of the identification process was designed to be inclusive rather than exclusive. Tippecanoe School Corporation students were placed in a pool of nominees if they met one of the following criteria: (a) a standardized group IQ score of 120+ on any one of three subtests; (b) a standardized group achievement test score greater than the 90th percentile in math concepts, total math, or total reading; or (c) a teacher nomination (Moon, Feldhusen, & Kelly, 1991). Additional information such as behavioral checklists and biographical information was gathered on all students in the pool. During the period that the study participants were in PACE, the selection process in TSC was school-based. The PACE teachers at each of the seven elementary schools selected the 10 students from each school who appeared most likely to benefit from the program by weighing all of the information that had been gathered on profile sheets for each nominee (Moon et al., 1991).

The PACE teachers. Most of the PACE teachers were graduate students in the Department of Education at Purdue specializing in gifted education. All participated in 2 to 4 days of annual in-service training each fall and in monthly staff meetings throughout the academic year. Because so many of the teachers were graduate students, PACE had a high staff turnover rate during the early years. All of the students in the study had at least two different PACE teachers and some had as many as four—a different teacher each year they were in the program (grades 3-6).

The PACE curriculum. PACE was implemented in all of the schools in approximately the same way during the 4-year period (Fall 1980–Spring 1985). The PACE teachers were trained in the Purdue Three-Stage Model and given a packet of curriculum materials that could be used to teach the thinking processes stressed by the model. A PACE library containing additional materials such as math manipulatives was also available. The PACE teachers were encouraged to develop units of instruction that would accomplish the goals of the program and were required to teach Stage I, II, and III skills (Feldhusen & Kolloff, 1979, 1986). Beyond that, little structure was provided. Thus the specific activities that the children experienced varied from teacher to teacher and school to school.

PACE began each year in early October and ended in late April. Each PACE teacher served one or two schools and worked from one to four days a week. The PACE teachers generally taught small groups of children grouped by grade level. In some of the smaller schools the PACE classes were cross-graded. Class sizes ranged from 6 to 15. The PACE students received an average of 2 hours per week of instruction over a period of 7 months, or a total of 56 hours of instruction a year. At the beginning of the year, Stage I activities (short, creative and critical thinking exercises) occupied most of the class time. As the year progressed, the students moved on to Stage II (creative problem solving), and Stage III (independent study) activities. No grades were given for PACE , but the students did receive a progress report twice a year. This report indicated growth in the affective and cognitive areas addressed by the program. Parent-teacher conferences were held once a year.

Involvement of PACE families. From the inception of the PACE program in the Tippecanoe Schools, efforts were made to involve the families of participating students and to enhance the ability of parents to nurture their children's talent. Every fall, parent meetings were held at each elementary school to explain the goals of the PACE program and suggest ways that parents could actively participate in their child's experience. Both the teachers and the director of PACE were available to talk with parents on an appointment basis throughout the school year. Parents were also encouraged to become involved in helping their children with Stage III projects. Each winter the director gave a 3-hour workshop on Stage III for parents. Parents who participated in this workshop were encouraged to volunteer their help in PACE classrooms.

In 1984, a guide was developed to inform parents about the program and suggest activities for reinforcing the thinking skills taught in PACE (Moon, 1984). New families were given a copy of the PACE Guide for Parents at annual meetings held at the beginning of the school year. The PACE staff attempted to maximize the positive effects of the program by encouraging families to be actively involved in nurturing their children's talents.

Sampling Procedure

Participants were selected for the follow-up study in two phases. A search of school records revealed that there were 43 gifted students in the cohort selected for study who had participated in the PACE program for at least three years while in elementary school. Nine of these students had moved away from the area leaving no forwarding address. The remaining 34 families were contacted both by mail and by telephone and asked to participate in the study. Twenty-three families (67%) agreed and returned completed student and parent questionnaires. The primary reason given for nonparticipation was the time commitment required.

In the second phase of the study, 10 of the 23 families that had responded to the questionnaire were asked to participate in a family interview. All 10 of these families agreed to participate. Criterion-based sampling procedures were used to select the interview students and their families (Goetz & LeCompte, 1984). The following selection criteria were used to choose families that would be likely to shed light on the assertions that had emerged from the first phase of the research:

1. Participants whose perceptions of PACE on the questionnaires seemed to be most positive and most negative (extreme-case selection).
2. Participants that indicated that PACE had had a catalytic (early years) effect on the student's later performance (theoretical selection).
3. Participants that had strongly emphasized program benefits of creativity, problem solving, or independent learning (theoretical selection).
4. Participants who represented certain special populations. Using this criterion two accelerated students, two Hispanic students, and one learning disabled student were included (unique case selection).
5. Finally, attention was paid to gender balance (the final sample contained four girls and six boys) and geographic balance (five of the seven elementary schools were represented).

Data Collection and Analysis

In the first phase of the research, the 23 former PACE students and their parents completed a questionnaire that included a 16-item Likert Scale designed to assess the extent to which the goals of PACE had been achieved. The questionnaire also included several open-ended questions designed to elicit perceptions about (a) evidence of special accomplishments, (b) the future plans of the students, (c) short- and long-term benefits of PACE, and (d) short- and long-term negative effects of PACE. These questionnaire data were analyzed using both case and cross-case analysis procedures (Moon, 1991b). In the second phase of the study, the 10 families that had been selected were interviewed in their homes by the researcher using a semistructured interview format. When all of the interviews had been conducted, a second set of case and cross-case analyses was conducted (Moon, 1991b).

FINDINGS

The findings concerning special accomplishments, future plans, and overall impact of the PACE program are summarized below. First, the wide variation in special accomplishments of the former PACE students during secondary school is described. Next, the future plans of the students are discussed. Gender differences were apparent in both areas. In the final section of this chapter, the reported benefits and negative effects of the PACE program are delineated. These included cognitive benefits, affective benefits, social benefits, problems with the pullout format, and interactions with family systems.

Special Accomplishments

The responses of the former PACE students were quite diverse. When asked to list evidence of special accomplishments in secondary school, some students neatly typed an entire page of activities while others wrote simply "none." As shown in Table 14.1, most of the former PACE students ($n = 20$, 87.0%) reported above-average

Table 14.1.   Levels of Accomplishment in the Six Years After PACE

Level	Male $n = 11$	Female $n = 12$	Total $n = 23$	Description
Multiple High Achiever	2	5	7	Exceptional performance in academics plus two or more other talent areas
High Achiever	2	2	4	Exceptional performance in academics and at least one other talent area
High Academic Achiever	4	0	4	Exceptional performance in academics only
Above Average Achiever	1	4	5	Above average performance in one or more talent areas
Average Achiever	0	1	1	Average performance
Underachiever	2	0	2	Clear evidence of under performance in one or more talent areas; no areas of above average or exceptional performance

or high levels of accomplishment in at least one talent area during the six years following PACE. One student reported merely average achievement levels and two showed signs of underachievement.

There were more than twice as many females ($n = 5$) as males ($n = 2$) who reported exceptional performance in academics and two or more other talent areas like music, sports, community service, and so on. These students were categorized as "multiple high achievers." Interestingly, one of the two males in this category was learning disabled, the only such student who participated in the study.

On the other hand, more males ($n = 4$) than females ($n = 0$) were categorized as "academic achievers." These were students who reported high levels of talent or achievement only in academics. All four of these males expressed unhappiness about their secondary school experience and two of them were also negative about their PACE experience. There were also more males ($n = 2$) than females ($n = 0$) who were categorized as underachievers. In general, males reported more dissatisfaction with their school experiences than females.

All three of the accelerants were males. One student was accelerated one year in junior high and two were admitted to college early. All three of these students expressed considerable dissatisfaction with the high school environment and were greatly relieved to have been able to enter college early. The student who had been accelerated in junior high school expressed less dissatisfaction with his high school experience than the two students who were admitted to college early.

Awards and honors were mentioned by 16 (69.6%) of the study participants. A few of the students had won awards in several talent areas. There were two valedictorians in the group. Both were female.

Categories of accomplishments listed by the students and their parents included awards, academics, sports, the arts, creative projects, school clubs, community activities, church activities, and leadership. The range of activities listed within these categories was very broad (Table 14.2).

Students' Future Plans

In response to an open-ended question about their professional future plans, all of the former PACE students indicated that they were planning to earn a college degree. Most (78%) intended to pursue graduate training. Specific graduate degrees mentioned as the highest expected degree by the participants included masters

Table 14.2. Sample Secondary Activities of Former PACE Students

Awards
Academic award
Academic team award
Art award
Chair prom, homecoming, etc.
Citizenship award
Dance award
Debate and speech award
History Projects
Honor Roll
Horsemanship award
Industrial arts award
Literary award
Midwest Talent Search award
Math award
Monetary prize
Music competition
National Merit Semi-Finalist
National Merit Finalist
Outstanding student award
Research Grant
Science fair award
Social Studies award
Sports award
Theatre award
Valedictorian
Who's Who American High School
  Students
Other

Academics
Academic teams
Acceleration
AP classes
Debate and speech teams
Honors classes

Sports
Baseball
Basketball
Golf
Gymnastics
Horseback riding
Swimming
Tennis
Track
Volleyball

Arts
Music
  Band
  Instrument

Music Camps
  State Competitions
  Voice
Visual Arts
Theatre

Creative Projects
Business endeavors
Clothing design
Creative writing
Crossword puzzles and word games
History Day
Independent Projects
4-H
Newspaper
Research Projects
Role Playing Games
Science Fair
Starting a business
Yearbook

School Clubs
Art Club
French Club
Japanese Club
Keyettes
Secret Admirers
Sunshine Society
SADD
Spanish Club
Speech Club

Community Activities
Church youth group
4-H
Exchange student program
Jobs (20-25 hours/week)
Teaching
University-based GT program

Leadership
Captain of an athletic team
Class officer
Counselor
Editor of Newspaper, Literary Magazine,
  Yearbook
Leadership conference
Leadership program (e.g., Junior
  Leaders, 4-H)
President of club
Student council

degrees ($n = 7$), law degrees ($n = 2$), medical degrees ($n = 4$), and doctoral degrees ($n = 3$).

There were pronounced gender differences in the educational plans of the former PACE students. In general, males had higher educational aspirations than the females. For example, almost twice as many males as females intended to continue their education beyond the masters level and four of the five students (80%) who were not planning on any graduate education were females.

When it came to personal plans, however, almost all of the females (91.7%) but less than half of the males (45.5%) wrote spontaneous comments about marriage when describing their personal goals. Similarly, almost all of the females (83.3%), but only a third of the males (36.4%), mentioned childrearing. A few males stated specifically that they were uncertain about or did not want to have children. For example, one wrote "Get married. Maybe have kids but not sure," and another said, "No plans or want for marriage." No females indicated similar resistance or uncertainty.

Specific career objectives listed by the former PACE students covered a wide range of occupations: architecture, business, medicine, engineering, law, politics, science, social work, writing, and teaching. Most of the students (69.6%) seemed to have fairly clear ideas about their future career goals. For example, one student wrote: "After I go to a 4-year college, I plan to work at least three years. Then I plan on getting my CPA license. I would also like one day to own my own accounting firm." Another said, "I would like to work in the art field. I would either like to work in New York City in advertising or as a cartoonist for Disney Studios." Still another wrote, "I hope to finish college and work along the coast as a marine biologist, doing work and research."

Perceptions of the Effects of the PACE Program

Most participants (82.6%) felt PACE had a positive impact on participating students. One student expressed the sentiments of many when he said, "In general I felt PACE was a good program and an advantage for me." In addition, most of the interview families, even the families who had been selected for an interview by extreme-case selection as one of the most "negative" cases, felt that PACE had been beneficial. Indeed, the quotation given above came from one of the "negative" cases.

In general, females were more positive than males about PACE. For example, when conducting the extreme-case selection of families for the interviews, all of the students were placed on a continuum from most positive to most negative. The three students who were most critical of the program were all males. Of the three most positive students, two were female and one was male.

Cognitive benefits. The greatest cognitive benefit of the PACE program appeared to be development of thinking skills. The skills the students gained while in PACE appeared to transfer to later learning situations. For example, one student wrote on her questionnaire: "PACE improved my thinking abilities which really helped me in secondary school." Another stated: "[PACE] developed my creativity early which therefore helped me in later years." Both of these students felt PACE had a significant influence on their lives.

PACE also seems to have shaped the *attitudes* of gifted students in ways that were perceived as beneficial. For example, one of the accelerants said, "The attitude I was first introduced to in PACE stuck with me making me a more mature thinker." In his family interview this student expanded on this concept by saying, "PACE was a catalyst for other things. It was the first step in . . . starting things rolling. It kind of set the tone for the rest of life." This student was the one participant who was accelerated during junior high school. He felt that PACE had had a "great effect" on his decision to accelerate. "I saw acceleration as being connected, being the same type of experience as being in PACE. [I hoped it would] put me in a position where I would start to enjoy regular school more."

Categories of cognitive benefits that had more short-term than long-term impact included challenge, interest, and variety. Comments relating to these categories tended to center around the students' memories of the contrast between PACE and the regular classroom. For example, one boy said, "PACE gave me a change in the day. It removed boredom from the everyday school day." A girl phrased the same concept more positively: "The program gave me a challenge. It was a change of pace from the regular routine of the classroom." Several students said that they appreciated the variety that PACE provided.

Affective benefits. PACE seems to have helped most of the participating students to develop more adequate self-concepts and to have encouraged them to set high-level goals for themselves. For some students and their parents, the development of self-concept appears to have been the most important benefit of participation in the program.

How did PACE enhance self-concept? It seems to have given students self-confidence and the courage to be different. One student said, "PACE gave me self-confidence—enough to go out and achieve goals for myself, and not to be ashamed for being labeled gifted." Another declared, "I learned it's not bad to be smart. It's fun! . . . I mean it's okay to be different; it's okay to be curious about everything; it's okay to be excited about learning . . . I think PACE helped a lot. That's where it all started."

PACE also seems to have helped students to clarify and confirm their abilities. Students framed this concept different ways. Some felt that PACE helped them know they could handle harder work. A student who was both gifted and learning disabled felt PACE helped to clarify his unique profile of intellectual strengths and weaknesses. The accelerant quoted earlier saw PACE as giving concrete meaning to abstract test scores and clarifying the differences between himself and others.

Only one student felt that PACE had a negative impact on self-concept. This student remembered getting "howls of dork and nerds" when the PACE students would leave the regular classroom. Instead of helping his identity development, he believed PACE had hurt it. PACE just "classifies you as one of those strange students that goes out . . . that's all."

Social benefits. Social benefits of PACE were not as evident to most of the participants as cognitive and affective benefits. The predominant social benefit of the program appears to have been the opportunity the program provided for interacting with gifted peers, many of whom remained friends during secondary school. With regard to nongifted peers, PACE appears to have been neutral in most cases. Other social benefits mentioned by a few of the participants included the development of leadership ability and the opportunity to work with others on a project. One parent mentioned that PACE had broadened his son's horizons by exposing him to complex social issues at an early age.

Pullout format. When asked to list short- and long-term hindrances of the PACE program, most students (87%) and parents (86.4%) indicated that the program had not hindered participating students in any way. Common responses were "none," "it didn't," and "in no way did PACE hinder me." When a negative effect was mentioned, it generally related to the pullout format. A typical student response regarding the pullout format was "I did miss some class, but the teachers were always helpful and it was not a problem." A typical parent response was "I don't think [PACE] hindered him, but he didn't like being pulled out of his regular class schedule." Most of the negative comments about the pullout format were phrased in qualified language, indicating that the problems created were perceived in retrospect as mild and short term.

Missed instruction was the most frequently mentioned concern. Two students and three parents mentioned missed instruction as a short-term problem and tended to perceive the problems they encountered as relatively mild. For example, one student said, "I missed some instruction from my teachers, but not enough to really hinder me." No students or parents mentioned missed instruction as a long-term negative and some students specifically stated that missed instruction had not been a problem for them. For example, in her family interview, one of the female students stated emphatically, "I had no problems with the pullout—I could make up the work, no problem!"

Interactions with family systems. In the 10 family interviews, possible interactions between PACE and the family systems of the PACE students were explored. All 10 families indicated that PACE had created subtle changes in their family environment. Most of these changes were positive. For example, most families ($n = 8$) said that PACE had provided enjoyable shared activities and inspired many interesting family conversations. As one mother put it, "[PACE] gave us something to share and talk about. . . . Anytime you stimulate family conversation and everyone working together on something, that's good. . . . It adds something."

PACE also appears to have influenced family structure and relationships by changing communication patterns, altering parental perceptions of the PACE student, and changing family alignments and boundaries. In some cases, these changes were positive. For example, three students felt PACE encouraged a closer relationship between themselves and a parent: "This sounds funny," stated one female participant, "but I think [PACE] brought my father and I closer 'cause . . . that's just . . . right up his alley . . . that was something really fun that I could do with my father . . . that . . . kept us close." However, for two others, PACE was perceived to have increased conflict or distance between family members. For example, in one family, PACE appears to have exacerbated existing conflict between siblings. The father in this family stated he felt PACE created friction between the PACE student and his brother: "I thought there were times when, in his relationship with his brother, he'd use PACE as sort of a weapon."

In seven of the 10 families interviewed, PACE functioned as an important link between home and school. "[PACE was a] sort of a link between the classroom, school, and me, and my family," stated one of the male participants. "I just thought it kind of connected it a little bit better." This linking seemed to occur because students were happier about school, parents were happier about what was happening in school, and the school and home environments became more congruent. These changes, in turn, gave families a more positive attitude toward the school. Many of the parents ($n = 6$) reported feeling very happy when their child was in PACE because he or she enjoyed the program so much. PACE seems to have given families something exciting to talk about, something to share, something in the school environment that families of gifted children could relate to with genuine enthusiasm.

DISCUSSION

For the most part, former PACE students who had been identified as gifted by a broad-based, multiple criteria procedure while in elementary school did show evidence of special accomplishment, creativity, and high ability during their secondary school years. In addition, all of the former PACE students had developed moderate to high educational aspirations. The PACE follow-up study appears to support the belief that there might be a relationship between early identification of gifted children and high performance in one or more talent areas as an adolescent, especially when the talents of the identified children are nurtured for at least three years by a theoretically sound enrichment program like PACE.

The gender differences were among the most interesting findings of the study. Although differences need to be interpreted with caution because of the small number of participants involved in the study, they do raise questions that could be addressed in future research. For example, the troubling gender differences that surfaced with regard to both secondary school accomplishments and future plans raise questions like: Why were so many of the boys dissatisfied with their secondary school experience? Of those who were dissatisfied, why did some seek acceleration as a remedy while others languished as underachievers? Why were girls more likely than boys to be developing multiple talent areas and achieving at very high levels by the end of secondary school? Is it possible that school learning is more suited to girls than boys?

The gender differences with regard to future plans are consistent with the findings of other scholars (in this volume, Arnold; Subotnik & Steiner; Benbow; Fleming & Hollinger). The gender differences in the future plans of the gifted youth in this study raise questions such as: Why didn't more of the boys include family in their future plans? Is this shortsighted, given the well-documented importance of family to middle-aged men? Why did so many of the girls seem to put family first and career second? What about the girls who "want it all"? Are they setting themselves up for failure, expecting too much of life and themselves? For both genders, are these genuine choices or merely socially conditioned responses? What relationship is there between the future plans of gifted adolescents and the actual choices they make for their lives?

The PACE follow-up study indicates that most of the former PACE students and their families perceived PACE as a positive and beneficial educational experience. These findings contradict some current trends in the field of gifted education. For example, pullout enrichment programs are currently out of favor with many educators because they are considered inadequate programming for gifted youth, but many of the former PACE students and their families seem to have perceived PACE as a life-changing educational experience. The students often remembered specific activities with great clarity and spoke of the program as laying a foundation for their outlook on life. A number of parents felt that PACE had transformed their children's self-concepts, giving them self-confidence and the courage to be themselves. Is it possible that researchers have been shortsighted? Have we reported little positive effect, when the true benefits of such programs can only be seen in the long term?

The findings concerning changes in the family systems of participating students suggest that it may be possible to maximize the impact of a gifted program by finding ways to facilitate positive interactions between a gifted program and the families of gifted students. A program for the gifted that can create positive changes in the family systems of participating students can multiply its impact at very little cost to schools. It may be cost-effective for school personnel to find ways to encourage the kind of sharing of activities and skills described by several of the families in this study.

RETROSPECTIVE AND LONGITUDINAL RESEARCH DESIGNS

The retrospective component of the PACE follow-up study proved helpful in illuminating differences between the short-term and long-term effects of PACE. Asking families to describe their perceptions of specific benefits and hindrances of a gifted program during different time periods provided useful information on the influence of PACE on talent development in specific individuals over time. The longitudinal component of the study provided information on the accomplishments and future plans of high school seniors who had been identified for a gifted program while in elementary school.

The qualitative research design enabled insights to emerge from the participants that might not have appeared had a priori theoretical constructs been imposed on the data. For example, the idea that a gifted program might help to improve the connections among the student, the family, and the school arose unexpectedly during the family interviews. Conducting both case and cross-case analyses allowed the researcher to examine both individual differences and common themes, providing a rich picture of the meaning of PACE for former PACE students.

Both retrospective and longitudinal qualitative research allow researchers in the field of gifted education to capitalize on the ability of gifted students to analyze and synthesize their experiences. In general, gifted individuals and their families are wonderful informants because they have excellent memories and enjoy expressing their views verbally. However, the strengths of retrospective and longitudinal designs for investigating research questions in gifted education are balanced by limitations. One of the most important limitations of such research is sample bias. Factors that may skew samples include the difficulty of tracking down potential participants who have moved, the unwillingness of some to take the time to participate in a research study, and the reluctance of others to open up their lives for investigation. All of these factors were operative to some extent in the PACE follow-up study.

The first author's previous experiences with the PACE program and intense immersion in the data were both strengths and weaknesses of this study. These prior experiences with PACE provided an in-depth awareness of the context of the program which was often helpful in interpreting the data. However, these experiences may also have introduced bias. Similarly, the first author's immersion in the data allowed insights to emerge that might have remained hidden, but also created the potential for bias. Efforts to contain researcher bias included the use of (a) *multiple instruments* (Likert scale questionnaire, open-ended questionnaire, and family interviews), (b) *multiple data sources* (individual students, individual parents, and families), and (c) *extreme-case sampling procedures* (both positive and negative cases in the interview sample).

Longitudinal and retrospective research designs offer investigators in the field of gifted studies powerful tools for examining talent development processes. The PACE follow-up study explored the later development of students who were identified as gifted in elementary school, examining the meanings that both parents and students ascribed to an elementary enrichment program over different time periods. Finally, through its longitudinal methodology, the study was able to address fundamental questions of long-term effects of early intervention in academic and creative talent development.

DIRECTIONS FOR FUTURE RESEARCH

The PACE follow-up study suggests numerous directions for future research. The gender differences in special accomplishments and future plans of these gifted adolescents give rise to many questions that could be addressed by future research. Similarly, the study suggests that more longitudinal research on program outcomes needs to be conducted.

Indeed, the new National Center for Research on the Gifted and Talented considers longitudinal research on the outcomes of gifted programming to be the number one priority on the national research agenda for the next decade (Gubbins & Reid, 1991; Reid, 1991). Many kinds of follow-up studies would be useful in carrying out this research agenda including experimental studies, quasiexperimental studies, predictive studies, and longitudinal and retrospective case studies like the PACE follow-up study. If other school districts across the country initiated such projects in partnership with trained researchers, the field could gradually build a clearer picture of the types of giftedness demonstrated in adolescence by children identified as gifted in elementary school, and the relative effectiveness of various programming options for different types of gifted children in a variety of settings.

REFERENCES

Albert, R. S., & Runco, M. A. (1986). The achievement of eminence: A model based on a longitudinal study of exceptionally gifted boys and their families. In R. J. Sternberg & J. E. Davidson (Eds.), *Conceptions of giftedness* (pp. 332–360). New York: Cambridge University Press.

Belcastro, F. P. (1987). Elementary pull-out program for the intellectually gifted—Boon or bane. *Roeper Review, 9*(4), 208–212.

Burns, D. E. (1988). The effects of group training activities on students' creative productivity. In J. S. Renzulli (Ed.), *Technical report of research studies related to the Revolving Door Identification Model*

(2nd ed., pp. 147–174). Storrs, CT: Research Report Series, School of Education, University of Connecticut.

Colangelo, N., & Brower, P. (1987). Labeling gifted youngsters: Long-term impact on families. *Gifted Child Quarterly, 31*(2), 75–78.

Colangelo, N., & Dettmann, D. F. (1983). A review of research on parents and families of gifted children *Exceptional Children, 50*(1), 20–27.

Cook, T. D., & Campbell, D. T. (1979). *Quasi-experimentation: Design and analysis issues for field settings.* Boston, MA: Houghton Mifflin.

Cornell, D. G. (1983). Gifted children: The impact of positive labeling on the family system. *American Journal of Orthopsychiatry, 53*(2), 322–335.

Cornell, D. G. (1984). *Families of gifted children.* Ann Arbor, MI: UMI Research Press.

Cornell, D. G., & Grossberg, I. N. (1986). Siblings of children in gifted programs. *Journal for the Education of the Gifted, 9*(4), 253–264.

Cornell, D. G., & Grossberg, I. N. (1987). Family environment and personality adjustment in gifted program children. *Gifted Child Quarterly, 31,* 59–64.

Cox, J., & Daniel, N. (1984). The pull-out model. *Gifted Child Today, 34,* 55–60.

Cox, J., Daniel, N., & Boston, B. O. (1985). *Educating able learners.* Austin, TX: Texas University Press.

Ehrlich, V. Z. (1978). *The Astor program for gifted children.* New York: Teachers College Press.

Ehrlich, V. Z. (1984). *The Astor program for young gifted children: Ten years later.* New York: Teachers College Press.

Feldhusen, J. F., & Kolloff, M. B. (1979). A three-stage model for gifted education. *Gifted Child Today, 4,* 3–5, 53–57.

Feldhusen, J. F., & Kolloff, M. B. (1986). The Purdue three-stage model for gifted education at the elementary level. In J. S. Renzulli (Ed.), *Systems and models for developing programs for the gifted and talented* (pp. 126–153). Mansfield Center, CT: Creative Learning Press.

Feldhusen, J. F., Kolloff, M. B., Cole, S., & Moon, S. M. (1988). A three-stage model for gifted education: 1988 update. *Gifted Child Today, 11*(1), 18–30.

Feldman, D. H. (1986). *Nature's gambit.* New York: Basic Books.

Fox, L. H., & Washington, J. (1985). Programs for the gifted and talented: Past, present and future. In F. D. Horowitz, & M. O'Brien (Eds.), *The gifted and talented: Developmental perspectives* (pp. 197–221). Washington, DC: American Psychological Association.

Gardner, H., & Nemirovsky, R. (1991). From private intuitions to public symbol systems: An examination of the creative process in Georg Cantor and Sigmund Freud. *Creativity Research Journal, 4,* 1–21.

Glaser, B. G., & Strauss, A. L. (1967). *The discovery of grounded theory: Strategies for qualitative research.* New York: Aldine.

Goetz, J. P., & LeCompte, M. D. (1984). *Ethnography and qualitative design in educational research.* San Diego, CA: Academic.

Green, K., Fine, M. J., & Tollefson, N. (1988). Family systems characteristics and underachieving gifted adolescent males. *Gifted Child Quarterly, 32,* 267–272.

Gubbins, E. J., & Reid, B. D. (1991, April). Research needs of the gifted and talented. In J. Renzulli (Chair), The *National Research Center on the Gifted and Talented: Present Activities, Future Plans, and an Invitation for Input and Involvement.* Symposium conducted at the American Educational Research Association, Chicago, IL.

Hackney, H. (1981). The gifted child, the family, and the school. *Gifted Child Quarterly, 25*(2), 51–54.

Heller, K. A. (1991). Perspectives on research on giftedness and talent: A global view. *World Gifted, 12*(4), 7–12.

Humes, C. W., & Campbell, R. D. (1980). Gifted students: A 15-year longitudinal study. *Gifted Child Quarterly, 24,* 129–131.

Keirouz, K. S. (1989). *The Parent Experience Scale: A measure designed to identify problems of parents of gifted children.* Unpublished doctoral dissertation, Purdue University, West Lafayette, IN.

Kolloff, M. B., & Feldhusen, J. F. (1981). PACE (Program for Academic and Creative Enrichment): An application of the three-stage model. *Gifted Child Today, 18,* 47–50.

Kolloff, M. B., & Feldhusen, J. F. (1984). The effects of enrichment on self-concept and creative thinking. *Gifted Child Quarterly, 28,* 53–57.

LeRose, B. (1986). The Lighthouse Program: A longitudinal research project. *Journal for the Education of the Gifted, 9,* 225–232.

Lincoln, Y. S., & Guba, E. G. (1985). *Naturalistic inquiry.* Beverly Hills, CA: Sage.

Moon, S. M. (Ed.). (1984). *PACE guide for parents.* Lafayette, IN: Tippecanoe School Corporation.

Moon, S. M. (1991a). Case study research. In N. K. Buchanan & J. F. Feldhusen (Eds.), *Conducting research and evaluation in gifted education: A handbook of methods and application* (pp. 157–178). New York: Teachers College Press.

Moon, S. M. (1991b). *The PACE Program: A high school follow-up study.* Unpublished doctoral dissertation, Purdue University, West Lafayette, IN.

Moon, S. M, Feldhusen, J. F, & Kelly, K. W. (1991). Identification procedures: Bridging theory and practice. *Gifted Child Today, 14*(1), 30–36.

Olenchak, R. F., & Renzulli, J. S. (1989). The effectiveness of the School-wide Enrichment Model on selected aspects of elementary school change. *Gifted Child Quarterly, 33,* 36–46.

Olszewski, P., Kulieke, M., & Buescher, T. (1987). The influences of family environment on the development of talent: A literature review. *Journal for the Education of the Gifted, 11*(1), 6–28.

Passow, A. H. (1989). Needed research and development in educating highly gifted children. *Roeper Review, 11,* 223–229.

Reid, B. D. (1991, June). National research needs assessment process. *The National Research Center on the Gifted and Talented Newsletter, 1*(1), 8–9.

Renzulli, J. S. (1977). *The enrichment triad model: A guide for developing defensible programs for the gifted and talented.* Mansfield Center, CT: Creative Learning Press.

Renzulli, J. S. (1987a). The positive side of pull-out programs. *Journal for the Education of the Gifted, 10,* 245–254.

Renzulli, J. S. (1987b). The difference is what makes differentiation. *Journal for the Education of the Gifted, 10,* 265–266.

Renzulli, J. S. (1988). *Technical report of research studies related to the Revolving Door Identification Model* (2nd ed., Vol. II). Storrs, CT: Research Report Series, School of Education, University of Connecticut.

Renzulli, J. S., & Reis, S. M. (1985). *The Schoolwide Enrichment Model: A comprehensive plan for educational excellence.* Mansfield Center, CT: Creative Learning Press.

Renzulli, J. S., & Reis, S. M. (1986). The Enrichment Triad/Revolving Door Model: A schoolwide plan for the development of creative productivity. In J. S. Renzulli (Ed.), *Systems and models for developing programs for the gifted and talented* (pp. 216–166). Mansfield Center, CT: Creative Learning Press.

Rimm, S. B. (1986). *Underachievement syndrome: Causes and cures.* Watertown, WI: Apple.

Rimm, S. B., & Lowe, B. (1988). Family environments of underachieving gifted students. *Gifted Child Quarterly, 32*(4), 353–359.

Schack, G. D. (1988). Creative productivity and self-efficacy in children. In J.S. Renzulli (Ed.), *Technical report of research studies related to the Revolving Door Identification Model* (2nd ed., pp. 51–94). Storrs, CT: Research Report Series, School of Education, University of Connecticut.

Skaught, B. J. (1988). The social acceptability of talent pool students in an elementary school using the Schoolwide Enrichment Model. In J. S. Renzulli (Ed.), *Technical report of research studies related to the Revolving Door Identification Model* (2nd ed., pp. 175–201). Storrs, CT: Research Report Series, School of Education, University of Connecticut.

Smith, J., LeRose, B., & Clasen, R. E. (1991). Underrepresentation of minority students in gifted programs: Yes! It matters! *Gifted Child Quarterly, 35,* 81–83.

Starko, A. J. (1988). Effects of the Revolving Door Identification Model on creative productivity and self-efficacy. *Gifted Child Quarterly, 32,* 291–297.

Strauss, A., & Corbin, J. (1990). *Basics of qualitative research: Grounded theory procedures and techniques.* Newbury Park, CA: Sage.

Urban, K. (1991, July). Research needs. In K. Urban (Chair), *Research on giftedness: Contributions of different approaches and methods.* Symposium conducted at the World Conference on the Gifted and Talented, The Hague, Netherlands.

Van Tassel-Baska, J. (1987a). The ineffectiveness of the pull-out program model in gifted education: A minority perspective. *Journal for the Education of the Gifted, 10*(4), 255–264.

Van Tassel-Baska, J. (1987b). Response to Renzulli: Advocating the pull-out model. *Journal for the Education of the Gifted, 10,* 267–269.

Vaugn, V. L., Feldhusen, J. F., & Asher, W. J. (1991). Meta-analysis and review of research on pull-out programs in gifted education. *Gifted Child Quarterly, 35,* 92–98.

Yin, R. K. (1989). *Case study research: Design and methods.* Newbury Park, CA: Sage.

15

Characteristics of High-Level Creative Productivity: A Longitudinal Study of Students Identified by Renzulli's Three-Ring Conception of Giftedness

Marcia Delcourt

This study focused on characteristics related to the creative and productive behavior of 18 secondary school students from districts employing Renzulli's Three-Ring Conception of Giftedness. All subjects had been identified for gifted programs in their respective schools. These particular students were recognized by their teachers for outstanding performance. Based on their interests either in or outside of school, they selected, pursued, and completed high-quality projects. Project examples included hosting a regional cable television show, conducting experiments in plant hybridization for a local florist, developing a computer program to analyze cancer growth for a group of chemical engineers, and publishing a poem in a national student magazine. The longitudinal qualitative design included two rounds of data collection. First, when each subject was still in high school, the family, the school, and the student served as data sources. The data collection methods incorporated document analysis, questionnaires, and a student interview. Second, after a 3-year period, a questionnaire was distributed by mail to each student. This information pertained to school and work experiences, career plans, and recent interests and projects. Reflecting on experiences from their respective programs for the gifted, students provided insights into how they obtained ideas for their projects, how their interest in investigation was sustained, and what they learned from their efforts.

The first part of this chapter provides an overview of the study, a description of the longitudinal design, and an overview of Renzulli's conception of giftedness. A review of the research design, sample, data collection process, analysis procedures, and results from the first and second data collection periods follows. The chapter concludes with a summary and discussion of the entire project and reflections upon the longitudinal nature of this research.

OVERVIEW AND BACKGROUND OF STUDY

Giftedness has been widely examined through the creative productivity of eminent adults (Goertzel, Goertzel, & Goertzel, 1978; MacKinnon, 1978; Roe, 1952; Sternberg, 1988; Treffinger & Renzulli, 1986). In many of these studies, scientific experiments, musical compositions, and architectural designs were examples of products representing creative and productive behavior. Generalizations from these data have been used to identify youth with potential for creative behavior. Examples of student investigations (Burns, 1990; Reis, 1981; Renzulli & Reis, 1986; Roeder, Haensly, & Edlind, 1982; Schack, 1986; Starko, 1988), numbers and types of awards (Walberg, 1969, 1971), and scores on tests of ideational creativity (Bogner, 1981; Ewing, Gillis, Ebert, & Mathews, 1975; Torrance, 1980) have provided estimates of future creative performances. Although researchers recognize that individuals may demonstrate characteristics indicative of creative and productive behavior across their lifespans, the relationship between gifted behavior in young people and in adults remains empirically uncertain (Milgram, 1984; Siegler & Kotovsky, 1986).

Contributing to this uncertainty is the issue of the criterion variable. What is an adequate assessment of creative productivity? When actual products are used to assess creative and productive behavior in students and adults, there remains controversy regarding the development of this behavior. Indeed, several researchers view creative productivity as a characteristic of adults, recognizing that youths may show potential for adult giftedness, but are more accurately classified as consumers of information rather than producers (Simonton, 1983; Tannenbaum, 1986). Other researchers believe not only that creative productivity is evidence of gifted behavior, but also that such behavior can be observed and nurtured in individuals throughout their lives (Renzulli & Reis, 1985, 1986).

Creative and productive behavior was investigated in this study for two main purposes: first, to describe the existence of the phenomenon in adolescents by locating secondary school students recommended as producers of information, and second, to examine longitudinally student behavior which elucidates the personal and

environmental developments associated with creative and productive behavior. Further, the longitudinal design provides the opportunity for assessing the long-term impact of a specific type of enrichment program.

Longitudinal Design

In this study, both a retrospective and longitudinal design are used
to provide information concerning subjects' behaviors. In this way,
a developmental view of creative productivity can be obtained as
students reflect on their childhood experiences and describe their
perspectives during high school and college.

According to Campbell and Stanley (1963), every research design
has limitations. The single cohort model used in this study is susceptible to interaction effects of treatment with setting and history
(Cook & Campbell, 1979). This means that conclusions and recommendations from this project may or may not be applicable to students at different times or in other settings. However, the triangulated methodology employed in the initial data collection period and
the longitudinal scope of this multicase study provide an in-depth
view of the phenomenon under investigation. This is unattainable
with any other design (Lincoln & Guba, 1985; Stake, 1987). In
addition, a precise description of the research design and methodology provides a strong foundation for applying the procedures in
other settings.

The Enrichment Triad Model: Promoting Excellence
in Education

Following Terman's original research, giftedness became synonymous with high IQ, and because of the high positive correlation
between scores from IQ and achievement tests, became related to
superior performance in school (Borland, 1986). This "schoolhouse
giftedness" (Renzulli, 1986) continues to be the focus of identification procedures in gifted and talented education (Hunsaker, Abeel,
& Callahan, 1991). In contrast to more specified procedures for
selecting gifted individuals, Renzulli promoted the identification
and development of gifted behavior. The term "gifted behavior" is
pivotal to Renzulli's conception of giftedness because it focuses on
the situation-specific nature of an individual's performances.

The Three-Ring Conception of Giftedness

The Three-Ring Conception of Giftedness is based on a broad range of research which has dealt with the identification and development of creative and productive behavior (Renzulli, 1986). Creative productivity involves applying one's abilities to an area of personal interest, the intended result being the "development of original materials and products that are purposely designed to have an impact on one or more target audiences" (Renzulli, 1986, p. 58). An audience consists of a forum for presenting one's ideas to interested individuals. This view of gifted behavior focuses on the interaction among three constructs: above-average ability, task commitment, and creativity. All three variables combine with environmental and personality factors and can be "brought to bear upon a multitude of specific performance areas" (Renzulli, 1978, p. 184). As a result of this process a person develops and exhibits "gifted behavior." Not all constructs remain stable for each person. The above-average ability cluster of traits tends to remain constant over time. Task commitment and creativity, on the other hand, tend to vary within individuals, at certain times, and under certain circumstances. In this way, the model considers individual differences and is used as a rationale for identifying above-average ability students who have the potential to develop creative and productive behavior. Students are nominated for special programming via status and action information. Status information refers to data such as grades and test scores. These data are usually gathered in the initial selection phase. Action information promotes ongoing recognition of students' gifted behaviors by peers, parents, and teachers. Renzulli and Reis (1986) recommended that 15–25% of the school population be selected for support services so as to include as many potentially creative and productive students as possible.

This conception of giftedness is part of a larger educational plan employing the Revolving Door Identification Model (RDIM; Renzulli, 1977), an identification model that is part of a widely accepted programming format (Mitchell, 1982). At the core of this program is the Enrichment Triad Model consisting of three types of activities: Type I (general exploratory activities), Type II (skill-building activities), and Type III (individual or small-group investigations of self-selected topics). All students nominated to the program receive the following services: (a) interest and learning style assessment, (b) opportunities for curriculum differentiation through "curriculum compacting," (c) Type I Enrichment, and (d) Type II Enrichment.

Students are provided the opportunity to pursue Type III Enrichment activities (Renzulli & Reis, 1986).

Several studies have been conducted to review this model's effect on creative productivity. Reis (1981) investigated the relationship between creative and productive behavior and an expanded view of giftedness. She found no significant differences in product quality between students in the top 5% of the sample and those in the next 15–20%. Also important is that 64% of the 1,162 subjects in Reis' study did not choose to complete an advanced level product. This observation led to the design of studies that focus on the characteristics and experiences of students who continuously choose to engage in self-selected investigations as well as those who never begin projects or those who do not complete them.

Gubbins (1982) identified four factors that interfered with product development (according to reports of program participants): low interest level; poor task commitment; inadequate time schedule; and lack of human and material resources. These findings highlight variables which impede productive behavior. Schack (1986) investigated factors that promote creative productivity. She employed Bandura's (1977) self-efficacy theory to support her belief that the greatest influence on a person's perceived ability to perform a behavior is past performance of the same or a similar task. Despite the application of a treatment designed to enhance abilities in research skills, Schack found no significant difference between the experimental and the control groups as far as the initiation of investigations of self-selected projects was concerned. Burns (1990), on the other hand, found that students trained in managing, planning, and focusing upon an investigation were more likely to initiate projects than were students who did not receive the training. Starko (1988) also investigated the relationship between creative productivity and project initiation. After comparing students who completed investigations of self-selected topics in school and those who did not, she concluded that "students who engage in creative productivity in school have higher self-efficacy with regard to creative productivity and are more likely to pursue creative productivity outside of school" (1986, p. 92). Starko's research highlights the need for studies focusing on transfer of similar performances from one situation to another. The home and school environments were also examined by Roeder et al. (1982). After conducting an analysis of the creative processes of four gifted and productive elementary school students, Roeder and her associates (1982) suggested that parents be more aware of their children's interests and needs, and that teachers encourage more risk taking and creative behaviors in their students. Few researchers have examined the behaviors of gifted students who consistently produce high-quality projects. The present study was conducted to investigate the development of consistent creative productivity.

METHODS AND PROCEDURES

Research Questions

These focal questions underlie the research design for this investigation of individuals' perceptions of their creative productive behavior: (a) What factors are associated with student creative and productive behavior? (b) What factors influence student creative and productive behavior over time? Are individuals more self-confident in initiating their own projects over time? Did they realize a gain in skills due to participation in the program for the gifted? Did they maintain their interests and career goals after leaving high school? What factors influence the elusive transition from being a consumer of knowledge to becoming a producer of knowledge? These questions guided this longitudinal study of individuals' perceptions of their creative and productive behavior.

Research Design

Part 1. This study employed a two-part qualitative research design with multiple case studies. Part 1 employed triangulation of data collection methods and sources (Jick, 1979; Mitchell, 1986) to overcome the weaknesses and biases that prevail in a single-method or source design. This technique provided checks for both reliability and validity (Smith, 1975). The sources of information were the student, the parents, and the school. Methods of data collection for each case included document analysis, questionnaires, and an interview schedule.

Triangulation was sought within the following plan:

1. School
   a. document analysis: gifted program policies, documentation of student abilities and achievements
   b. checklist and description of student behaviors and activities

2. Student
   a. survey of attitudes toward school
   b. questionnaire regarding the student's perceptions of his or her creative and productive behavior
   c. structured interview schedule, tape-recorded and transcribed
3. Parents
   a. questionnaire for family background of the student
   b. questionnaire regarding the parents' perceptions of the student's creative and productive behavior

Data were also collected describing student self-efficacy for creative productivity, learning preference, and self-concept, and are reported elsewhere (Delcourt, 1988). Except for the document analysis, all methods listed above are classified as reactive measures (Webb, 1966), in that the source (student, teacher, parent) may consciously or unconsciously alter the data as a result of involvement in the study. In order to reduce possible Hawthorne effects, the assessments of self-concept and attitudes toward school were administered prior to collecting any other information, and with the subjects grouped among other students who were not participating in the study.

Part 2. A follow-up questionnaire was distributed by mail three years after initial data collection to investigate the interests, career goals, academic attainment, and creative and productive patterns of these individuals. Additional questions were mailed to each subject to clarify their responses.

Sample

Part 1. The sample for Part 1 consisted of 18 students in grades 9 through 12 from four sites in three different states. There were eight females in the study: none in grade 9, one in grade 10, five in grade 11, and two in grade 12. Of the 10 males in the project, one was in grade 9, two were in grade 10, five were in grade 11, and three were in grade 12. All sites were recommended by experts in the field of gifted and talented education and were located in typical high schools rather than special schools for the gifted. Each program employed the Enrichment Triad Model (Renzulli, 1977) which encourages productivity within student-initiated interest areas. Program services at the sites also included Advanced Placement courses, honors classes, special seminars, and mentorships, as well as opportunities for individual investigations.

At all four sites, one teacher of the gifted coordinated the enrichment program. Each had completed coursework in gifted and talented education. These teachers were given a checklist of creative and productive behaviors and asked to nominate students for the study who had produced at least three performances or products. Only high school students were included in the study because their age and experience provided more pertinent information for exploring creative processes over time. To ensure student familiarity with the goals of the program for the gifted and talented, only subjects with four or more years of participation in a program were eligible. The impact of a project was also assessed by categorizing the type of audience as local, regional, state, or national.

Students were selected based on their outstanding performances. Student projects were used to make decisions in the nomination process. The projects of one twelfth grade student included the organization of a humanities seminar for high school students, teachers, and college professors; the organization of an internship to serve as a research assistant to a state senator; the founding of a newspaper for student political awareness; and the organization of a global issues conference for regional high school students. A tenth grade student interested in science created a movie on several linked computers that won a regional media festival award; developed an electrical circuit for a regional creative competition; wrote and was awarded a grant to investigate holograms; and wrote a computer program and paper about a specific type of cancer growth pattern which was presented to professors and deans of an engineering school.

Part 2. During initial data collection in Part 1, students were asked if they would allow future contact. All but one student agreed. Because this student was the only subject in the ninth grade at the beginning of this project, all subjects had graduated from high school and begun college by the time the follow-up investigation was conducted in Spring 1991. During the second data collection period, subjects ranged in age from 19–21 years. Surveys were mailed to all 17 students. When two of the surveys were returned with no forwarding address, letters of inquiry were sent to teachers in the cooperating schools, and phone directories for each location were consulted. This search did not produce the addresses of these subjects. After two rounds of surveys were mailed to nonrespondents, 8 out of 15 students had returned their completed forms, testifying to the difficulty of locating subjects as well as maintaining their commitment to a project after an extended period of time (Dillman, 1978; O'Tuel, 1991).

Data Collection

Instrumentation: Part 1. Parents completed two questionnaires. One of these described family background including parents' occupations and educational levels. The second survey asked about the quantity and quality of student projects completed in and outside of school, as well as the amount of effort invested in these projects by the student. A parallel form of this survey was completed by the students.

Each student participated in a 1 ½- to 2-hour interview which was audiotaped and later transcribed. The 36 interview questions were divided into three categories based on family background and childhood interests, educational experience, and project development. Each student responded to all questions. Follow-up questions were used to clarify responses during the course of the interview and each student received a copy of the transcription in order to make any corrections. All questionnaires are available in the original report of this research (Delcourt, 1988).

The School Sentiment Index (Attitudes Toward School K-12; 1972) for high school students was also completed by each subject. Originally composed of 82 items within 7 categories, a selection of 59 items among the following 6 subscales was retained for the purposes of this study: general attitudes toward school, teacher-mode of instruction, teacher-authority and control, teacher-interpersonal relationship with students, attitudes toward learning, and peer relationships. Items from the social structure and school climate subscales were deleted since they did not reflect the intent of this research. Using a 4-point Likert response format, descriptors ranged from strongly disagree (1) to strongly agree (4). A total internal consistency coefficient of .88 was reported in the manual for this instrument (Attitudes Toward School K-12; 1972). Estimates of internal reliability for the original subscales ranged from .68 to .88. These are acceptable values given that coefficients of .70 and above are recommended by Gable (1986) for affective measures.

Instrumentation: Part 2. Subjects were sent a 26-question survey focusing on their interests, educational and work experiences, career plans, and projects. Each packet included a cover letter summarizing the study and its importance, a copy of the survey, postage for forwarding the survey, a self-addressed stamped envelope for their response, and a small notepad as an incentive. A second round of surveys was sent to nonrespondents. Upon receiving each returned survey, another 5-question survey was sent to elaborate on earlier responses. Along with this survey, each student received a summary of the initial research.

Analysis

Part 1. Confidentiality was assured and a coding system employed for all data sources. Analysis of the data proceeded with the formation of case records (Patton, 1980). The unit of analysis was the student. The more subjective information obtained from questionnaire and interview data underwent content analysis to uncover patterns and themes (Spradley, 1979). This process was refined by the use of *The Ethnograph*, a computer program designed to organize data analysis by sorting text according to researcher codes (Seidel & Clark, 1984; Seidel, Kjolseth, & Seymour, 1988). For readers not familiar with this software, the steps used to incorporate the program into the content analysis process are as follows: (a) the researcher transcribes the data and makes the text compatible with *The Ethnograph* program format, (b) the software automatically numbers each line, (c) the researcher codes each line or group of lines in the text according to one or more themes, and (d) the computer is used to search for, sort, and print all instances of one or more themes in a given number of case records. All codes appear with the designated text sequences. By employing *The Ethnograph*, concepts were more quickly and systematically sorted and retrieved. Patterns among the data were examined through the processes of convergence and divergence. Convergence refers to the ability of a category to "hold together" (Patton, 1980, p. 311). Divergence links the category to existing information, sometimes raising additional hypotheses (Lincoln & Guba, 1985). In order to evaluate the consistency of responses, all data sources and methods were compared or triangulated (Mitchell, 1986). After analyzing all records individually, they were compared and contrasted in terms of patterns, themes, and categories (Miles & Huberman, 1984; Swanson-Kauffman, 1986).

Part 2. Responses to the follow-up survey were analyzed by searching again for patterns and themes within and across cases, and by comparing this information to earlier responses (Spradley, 1979). There was no need to use *The Ethnograph* computer program since this information was not as lengthy or complex as the earlier data.

RESULTS AND DISCUSSION: PART 1

Results are reported in three general categories: demographic data and family background, educational experiences, and student perceptions. Scores from selected instruments represent descriptive information. The qualitative design of this study did not support the use of inferential statistical procedures.

Demographic Data and Family Background

Both parents were likely to have pursued an education after high school and to be employed in a professional occupation. This was not viewed as a predictor of creative productivity but as a descriptor of each family's socioeconomic status. This sample contained 8 females (44%) and 10 males (56%). Career choices were placed into two broad categories: arts and humanities (writing, acting, photography, filmmaking) and sciences (computer science, mathematics, medicine, psychology/psychiatry). From this sample, only one male chose a career in the humanities, based upon his interest in film. Another male was undecided, but the rest intended to pursue careers in the areas of mathematics or science. The careers selected by males included political scientist/economist, aerospace engineer, computer scientist/military officer, Air Force pilot, scientist/mathematician, astrophysicist, Navy pilot, and landscape architect/ engineer. This contrasts with four females out of eight who planned to major in mathematics or science. Careers selected by the females were civil rights activist, wildlife photographer, international relations expert/linguist, writer, pediatrician/physical therapist, psychologist, psychiatrist, accountant. Sex-role stereotyping may have influenced choice of career path with fewer women selecting careers in mathematics or science (Reis, 1987).

Parental support. Parental support was investigated using two sources: the parents and the students. Replies to the parent questionnaire were compared with student interview responses to establish consistent patterns and themes. When asked if they thought their parents were supportive of their projects and interests, 11 students indicated "yes," 3 were in partial agreement, and 4 replied "no." All students who responded positively added that they felt free to select any topic which interested them. When the parents of these students responded to their questionnaires, they indicated they were pleased with the projects that their children pursued. Many of these parents also stated that they were proud of their children, and that they encouraged these .interests in their sons or daughters. When asked "What do you think motivates your child outside of school?" they responded with insights into their children's behaviors. The following are parents' remarks about three different children.

Doing one's best is stressed in our household. He always tries to reach for his dreams and he always does the best he can.

He is motivated by inherent intellectual curiosity in a very strong, driving personality. These characteristics were obvious in him from early infancy, and I have tried to foster them while helping him learn to live with the demands of the natural world and of society.

She really feels she wants to effect change in the world and believes grassroots organizations are the way to do it.

The four students who were disappointed by the support they received from home also reported parental pressure to excel in school. Two of these four parents mentioned their disappointment in their child's school performance. In general, when parents are interested in their child's performance both in and out of school, the student perceives his or her parents as being supportive. Parents viewed as unsupportive placed greater emphasis on grades than on their child's interests and projects.

Independence was mentioned by the students as they described their freedom to choose and investigate topics. Paired with parental support, this may be viewed as *interest without interference*. These students knew that their parents approved of their work both in and out of school, discussed their projects with their parents, occasionally asked them for ideas, and were largely unhampered in pursuing projects through their own methods. One student said that it was nice to know that no one was "looking over her shoulder all of the time." Another student credited her parents with helping her to become independent, "They've [parents] been pretty supportive of me. I tell them that they don't have a reason to limit me. I gained more independence by going out on my own." Early readers ($n = 13$) also mentioned the importance of learning to love books and of having their parents read to them regularly.

Parental support may take several forms. In addition to encouraging independence, parents in this study provided their children with supportive elements also found in other studies such as encouragement to take risks (Getzels & Jackson, 1962), to explore ideas early in life (McCurdy, 1960), and to experience the value and love of learning (Barbe, 1988).

Childhood interests. Childhood includes primary and elementary school years and the period before a student entered school. In describing their childhood interests, 13 of the subjects said they were early readers, and 12 of the students had an interest in music when they were children. A majority of the students ($n = 13$) intended to pursue careers that were related to topics of interest formed early in childhood (see Table 15.1). The following accounts describe examples of these relationships between early interests and career plans:

> Basically, it was science right from the start. (Current Career Objective—engineer, landscape architect, specifically investigating plant hybridization)

> A lot of my interests, at an early age, came from camping. A major interest of mine is camping and wilderness survival. It's something I'm going to pursue as part of my career. (Current Career Objective—wildlife photographer)

> I cannot remember a single time when I wasn't interested in technology. (Current Career Objective—astrophysicist)

The degree to which others have influenced these students to pursue specific lines of interest is unknown. Both parents and teachers may have been instrumental in distributing attention and resources to assist in the development of specific student interests. Bloom (1982; Bloom & Sosniak, 1981) referred to these interests and proclivities as "markers." This pattern of retaining an interest area from childhood that subsequently plays an important role in career selection was also found in a longitudinal study of creative individuals conducted by Torrance (1981). In that particular project, individuals identified as highly creative appeared to have "fallen in love" (p. 61) during their elementary school years with a particular topic to which their career was later related. As the students made their career choices after high school, the second part of this study documented whether or not they continued with the same interest areas they began in childhood.

Educational Experiences

As program selection criteria were reviewed, an investigation was made of variables concerning school in general, and the students' participation in the program for the gifted and talented, in particular. An examination of students' interests, attitudes, relationships, motivation, and learning patterns in relation to school was also conducted.

Program selection criteria and student records. All four sites based their programs upon multiple selection criteria. Even

Table 15.1. Past, Present, and Future Student Interests

Student	Art[a]	Collections	History/Politics	Music[b]	Outdoor Activities	Reading	Science	Sports	Travel	Other	Major Area of Interest	Possible Career
1		X	X			X				money	politics, economics	major in political sciences, economics
2	P			1						children	science, drama, children	pediatrician or pediatric physical therapist
3			X	1		X					politics	civil rights activist through medicine, writing, and philosophy
4				1		X		X			engineering, computers	aerospace engineer
5						X		X		TV/movies	movie-making, script-writing	film-directing, screen-writing
6	P				X						outdoor activities, photography	wildlife photographer
7				1	X	X		X	X	computers	swimming, computers, ham radio, outdoor activities	outdoor job or computer science or military
8	P			1		X					writing, foreign language	international relations
9			X			X		X		chess	history, writing	Air Force
10		X				X			X	Boy Scouts	mathematics, holography	major in science and mathematics
11						X				writing	writing, observing behavior	psychology or psychiatry
12				T		X	X				computers, science	astrophysicist
13				3		X				writing	writing	writing
14				1						flying	aviation, designing structures	Navy pilot
15	P			2							drama, music	psychology with hobbies in acting and music
16				1		X				TV/writing	writing	undecided
17	V			3		X					writing, drawing bookkeeping (summer job)	accountant
18	V			1	X	X	X	X			horticulture, computers visual art	landscape architect or engineer

Art[a] – Visual Arts = V, Performing Arts = P
Music[b] – Number of instruments are indicated
T = Technical aspects of music

though the identification systems for each program used either achievement scores, IQ test scores, or grades as criteria, "alternate pathways" were also considered. These nontraditional methods for selection into programs for the gifted and talented included parent, peer, and self-nomination; writing samples; and estimates of creative behavior.

No one criterion determined selection into the program at any site. If, however, an IQ cutoff score of 130 had been employed, at least six students would have been eliminated from the program for the gifted and talented. The 12 IQ test scores received ranged from 104 to 154 (mean = 133). Because all students qualified as high creative producers, this score range supports the use of multiple criteria which do not overstress intelligence test scores. Although conceptions of giftedness vary (Sternberg & Davidson, 1986), a current trend toward the assessment of more complex student behaviors and products seems to refocus the role of ability test scores to one among other important characteristics of giftedness rather than the criterion by which to compare all other variables (Renzulli & Delcourt, 1986).

Attitudes Toward School. Students received the School Sentiment Index (Attitudes Toward School K-12, 1972). Most students had positive attitudes toward school and related their motivation in school to both internal (self-motivation, love of learning) and external variables (grades, getting into college). When asked what motivates them in school, students made these comments:

It makes me feel good about myself when I realize that I am working hard to accomplish something. So that tends to motivate me.

I just like to learn. I want to get good grades at it because I just care about doing it right, for the future.

You have to motivate yourself. Someone else can't do it for you. I think the biggest thing that motivates me would be getting into college. It's just like a stepping ladder. Getting good grades would mean getting into a good college, which would mean getting a good position.

Those reporting negative attitudes during the student interviews also have lower scores on the inventory. The following passages from students with below-average scores on this index illustrate this:

I don't really know what motivates me. I guess just being able to get out of here [school] at the normal time.

In general, I learn everything, it's a matter of getting the homework in. I was about to give up on it all and drop out. I really didn't get much work done, and so I didn't understand anything.

(What motivates you in school?) Getting out, which is not a very lofty motivation. Because in order to get out, you have to pass. That's what I'm doing, I'm just passing.

These students were three of the four participants who had below-average scores on the attitudes toward school inventory and reported lack of parental support as well as an increase in parental pressure to excel in school. Because two of these gifted students were also receiving lower grades than would be expected, they fit one description of an underachiever defined by Whitmore (1980), a student with high ability, but low school achievement. This indicates the need for research on the interaction between parental recognition for student interests and projects, pressure to excel academically, and attitudes toward school.

Relationships. A majority of the subjects spoke positively about their teachers and peers. These relationships were viewed realistically, because the students recognized that they would not get along well with every teacher or in every social group. Students usually had the same group of friends over a period of several years and had several peer groups according to their different interests (i.e., drama club participants, ham radio operators, emergency medical technicians).

All students realized that others might dislike them because they are "smart." Explaining this situation, one subject said: "There just aren't a whole lot of people who I'm going to be able to have a prolonged relationship with, and really enjoy the relationship, you know? It's tough." The same student stressed the need to understand one's abilities in relation to others.

Like I said in the beginning, perspective is what counts. You have to see everything in perspective or you just get so deeply involved [in your own work] that you just can't see out. You're in a "black hole of society."

Student interests in relation to school. Although most students had interests in the same content areas as their favorite school subject (see Table 15.2), few students related their independent investigations to school or regular curriculum activities. Nonetheless, a consistency was noted between most-liked class, favorite project, and potential career.

Teachers played an important role in subject area preference. Five students related their least-liked course to their least-liked teacher. Everyone in the sample said that teachers "make a difference" in a course. This means that the teacher determines how challenging and enjoyable the course will be, and structures the pattern for presenting information.

Learning. When asked about their learning processes, students said they learned best through reading, research, discussion, and application of content. As reported by these students, these methods are not regularly and satisfactorily employed throughout the school setting.

Factors affecting motivation in school were more often externally oriented, such as parental pressure for grades and pressure to get into college. Outside of school, motivation was most often internally oriented by interest, task commitment, and self-motivation. Not surprisingly, recommendations for improving school focused on student interests. Comments included increasing the course selection to provide advanced level courses (i.e., calculus II and creative writing II), and offering a variety of new topics for exploration (i.e., photography and electronics).

Student Perceptions

This section reviews student accounts of project planning and development. Topics include favorite projects, project planning, advice to new students, and the role of the audience.

Most and least-preferred projects. Many students have completed projects in more than one area, yet their favorite project usually related to their favorite school subject, present area of interest, and potential career path. In describing their most successful investigations, student responses included the following criteria:

1. Genuine interest in the topic (seen as vital)
2. Self-satisfaction and enjoyment
3. Audience recognition and helpful feedback
4. Opportunities for creative expression
5. The project did what it was supposed to do; "It worked."

Table 15.2. Favorite School Subject Areas and Projects Compared with Present and Future Student Interests: Selected Examples

Student	Favorite School Subjects	Topics for Favorite Project(s)	Major Area of Interest	Possible Career
1	mathematics	writing computer programs, collecting and displaying baseball cards, research of Newton's Laws of Motion	economics and politics	major in political science and economics
2	biology and chemistry	developing and presenting stories to children	science, drama, children	pediatrician, pediatric physical therapist
3	history	working for peace in local and state government groups	politics	civil rights activist through medicine, writing, and philosophy
4	mathematics	a computer program related to chemical engineering, creating a battery-powered car	engineering, computers	aerospace engineer
5	English, creative writing	video filming	movie-making, script-writing	film directing, screenwriting
6	photography	photographic portfolio and displays	outdoor activities and photography	wildlife photographer
7	science, chemistry, computers	computer programs	swimming, computers, ham radio, outdoor activities	outdoor job or computer science, or military career

8	English and foreign languages	creative writing for a skit	writing, foreign languages, dancing	international relations
9	history	computer programming	history, writing	Air Force
10	mathematics	holographic displays	mathematics, holography	majoring in science and mathematics
11	English and social studies	writing poetry	writing, observing behavior	psychology, psychiatry
12	science	a computer program about fractal patterns	computer science	astrophysicist
13	geometry	publishing poetry, creating puppet show	writing	writing
14	science	acting in a play, designing structures for a problem-solving program	aviation, designing structures	Navy pilot
15	English, creative writing	writing and producing a play	drama, music	psychology with hobbies in acting and music
16	English, creative writing	editing a school literacy magazine, writing	writing	undecided
17	mathematics	creating a play—drawing and writing	writing, drawing, bookkeeping	accountant
18	science	all projects involving art and science	horticulture, computers, visual art	landscape architect or engineer

Least-liked projects were identified by the following criteria:

1. Lack of group or personal commitment
2. Lack of interest in the topic
3. Inadequate amount of time for working on the project
4. Poor selection of human and material resources
5. Inadequate information or skills prior to commencing an investigation.

These criteria are similar to those described by Haensly and Roberts (1983) in a study of the creative processes of professionals in six different fields. In their study, the subjects reported the following necessary ingredients for successful product development: task commitment, the ability to select an appropriate audience for presenting one's contribution, and energy to overcome obstacles such as lack of time, money, or cooperation. The criteria used to define least-liked projects also agree with Gubbins's (1982) identification of four factors that interfered with product development: low interest level, poor task commitment, inadequate time commitment, and lack of human and material resources.

Getting ideas. These students continuously explored their many interests as they actively sought project ideas through a variety of techniques, including reading, sharing information with others, and taking courses both in and out of school. The concept of "falling in love" with a topic appeared frequently in the interviews as demonstrated by a student who explains how he first became interested in fractal geometry.

> I really enjoyed that project. . . . It started in June. It was kind of almost "romantic" because I saw this article in *Scientific American* . . . and I said, "Gee, that's neat." And it just kind of built on itself.

A majority of the subjects ($n = 15$) said they investigated topics which they already liked or knew something about. They recognized many of their strengths and weaknesses and built upon topics which were already of interest. As one student put it, "What I want to do is defined by what I've enjoyed doing." After students got ideas, "think time" played an important role in product development. One student referred to this as "mind intervention." The following response illustrates how a student employed incubation while deciding to investigate the difference between diamonds and graphite.

> It starts out as an insignificant thing. You think: "Why is that dia-
> mond hard?" But then it will just develop . . . your mind will just keep
> turning the idea over and over. . . . If you get to the point where you
> just can't figure it out and you really want to know, then it starts to
> seem important to you and you think, "This is something I should try
> and figure out."

Another student, who set aside time each day for thinking, came
upon ideas in the following manner:

> I don't consciously sit down and say: "What project am I going to do
> next?" It starts as a like, or a thought and just turns into a project."

In addition to being examples of "getting ideas," these quotations
provide insight into how a student might select a topic based upon
an area of interest and how a topic could become a self-selected
investigation. These types of investigations cannot be predicted in
advance, but a supportive environment can assist the process.

After beginning a project, a few students work steadily until completion, but most take breaks along the way. These breaks are not
periods of disinterest. Fourteen students reported consciously stopping work on a project in order to "get away from it." These periods
of incubation occur at regular intervals during the process, as the
students accomplish subtasks related to the completion of their
goals.

Planning. Most of the students do not regard planning in a lock-
step fashion. They do not consider their approach to these activities
as structured. This attitude is reflected in the following quotations:

> You see, I don't plan. When I'm writing, I might think of an outline of
> what I wanted to do. I don't go step by step. I just write and I go over it
> and maybe change a few things. It gets the job done. But it's certainly
> not ordered. I'm not saying I'm totally unstructured, I do it in sections.

> There's no schedule. I try to break it down into smaller pieces to make
> it easier, but there's no formal plan that I spend hours working on to
> get everything straightened out and [to figure out] the amount of time
> I'm going to spend on everything.

This ability to have a goal in mind and to break a task into its
component parts while maintaining a tolerance for the partial suc-
cesses along the way is a characteristic of expert problem solvers

(Larkin, Heller, & Greeno, 1980). Although all students in this study employed problem-solving behaviors to complete their projects, most students ($n = 12$) made a point of detailing this less structured format during their interviews.

Time and energy spent on projects. Given the quality and quantity of the projects, it is not surprising that these students allocated a great deal of time and energy to working on their investigations. Students reported spending between 1 and 10 hours a week working on a project, including thinking time. One student explained that his devotion to a project is sporadic:

> If interest comes and something is really happening at a certain time, it will be a lot. It could be five hours a day, late into the night. If nothing is happening, nothing happens for weeks.

The time and energy spent on an investigation depends on the student's interest and commitment. Deadlines for projects may be imposed by a formal organization, but the distribution of effort is largely determined and controlled by the student.

The role of the audience. Students in this study believed that it was essential to show their work to the appropriate audience. These are people who understand the topic, appreciate the student's effort, and supply constructive criticism, not just flattery. An audience might consist of all subscribers to a national publication, a group of interested community members, or a mentor. When asked why an audience was necessary, subjects responded.

> Because you don't really have anybody's comment on what you've done. If you just do it yourself, you can't really say as easily that some things should have been better, because you're looking at the fact that you worked for a long time on this, and worked really hard, so it's got to be the best possible. So it usually takes someone else, on the outside, to get you thinking about some of the mistakes that were made or things that could have been done better.

> Actually, it's one of the rewards, being able to explain something to somebody and having them understand it. You get a real sense of satisfaction out of being able to show your understanding for [your project] and create an understanding in other people. You've just given them something. It's a gift!

Advice to a new student. When asked to supply advice, students responded in this manner:

1. Choose a topic of interest (unanimous response)
2. Have task commitment/"stick-to-itiveness"
3. Don't choose a topic to please other people, select something you want to do
4. When working in groups, make certain that everyone in the group gets along and is interested in the topic
5. If you don't like the topic, get out.

The effects of working on projects. In general, students attributed positive changes over time to the activities in their respective programs for the gifted and to being involved in the projects themselves (see Table 15.3). They remarked that engagement in these projects should have favorable future effects. These effects are internalized as students have more confidence in evaluating their own behavior. The secondary reinforcement of receiving a formal grade is rarely applied in these programs and is not important, as this student explains: "I grade myself. . . . If I really like what I'm doing, I have an 'A' in myself."

Table 15.3. Student Responses to the Interview Question: "How Do You Think Your Ability to Work on These Projects Has Changed Over Time?"

1. The Project itself resulted in:
   a. increased interest and task commitment
   b. improved quality of projects completed later
   c. the ability to get more ideas
   d. better organizational strategies
   e. future selection of more challenging projects
   f. the ability to accept criticism more realistically.

2. Skill acquisition or development occurred in the areas of:
   a. research
   b. writing
   c. communication
   d. technical abilities.

3. General personality traits showed improvement in:
   a. self-satisfaction
   b. patience
   c. self-assurance
   d. responsibility
   e. attitude toward learning
   f. independence
   g. enjoyment
   h. passion for a topic.

4. Potential careers were explored.

Why work on this type of project? Students agreed that the projects assisted in meeting the following needs: interest and inquisitiveness, self-satisfaction, increased learning, challenge, and self-expression.

> Why do I write (computer) programs? When I see something, and I don't know how it works, I wonder. So that may be part of it.

> As I said, my motivation for writing is expression. If I can find something better, that's what I'm going to do. It's not something I do because I want a grade, or something I do because I want money out of it. It's something I have to do, because if I don't, I lose those ideas. If I lose those ideas, then I don't know what exactly I have lost.

No single answer exists as to why someone creates. It is a combination of variables based upon a deep interest, and it seems to originate in taking advantage of personal characteristics, directing energy toward a particular topic, and using imagination for exploring and developing new ideas.

RESULTS AND DISCUSSION: PART 2

This part of the study reviews the responses of eight college students (2 females, 6 males) who were originally identified for their high creative productivity when they were in secondary school. At the time of the follow-up study, these participants ranged in age from 19–21 years. Upon graduating from high school, all students were acknowledged for their scholastic abilities. Six students had been awarded scholarships and one had received a fellowship. The sample included one presidential scholar, one valedictorian, and one salutatorian. Two students are presently serving in the military.

Regarding their scholastic standings, all students were in their first, second, or third year of college with grade point averages ranging from 2.88 to 3.80 on a 4-point scale. Students maintained career objectives in college similar to their career plans three years ago in high school. The only shifts in declared major area of study were seen when two students changed from one area of science to another and when a female subject stated that she has no further career goals after college beyond having a family (see Table 15.4). This consistency in field of interest from high school to college is not easily attained by many young adults (Phifer, 1987). Time and effort spent exploring interest areas seemed to be important career decision-making strategies for students in this study.

Table 15.4.   Past and Present Student Interests and Career Plans

High School		College	
Major Areas of Interest	Possible Career	Declared Major	Career Plan
science, drama, children	pediatrician or physical therapist	zoology	M.D. or physical medicine
engineering, computers	aerospace engineer	chemistry	forensic scientist
swimming, computers, ham radio, outdoor activities	outdoor job or computer science or military	physics/ computers military	teacher of physics and computer science
writing, foreign language, dancing	international relations	history/political science	home-maker
history, writing	Air Force	international studies	government service, foreign related
mathematics, holography	major in science and mathematics	mathematics	actuarian
computers, science	astrophysicist	computer science	computer science applied to artificial intelligence
aviation designing structures	Navy pilot	oceanography, U.S. Marine Corps aviation	Marine Corps, aviation

When these students were in high school three years ago, their career choices were already related to their childhood interests. This was the case for 13 out of 18 students in the original sample. The fact that their career plans have remained stable during high school and college reflects the propensity in such students to develop specific interests early in life and to pursue them through young adulthood. It is also important to mention that these students had a variety of interests in childhood (refer to Table 15.1) and felt that their respective programs for the gifted provided opportunities for exploration of topics. Two students regretted not having been introduced to a variety of topics when they were children. One student explains why his childhood activities may not have been related to his present career selection:

> I can't see where my present interests are really related to my early
> (childhood) interests. I think this may be because at such an early age

> I was not exposed to math and sciences in elementary school . . . Only
> after advancing in school was I introduced to the sciences and math,
> subjects which I am more advanced in now.

Without the opportunity to explore different topics or cognitive processes, students may not realize their interests or abilities. The
same student remarked that his interest area was related to the way
he processes information.

> I think that these topics are of interest to me because they are all
> logically oriented in nature. I have a very logical manner of thinking
> and thus [these types of] topics will be of the most interest to me.

When completing the follow-up survey, each student was asked to
describe the progress of their hobbies and projects since the last
contact. Their average number of hobbies was six, including owning
and operating a small sailing yacht, making crafts, collecting baseball cards, playing rugby, and painting. Students reported not being
able to pursue these hobbies as much as they would have liked
because of the demands on their time for completing college-related
projects.

The follow-up survey did not provide a particular definition of the
terms *project, product,* or *Type III activity.* Subjects were asked to
describe the sources, types, and outlets of the projects that they
pursued according to their interests. In many cases, these interest
areas converged with courses and career plans as reported by the
college students. The average number of projects completed by students over a 3-year period was 2.3. Only one student reported that
he did not complete any projects over this time span. He did, however, engage in many sports activities and was very involved in
attaining his piloting credentials as part of his military training.
Another student responded that while her favorite activities involved creative writing, she has not sought to present her work in
any particular forum since high school. For the remainder of the
students, two completed one project each, another two reported that
they each were involved in three projects, one student completed
four projects, and one student reported finishing over six projects in
the past three years. These projects were related to areas of interest
based on job or course activities which were either assigned or self-
selected topics. Projects included a presentation about a company's
pollution record (college class), a computer program "to translate
'semantic frames' in French" (work), a research paper on "the effects
of calcium and other factors on osteoporosis" (college class), and a
publication in a literary magazine (personal interest in high school).

Following perhaps a less characteristic pattern, one student who completed three projects over the past three years remarked that he was "not quite as project-oriented" as other students. He stated that his "projects are geared toward self-expression and fulfillment . . . rather than an immediate contribution to a specific area." He explained that his chosen career path in international relations has meant that his activities were necessarily different from the projects of students who focused on science (independent research) or humanities (creative expression). This subject stated that he felt "isolated to a certain extent" because his interest area and projects were not easily categorized, suggesting that for more abstract areas of study, the concept of "project" may require redefinition.

In general, students reported that they did not have the time to pursue large-scale projects totally unrelated to their present schedules. In fact, several students mentioned that given more time, they would have liked to pursue more of the same type of research. Although this may not seem surprising, these same students reported almost no connection between their favorite projects and assignments in high school. It appears that these students were able to explore areas of strengths and interests throughout the years in their respective gifted programs, to relate these interests to possible careers during high school and are now satisfied with the merging of their interests, college courses, and career plans. When asked whether or not their ability to work on these projects changed over time, respondents reported being better organized and more efficient, largely because of their past participation in these activities.

Students were also asked to describe the future effects of completing these activities. Because the projects were usually job- or course-related, students saw them as vehicles for demonstrating that they can do well in their major areas of study. Their hope is that this will eventually lead to a fulfilling career. Students also said that they were engaged in these projects to learn more about their selected areas of study and to understand themselves better.

In looking back at their respective programs for the gifted, students responded to the following question, "How do you think your program for the gifted influenced you over time?" All students in the sample participated in programs with a pullout component and they all said that leaving the regular classroom helped to decrease the drudgery of many class activities. They indicated that it was intellectually stimulating to meet with students who had similar interests and abilities.

I began studying in a gifted program in late elementary school (5th grade). The times spent in this program over the next few years played an essential role in my intellectual development as only in the gifted program was I able to explore areas of my specific interests and develop an important background for my future studies.

I think it was good to be in a gifted program and to get away from frustrating and tedious school routines. We got to apply learning in real places in the community.

It seems to me that the best (and certainly most important) effects of the program have been its secondary ones . . . It was the opportunity for personal growth and experience that has affected me the most as of today.

These comments support the efforts of teachers of the gifted to provide time for gifted students to explore new topics. However, these remarks also suggest that a pullout program is not enough to meet the needs of high-ability students; the regular curriculum must also be addressed. Although some of these students reported having challenging high school classes, many said that they were not intellectually stimulated in most of their courses.

When asked what advice they would give to people who are influential in the field of gifted education, their responses focused on student needs: exploring interests, learning how to think, becoming independent, learning how to work with others, and learning that gifted "does not imply better." These students also shared their insights into what they wanted most from life. Besides having satisfying, well-paying jobs, they wanted fulfilling lives in which they could make a significant difference in their environments. Future marriage and family plans were mentioned by one male respondent and both females. Other subjects made these comments:

(What do you want most out of life?) To comprehend it. Seriously, to make a difference in understanding it. (Career—Government Service)

The only thing I want out of life is to be remembered as someone who cared for and helped others. If, in my life, I make a decision that makes someone else's life better, I will have accomplished the most important task. (Career—Forensic Scientist)

SUMMARY AND CONCLUSIONS

The first phase of this longitudinal study identified 18 secondary school students who exhibited creative and productive behavior by consistently engaging in firsthand investigations of self-selected topics both in and out of school. After a 3-year period, 17 students were sent surveys as part of a follow-up study. Based upon each student's level of involvement with his or her investigations and the quality of the projects, this study supports the theory that adolescents and young adults can be producers of information as well as consumers. While their processes and products differ in scope, students identified as creative producers are developing projects to their own satisfaction. By recording the types of audiences for these projects, it should be noted that a criterion of product quality extends beyond the producer since these projects were also comparable to the work of students at local, regional, state, and national levels and occasionally comparable to the achievements of adults.

For the first data analyses, a qualitative investigation using triangulation of data methods and sources produced remarkably clear patterns and themes among the subjects. Data sources included family background, school environment, and a student's present and retrospective perceptions of his or her project development. Considering the home environment, students identified independence as necessary to pursue their interests. Combined with parental support, this factor of independence was defined as parental "interest without interference." A small number of students reporting a lack of parental support tended to have more negative attitudes toward school and felt excessive pressure from their parents to excel academically. The degree of parental influence in maintaining specific interest areas throughout childhood is unknown. However, most students in the sample retained interests from childhood which were often determinants of their career selections. This pattern was maintained as students selected their major field of study in college. For most of them, there remained a link between having a variety of early interests and developing one of these areas into a career.

After a 3-year interval, subjects were sent a questionnaire focusing on their interests, educational and professional experiences, career plans, and projects. Results indicate that students maintained similar or exact career goals from their plans in high school and major fields of study in college. As college students, they were satisfied completing projects related to their courses or their professions. These assignments coincided with their interests and goals. This apparently made their investigations easier to complete. By contrast, three years ago they reported little or no relation between personally instigated and high school projects. Some students were not particularly concerned with high levels of attainment in their careers, but rather with good relationships with friends and family. Overall, the young adults who participated in the follow-up study reported being satisfied with their academic and professional choices. Perceptions of their professional success will be sought in a future study.

In each high school, student selection procedures in the programs for the gifted employed multiple criteria across several categories of behaviors. Strict cutoff scores on ability tests were not used to exclude students from any of the programs. As this study revealed, of the 12 IQ test scores collected, the values ranged from 104 to 154 (M = 133). Because all students qualified as high creative producers, the present results support the use of multiple criteria which do not overstress intelligence test scores.

When in high school, students responded to interview questions about school activities and their projects. Students believed that there were three categories of project environments: (a) assignments as part of regular classes, (b) activities in the program for the gifted, and (c) projects the student really wants to do in his or her free time. More overlap existed between categories (b) and (c) than between (a) and either (b) or (c). Projects completed as school assignments were often referred to as "routine" or "regular" and not normally related to creative activities. Even when there appeared to be a more obvious connection between most-liked course (i.e., history) and favorite project topic (i.e., political science), most students separated school-related topics from personal projects. In addition, their motivation appeared more externally oriented for school activities and more internally oriented where self-selected projects were concerned. This pattern changed when students attended college because their assignments as part of regular classes were also the activities that they really enjoyed. This suggests that if teachers want their students to become more internally oriented toward school, they may also want to incorporate more student interests and student selection of topics into the curriculum.

As secondary school students, the separation between school and outside interests did not seem to affect attitudes toward school because a majority of students had above-average scores on the School Sentiment Index. Those few with lower scores on the attitudes measure, however, made profound statements about the difficulty of contributing, even minimally, to class assignments. One student, who worked on several projects at a time outside of school, remarked that working on his worst one was better than going to school. These projects were obviously valuable creative outlets for all of these individuals. Once in college, students reported that interests, course assignments, and career goals focused on the same activities. This assisted students in the organization and concentration invested in their projects.

During high school, students noted that completed projects needed to be shared. They found it imperative to locate peer groups, though not necessarily same-age peers. For this purpose, they sought membership in both formal and informal groups related to specific topics. Three years later, audiences were likely to be college classmates and many projects were course assignments. In general, the subjects were realistic about their relationships with others, desiring strong friendships, but they were also particular about finding people with similar interests. Throughout the study, students agreed that as they worked on their projects over time, they gained perspective on how they learned best and planned their projects.

The students in this sample explored their interests and discovered their learning patterns over a period of time. Their creative productivity could be viewed in three phases. First was a period in which they were presented with a variety of ideas, topics, books, and activities. As young children, their parents read to them regularly and encouraged their interests and independent behaviors. Second, participation in both their respective programs for the gifted and talented and in their projects clearly assisted them in improving the quality of their investigations, increasing their general skills, enhancing their personal characteristics, and exploring potential careers. During this phase, they tended to dissociate school activities from favorite projects. In the third phase, interests, academic programs, and career plans of these college students seemed to merge, allowing them to focus their time and energy toward a specific goal.

Why offer opportunities for students to become producers of information as well as consumers? Student involvement in creative and productive activities through Triad programs provided them with the opportunities to explore interest-based projects (Type III activities) on a long-term basis and to relate these interests to potential career plans. As two students described it:

> Over time, I am more likely to see the "big picture" applications of what I learn.

> I don't know. I guess it's basically the idea that these things [projects] really do make a difference, that they're significant.

When students know that they can make significant contributions through their projects, they derive a sense of pride from their actions and are more likely to exhibit these types of behaviors in the future. As these activities continue, students gain confidence and expertise on the path to becoming creative and productive adults.

Importance Of Longitudinal Research

The only way to gather developmental data about possible changes in behavior is to follow the same cohort over a period of time (O'Tuel, 1991). This research design has certain disadvantages, but also some undeniable rewards. Probably the most disappointing aspect of a follow-up study is subject attrition. One advice would be to contact the subjects at regular intervals, even if in-depth information is not required for the study. An annual note should be sent with a return postcard requesting notification of any changes in address, and perhaps also a brief survey to determine current activities. For this study, information was sent to students and teachers after one year, and follow-up surveys after three years. This was not enough to encourage further participation from certain individuals.

The rewards of this type of research include the human relationships established by regular contacts with the subjects, as much as the discovery of their perspectives. Within this study, for example, some students also attached personal notes to the surveys or made jokes about their fields of interest. One student said that he greatly appreciated reading the summary of the first round of data collection because it helped him to know that there were other students with similar "interests, problems, and experiences."

It is also exciting to read how enthusiastic certain subjects are in pursuing their interests. One might wonder whether the patterns determined in this study will still be observable in the future. This degree of uncertainty is a characteristic of longitudinal research, given that it obviously reflects the circumstances of an individual's life.

Areas for Further Investigation

Research should always be directed toward theory building. This study was based upon the theory that students identified by the Three-Ring Conception of Giftedness are likely to develop their creative and productive behaviors when encouraged to do so. It examined the characteristics of individuals identified for their high levels of creative and productive behaviors and followed these students from their high school programs to college. The next phase of this research will provide information about the creative productivity of these individuals as they start their professional life. Directions for future investigations include expanding the sample size, providing a comparison group, applying results as program strategies, and examining new combinations of variables. Subjects representing a wide range of ethnic groups, school programs, and community settings should also be studied. These recommendations are by no means exhaustive. They should, however, be considered for continuing this investigation of creative productivity in young adults and for exploring further implications both in terms of theory and educational programs.

REFERENCES

Attitudes toward school K-12. (1972). Los Angeles, CA: Instructional Objectives Exchange.

Bandura, A. (1977). Self-efficacy: Toward a unifying theory of behavior change. *Psychological Review, 84,* 191–215.

Barbe, W. (1988). Pain or pleasure in the gifted child family. *Gifted Child Today, 11*(1), 6–8.

Bloom, B. S. (1982). The role of gifts and markers in the development of talent. *Exceptional Children, 48*(6), 510–522.

Bloom, B. S., & Sosniak, L. A. (1981). Talent development vs. schooling. *Educational Leadership, 39,* 86–94.

Bogner, D. (1981). Creative individual education programs (IEPs) from creativity tests. *Creative Child and Adult Quarterly, 6,* 160–162.

Borland, J. H. (1986). IQ tests: Throwing out the bath water, saving the baby. *Roeper Review, 8,* 163–167.

Burns, D. E. (1990). The effects of group training activities on students' initiation of creative investigations. *Gifted Child Quarterly, 34,* 31–36.

Campbell, D. T., & Stanley, J. C. (1963). *Experimental and quasi-experimental designs for research.* Boston, MA: Houghton Mifflin.

Cook, T. D., & Campbell, D. T. (1979). *Quasi-experimentation: Design and analysis issues for field settings.* Boston, MA: Houghton Mifflin.

Delcourt, M. A. B. (1988). *Characteristics related to high levels of creative/ productive behavior in secondary school students: A multi-case study.* Unpublished doctoral dissertation, University of Connecticut, Storrs, CT.

Dillman, D. A. (1978). *Mail and telephone surveys.* New York: Wiley.

Ewing, J. H., Gillis, C. A., Ebert, J. N., & Mathews, H. M. (1975). Profile of perceptual-cognitive traits and personality style of possible relevance to creative productivity. *Perceptual and Motor Skills, 40,* 711–719.

Gable, R. K. (1986). *Instrument development in the affective domain.* Boston, MA: Kluwer-Nijoff.

Getzels, J. W., & Jackson, P. W. (1962). *Creativity and intelligence: Explorations with gifted students.* New York: Wiley.

Goertzel, M. G., Goertzel, V., & Goertzel, T. G. (1978). *Three hundred eminent personalities.* San Francisco, CA: Jossey-Bass.

Gubbins, E. J. (1982). *Revolving Door Identification Model: Characteris-*

tics of talent pool students. Unpublished doctoral dissertation, University of Connecticut, Storrs, CT.

Haensly, P. A., & Roberts, N. M. (1983). The professional productive process and its implications for gifted studies. *Gifted Child Quarterly, 27,* 9–12.

Hunsaker, S. L., Abeel, L. B., & Callahan, C. M. (1991). *Instrument use in the identification of gifted and talented children.* Paper presented at the meeting of the Jacob K. Javits Gifted and Talented Education Program Grant Recipients, Washington, DC.

Jick, T. D. (1979). Mixing qualitative and quantitative methods: Triangulation in action. *Administrative Science Quarterly, 24*(4), 602–611.

Larkin, J. H., Heller, J. I., & Greeno, J. G. (1980). Instructional implications of research on problem solving. *New Directions in Teaching and Learning, 2,* 51–65.

Lincoln, Y. S., & Guba, E. G. (1985). *Naturalistic inquiry.* Beverly Hills, CA: Sage.

MacKinnon, D. W. (1978). *In search of human effectiveness: Identifying and developing creativity.* Buffalo, NY: Creative Education Foundation.

McCurdy, H. G. (1960). The childhood pattern of genius. *Horizon, 2,* 33–38.

Measures of self concept K-12. (1972). Los Angeles, CA: Instructional Objectives Exchange.

Milgram, R. M. (1984). Creativity in gifted adolescents: A review. *Journal for the Education of the Gifted, 8*(1), 25–42.

Miles, M. B., & Huberman, M. A. (1984). *Qualitative data analysis.* Beverly Hills, CA: Sage.

Mitchell, B. M. (1982). An update on the state of gifted/talented education in the U.S. *Phi Delta Kappan, 63,* 357–358.

Mitchell, E. S. (1986). Multiple triangulation: A methodology for nursing science. *Advances in Nursing Science, 8*(3), 18–26.

O'Tuel, F. S. (1991). Developmental and longitudinal research. In N.K. Buchanan & J. F. Feldhusen (Eds.), *Conducting research and evaluation in gifted education: A handbook of methods and applications* (pp. 95–113). New York: Teachers College Press.

Patton, M. Q. (1980). *Qualitative evaluation methods.* Beverly Hills, CA: Sage.

Phifer, P. (1987, October). *College majors and careers: How to select a college major.* Paper presented at the annual meeting of the Michigan Association for Counseling and Development, Grand Rapids, MI.

Reis, S. M. (1981). *An analysis of the productivity of gifted students participating in programs using the Revolving Door Identification Model.* Unpublished doctoral dissertation, University of Connecticut, Storrs, CT.

Reis, S. M. (1987). We can't change what we don't recognize: Understanding the special needs of gifted females. *Gifted Child Quarterly, 31,* 83–89.

Renzulli, J. S. (1977). *The Enrichment Triad Model: A guide for development of defensible programs for the gifted.* Mansfield Center, CT: Creative Learning Press.

Renzulli, J. S. (1978). What makes giftedness? Reexamining a definition. *Phi Delta Kappan, 60,* 180–184, 261.

Renzulli, J. S. (1986). The Three Ring conception of giftedness: A developmental model for creative productivity. In R. J. Sternberg & J. E. Davidson (Eds.), *Conceptions of giftedness* (pp. 53–92). New York: Cambridge University Press.

Renzulli, J. S., & Delcourt, M. B. (1986). The legacy and the logic of research on the identification of gifted persons. *Gifted Child Quarterly, 30,* 20–23.

Renzulli, J. S., & Reis, S. M. (1985). *The Schoolwide Enrichment Model: A comprehensive plan for educational excellence.* Mansfield Center, CT: Creative Learning Press.

Renzulli, J. S., & Reis, S. M. (1986). The Enrichment Triad/Revolving Door Model: A schoolwide plan for the development of creative productivity. In J. S. Renzulli (Ed.), *Systems and models for developing programs for the gifted and talented.* Mansfield Center, CT: Creative Learning Press.

Roe, A. (1952). *The making of a scientist.* New York: Dodd, Mead.

Roeder, C., Haensly, P. A., & Edlind, E. P. (1982). *The secret ingredients in gifted children's productivity.* Paper presented at the conference of the National Association for Gifted Children, New Orleans, LA.

Schack, G. D. (1986). *Creative productivity and self-efficacy in children.* Unpublished doctoral dissertation, University of Connecticut, Storrs, CT.

Seidel, J. V., & Clark, J. A. (1984). The Ethnograph: A computer program for the analysis of qualitative data. *Qualitative Sociology, 7*(1 & 2), 110–125.

Seidel, J. V., Kjolseth, R., & Seymour, E. (1988). *The Ethnograph: A program for the computer assisted analysis of text based data* [Computer Program]. Littleton, CO: Qualis Research Associates.

Siegler, R. S., & Kotovsky, K. (1986). Two levels of giftedness: Shall ever the twain meet? In R. J. Sternberg & J. E. Davidson (Eds.), *Conceptions of giftedness* (pp. 417–435). New York: Cambridge University Press.

Simonton, D. K. (1983). Creative productivity and age: A mathematical model based on a two-step cognitive process. *Developmental Review, 4,* 77–111.

Smith, H. W. (1975). Triangulation: The necessity for multimethod approaches. In W.H. Smith (Ed.), *Strategies of social research: The methodological imagination* (pp. 271–292). Englewood Cliffs, NJ: Prentice-Hall.

Spradley, J. P. (1979). *The ethnographic interview.* New York: Holt, Rinehart & Winston.

Stake, R. E. (1987). Case study method in social inquiry. *Educational Researcher, 7,* 5–8.

Starko, A. J. (1986). *The effects of the Revolving Door Identification Model on creative productivity and self-efficacy.* Unpublished doctoral dissertation, University of Connecticut, Storrs, CT.

Starko, A. J.(1988). Effects of the Revolving Door Identification Model on creative productivity and self-efficacy. *Gifted Child Quarterly, 32,* 291–297.

Sternberg, R. J. (Ed.). (1988). *The nature of creativity: Contemporary psychological perspectives.* New York: Cambridge University Press.

Sternberg, R. J., & Davidson, J. E. (Eds.). (1986). *Conceptions of giftedness.* New York: Cambridge.

Swanson-Kauffman, K. M. (1986). A combined qualitative methodology for nursing research. *Advances in Nursing Science, 8*(3), 58–69.

Tannenbaum, A. J. (1983). *Gifted children: Psychological and educational perspectives.* New York: Macmillan.

Torrance, E. P. (1980). Growing up creatively gifted: A 22-year longitudinal study. *The Creative Child and Adult Quarterly, 25,* 55–61.

Torrance, E. P. (1981). Predicting the creativity of elementary school children (1958-80) and the teacher who "made a difference." *Gifted Child Quarterly, 25,* 55–61.

Treffinger, D. J., & Renzulli, J. S. (1986). Giftedness as potential for creative productivity: Transcending IQ scores. *Gifted Child Quarterly, 8,* 150–154.

Walberg, H. J. (1969). A portrait of the artist and scientist as young men. *Exceptional Children, 36,* 5–11.

Walberg, H. J. (1971). Varieties of adolescent creativity and the high school environment. *Exceptional Children, 38,* 111–116.

Webb, E. J. (1966). *Unobtrusive measures: Nonreactive research in the social sciences.* Chicago, IL: Rand McNally.

Whitmore, J. R. (1980). *Giftedness, conflict, and underachievement.* Boston, MA: Allyn & Bacon.

16

Lessons from Contemporary Longitudinal Studies

Karen D. Arnold
Rena F. Subotnik

The fruits of potential genius are indeed beyond price. The task ahead is not simply that of finding how gifted children turn out; it is the problem rather of utilizing the rare opportunities afforded by this group to increase our knowledge of the dynamics of human behavior, with special reference to the factors that determine degree and direction of creative achievement.

—Terman & Oden, 1947, p. 381

WHAT HAVE WE LEARNED ABOUT GIFTEDNESS AND TALENT FROM CONTEMPORARY LONGITUDINAL STUDIES IN GIFTED EDUCATION?

Eighty years after the *Genetic Studies of Genius* began, Terman's claims for the value of longitudinal study of giftedness remain persuasive. The contemporary longitudinal research literature represented in this volume extends our understanding of the dynamics of giftedness and the correlates of achievement. The collection also exposes the obstacles that continue to impede the full utilization of repeated measures methodology nearly a century after the inception of the first long-term study of the gifted. Analysis spanning the 14 studies reveals common discoveries about giftedness and important insights regarding the practice of longitudinal research. The studies' goals and outcomes can be categorized into two major domains: conditions for the manifestation of talent, and the impact of gender on the fulfillment of promise.

Conditions for the Manifestation of Talent

Timing. The longitudinal literature in this volume underlines the inextricable link between identification and timing. Casting various screening nets will collect different cohorts at different developmental points. For example, the concept of using the SAT-M before the age of 14 is crucial to the legitimacy of the SMPY model because a majority of educational institutions tend to track students in mathematics once they have completed the elementary school curriculum. Course taking therefore plays a larger role in middle and secondary school gifted identification.

Perleth and Heller discovered that "underachievers" in their study population rose grandly to the occasion for the *Abitur*, or final examinations leading to university admission. These students were motivated by challenges they perceived as vital; Perleth and Heller's tests paled in comparison to the *Abitur*. Another noteworthy conclusion from the Perleth and Heller, Hany, and Cramond studies was that the contribution of domain specific tests in predicting achievement increases with the age of subjects.

Scripp and Davidson identified the central role of music sightreading in the transformation of performance talent into high level musicianship. Sightsinging tends not to be introduced before the conservatory level in music education. Scripp and Davidson's work leads to speculation about the possible influence earlier study of sightreading without an instrument might have on the development of musical performance.

Some novice scientists in Subotnik and Steiner's study had conducted independent experiments in late elementary school. By the time they competed in the Westinghouse Science Talent Search, a large majority had learned that working under the supervision of a powerful and experienced professional scientist, despite limited opportunities to select research questions, was a strategic means to successful competition. These examples point to the importance of longitudinal investigation in determining ideal opportunities for identification in various talent domains.

Interests. Interests and after-school pastimes are too often ignored by teachers as signposts of talent or keys to instruction for underachievers. Milgram and Hong, and Delcourt noted stability of interests in their subjects who were most accomplished in terms of creative productivity. Data on subjects' favorite academic topics as well as out-of-school leisure-time activities appear to be an excellent source of information for future longitudinal researchers.

Program goals. Differentiated programs were, for the most part, successful in meeting goals for participants according to Moon and Feldhusen, Fleming and Hollinger, Delcourt, and Rudnitski. Although conclusive support for these results was limited by a lack of control groups, student outcomes appeared to vary as a function of programmatic goals and underlying theoretical models. In each case, identification was closely tied to objectives and to instruction. Although it is common knowledge in our field that these three dimensions are related, long-term empirical evidence to that effect has previously been unavailable.

Mentoring. Studies that focus on talent development address the question of how experts enhance the gifts of the novices they mentor (Bloom, 1985; Zuckerman, 1977). Many of Rudnitski's graduate leadership program participants admired and worked closely with at least one of their two project directors. Other subjects found program participants from earlier cohorts who provided needed guidance and advice. These mentors were able to create opportunities for Fellows in the Graduate Leadership in Education Program that led to the acquisition of desirable jobs and recognition in the community.

Fleming and Hollinger served as agents for change among Project CHOICE women. Their intervention strategies mediated to a considerable degree the effects of socioeconomic background on participants' later educational and occupational choices. Subotnik and Steiner identified four responsibilities fulfilled by mentors of Westinghouse Science Talent Search winners: role model, emotional support, intellectual sparring partner, and professional networker. Further, in keeping with the literature on mentoring, Subotnik and Steiner noted that at the advanced degree program and professional level, mentors select from among promising young individuals those who might serve as good "investments" in the mentor's future influence in the field. Differential experiences with mentors is a rich area for future exploration in longitudinal research, and a significant component of schooling that is missing from too many educational programs for gifted students.

Labeling. Moon and Feldhusen discussed the changing dynamics of family relationships when children were identified as gifted in school. Rudnitski's subjects described feeling professionally confident and proud to be associated with the GLEP fellowship program. They believed that association with the project opened doors for them that might have otherwise been closed. Subotnik and Steiner's subjects reported receiving public acclaim and possibly more selective college admission upon being named a Talent Search winner, but said they were virtually ignored as a nationally recognized source of talent once they began their undergraduate career. Many valedictorians in Arnold's longitudinal study felt that their labeling as the best high school student rested on their academic record instead of intellectual giftedness. Further study of the long-term effects of labeling requires matched control groups and complicated treatment designs, but is essential to the basic implementation of policy in our field. The effects of being labeled as a potential leader or scientist, for example, cannot be conclusively determined without investigating the outcomes of nonlabeled individuals with similar potential.

Family context. The values that individuals bring to their educational experiences are central to achievement. Teachers despair over the minimal influence they believe they have over important background variables, and attempts to promote educationally supportive family structures tread uneasily near sensitive questions of conflicting cultural priorities. Albert, Moon and Feldhusen, Delcourt, and Fleming and Hollinger employed family beliefs and aspirations to explain differences in outcomes and to propose intervention strategies.

Desired outcomes. The philosophical underpinnings of gifted education are based either on providing special services to gifted and talented students whose needs are not met in the regular classroom, or on identifying and developing talents that might enrich society (see further discussion of this point below). Definitions of success in most of the research projects described in this volume lie in the realm of professional achievement; for the most part, study subjects were in postsecondary education and beyond. Expectations for future attainment of eminence are tentative at this point, as most of the study cohorts are still young adults. The researchers associated with these studies anticipate that some proportion of their subjects will make major contributions to various fields of specialization, if not to society as a whole.

Perleth and Heller, and Moon and Feldhusen, whose subjects are of school age, focused on general academic achievement as a primary dependent variable. Davidson and Scripp explored the development of musical talent with primary-age children, and Hany investigated the identification of technical creativity in middle and high school students. Study of the use of general tests of intelligence and creativity with populations of adults has been extensively explored during this century. Identification of domain-specific talent in school-age populations has now become an open arena for future predictive validity studies.

In sum, material essential to the development of sound policy for work with gifted and talented children, adolescents, and adults has been provided by the studies described in this volume. A remaining challenge is the application of some of these principles to under-represented populations in current gifted programs or talent cohorts who, without special recognition, might face severely limited educational opportunities.

Impact of Gender on the Fulfillment of Promise

Gender emerges as the single most salient variable across studies. Researchers consistently reported differences between gifted males and females in findings ranging from test validity and educational outcomes to career choice and implementation. Cramond, for example, found that the TTCT was more predictive of creative behavior in males than females. Studies by Perleth and Heller, Delcourt, Subotnik and Steiner, and Lubinski and Benbow revealed gender differences in early interests, an important finding given the research evidence for the role of interests in adult attainment. Several of the studies, including Lubinski and Benbow's large-sample work, showed girls and women selecting mathematics and science careers less frequently than males.

Hany reported that technical creativity was differentially related to physics background and achievement for boys and girls, including the puzzling finding that young women with particularly strong physics records scored lower than less gifted peers on tests of technological problem solving. Also disturbing was Moon and Feldhusen's discovery that their gifted male subjects were more dissatisfied with their school experiences than girls but nevertheless maintained higher educational aspirations than equally talented girls. Lubinski and Benbow's mathematically talented women, similarly, earned higher college grades than SMPY males but were less likely than men to major in mathematics or science or to attend graduate school. Female high school valedictorians, according to Arnold's findings, lowered their intellectual self-esteem during their undergraduate years despite superb academic performance.

Taken together, these findings strongly suggest that gifted girls and women respond differently than equally able males to the same measurement instruments and educational experiences. Supporting this contention is the repeated research discovery that the lack of opportunities for intellectual and professional mentoring is a significant barrier to the realization of promise in talented women. Compelling policy implications follow from these findings. Reexamination of identification methods for females, and the design of programs which foster self-esteem, high aspirations, and connections with mentors are critical to meet the needs of gifted girls and women.

LONGITUDINAL METHODOLOGY

The collected studies in this volume document both the advantages and the challenges of repeated measures research in gifted education. The variety of data sources, relationship of theory to research, and study design illustrate most of the key issues in conducting longitudinal investigations.

Data Sources

Several of the chapters reported on studies that draw from more than one type of data. Triangulation of data sources strengthens the validity and reliability of study findings and provides context for outcomes measures. Perleth and Heller administered a variety of test instruments and conducted interviews in their study of German school children and adolescents. Arnold's high school valedictorians completed both mailed survey instruments and interviews, and provided standardized college admissions test scores. In her study of past gifted program participants, Delcourt analyzed documents, administered questionnaires, and conducted interviews in and outside of school with students and their parents. Albert paired psychometric measures with in-depth interviews and observable behaviors and products.

Other chapters also demonstrated the value of triangulating data sources in order to form a convergent picture of the gifted individual and his or her development. Follow-up studies have highlighted the shortcomings of paper-and-pencil tests in predicting long-term outcomes, the importance of personality, gender, and family context on the experience of educational programs, and the role of mentoring on the fulfillment of promise. Beyond research, however, the notion of multiple data sources has policy implications for identification, program design, and evaluation in gifted education. As in research, educational identification, evaluation, and interventions that rely on performance-based measures and contextual information should prove more valuable than single indicators of potential or gifted behavior.

Qualitative and quantitative data provide different, but highly valuable, contributions to the understanding of gifted development.

Large-scale quantitative data sets, reported by Cramond, Lubinski and Benbow, and Perleth and Heller allowed testing of complex theoretical constructs and causal modeling of the development of giftedness and its nurturing conditions. Regression analyses, structural equation models, and fine-grained intergroup comparisons require large sample sizes and quantitative forms of information. The use of normed instruments like the SAT allows comparison of gifted cohorts to representative national samples. Although subjects might more honestly convey their fears and struggles in an anonymous questionnaire, these studies also utilized interviews of selected subsamples in order to contextualize quantitative findings and to generate hypotheses for further study.

The value of qualitative data is equally clear. The voices of gifted students themselves are powerful illustrations of group patterns, reminders of the uniqueness and exceptionality of gifted subjects, and persuasive indicators of the personality and contextual variables that mediate the expression of ability. The Fleming and Hollinger study, for instance, illustrated the limiting effect of stereotyped gender roles and class-related expectations in their compelling quotations from the brilliant young woman who aspired to be a hairstylist. The role of Project CHOICE in this woman's eventual pursuit of a career in medicine was clearly expressed through the combination of individual case material with quantitative group findings. Ideal for hypothesis and theory generation, interview designs begin with the perceptions and concerns of study participants themselves, and accommodate the rich, untidy variety of life influences that are so difficult to capture in paper-and-pencil instruments. Delcourt, for example, was able to show the sometimes complex pattern associated with ongoing creative project production by considering contextual information about family support and by comparing adolescent project production to school requirements. Scripp and Davidson provided readers with conservatory students' changing reflections and records of performance as they are exposed to challenges of singing music at sight. In short, qualitative data yield rich, contextual information and preserve individual voices and variability amid group patterns.

Interview studies lead inevitably to the formation of acquaintances and ties between researchers and study participants. A potential source of study bias and selective attrition, personal relationships with research participants are, nonetheless, consistently cited by investigators as one of the greatest joys in doing longitudinal work. Both Arnold and Subotnik have coauthored manuscripts with members of their study cohort, including Cynthia Steiner in this volume. Such relationships result in deeper, more personal revelations from subjects. Arnold attributes the retention of all 81 valedictorians in her 15-year study to the personal relationships she and her co-researcher, Denny, have developed with the project members.

Again, policy implications flow from research findings. The personal ties and self-exploration that result from open-ended conversations about issues that matter to students offer a model for the problematic area of gifted student guidance and mentoring. In the classroom, performance-based assessment of cognitive strategies and education for problem finding could benefit from the use of structured interviews. The qualitative data in this collection are nearly all interview and case study material. Ethnographic techniques such as participant observation of classroom and peer group dynamics offer other potentially important sources of data for longitudinal research.

Theory and Research

Theory plays varying roles in the longitudinal research literature. Cramond's account of the development of the Torrance Tests of Creativity and Milgram and Hong's study of creative accomplishment in adults each tested models of creativity. Davidson and Scripp's work was based on Gardner's Multiple Intelligence Theory (Gardner, 1983). The work of Perleth and Heller and of Hany tested comprehensive causal models of multidimensional giftedness and technical creativity, respectively.

The chapters on program effects investigated the outcomes of theoretically driven interventions, offering an indirect test of the underlying theories themselves. Finally, qualitative studies such as those of Arnold, and Subotnik and Steiner, attempted to generate theory from extensive qualitative data.

Research Issues in Longitudinal Design

Virtually all of the problematic issues in longitudinal research methodology are apparent in the literature on giftedness. Most of the researchers faced subject attrition, for instance, and experienced challenges in reducing and analyzing large amounts of data. Only the multiple cohort studies of Cramond, Perleth and Heller, and Lubinski and Benbow began to address historical threats to validity. Even Perleth's study, however, tested cohorts so close in age that their general social context was quite similar. The effects of changing gender roles on the women of Project CHOICE, the influence of the Reagan years on the career paths of high school valedictorians, and the funding environment for gifted education are historical effects that undoubtedly affected the development and outcomes of study subjects in the work of Fleming and Hollinger, Arnold, and Rudnitski.

Time-of-measurement effects were dramatically portrayed by the subject attrition in the TTCT study due to the Vietnam War, in the collection of Milgram and Hong's data during the Yom Kippur War in Israel, and in the replication of Hany's technical creativity study in Beijing around the time of the Tienanmen Square incident. Milder instances of time-of-measurement effects included Perleth and Heller's data collection during students' examination preparation, and Fleming and Hollinger's inadvertent formation of control groups through the inability of some subjects to negotiate a major snow storm.

In addition to its importance in guiding educational policy and program design, the difficulty in defining criterion variables is a problem in research. Definitions of desirable outcomes vary by study. Lubinski and Benbow defined success in terms of math-related careers and attainment of the doctorate. Milgram and Hong, Delcourt, and Cramond sought evidence of creative accomplishment. Subotnik and Steiner's criterion variable was pursuit of a research career in science; Arnold, and Fleming and Hollinger measured general occupational levels.

In addition to defining criterion variables, operationalizing "success" poses a challenge to researchers. Hany, for example, expressed the possibility that the poor empirical fit of his model of technical creativity might be due to the measurement of technological education by the proxy of physics instruction. Just as intervention outcomes relate strongly to specific program goals, longitudinal research results rely on the definition and operationalization of outcome measures of success.

A final research issue addressed by the study authors is the issue of comparison or control groups. Hany's study was exemplary in this respect, utilizing same-age comparison groups of average- and high-intelligence subjects. Davidson and Scripp, similarly, compared musically gifted and nongifted children. The collected research demonstrates the value of internal comparison groups in designs without formal control groups. Nearly all of the researchers compared men and women, for instance. Fleming and Hollinger compared students by schools; Subotnik and Steiner contrasted subjects who leave and those who remain in science; and Arnold compared vocational groups of academically talented males. Such within-sample comparisons can guide educational practice by providing important insights into differences within gifted populations. In short, the collected studies illustrate both the methodological challenges of longitudinal research in gifted education and the diverse solutions posed by scholars with varied methodological orientations, data sources, study populations, and central variables.

DIRECTIONS FOR FUTURE RESEARCH

What We Study

Researchers choose study variables to explore according to long-term goals for gifted education that can be categorized into two philosophical orientations. One thrust calls for wide-sweeping identification of those students with academic or creative potential who might be missed in narrowly drawn searches for giftedness or whose educational needs are being ignored or suppressed by the regular classroom environment (e.g., Baldwin, 1987; Frasier, 1991; Wright & Borland, 1992). Fulfilling this goal would result in improving the intellectual and emotional life of each identified child. Secondarily, of course, the community benefits by successfully challenging a larger proportion of its students. Implementation of this philosophy might include full-time or part-time placement of gifted students in homogeneously grouped classrooms, or teacher training for individualized instruction within the regular classroom. From a psychometric perspective, new methods to identify gifted females, children from diverse language backgrounds, students with physical and cognitive disabilities, and from nonmainstream groups would continue to receive priority, while currently employed identification methods would be pursued rigorously for predictive validity with previously underrepresented groups.

A second philosophical orientation is directed toward fulfilling community or global needs. Those researchers and practitioners concerned about the development of talent are interested in locating specific behaviors or products that reflect extraordinary gifts in a specific domain (e.g., Bloom, 1985; Feldhusen, 1992; Renzulli, 1986; Subotnik, Kassan, Summers, & Wasser, 1993; Tannenbaum, 1983). This perspective focuses on the individual as a means to the enrichment of society. Additionally, talented individuals gain satisfaction and fulfillment from the exercise of their gifts and from public recognition. Scholars and educators in this context might address such questions as: How early can extraordinary talent be recognized in various fields? How specialized should training for talent development be and at what age should it begin? What are the best ways to structure learning in specific talent areas in order to maximize individual performance? Questions from both philosophical perspectives are innately longitudinal.

Each of the two perspectives carries implications for gifted education. If the goal of education is the broadest possible recognition of potentially gifted individuals, efforts should focus on comprehensive identification methods and special programs for children. Matching educational provisions to the needs of exceptional students should be initiated soon after the beginning of a child's school career and be flexible throughout the entire span of elementary and early secondary years. Identification methods should be comprehensive, multidimensional, and tailored to reflect the community being served, keeping in mind that communities change over the course of time.

If talent development is the focus, policy makers and program developers need to target talent areas, operationalize criteria for excellence, select cohorts of respected judges, and identify teachers for each level of mastery. Educators must be prepared to change policies if outstanding products and successful competition do not ensue. In this talent development approach, research and educational programs will more rarely begin in the early elementary years, and will more often include secondary and postsecondary subjects.

The studies included in this volume have established a baseline for facilitating the acquisition of gifted education goals. By further diversifying study samples and talent domains, still greater insights can be brought to bear on the field.

Methodology

The variety of possible research designs is a strength of longitudinal studies of giftedness. The research described in this volume employs diverse data sources, samples, and central variables. The literature as a whole, however, needs to move toward more comprehensive designs in order to fulfill the promise of longitudinal methods for definitive findings about the development of giftedness. Overcoming threats to validity in repeated measures research requires investigations that adequately address historical and time-of-measurement effects through multiple-cohort studies. A single-cohort study restricts generalization to individuals at one point of history and to those experiencing a contemporary series of events. The effects of the Women's Movement on the career choices of high school girls in the 1970s, for instance, cannot be adequately determined without a comparable sample from a different time period. Schaie (1983) stated that new longitudinal follow-ups of single cohorts are acceptable only for investigations of previously unstudied populations. Most of the reports in this book are precisely that—intensive studies of unusual groups which have never been studied longitudinally. Information from these single-cohort inquiries yields valuable information about gifted individuals and groups that can form the basis for subsequent research and theory generation.

Multiple-cohort studies, such as those of Cramond, Lubinski and Benbow, and Perleth and Heller reflect ideal longitudinal designs. Researchers may also add new cohorts to existing studies. Subotnik, for example, is currently seeking to establish a new cohort of Westinghouse Science Talent Search winners. Two longitudinal studies with different cohorts and time periods can sometimes be used for comparison and to address historical threats to validity. Careful replication of sampling, and test and interview items is necessary for direct comparison of cohorts in different studies, but general outcomes from similarly identified individuals can serve as a beginning point in controlling for historical effects. Although the need for multiple cohorts is clear, the required financial support and human labor are so extensive that comprehensive study designs will only take place in a research environment that strongly values and adequately funds longitudinal work.

In addition to the limitations of single-cohort studies, much of the longitudinal literature on giftedness suffers from small sample size. In certain methodologies, particularly ethnography, small samples are appropriate and valuable for theory generation. Small-sample studies, however, restrict generalizability to larger populations. As in cross-sectional research, longitudinal samples also need to be diverse in terms of social class, gender, and ethnic representation in order to control for important independent variables that affect outcomes. The Fleming and Hollinger chapter provided findings from a sample that included individuals from varied social classes and cultural backgrounds. The work of Perleth and Heller, and Hany, points to the important potential of comparing the development of giftedness across nations. Replications of their studies in Russia, Korea, and the People's Republic of China will enable direct investigation of cultural and national differences in gifted individuals.

Theoretical and Developmental Concerns

Terman's work has been criticized for its weak theoretical base (Baird, 1982; Chapman, 1988; Gould, 1981; Shurkin, 1992). The relationship between research and theory remains problematic in the current longitudinal literature on giftedness. The two German studies in this volume explicitly test theoretical models of giftedness and use empirical findings to reconsider theory. This dialectical approach, in which researchers move back and forth between research and theory, is ideal for repeated measures studies, allowing modification of data collection in light of previous findings. Most of the other research projects described here drew from theory but were less directly tied to the testing and generation of specific theoretical models.

Despite the ideal fit between long-term studies and developmental research, little existing literature is genuinely developmental—that is, investigating patterns of intraindividual change over time. The work of Davidson and Scripp on the evolution of musical reasoning represent the most purely developmental studies in the book. Research in this tradition is critical for informing educators and policy makers about the ways in which gifted individuals change, the nature and timing of interventions, and the cognitive and psychosocial differences between gifted students and their peers. Further developmental work could enable us to investigate such issues as whether the critical learning period in humans varies in timing or duration as a factor of intelligence.

Another limitation in the longitudinal research literature is the lack of control groups for many studies. Sample size, with all its associated costs, is an obstacle in forming control groups for multiple-cohort studies. Designing appropriate comparison groups for exceptional individuals is also a problem, as is the withholding of special opportunities from gifted students. For definitive study designs, however, appropriate control groups are essential.

Program outcomes research is extraordinarily important, given the resources required by differentiated educational efforts. Unfortunately, few studies investigate the medium- and long-term outcomes of special programs for talented and gifted. The studies of Delcourt, Rudnitski, and Moon and Feldhusen represent promising directions for program research. Like many of the studies presented in this volume, however, intervention follow-ups need larger samples and carefully selected control groups. Disentangling the effects of specific educational experiences and special programs from other life experiences calls for particularly sophisticated designs.

Research on comparative identification methods is another promising and underutilized area for outcomes study. Albert's work comparing boys with high IQ to those with high mathematics aptitude scores is a good example of a design that allows for the direct comparison of identification methods.

Gifted education includes a vigorous and diverse longitudinal research literature. Despite the nearly 80-year history of longitudinal research on the gifted, however, current studies in this tradition generally suffer from historical effects that threaten their validity, and from small and circumscribed samples that restrict their generalizability. The literature in this volume must be viewed in terms of the immense challenges of conducting longitudinal studies and the extraordinarily important preliminary evidence for the testing and generation of developmental theory.

CONCLUSION

In the final analysis, have we indeed moved beyond Terman? As the premiere longitudinal investigation of a gifted population, the Terman study set a standard of comprehensiveness, large study sample, and societal influence that is difficult to supersede. In spite of the Terman study's large number of research associates and rich sources of funding support, the data are still being organized for more accurate statistical analysis and examined for more challenging research questions. Further, the *Genetic Studies of Genius* and its more current follow-ups did not address key questions of concern in today's social, political, and historical climate, or issues of central importance in the future. The investigations in this book have established a groundwork for answering previously unanswered questions: Are we identifying the "right" people? What are the outcomes associated with various forms of identification and intervention?

Over the course of his long career, Terman's perspective on high IQ as a source for potential genius changed to allow personality, interest, special abilities, and opportunity to play a growing role in adult achievement. In filling a vacuum left by Terman, this collection of contemporary studies can guide policy and program development based on the conditions and interventions that contribute to the fulfillment of talent.

REFERENCES

Baird, L. L. (1982). *The role of academic ability in high level accomplishment and general success* (College Board Report Vol. 82, No. 6). Princeton, NJ: Educational Testing Service.

Baldwin, A. Y. (1987). Undiscovered diamonds: The minority gifted child. *Journal for the Education of the Gifted, 10*(4), 271–285.

Bloom, B. S. (Ed.). (1985). *Developing talent in young people.* New York: Ballantine Books.

Chapman, P. D. (1988). *Schools as sorters: Lewis Terman, applied psychology, and the intelligence testing movement 1890–1930.* New York: New York University Press.

Feldhusen, J. (1992). Talent identification and development in education. *Gifted Child Quarterly, 36,* 123.

Frasier, M. (1991). Disadvantaged and culturally diverse gifted students. *Journal for the Education of the Gifted, 14*(3), 234–245.

Gardner, H. (1983). *Frames of mind.* New York: Basic Books.

Gould, S.J. (1981). *The mismeasure of man.* New York: W. W. Norton.

Renzulli, J. S. (1986). The Three–Ring conception of giftedness: A developmental model for creative productivity. In R. J. Sternberg & J. E. Davidson (Eds.), *Conceptions of giftedness* (pp. 53–92). New York: Cambridge University Press.

Schaie, K. W. (1983). *Longitudinal studies of adult psychological development.* New York: Guilford Press.

Schurkin, J. S. (1992). *Terman's kids: The groundbreaking study of how the gifted grow up.* Boston, MA: Little, Brown.

Subotnik, R. F., Kassan, L., Summers, E., & Wasser, A. (1993). *Genius revisited: High IQ children grown up.* Norwood NJ: Ablex.

Tannenbaum, A. J. (1983). *Gifted children: Psychological and educational perspectives.* New York: Macmillan.

Terman, L. M., & Oden, M. H. (1947). The gifted child grows up. *Genetic studies of genius* (Vol. IV). Stanford, CA: Stanford University Press.

Wright, L., & Borland, J. (1992). A special friend: Adolescent mentors for young, economically disadvantaged, potentially gifted students. *Roeper Review, 14*(3), 124–129.

Zuckerman, H. (1977). *Scientific elite: Nobel laureates in the United States.* New York: Free Press.

Author Index

Subject Index